1996

PERIODICAL LITERATURE IN NINETEENTH-CENTURY AMERICA

•

PERIODICAL LITERATURE IN NINETEENTH-CENTURY AMERICA

•

Edited by Kenneth M. Price
and Susan Belasco Smith

•

University Press of Virginia
Charlottesville and London

The University Press of Virginia
Copyright © 1995 by the Rector and Visitors
of the University of Virginia

First published 1995

Library of Congress Cataloging-in-Publication Data

Periodical literature in nineteenth-century America/edited by Kenneth M.
Price and Susan Belasco Smith.
    p.   cm.
    Includes index.
    ISBN 0–8139–1629–1 (alk. paper). — ISBN 0–8139–1630–5 (pbk. :
alk. paper)
    1. American literature—19th century—History and criticism.
2. Periodicals, Publishing of—United States—History—19th century.
3. Literature and society—United States—History—19th century.
4. Authors and publishers—United States—History—19th century.
5. Literature publishers—United States—History—19th century.
6. American periodicalspublishers—History—19th century.   7. Social history
in literature.   I. Price, Kenneth M.   II. Smith, Susan Belasco,
1950–
PS201.S58   1995
810.9′003—dc20   95-21204
                                                                    CIP

Printed in the United States of America

CONTENTS

•

CONTENTS

PERIODICAL LITERATURE IN NINETEENTH-CENTURY AMERICA

•

INTRODUCTION
Periodical Literature in Social and Historical Context

SUSAN BELASCO SMITH AND
KENNETH M. PRICE

•

THE decades between the 1830s and the 1890s transformed the American literary marketplace. In the 1830s technological developments in papermaking, the widespread use of the cylinder press, cheaper postal routes, rising literacy rates, and wide distribution by railroad altered the course of publication and deeply affected writers and readers alike. Periodicals became easier to produce and sustain as consumable commodities for a market of incalculable potential. At the same time, inexpensive and widely available copies of printed texts profoundly changed the profession of authorship and the nature of the readership. The periodical—far more than the book—was a social text, involving complex relationships among writers, readers, editors, publishers, printers and distributors.

When Ralph Waldo Emerson delivered an address on "The Fugitive Slave Law" in New York City on 7 March 1854, he was acutely aware of reporters in his audience turning his lecture into news for the daily papers and thus disseminating his words far beyond his immediate audience. Emerson took the occasion to reflect on the revolution that the periodical press was bringing about in America: "For who are the readers and thinkers of 1854? Owing to the silent revolution which the newspaper has wrought, this class has come in this country to take in all classes. Look into the morning trains which, from every suburb, carry the business men into the city to their shops, counting-rooms, work-yards and warehouses. With them enters the car—the newsboy, that humble priest of politics, finance, philosophy, and religion. He unfolds his magical sheets—twopence a head his bread of knowledge costs—and instantly the entire rectangular assembly, fresh from their breakfast, are bending as one man to their second breakfast. There is, no doubt, chaff enough in what he brings; but there is fact, thought, and wisdom in the crude mass, from all regions of the world."[1] Although not usually known for an interest in contemporary trends, Emerson is remarkably perceptive here and correctly acknowledges the profound social changes that the "magical sheets" of the newspapers would produce. In this passage, he predicts the pattern of reading of the future and the centrality of the periodical in that pattern.

I

DURING the decades treated in this collection, periodical publication soared, especially when compared with the years immediately following the Revolutionary War. With some asperity, Noah Webster remarked about his *American Magazine* (1787–88), which never had a circulation exceeding five hundred, that the "expectation of failure is connected with the very name of a Magazine."[2] Early periodical publishers were plagued by numerous problems: the lack of a sufficiently literate population to create a demand for reading materials, a dearth of authors willing to write original contributions for new and tenuous ventures, inadequate distribution systems for the dispersed population of the new republic, and various problems in printing and manufacturing. Not surprisingly, 60 percent of the magazines that Frank Luther Mott classifies as belonging to the early period of magazine history (1741–94) did not survive their first year.[3] Newspapers fared somewhat better; about 450 new papers were begun in a twenty-five-year period following the Revolutionary War. While many of these were short-lived, the advent of daily papers (in 1783) helped to create an increasingly loyal readership.[4] The passage of the Postal Act of 1794 helped magazine publishers by permitting the distribution of magazines in the mails "when the mode of conveyance and the size of the mails will permit of it."[5] Although using the post office for delivery raised the cost of magazines—the yearly postage for a monthly ranged from forty-eight to ninety-six cents, depending on the distance—more magazines were founded. By 1825, there were some one hundred magazines in circulation in the country, most of them distributed through the mail. The growth of cities as well as the expansion of the country with the purchase of the Louisiana Territory in 1803 increased the demand for newspapers; by 1833, there were approximately 1,200 newspapers in existence, of which sixty-five were published on a daily basis.[6]

Apart from better distribution systems, a number of other factors helped to spur the growth in periodical publication during the first third of the nineteenth century. The development of common schools led to

4

an increasingly literate population. The American economy grew rapidly, and the population consequently became more leisured and more willing to seek entertainment. The growing interest in a national literature and the desire to challenge negative accounts of life in America put forth by Frances Trollope, Charles Dickens, and others spurred writers like Edward Everett and James Kirke Paulding to respond in what is sometimes called the Paper War with England in 1819–20. When the *Quarterly Review* published a review that included the comment that "Americans are inherently inferior," the *Atlantic Magazine,* under the editorship of William Cullen Bryant and Henry J. Anderson, responded, "The best way to receive the rhapsodies of the *Quarterly* about the barbarism of the United States is with laughter at their blunders, if made ingenuously, and with commiseration, if they proceed from malice."[7]

The 1820s saw rapid development of periodicals in the United States. The Erie Canal, completed in 1825, created a link from New York to Buffalo that changed the nature of routes to the west and consequently drew the Northeast and the West closer together both economically and politically. The election of the first populist president, Andrew Jackson, in 1828 marked important changes in the nature of the presidency as well as in government policies. It was an era of enlargement and extension, and the growth in the number and scope of periodicals reflected the mood of the country. By 1840, some 1,500 ongoing periodicals of various kinds existed in the country; as the *New-York Mirror* proclaimed, "This is the golden age of periodicals!"[8] In comparison, George Palmer Putnam reported at the Association of New York Publishers convention in 1855 that only about one hundred books a year were published between 1830 and 1842, and nearly half of them were foreign reprints.[9] Even a brief survey of the circulation numbers of a few periodicals tells the story of the dominance of the periodical. *Godey's Lady's Book* maintained a list of 70,000 subscribers by 1851 and reached 150,000 just before the Civil War. In the 1860s Robert Bonner's *New York Ledger* reached a circulation of 400,000. By the 1870s, the inexpensive weekly magazines, an estimated 4,295 of them, had a combined circulation of 10.5 million, a staggering figure given the fact that the population of the United States was only 30 million in 1870.[10]

Periodicals helped significantly in establishing American literary culture as an author-sustaining formation. Some writers of extraordinary power had appeared before this time, but they lacked developed institutions to insure that they could earn an adequate income through writing. At one extreme was Washington Irving, who had published four books before 1825 and was able to make most of his living with his writing; on the other hand, Nathaniel Hawthorne earned only $108 for one year of steady publication in the 1830s. The emergence of the penny press and the publication of weeklies in the 1840s gave rise to newspapers that published fiction either exclusively or along with news as well as to a variety of magazines and journals that mixed popular and elite forms. Some writers, such as Fanny Fern and Lydia Maria Child, who were among the first women to write regularly for newspapers, made increasingly good incomes from their articles and columns in such periodicals.[11] In fact few prominent nineteenth-century authors did not, at some point, write for a magazine, journal, or newspaper, with titles as well known as the *Daily Alta California* and *Harper's Monthly* or as obscure as the "Leviathan" newspapers and the *Literary World.*

Periodicals quickly came to play a central role in communication, information, and entertainment. William Kirkland, a contemporary critic and reviewer for *Godey's Lady's Book,* observed that periodicals were rapidly becoming the pervasive reading material of the day: "A large percentage of books published scarce find a purchaser; numbers of those purchased are never read and many that *are* read, are read by one or two persons, while with periodicals the *un*-read are the exception. One has but to look into circulating libraries, reading-rooms and the like places to see that an extensive class of readers finds time or inclination for little else."[12] The ubiquitousness of the periodical made it a natural forum for the dissemination of general education. Mary Abigail Dodge (Gail Hamilton), who wrote at various times for the *National Era,* the *Independent,* the *Congregationalist,* the *New York Tribune,* the *North American Review,* and *Harper's Bazaar,* commented that there were many readers "who without the magazines would not only not read Bacon and Plato, but would not read anything."[13] Similarly, Margaret Fuller, whose career was fundamentally shaped by her experiences as an editor of the *Dial* and as a writer for the *New York Tribune,* stressed the educational mission of the periodicals: "The most important part of our literature, while the work of diffusion is still going on, lies in the journals, which monthly, weekly, daily, send their messages to every corner of this great land, and form, at present, the only efficient instrument for the general education of the people."[14] The abolitionists seized on the periodical form and frequently established their own newspapers, such as the *Liberator* and the *National Era,* to publicize and gain support for the antislavery movement. Later in the century, Dana Estes, a publisher who testified before a Senate committee considering international copyrights, commented on the economic importance of the periodicals to the profession of authorship as well as on the pervasiveness of the form in disseminating works of literature: "It is impossible to make the books of most American authors pay unless they are first published and acquire recognition through the columns of the magazines."[15] And, as Joan Hedrick has pointed out in her recent biography of Harriet Beecher Stowe, the tradition of "parlour literature" in the nineteenth century—the practice of reading for informal gatherings of family and friends—made books and especially periodicals a central source of entertainment in the home. The works of British and American fiction and poetry in the periodicals—those of Dickens, Thackeray, Tennyson, Stowe, Longfellow, Helen Hunt Jackson, and E.D.E.N. Southworth, to name only a few—were a staple of such evenings.

Between the 1830s and 1890s, American periodicals displayed a healthy heterogeneity, since even the most prestigious magazines, including *Harper's Monthly, Putnam's,* and the *Atlantic,* mixed popular and elite forms, a distinction that was perhaps more blurred then than it is today. In writing for periodicals, many authors sought—and some found—a broad audience without sacrificing artistic integrity. This book closes at the end of this era, before the development in the 1890s of chapbooks with restricted circulation and magazines like *McClure's, Munsey's,* and the *Ladies' Home Journal,* which lowered prices, gained enormous circulations, and funded themselves not through subscriptions but through advertisements. These mass magazines had a place for literature, too, though in them culture was organized so that literature was put to the service of commodities and used to draw readers through pages framed with advertising copy.[16] Likewise, the development of competing national news bureaus, the concomitant emphasis on the marketing of news, and the expansion of large city newspapers such as the *Louisville Courier-Journal,* the *Los Angeles Times,* and, of course, the *New York Times* (whose motto became "All the News That's Fit to Print" in 1896) tended to reduce and eventually eliminate the space that was previously devoted to fiction and poetry.

II

IN the past ten years there has been increasing interest in an emerging field in literary study known as the history of the book. In general, the history of the book is a study of the context of printed texts in a variety of forms (books, magazines, newspapers, journals, reviews, and pamphlets) and how those texts are produced, received, and interpreted. Strongly antiformalist in origin and intent, the theory and practice of book history draws on a variety of disciplines, ranging from history to anthropology, sociology to linguistics, and literature to politics. Signs of the field's vitality are everywhere. In a recent article in the *Chronicle of Higher Education,* Karen Winkler lists a variety of developments that signal an emerging discipline: the formation of the Society for the History of Authorship, Reading, and Publishing; a National Endowment for the Humanities grant to the American Antiquarian Society for a multivolume history of the book in American culture; new academic programs in book history at the Pennsylvania State University and the University of South Carolina; the establishment at the University of Paris of "Scriptor," an electronic bibliography of resources in the history of writing; and the announcement of encyclopedias on publishing and book history forthcoming from both Garland and Henry Holt publishing companies. In addition, some two dozen books on the topic have been published since 1984, including Cathy N. Davidson's *Reading in America: Literature and Social History* (Baltimore: Johns Hopkins Univ. Press, 1989); Susan Coultrap-McQuin's *Doing Literary Business: American Women Writers in the Nineteenth Century* (Chapel Hill: Univ. of North Carolina Press, 1990); Richard D. Brown's *Knowledge Is Power: The Diffusion of Information in Early America, 1700–1865* (New York: Oxford Univ. Press, 1989), Carl F. Kaestle's *Literacy in the United States: Readers and Reading since 1880* (New Haven: Yale Univ. Press, 1991); and Richard H. Brodhead's *Cultures of Letters: Scenes of Reading and Writing in Nineteenth-Century America* (Chicago: Univ. of Chicago Press, 1993).[17] Scholars engaged in these projects have tended to focus on the single or multivolume book; from that departure point, they investigate the relationships among authors, publishers, and readers; the nature of the literary marketplace; and the effects of copyright laws and various print technologies. Such investigations, however, reveal only part of the history of books and reading, especially for nineteenth-century America.

Other equally important signs of the times point toward the study of American periodicals as an important field of inquiry in the history of the book. The founding of the Research Society for American Periodicals in 1990, the establishment of the journal *American Periodicals,* and the increasing academic interest in the sources of the "new" journalism of contemporary culture, as well as the publication of books such as Frankie Hutton's *The Early Black Press in America, 1827–1860* (Westport, Conn.: Greenwood, 1992) and Gerald J. Baldasty's *The Commercialization of the News in the Nineteenth Century* (Madison: Univ. of Wisconsin Press, 1992), all point to the enthusiasm for study of American literature as it frequently appeared in the nineteenth century in its original, periodical context. In *Investigating Victorian Journalism,* Lyn Pykett quotes one of James Mill's remarks in the *Westminster Review* (1824): "It is indeed a

8

subject of wonder, that periodical publications should have existed so long ... without having become subject to a regular and systematic course of criticism."[18] Readers of American literature can immediately recognize the truth and the irony of such a statement—170 years later.

This collection of essays and the scholars whose work is represented here contribute to the effort to establish such a "systematic course of criticism" and to develop a multidimensional history of the book. Although the essays have been arranged chronologically, loosely covering the decades from the 1830s through the end of the century, all of them reveal the ways in which literary analysis can be enriched when it encompasses social history, publishing contexts, the literary marketplace, and the relationships between authors and editors, among other matters. The contributors examine a variety of types of periodicals, including such powerful magazines as the *Atlantic Monthly*, newspapers as limited in readership as the *National Era*, and examples from the eastern, southern and western United States.

The term *periodical* is itself loosely defined and includes newspapers, reviews, weeklies, magazines, monthlies, pamphlets—in short, those publications that, in Mott's formulation, "possess periodicity"; in other words, we define periodicals as publications that are issued at intervals that are more or less regular. Such a definition points to the instability of the term *periodical* and of the form itself. In fact, what constitutes the *text* of a work published in a periodical is problematic. Nineteenth-century authors generally had little or no control over the final editing and printing of their work; for example, when Margaret Fuller wrote her dispatches from Europe for the *New York Tribune* in 1846–50, she only saw the published versions when a relative or friend sent them to her. Since no manuscripts or copy texts survive, the published versions of her dispatches in the newspaper must constitute the final text of her work. But the nature of periodicals raises other textual problems. Is a periodical a single text or is it the sum total of the many texts that appear in competing columns and pages? Some scholars of Victorian periodicals have argued that separating a particular article or story from the original context is a distortion and prefer instead to consider the text of a periodical an issue or number or even the entire run of a periodical from start to finish. Yet another question concerns the democratic nature of the periodical and the way in which readers are invited to be unusually active participants in the readings. In her provocative "Towards a Theory of the Periodical as a Publishing Genre," Margaret Beetham has drawn on contemporary criticism of television and other popular modes to draw a distinction between the "closed" form of books, which asserts "the dominant structures of meaning by closing off alternative options and offering the reader or viewer only one way of making sense of the text," and the "open" form of periodicals, "which refuses the closed ending and allows for the possibility of alternative meaning."[19] Beetham suggests that books, with firm bindings and solid feel, are very different from the flexible covers and consumable nature of newspapers or magazines. As such, periodicals may be seen as democratic and nonhierarchical, and yet, as many of our contributors demonstrate, this perception is open to question and challenge.

Studying literature in periodical contexts can yield new discoveries about writers as familiar as Margaret Fuller, Walt Whitman, Herman Melville, and Emily Dickinson. For example, in the first essay in this collection, "From *Dial* Essay to New York Book: The Making of *Woman in the Nineteenth Century*," Larry J. Reynolds explores those pressures—biographical, sociohistorical, generic—that affected Fuller most strongly as she revised "The Great Lawsuit" in the fall of 1844. Reynolds analyzes how she was pulled in two directions: both toward her new readers and backward toward her former *Dial* circle of educated friends. Similarly, David Reynolds considers how periodicals shaped the early writings of Walt Whitman. In "From Periodical Writer to Poet: Whitman's Journey through Popular Culture," Reynolds moves beyond the cursory treatment usually accorded to Whitman's pre–*Leaves of Grass* work. He argues that the twenty-four pieces of fiction and nineteen poems Whitman published before 1855 show him experimenting with a variety of popular genres and that a major poem like "Song of Myself" represents a collation of strategies and voices Whitman had learned as a writer for popular periodicals.

The work of Herman Melville and Emily Dickinson was also shaped by periodicals. In "Magazine Practices and Melville's *Israel Potter*," Sheila Post-Lauria shows that the interests of another prominent writer were much more congruent with magazine practices than has been thought. When Melville turned to magazine writing in 1853, he participated in the two distinct literary environments of *Harper's Magazine* and *Putnam's Monthly*. The unusual composition history of *Israel Potter* illustrates how Melville altered his style when writing for *Harper's* and *Putnam's*. Of all the author's periodical fiction, this narrative of a Revolutionary War "hero" remains the only work by Melville that, having been rejected by one magazine, was reconceived to meet the editorial policies of its competitor. Examining Melville's magazine fiction in its periodical context reveals how the author's creativity was stimulated rather than hampered by magazine practices. In "'Don't Tell! They'd Advertise': Emily Dickinson in the *Round Table*," Robert J. Scholnick takes on that most private of nineteenth-century poets and explores the publication of the poem "Some Keep the Sabbath" in a New York weekly founded by Henry E. Sweetser and Charles H. Sweetser. Although Dickinson was distantly related to the Sweetsers, Scholnick shows that the poem appeared in the magazine for more than family reasons. Using as his departure point the Sweetser brothers' "attack on the corrupting conditions of publishing and literary reviewing," Scholnick provides a new contextual understanding for Dickinson's work.

Approaching texts in their original periodical contexts encourages critics to reach beyond the careers of individual, well-known authors. The workings of the marketplace, the vagaries of reception history, and the oddities of canon formation are illuminated if we focus not solely on "major" figures but also on neglected writers, texts, and periodicals. In "Addressing or Redressing the Magazine Audience: Edmund Quincy's *Wensley*," Ezra Greenspan treats an overlooked author, the abolitionist Edmund Quincy. *Wensley* was one of the first feature works of serial fiction published in *Putnam's Monthly*. This magazine self-consciously promoted American letters, refusing to publish works of foreign authors. Quincy's novel was successful; John Greenleaf Whittier judged it "the most readable book of the kind since Hawthorne's *Blithedale Romance*." The book nonetheless fell out of sight until Greenspan resurrected it from obscurity. Expansions of the canon have usually turned to socially disadvantaged groups. In contrast, Greenspan's work is an intriguing reconsideration of a New England white male as well as a reminder that changing patterns of taste are as important as race and gender when we consider the reasons why works fall into obscurity.

Other contributors to this collection advance the understanding of women writers by exploring how they created authorial roles in response to periodical practices. In "Not Just Filler and Not Just Sentimental: Women's Poetry in American Victorian Periodicals, 1860–1900," Paula Bennett argues that magazines were crucial to the development of women's poetry in the United States. Bennett examines the poetry published primarily in the latter half of the nineteenth century, studying the innovative works of little-known poets such as Sarah Piatt, as the forerunners of literary modernism. "Uncommon Discourse: Fanny Fern and the *New York Ledger*," by Joyce Warren, sheds light on questions of taste and milieu in mid-nineteenth-century America. She points out that when Robert Bonner, owner of the *Ledger*, a small businessman's newspaper, resolved to create a paper of vital interest to a wide reading public, he hired Fanny Fern as an exclusive columnist. A year later, at the end of 1856, circulation had soared to 180,000, the largest of any American paper at the time. This chapter explores the interaction between Fern and the *Ledger*—that is, the way the newspaper shaped her writing and how she shaped the overall tone of the paper. In another treatment of a highly successful woman periodical writer, Carolyn Karcher takes up the development of children's literature in the United States by discussing "Lydia Maria Child and the *Juvenile Miscellany:* The Creation of an American Children's Literature." On the surface, the materials published in this magazine conformed to the conservative social mission of nineteenth-century children's literature and reinforced the dominant society's hierarchies of class, race, and gender. Karcher demonstrates the subtle ways in which Child undermined the ideology of the white middle class and advanced her own vision of racial equality.

The issue of slavery became increasingly important to northern writers after the passage of the Compromise of 1850. Harriet Beecher Stowe was prompted to write *Uncle Tom's Cabin* in response to a part of that compromise, the passage of the Fugitive Slave Law. In "Serialization and the Nature of *Uncle Tom's Cabin*," Susan Belasco Smith reassesses Stowe's novel by considering the periodical in which it originally appeared as a serial, the antislavery newspaper the *National Era,* edited by Gamaliel Bailey. In promoting the antislavery cause, *National Era* couched its overall argument in the domestic imagery of the union as a house and the American citizens as a family. Bailey wanted to engage his readership on moral grounds, for he saw slavery as a threat to the republican value of liberty beginning at the level of the American family—both Northern and Southern. *Uncle Tom's Cabin* was a perfect illustration of that perspective and, as Smith suggests, Stowe's argument against slavery, offered through the graphic images of the domestic implications of slaveholding, gained considerable power by unfolding from week to week in the pages of a family newspaper.

Southern writers were similarly engaged in the controversy over the extension of slavery. Patricia Okker's "Serial Politics in William Gilmore Simms's *Woodcraft*" focuses on the serial *The Sword and the Distaff,* which was later published as in book form as *Woodcraft.* Simms's first serial novel published in a Southern periodical was an attempt to establish a Southern serial novel distinct from its counterparts in the north, especially *Uncle Tom's Cabin.* The essay also explores Simms's response to two dominant strains in serial fiction of the 1850s: the fast-paced adventure story and slower-paced didactic fiction. Like Smith's essay on Stowe, Okker's essay on Simms both illuminates issues that emerge when fiction is serialized and clarifies sectional issues (particularly those related to slavery).

Other essays illuminate racial and sectional relations after the Civil War. Kathleen Diffley's "Home from the Theatre of War: The *Southern Magazine* and Recollections of the Civil War" studies the narratives of the rebellion that emerged after the war and especially after the establishment of the International Copyright Association in 1868. Under newly favorable conditions for authorship, the magazine trade burgeoned outside eastern publishing centers, and a distinctly regional literature arose. The perennially resurgent commercial center of Baltimore became a magnet for displaced secessionists after Appomattox and therefore welcomed the arrival in 1868 of the *New Eclectic* (eventually rechristened the *Southern Magazine*). The pages of the journal provide a window on the war from the perspective of those who lost. Also reflecting on the aftermath of the Civil War, Janet Gabler-Hover treats the "North-South Reconciliation Theme and the 'Shadow of the Negro' in *Century Illustrated Magazine*." From November 1884 through November 1887, *Century* conducted a Civil War series, an immensely popular experiment that boosted circulation dramatically. The series attempted to treat the war from a nonpolitical point of view and to "soften controversy." This chapter explores how the effort by *Century* to unify North and South influenced the selection of fiction and the mentoring of authors. Gabler-Hover also examines whether the magazine's support of intersectional unity damaged African-American prospects for equality, since the blurring of division between the sentiments of Northern and Southern whites may have assisted in the nation's evasion of the real racial issues that still divided it. Kenneth M. Price's "Charles Chesnutt, the *Atlantic Monthly*, and the Intersection of African-American Fiction and Elite Culture" contextualizes Chesnutt's problematic relationship with Thomas Bailey Aldrich, editor of the *Atlantic Monthly* from 1880 to 1890. A conservative editor devoted to the genteel tradition, Aldrich is infamous for having written "The Unguarded Gates," a poetic plea for restriction of immigration, a "cry to keep out the alien sinister races." Yet Aldrich also (inadvertently) advanced the cause of African-Americans when he published three stories by the unknown Charles Chesnutt. Price indicates that Chesnutt's groundbreaking work in the *Atlantic* should be read not only against Joel Chandler Harris's Uncle Remus stories but also against the backdrop of the *Atlantic*'s own racial discourse in the 1880s. The conservative—and at times reactionary—sentiments expressed in the magazine help to explain Chesnutt's reliance on elaborate distancing devices in his tales.

Sectional issues can take on a new prominence and clarity when viewed through the lens of the periodical press. In "Ambrose Bierce and the Transformation of the Gothic Tale in the Nineteenth-Century American Periodical," Gary Hoppenstand explores Bierce's role as one of San Francisco's most important authors prior to the turn of the century. Hoppenstand studies the powerful influence Bierce exerted on West Coast periodicals and on the San Francisco community of fantasy and scientific authors. Bierce's tales were disseminated by magazines and newspapers, which substantively dictated the style and content of Gothic fiction. In contrast to European models, the American Gothic tale became sparser and less ornate, influenced by the evolving journalistic vernacular of a print media pressured by publication deadlines, considerations of space, and the changing tastes of an expanded readership.

In nineteenth-century America, most literary works were written for and read in various kinds of periodicals, yet periodicals have received surprisingly little attention in the emerging history of the book. Studying periodicals allows us to examine the intersection of history and literature in a way that challenges traditional academic fields. Periodicals, once seen as the reflection of a culture and mined for background detail, are now recognized as central components of culture. In tracing the progress of what Emerson had termed the silent revolution, the essays in this volume approach American texts not as if they exist in timeless artistic isolation but rather as works emerging from contestation in the junctures where highbrow meets lowbrow, where commerce meets artistry. Indeed, the essays suggest that the distinctions between highbrow and lowbrow and between commerce and artistry were far less clear to periodical writers of the nineteenth century than those distinctions have often seemed to academic audiences of the twentieth century.

IN preparing this collection of essays, we have been fortunate to have the support and assistance of a number of colleagues and friends. We are grateful to the program committees of the Modern Language Association annual convention, the American Literature Association, and the Research Society for American Periodicals for providing opportunities for us and our contributors to present many of the ideas that are represented in these essays. For timely suggestions and encouragement, we are grateful to Martha Banta, Nina Baym, Alfred Bendixen, Robert C.

Bray, Cathy Davidson, Jeffrey D. Groves, Robert Scholnick, Merton Sealts, Ellery Sedgwick, and Jean Fagan Yellin. Michael O'Brien deserves special thanks for insightful suggestions about the scope of the essays. Our most important personal debts are to Linck C. Johnson for his astute criticism and excellent advice and to Renée Price for her good counsel and strong support. A faculty development leave awarded to Susan Belasco Smith by California State University, Los Angeles, provided time and support at a crucial stage in the editing of the collection. Cathie Brettschneider, our editor at the University Press of Virginia, has been a model of professionalism; we are thankful for her interest in our project and for her work in helping us bring it forward.

More formally, we wish to acknowledge the following libraries and publishers for their permission to use manuscripts and previously published materials: the Richard Watson Gilder Papers, Rare Books and Manuscripts Division, the New York Public Library; the Astor, Lenox, and Tilden Foundations; the Edmund Quincy–Charles Briggs Correspondence, the Massachusetts Historical Society; Duke University Press for extracts from chapters 3 and 7 of *The First Woman in the Republic: A Cultural Biography of Lydia Maria Child,* by Carolyn Karcher; the publishers and the Trustees of Amherst College for *The Poems of Emily Dickinson,* Thomas H. Johnson, eds., copyright 1951, 1955, 1979, 1983 by the president and the fellows of Harvard College; Little, Brown, and Company for *The Complete Poems of Emily Dickinson,* ed. Thomas H. Johnson, copyright 1929 by Martha Dickinson Bianchi, copyright renewed 1957 by Mary L. Hampson; and Rozanne Veeser, McFarlin Library, University of Tulsa, and Malcolm Germann and Betty Smith, Ablah Library, Wichita State University, for their assistance with interlibrary loan arrangements.

NOTES

1. Ralph Waldo Emerson, in "The Fugitive Slave Law," *The Collected Works of Ralph Waldo Emerson,* 12 vols. ed. Edward W. Emerson (Boston: Houghton-Mifflin, 1906), 11:218.

2. Frank Luther Mott, *A History of American Magazines, 1885–1905,* 5 vols. (Cambridge: Belknap Press of Harvard Univ. Press, 1957), 1:13, and Edward E. Chielens, ed., *American Literary Magazines: The Eighteenth and Nineteenth Centuries* (Westport, Conn.: Greenwood, 1986), 12–15.

3. Mott, *History,* 1:21.

4. Frank Luther Mott, *American Journalism: A History, 1690–1960,* 3d ed. (New York: Macmillan, 1962), 115.

5. Mott, *History,* 1:119.

6. Mott, *American Journalism,* 167.

7. Quoted in Mott, *History* 1:189.

8. Mott, *History,* 1:341.

9. Quoted in Ronald J. Zboray, "Antebellum Reading and the Ironies of Technological Innovation," in *Reading in America: Literature and Social History,* ed. Cathy N. Davidson (Baltimore: Johns Hopkins Univ. Press, 1989), 180.

10. Robert E. Spiller et al. *Literary History of the United States,* 3d ed. (New York: Macmillan, 1963), 805–6.

11. Richard H. Brodhead, "Literature and Culture," in *Columbia Literary History of the United States,* ed. Emory Elliott (New York: Columbia Univ. Press, 1988), 468–69.

12. William Kirkland, "British and American Monthlies," *Godey's Lady's Book* (1845): 271, quoted in Sheila Post-Lauria, "Writing for the Magazines: Creativity in the Antebellum Periodical Marketplace," unpublished ms., 1.

13. Mary Abigail Dodge (Gail Hamilton), *Skirmishes and Sketches* (Boston, 1865), 228, quoted in Mott, *History* 1:2.

14. Margaret Fuller, *Papers on Literature and Art* (New York: Fowler and Wells, 1852), 137–38.

15. Dana Estes, Senate Reports, quoted in Mott, *History,* 1:3.

16. Brodhead, "Literature and Culture," 475–76.

17. Karen J. Winkler, "In Electronic Age, Scholars Are Drawn to Study of Print," *Chronicle of Higher Education* (14 July 1993), A7.

18. Lyn Pykett, "Reading the Periodical Press: Text and Context," in *Investigating Victorian Journalism,* ed. Laurel Brake, Aled Jones, and Lionel Madden (New York: St. Martin's, 1990), 3.

19. Margaret Beetham, "Towards a Theory of the Periodical as a Publishing Genre," in ibid., 27.

1

FROM *DIAL* ESSAY TO NEW YORK BOOK
The Making of *Woman in the Nineteenth Century*

LARRY J. REYNOLDS

•

MARGARET Fuller's life and writings pose a multitude of riddles that remain unsolved. Perhaps the most intriguing of these, in this age of ideological critique, concerns her system of values and beliefs. As her friend James Freeman Clarke put it in 1839, "Her complex & various nature draws her in many directions. Her sense of the beautiful & keen discriminating mind, cause her to be exclusive in her tastes & aristocratic in her principles. Her practical tendency takes her back to the multitude. . . . What a Sphynx is that girl! who shall solve her?" As he ponders Fuller, Clarke predicts, "When she gets her principles & feelings in harmony she will do something."[1] Perhaps the most important thing Fuller subsequently did was to write *Woman in the Nineteenth Century* (1845), which has long served as a foundational text for the women's rights movement in America; whether this work successfully harmonizes Fuller's aristocratic principles and democratic feelings, however, remains an open question.[2]

Digressive, allusive, at times boldly philosophical, *Woman*, despite its straightforward title, is the most challenging and erudite expression of Fuller's views on the quest for human perfection. First published in the July 1843 *Dial* as an essay entitled "The Great Lawsuit: Man *versus* Men. Woman *versus* Women," the book advances the thesis that to achieve full intellectual and spiritual development, women must develop self-respect and learn self-help. It catalogs the many barriers to this project and urges American society to grant women the freedom and equality they deserve, not as concessions, but as rights. "We would have every arbitrary barrier thrown down," Fuller declares. "We would have every path laid open to woman as freely as to man."[3]

Now considered "one of the most important statements of feminist method and theory in history,"[4] *Woman* was transformed from essay to book in the fall 1844, a time of major change in Fuller's life and career. Having just accepted a job on a daily newspaper, the *New York Tribune,* known for its interest in social reform, she was turning her attention away from her relations with a circle of intimate friends and toward the plight of the lowly and oppressed. Her trip to Chicago and the Great Lakes in the summer of 1843 had given her new insight into the hardships of women on the frontier and into the injustices suffered by the American Indian. Also, as Christina Zwarg has recently shown, her trip strengthened her feminism "by forcing her to encounter the problematic grounding of any feminist argument,"[5] especially the limitations of her own cultural position. As Fuller began working on *Woman,* she travelled to Sing Sing, where she visited with female prisoners seeking "information of those who had been tempted to pollution and sorrow."[6] Her visit, she wrote them, inspired "great interest in your welfare and hope for your improvement" (*L,* 3:238). Despite this interest and hope, however, the book into which she incorporated their experiences displays even more evidence of Fuller's exclusive tastes than does "The Great Lawsuit." As Madeleine Stern has observed, "From Greek mythology and Spanish ballads, from the worship of the Virgin Mary and the legends of the Drachenfels, from the Macaria of Greece and the Britomart of Spenser, from Xenophon and Socrates, Euripides and Sophocles, from the Scandinavian sagas and from Goethe, from Spinoza and Eugène Sue, [Fuller] draws that 'catalogue of instances' that elucidates the nature of woman."[7] Such elucidation, which enlarged "The Great Lawsuit" to book length, seems addressed to the few, not to the multitude. Fuller herself sensed this, informing her friend William Henry Channing, "The writing, though I have tried to make my meaning full and clear, requires, shall I say? too much culture in the reader to be quickly or extensively diffused" (*L,* 3:241–42).

Responses to the book confirmed Fuller's opinion. One of Fuller's working-class contemporaries, the author of "Stray Leaves from a Seamstress's Journal," pointed out the "veil" between Fuller and "the rude, practical, every-day working world. She may write, and teach, and call herself a laborer, but this brings her only into distant relationship with us." As for *Woman,* the seamstress declared, "This book is for the educated few, it is rich in classic lore, and though there are many expressions of universal sympathy, it fails in practicality, and will be useful only to one class" (*Una,* Oct. 1853, 150). How and why did *Woman* become such a work, one that exudes sympathy for oppressed humanity, especially woman, and yet demands "too much culture" from a mass audience to be understood? This essay will address these questions by focusing on

Fuller's sense of audience during key stages of the book's composition, especially as it was originally written for the *Dial* in the winter 1842 and then revised and completed during her move from New England to New York City in 1844. I do not seek to "solve" the riddle of Fuller but rather to suggest reasons why *Woman* became the book that it did.

I

To begin to understand the making of Fuller's *Woman* requires a new narrative about the emergence of the *Dial* itself. Early commentary, as well as later scholarship, has consistently regarded this periodical as a product of the Transcendental Club, established to provide a public outlet for its members' philosophical and religious views. Bronson Alcott in his journals and reminiscences offers this account, which later commentators have followed, most notably Joel Myerson. As Myerson tells it, the club was formed in June 1836 by a group of Unitarian ministers—Ralph Waldo Emerson, Frederic Henry Hedge, George Putnam, and George Ripley—who "wished to assemble 'certain likeminded persons of our acquaintance for the free discussion of theological & moral subjects.'"[8] This group, later "swollen by the addition of Emerson's friends," including Alcott, Fuller, and Henry David Thoreau, decided to start a periodical of their own, because they "found all possible existing avenues of expression cut off from them."[9] In the fall of 1839, the subject of a journal was discussed at a meeting of the club, Alcott suggested the *Dial* as its name, and "Fuller was appointed editor." Thus, "the Transcendental Club, having provided its members with a body of sorts, was now preparing to supply them with a voice with which to be heard."[10] When Myerson turns to early issues of the *Dial,* however, he encounters a problem and must offer a discontinuous narrative, explaining that "somewhere between agreeing to establish a journal and actually getting an editor and a publisher and soliciting contributors, the Transcendental Club as a driving force dropped from sight, to be replaced by Fuller, Emerson, Ripley, and their—more often than not—nonministerial friends."[11] But these friends—Samuel Ward, Ellen Hooper, William Ellery Channing, Carrie Sturgis, and others—had been there all the time, and the "driving force" impelling them toward periodical publication was Fuller, not the Transcendental Club. For Myerson, the story of the *Dial* is one of loss and reversal, because he views Fuller as an unsuccessful functionary rather than a central organizing figure. In his view, her editorship arose because her "own natural desire to be at the center of attention coincided with her wish to help the Transcendentalists."[12]

What Myerson and others have failed to appreciate is that although the idea of the *Dial* emerged from conversations that occurred at meetings of the Transcendental Club, the journal itself grew out of the coterie publishing practices of a small group of friends, the Fuller circle if you will, who had been sharing "pacquets" or "portfolios" of materials with one another for several years. Fuller created this circle on her own initiative, and the pacquets they exchanged, which constituted the *Dial* in embryo form, contained a varying mixture of letters, poems, journal entries, critical essays, prints, and books and periodicals loaned by one member to another. Many of these original pieces later appeared in the *Dial*. Formed in 1836, soon after Fuller's first meeting with Emerson, the circle included Emerson, Sturgis, Ward, Anna Barker, Hooper, Ellery Channing, William Henry Channing, Timothy Dwight, and several others. Some of these individuals were members of the Transcendental Club; some not.[13] Unlike the club, whose primary interests were religious and public, those of the Fuller circle were literary and personal. As Charles Capper has pointed out, "Fuller initially looked to Transcendentalism, not primarily, as many did, to give birth to a new theology or church, but rather to help stimulate a cultural awakening."[14] This awakening, moreover, would arise through personal experience, as opposed to philosophical speculation, and would begin with private expression. As Fuller explained after sending one pacquet to Emerson in 1839, the papers were "some grove of private life, into which you might step aside to refresh yourself from the broad highway of philosophy" (*L*, 2:99).

For Fuller, the different materials she and her friends exchanged constituted an ongoing discussion or dialogue, leading to a better understanding of topics such as friendship, love, marriage, and the union of souls. The mode and matter of exchange thus matched one another. Through her efforts, especially the introduction of her friends to Emerson, Fuller effected a major shift in his career, turning his attention from philosophy and religion to lived experience. A letter she wrote to him on 24 November 1839 reveals the rich intertextuality of her efforts and the coterie publishing they involved: "I send you the canto in the poem of Caroline which I half promised. I have had many doubts about it, but finally I see so much beauty here that I cannot be willing not to share it with you, especially as I cannot hope to share it with any other person. I have given her last letter of the winter that you may better appreciate the flux and reflux of mind. Next to this read the two passages in my journal where I have turned the leaf, they were read by her and to the conversations which sprung from them several passages in her letter refer. To make the whole complete you should see a letter of mine upon the wind; but neither C. nor I has that now. . . . I thought this chapter out of my poetical journal might interest you now all the verses, even the translns bear some reference to Anna, W[ard]. and myself" (*L*, 2:98–99). The *Dial* should be regarded as an outgrowth of this kind of exchange, and Fuller's contributions to the *Dial*, especially "The Great Lawsuit," as her part of an ongoing, intertextual conversation with a group of like-minded friends.

Unlike Alcott, whose egocentricity blinded him to Fuller's formative role on the *Dial*, Emerson understood the way in which the journal fulfilled Fuller's desire to engage her friends in an intimate project of cultural growth; nevertheless, when he told his own public story about the *Dial*, he suppressed part of this knowledge. In his essay "Historic Notes of Life and Letters in New England" (1880), Emerson identified the transcendentalists as "two or three men or women who read and wrote, each alone, with unusual vivacity." He added, "As these persons became in the common chances of society acquainted with each other, there resulted certainly strong friendships, which of course were exclusive in proportion to their heat; and perhaps those persons who were mutually the best friends were the most private and had no ambition of publishing their letters, diaries or conversation."[15] What Emerson omits when taking this passage from his journal is the statement that "Margaret with her radiant genius & fiery heart was perhaps the real centre that drew so many & so various individuals to a seeming union."[17]

When he wrote the prospectus for the *Dial*, Emerson indicated the original purpose of the journal, linking it to a circle of friends: "As we wish not to multiply books, but to report life, our resources are therefore not so much the pens of practised writers, as the discourse of the living, and *the portfolios which friendship has opened to us*. From the beautiful recesses of private thought; . . . from the secret confession of genius afraid to trust itself to aught but sympathy; from the conversations of fervid and mystical pietists; from tear-stained diaries of sorrow and passion; from the manuscripts of young poets; and from the records of youthful taste commenting on old works of art; we hope to draw thoughts and feelings, which being alive can impart life" (emphasis added).[17] In his 1840 *Dial* essay on "New Poetry," Emerson announced a "revolution in literature" that "is now giving importance to the portfolio over the book," and he generalized his personal experience by declaring that "a wider epistolary intercourse ministers to the ends of sentiment and reflection than ever existed before" (Oct. 1840, 220). When he took over the editorship of the *Dial* from Fuller in 1842, Emerson cited this "epistolary intercourse" as his main reason for doing so, saying he valued the *Dial* "as a portfolio which preserves & conveys to distant persons precisely what I should borrow & transcribe to send them if I could."[18]

When Fuller began to edit the *Dial*, the pacquets that had passed between her and Emerson moved out of their circle into the hands of George Ripley (who had agreed to help Fuller with the financial end of the *Dial*) and the printers, at first Weeks, Jordan, and Co., then Elizabeth Peabody. As she and her friends went public with their writing, she expressed disappointment about the alterations and anonymity that seemed necessary because "these journals have something of the market-place vulgarity after all" (*L*, 2:133). Yet one sees her struggling to imagine the audience for the *Dial* not as the public at large but rather as a large circle of ideal friends. For her, the American public was hopelessly vulgar and ignorant, and she was reluctant to address it at this time. In 1836 she had explained her refusal to write for the *American Monthly* by declaring, "I am *not* willing to have what I write mutilated, or what I ought to say dictated to suit the public taste."[19] A few years later, she declared, "What a vulgarity there seems in this writing for the multitude! We know not yet, have not made ourselves known to a single soul, and shall we address those still more unknown?"[20] In her account of the correspondence between Bettina Bretano and her friend Günderode, Fuller suggests how she conceptually resolved the tensions involved in placing private expression before the public: "Those who write in the spirit of sincerity," she asserted, "write neither to the public nor the individual, but to the soul made manifest in the flesh, and publication or correspondence only furnish them with the occasion for bringing their thoughts to a focus" (*Dial*, Jan. 1842, 321).[21] Thus, Fuller managed to make all readers of the *Dial* into an audience of idealized presences.[22]

II

JUST as the *Dial* itself grew out of the coterie publishing of the Fuller circle, "The Great Lawsuit" grew out of the circle's intertextual conversations, especially those about human relations, which became an obsession for them during 1839–42. How should men and women relate to one another? What constitutes a perfect union? A permanent marriage? The ideal friendship? Thoreau responded first to these questions with his poem "Friendship," which he gave to Emerson in November 1839 and Fuller published in the October 1841 *Dial*. Emerson began to write his essay with the same title as early as the winter 1839, drawing on his correspondence with Fuller, Ward, and Sturgis. The triangular relationship between Emerson, Fuller, and Sturgis, along with its stresses and strains, provoked Fuller's own thoughts on the subject. The marriage of Ward and Anna Barker in October 1840 not only precipitated the well-known religious awakening in Fuller's life but also stimulated discussion within her circle about the union of souls.[23] Other marriages that informed this discussion included those of her sister, Ellen, and Ellery Channing (in September 1841), Sophia Peabody and Nathaniel Hawthorne (in July 1842), and Mary Peabody and Horace Mann (in May 1843). Fuller discussed the topic of marriage with both of the Hawthornes, and during the summer of 1842 she discussed marriage with Emerson at length, affecting his own marriage as she did so.

From August through September, she spent time walking and talking with Emerson (making his wife, Lidian, jealous on at least one occasion of which we know) and struggling to clarify the differences between his thought and her own. Fuller's journal entry for 1 September records Emerson's rarified approach to his second marriage: "We got to talking, as we almost always do, on Man and Woman, and Marriage.—W[aldo]. took his usual ground. Love is only phenomenal, a contrivance of nature, in her circular motion. Man, in proportion as he is completely unfolded is man and woman by turns. The soul knows nothing of marriage, in the sense of a permanent union between two personal existences. The soul is married to each new thought as it enters into it."[24] A week later Fuller revealed her continuing interest in Emerson's thoughts on marriage and through her imagery showed the romantic appeal he exerted upon her despite of—or perhaps because of—his aloof serenity: "Waldo came into my room to read what he has written in his journal about marriage, & we had a long talk. He listens with a soft witful look to what I say, but is nowise convinced. It was late in a dark afternoon, the fine light in that red room always so rich, cast a beautiful light upon him, as he read and talked. *Since* I have found in his journal two sentences that represent the two sides of his thought. . . . I shall write to him about it."[25]

"The Great Lawsuit" was part of Fuller's answer to Emerson. When she returned to Cambridge in the fall, she wrote to him that she wished to find expression for "much that has passed in my mind and which I should like you to know." She had done some writing, she told him, and "got along well enough till the point of division came, where I wanted to show that the permanent marriage cannot interfere with the soul's destiny." "There lies the paper," she concluded, "and I expect the hour may yet come when I can make out my case, if so, it will be sent" (*L*, 3:96). By the end of the winter of 1842–43, she had finished her case, her lawsuit, which not only argued on behalf of "permanent marriage" but also critiqued inferior pairings and justified the woman who chose not to marry at all. In "The Great Lawsuit," she wrote, "Saints and geniuses have often chosen a lonely position, in the faith that, if undisturbed by the pressure of near ties they could give themselves up to the inspiring spirit, it would enable them to understand and reproduce life better than actual experience could" (*Dial,* July 1843, 36). As for marriage, Fuller catalogs a number of types that fail to realize the full potential of either the husband or the wife. The first she mentions is a household partnership, much like the Emersons, based on mutual esteem and mutual dependence: "The wife praises her husband as a 'good provider,' the husband in return compliments her as a 'capital housekeeper.' This relation is good as far as it goes" (28). The second is a closer tie taking the form of immature intellectual companionship or mutual idolatry: "To themselves they seem the only wise, to all others steeped in infatuation. . . . To men the woman seems an unlovely syren, to women the man an effeminate boy" (28). The third type of marriage is mature intellectual companionship, often involving literary men and artists who have "found in their wives companions and confidants in thought no less than in feeling" (28). The fourth and highest is a religious union that goes beyond the other three relations by involving a joint spiritual quest.[26]

For Emerson, individuals would inevitably be alone in their quests for spiritual elevation; the best one could hope for was temporary union with another person, until one partner or the other moved on to a higher state of enlightenment. "All loves, all friendships are momentary," he recorded in his journal. "*Do you love me?* means at last *Do you see the same truth I see?* If you do, we are happy together: but when presently one of us passes into the perception of new truth, we are divorced and the force of all nature cannot hold us to each other."[27] For Fuller, the pursuit of truth could indeed mean forsaking ordinary human relations. Nevertheless, unlike Emerson, she believed in the possibility of marriage to enable and inspire. His tragedy, she believed, was accepting the appearance of marriage for the reality and then generalizing from his own experience. In her 1844 journal, she wrote, "I shall never forget that my curse is nothing compared with that of those who have entered into those relations but not made them real: who only *seem* husbands, wives & friends. H[awthorne]. was saying as much the other evening."[28]

Though Emerson gave insufficient attention to the ways in which the life experience of one individual could enrich that of one's friend or spouse, he nevertheless entertained remarkably open and flexible notions of gender. For him, as for her, the masculine and feminine flowed into one another, and in *Woman,* she clarifies the nuances in their thoughts on this important topic. Whereas Emerson believed that one becomes male and female in turn during moments of pure spirituality, Fuller understood that gender as defined in the material world, while fluid, nevertheless had historical consequences. She noted recent interest in the idea "that, in the metamorphoses of life, the soul assumes the form, first of man, then of woman, and takes the chances, and reaps the benefits of either lot. Why then, say some, lay such emphasis on the rights or needs of woman?" Her answer to this question is that "It is not woman, but the law of right, the law of growth, that speaks in us, and demands the perfection of each being in its kind, apple as apple, woman as woman" (162). In other words, the divinity within all material forms, including the body, the household, and the state, impels the ongoing perfection of these forms, despite their illusory and impermanent nature. Spiritual growth and social reform are thus bound inextricably together, and the "lawsuit" she has filed is against all who would obstruct "the holy work that is to make the earth a part of heaven" (v–vi). Whereas Emerson would have us transcend the material to realize our divinity, Fuller would have us realize our divinity by perfecting the material.

Soon after Fuller's essay appeared in the July 1843 *Dial,* Emerson informed her of its positive reception: "'The Great Lawsuit' is felt by all to be a piece of life, so much better than a piece of grammar. H. D. Thoreau, who will never like anything, writes, 'Miss F's is a noble piece, rich extempore writing, talking with pen in hand.' Mrs Sophia Ripley writes that 'Margaret's article is the cream of herself, a little rambling, but rich in all good things' and Ellery [Channing] testifies his approbation very distinctly & without qualification." As for his own opinion, Emerson told Fuller, "I think the piece very proper & noble, and itself quite an important fact in the history of Woman: good for its wit, excellent for its character—it wants an introduction; the subject is not quite distinctly & adequately propounded."[29] Perhaps because of this comment, Fuller decided to expand her essay into a book, or "pamphlet," as she called it. She began this task in the summer 1844 after publishing *Summer on the Lakes, 1843,* but at first made little progress. Her difficulty grew out of the change in vocation she was about to make. Impressed by *Summer on the Lakes,* Horace Greeley had offered Fuller a position on the *New York Tribune.* Though she would eventually accept the offer and do some of her most lucid and powerful writing for him, the prospect of working on a newspaper unsettled her. The step from addressing her good friends to addressing a mass of uncultured readers seemed almost too great to take.

III

BELL Gale Chevigny has ably discussed the trajectory of Fuller's career, emphasizing its centrifugal evolution, with each outward movement displaying more and more political involvement.[30] I would like to underscore the tension and contradictions associated with another key stage in this evolution. When Fuller went to Fishkill Landing to make "The Great Lawsuit" into a book, she was at a turning point in her career. As she stood overlooking the Hudson, with the high culture of the *Dial* behind her and the popular culture of the *Tribune* before her, her conscious intentions conflicted with her subconscious desires, which resulted in her new book becoming both less and more than she intended.

Although Fuller would never express regret about becoming a journalist, the job represented a lowering that both she and her Concord friends had difficulty adjusting to. Soon after Greeley offered Fuller the job on his newspaper, she experienced symptoms of stress associated with the decision she had to make. On 8 September, she wrote in her journal, "This past week has been one of the most suffering I ever spent, as the pain has never ceased, night or day. . . . I dared not write in the pamphlet for fear of exasperating my head by thought" ("Impulses," 114). Two days later, she recorded: "Woke much depressed. I do not see clearly what course to take, & that is even more trying than not to have energy to act as one has decided to be best" (115). That same day she wrote Greeley a long letter but expressed fear that it was "not the right one" (116). The letter never made it into the mail, but five days later, on 15 September, Greeley himself showed up in Cambridge, and Fuller agreed to go to New York and at least try the new job. When she visited Concord on 22 September, both Hawthorne and Emerson professed to find the *Tribune* position promising, but the next night Fuller had a nightmare related to her continued uncertainty. In the dream, Carrie Sturgis was lost on the seashore and Fuller unable to save her. Fuller wrote in her journal, "My feet seemed rooted to one spot: and my cloak of *red silk* kept falling off when I tried to go. At last the waves would wash up her dead body on the hard strand & then draw it back again. It was a terrible dream" (119). The nightmare seems to reveal Fuller's fear of being overwhelmed and drowned by vast impersonal forces. Her paralysis in the dream and the loss of her protecting cloak also seem clearly linked to a sense of powerlessness and vulnerability, and not surprisingly, in the same journal entry, she relates, "This morning letter from N Y about our going" (119).

Fuller understood all that was implied in the decision to write for a newspaper having thousands of lay readers as opposed to a literary journal read by a small group of highly educated friends. *Summer on the Lakes, 1843* marked her first step toward a mass audience, but the travel-writing genre held a status that journalism did not. Her friend Ellery Channing held strong negative feelings toward the profession, which he had entered several months ahead of Fuller. After working briefly at the *Tribune,* Channing visited Fuller in Fishkill while she was writing *Woman* and soon afterward described his plight in imagery similar to hers—that is, as a drowning and annihilation. He was, he wrote to Emerson, the "prey of Newspaper wages" and "deeply sunk in oceans of stupidity, in blank wastes of Newspaper deserts, my faculties all begummed, seriously dried, dessicated, & without any species of intelligence, save the last floating remnants of a kind of childish Affection."[31]

At Fishkill Landing, Fuller dealt with her decision to go to New York with a final outpouring of cultural knowledge that few others could match. Somehow the place itself liberated her to respond energetically to the problems of a new career and mass society. In letters to friends, she emphasized the elevation of the site and made the high hills behind the town into lofty mountains. In her letters and in the book itself, she used high ground as a spatial metaphor to suggest the quality of her work and its elevating effects. "The boldness, sweetness, and variety here, just what I like," she wrote. "How idle to pretend that one could live and write so well amid fallow flat fields! This majesty, this calm splendor, could not but exhilarate the mind, and make it nobly free and plastic" (*L,* 4:232). On 17 November 1844, she wrote to her friend William Henry Channing, "At last, my dear William, I have finished the pamphlet. The last day it kept spinning out beneath my hand. After taking a long walk early on one of the most noble exhilarating sort of mornings I sat down to write and did not put the last stroke till near nine in the evening Then I felt a delightful glow as if I had put a good deal of my true life in it, as if, suppose I went away now, the measure of my footprint would be left on the earth" (*L,* 3:241–42).

When Fuller's book took on a life of its own, it contradicted her conscious intention of writing for a new audience of lay readers, as can be seen throughout her revisions; however, her change of title and her comment upon it reveal the pull she felt in the opposite direction. In the preface she declares, "Objections having been made to the former title, as not sufficiently easy to be understood, the present has been substituted as expressive of the main purpose of the essay; though, by myself, the other is preferred, partly for the reason others do not like it, *i.e.*, that it requires some thought to see what it means, and might thus prepare the reader to meet me on my own ground" (*Woman*, v). Fuller's statement, of course, raises questions of audience and purpose. Does she want to move to her readers' ground so as to be understood, or does she seek to raise them to her own level to stimulate their thought? The answer seems to be both.

While at Fishkill Landing, Fuller tried to negotiate between an emerging egalitarianism associated with her new job in New York City and a residual intellectual elitism associated with her Concord-Cambridge-Boston circle of friends. She clearly cared about the lowly and oppressed, and sections she added in 1844 dealing with abused wives, female slaves, prostitutes, old maids, and female factory workers all give evidence of her democratic feelings; however, other passages she added about Swedenborg, Fourier, Goethe, Renaissance drama, Greek myth, Spanish ballads, Rhine legends, and Native American stories plus eight appendixes quoting from Apuleius, Petrarca (in Italian), John Lockhart, Spinoza, Euripides, and others hark back to the exclusive tastes of her *Dial* circle. The overflowing extravagance Fuller displayed while writing her book serves to defend against disdain from this circle and against the leveling of the multitude. In the poem that concludes *Woman*, Fuller urges the reader to cherish "your best hopes as a faith" and

> Ask for the Castle's King and Queen;
> Though rabble rout may rush between,
> Beat thee senseless to the ground,
> In the dark beset thee round;
> Persist to ask and it will come,
> Seek not for rest in humbler home;
> So shalt thou see what few have seen,
> The palace home of King and Queen.

In her discussion of this "monarchist vignette," Julie Ellison has observed that "the mob represents both internal and external resistance; its chthonic energy, which threatens unconsciousness, dark confusion, and claustrophobia, conveys the psychological as well as the social price of blowing one's own horn."[32] Given Fuller's situation in November 1844, it seems likely that the poem alludes as much to an anticipated loss of identity in mass society as it does to the price of outspoken feminism.

The "rabble rout" in Fuller's poem is ungendered. The book as a whole, however, does focus on gender issues. Her additions reveal a shift in imagined audience from a circle of male and female friends to American women in general, and *Woman* thus becomes a far more feminist work than the essay from which it originated. "The Great Lawsuit" assumes an audience of men and women, and Fuller's good friends Emerson, Clarke, Ellery Channing, William Henry Channing, and even Hawthorne were surely as much on her mind as she wrote as the women who had been attending her course of Boston "Conversations." In the preface to *Woman*, dated November 1844, Fuller alludes to her male friends, asking other men to share their outlook: "From men I ask a noble and earnest attention to any thing that can be offered on this great and still obscure subject, such as I have met from many with whom I stand in private relations" (v). The some ninety pages she added to the essay, though, shift her focus to women's rights, and in the new material she addresses women almost exclusively, offering them counsel and encouragement.[33] She tells them that they are responsible for their fates, that they need to help themselves and not rely upon men. As she turns to the topic of prostitution, she says, "O men! I speak not to you. . . . You need to teach and warn one another. . . . But to you, women, American women, a few words may not be addressed in vain. One here and there may listen" (119–20). Similarly, in her discussion of "coquettish attraction," she writes, "to you, women of America, it is more especially my business to address myself on this subject" (127). Finally, near her conclusion, she declares, "Women of my country!—Exaltadas!" (152).

Despite these passages, not all American women could hope to understand Fuller's words, and by turning to obscure works of history and literature in a final burst of cultural enthusiasm, Fuller returned to the spirit that had impelled the work in the first place. After Fuller left Fishkill Landing and went to New York City in December 1844, her first assignment was to review Emerson's *Essays, Second Series,* which had just appeared. In reviewing the work of her friend, she justifies the challenging features of the book she has just completed. She contrasts Emerson with popular writers who write down to their audiences, "who lend all their efforts to flatter corrupt tastes and mental indolence, instead of feeling it their prerogative and their duty to admonish the community of the danger and arouse it to nobler energy." She claims that Emerson's goal is "to raise his mind as high as he can toward the heaven of truth, and try to draw up with him those less gifted by nature with ethereal lightness." Though she criticizes his lack of earthiness, his having "raised himself too early to the perpendicular," she nevertheless places him among an intellectual elite: "He belongs to that band of whom there may be found a few in every age, . . . who worship the one God only, the God of Truth."[34]

Once on the *Tribune*, Fuller put a distance between herself and Emerson, turning to "those less gifted by nature," seeking to educate them in more direct fashion. In 1845 she wrote to a correspondent from New York City, "I am pleased with your sympathy about the Tribune, for I do not find much among my old friends. They think I ought to produce something excellent, while I am satisfied to aid in the great work of popular education. I never regarded literature merely as a collection of exquisite products, but rather as a means of mutual interpretation" (*L*, 4:39). A new style accompanied this new attitude, and one could not ask for a more clear and direct prose than that Fuller developed while working on the *Tribune*.

Fuller credited her new friend Horace Greeley with this change, declaring, "He teaches me things, which my own influence on those who have hitherto approached me, has prevented me from learning" (*L*, 4:40). The mutual admiration that developed between them signaled the end of the "Fuller circle" and the beginning of a new stage in Fuller's sociopolitical development. In the spring 1845, Fuller told her brother, Eugene, "Mr. Greeley I like, nay more, love. He is, in his habits, a slattern and plebeian, and in his heart, a nobleman" (*L*, 4:56). This nobleman, whose love of working people knew no bounds, appreciated the reforming impulse at the heart of *Woman*, commenting, "If not the clearest and most logical, it was the loftiest and most commanding assertion yet made of the right of Woman to be regarded and treated as an independent, intelligent, rational being."[35] By opening the profession of journalism to Fuller and treating her with the greatest respect, Greeley was rewarded by having the *Tribune* become the periodical in which she at last published her most powerful prose and established herself as the most radically democratic writer of the American Renaissance.

NOTES

I would like to thank Bell Chevigny, Jeffrey Cox, Susan Egenolf, Thomas Mitchell, Kenneth Price, and Susan Belasco Smith for their useful responses to earlier drafts of this essay.

1. Quoted in Charles Capper, *Margaret Fuller: An American Romantic Life*. vol. 1, *The Private Years* (New York: Oxford Univ. Press, 1992), 314.

2. The strongest argument on behalf of *Woman* as a harmonizing work has been made by David M. Robinson, "Margaret Fuller and the Transcendental

Ethos: *Woman in the Nineteenth Century*" *PMLA* 97 (1982): 83–98, which argues that "the work ... stands as a translation of transcendental idealism into the social and political realm" (84). For Robinson, "The vision of harmony, based on the belief in the possibility of a society that would make self-culture possible, ultimately fuels Fuller's social criticism" (94). Bell Gale Chevigny, on the other hand, has argued that the book "is rife with unresolved issues and contradictions. Not the least of these is that it simultaneously pays tribute to Transcendentalism and signals her break with that movement" ("To the Edges of Ideology: Margaret Fuller's Centrifugal Evolution," *American Quarterly* 38 [1986]: 173–201; quotation, 183). For Chevigny, Fuller's emerging feminism "was ill-reconciled with Transcendentalism" and thus what emerges in the book "is a revealing incoherence" (183).

3. *Woman in the Nineteenth Century,* ed. Joel Myerson, with an introduction by Madeleine Stern (Columbia: Univ. of South Carolina Press, 1980), 28. Hereafter cited parenthetically.

4. Barbara Welter, *Dimity Convictions: The American Woman in the Nineteenth Century* (Athens: Ohio Univ. Press, 1976), 180.

5. Christina Zwarg, "Footnoting the Sublime: Margaret Fuller on Black Hawk's Trail," *American Literary History* 5 (1993): 616–42; quotation, 637.

6. *Letters of Margaret Fuller,* ed. Robert N. Hudspeth, 5 vols. to date (Ithaca: Cornell Univ. Press, 1983–), 3:237. Subsequent references will be cited parenthetically as *L*.

A number of twentieth-century critics have defended the difficult features of Fuller's book on aesthetic, psychological, and political grounds. See especially, Marie Mitchell Olesen Urbanski, *Margaret Fuller's "Woman in the Nineteenth Century": A Literary Study of Form and Content, of Sources and Influence* (Westport, Conn: Greenwood, 1980); Jeffrey Steele, "The Call of Eurydice: Mourning and Intertextuality in Margaret Fuller's Writing," in *Influence and Intertextuality in Literary History,* ed. Eric Rothstein and Jay Clayton (Madison: Univ. of Wisconsin Press, 1991), 271–97; Stern, introduction to *Woman:* and Julie Ellison, *Delicate Subjects: Romanticism, Gender, and the Ethics of Understanding* (Ithaca, N.Y.: Cornell Univ. Press, 1990), 266–87.

7. Stern, introduction to *Woman,* xv.

8. Joel Myerson, "A History of the Transcendental Club," *ESQ* 23 (1977): 27–35; quotation, 27.

9. Ibid., 29; Joel Myerson, *The New England Transcendentalists and the "Dial": A History of the Magazine and Its Contributors* (Rutherford, N.J.: Fairleigh Dickinson Univ. Press, 1980), 35.

10. Myerson, "A History," 32.

11. Myerson, *The New England Transcendentalists,* 36.

12. Ibid., 37.

13. For a list of those who attended meetings of the Transcendental Club, see Joel Myerson, "A Calendar of Transcendental Club Meetings," *American Literature* 44 (1972): 197–207. (Emerson, William Henry Channing, and Dwight at-

tended regularly; Ward may have attended once.) For a list of contributors to the *Dial,* see the appendix to Myerson's *New England Transcendentalists.* Prominent members of the club who did not publish in the *Dial* included George Putnam, Cyrus Bartol, Convers Francis, and Caleb Stetson; members of the Fuller circle involved with the *Dial* but not the Transcendental Club included Ward, Sturgis, Hooper, and William Ellery Channing.

14. Capper, *Margaret Fuller,* 1:313.

15. *The American Transcendentalists: Their Prose and Poetry,* ed. Perry Miller (Garden City, N.Y.: Doubleday, 1957), 15.

16. Ralph Waldo Emerson, *The Journals and Miscellaneous Notebooks of Ralph Waldo Emerson,* ed. Linda Allardt, David W. Hall, and Ruth Bennett (Cambridge: Belknap Press of Harvard Univ. Press, 1982), 16:22.

17. *The Transcendentalists: An Anthology,* ed. Perry Miller (Cambridge: Harvard Univ. Press, 1950), 250.

18. *The Letters of Ralph Waldo Emerson,* ed. Ralph L. Rusk (New York: Columbia Univ. Press, 1939), 3:37.

19. *Memoirs of Margaret Fuller Ossoli,* ed. R. W. Emerson, W. H. Channing, and J. F. Clarke, 2 vols. (1852; rpt. New York: Burt Franklin, 1972), 1:168.

20. Ibid., 1:296.

21. After she went to work on the *Tribune,* she rephrased this idea, asserting that in writing for the newspaper, "we address not our neighbor, who forces us to remember his limitations and prejudices, but the ideal presence of human nature as we feel it ought to be and trust it will be. We address America rather than Americans" (*Margaret Fuller, American Romantic: A Selection from Her Writings and Correspondence,* ed. Perry Miller [Garden City, N.Y.: Doubleday, 1963], 248).

22. In his biography, Capper traces Fuller's remarks about the "vulgarity" of her audience to her "paralyzing uncertainty" about her abilities as a writer: "She knew the fundamental problem lay, not just in writing for an audience, but with herself—in particular with her inability to *imagine* a sympathetic or congenial audience" (*Margaret Fuller,* 336–37).

23. For excellent discussions of the intense friendships that arose among the Fuller circle during 1839–42, see Bell Gale Chevigny, *The Woman and the Myth: Margaret Fuller's Life and Writing* (rev. ed. Boston: Northeastern Univ. Press, 1994), 66–80; Anne C. Rose, *Transcendentalism as a Social Movement: 1830–1850* (New Haven: Yale Univ. Press, 1981), 174–84; and Dorothy Berkson, "'Born and Bred in Different Nations: Margaret Fuller and Ralph Waldo Emerson,'" in *Patrons and Protégées: Gender, Friendship, and Writing in Nineteenth-Century America,* ed. Shirley Marchalonis (New Brunswick, N.J.: Rutgers Univ. Press, 1988), 3–30.

24. Joel Myerson, "Margaret Fuller's 1842 Journal: At Concord with the Emersons," *Harvard Library Bulletin* 21 (1973): 320–40; quotation, 330.

25. Ibid., 335.

26. It seems likely that Sophia and Nathaniel Hawthorne provided the model for Fuller's third category of marriage if not her fourth; nevertheless, Sophia found Fuller's article offensive and wrote to her mother, "What do you think of

the speech which Queen Margaret Fuller has made from the throne? It seems to me that if she were married truly, she would no longer be puzzled about the rights of woman. This is the revelation of Woman's true destiny and place, which never can be *imagined* by those who do not experience the relation" (Julian Hawthorne, *Nathaniel Hawthorne and His Wife*, 2 vols. [Boston: Houghton Mifflin, 1884], 1:258).

There are a number of explanations for Sophia's critical response to Fuller's essay, but defensiveness about her own marital situation is perhaps a key one. The ongoing discussion within the Fuller circle about friendship, marriage, and the union of souls made almost everyone in Concord self-conscious about establishing the perfect union. Thus, when Fuller posited a hierarchy of marriages, she aggravated the anxiety the new Adam and Eve at the Old Manse already felt. While couples such as Sam and Anna Ward or Horace and Mary Mann seemed to be prosperous and happy, the Hawthornes were struggling with a poverty they found embarrassing. Moreover, the Peabodys of Boston put the couple on edge by reporting on the happiness of others, especially Sam and Anna.

27. *The Journals and Miscellaneous Notebooks of Ralph Waldo Emerson*, ed. A. W. Plumstead and Harrison Hayford (Cambridge: Belknap Press of Harvard Univ. Press, 1969), 7:532.

28. Martha L. Berg and Alice de V. Perry, eds., "'The Impulses of Human Nature': Margaret Fuller's Journal from June through October 1844," *Massachusetts Historical Society Proceedings* 102 (1990): 38–126; quotation, 92. The textual history of his entry reveals Emerson's sensitivity to its truth. As Berg and Perry note, when he copied it into his own journal after Fuller's death, he changed the "H." to "W.," thereby appropriating Hawthorne's role as sharer of Fuller's opinion. When Emerson put the entry into the *Memoirs*, he removed the last sentence altogether, thus thoroughly protecting his marriage from Fuller's public consideration.

29. *Letters of Ralph Waldo Emerson*, 3:183.

30. See Chevigny, "To the Edges of Ideology" and *The Woman and the Myth*.

31. Francis B. Dedmond, ed., "The Selected Letters of William Ellery Channing the Younger (Part One)," in *Studies in the American Renaissance 1989* (Charlottesville: Univ. Press of Virginia, 1989), 211.

In private, Emerson shared Channing's estimate of newspaper work. In a 2 December 1844 letter to Sam Ward, he referred to Channing's and Fuller's new careers: "The Tribune office may be good treatment for some of his local distempers, but it seems a very poor use to put a wise man & a genius, to. Is it any better with Margaret? The Muses have feet, to be sure, but it is an odd arrangement that selects them for the treadmill. Our grand machine of Society must be sadly disjointed & ricketty, if this is its best result; and it is" (*Letters of Ralph Waldo Emerson*, 7:618).

32. Ellison, *Delicate Subjects*, 262.

33. For a complex and acute discussion of the ambiguous gender of *Woman*'s narrator and its "positionality and activity in relation to its subjects and readers,"

see Mary E. Wood, "'With Ready Eye': Margaret Fuller and Lesbianism in Nineteenth-Century American Literature," *American Literature* 65 (1993): 1–18.

34. "Emerson's Essays," reprinted in *The Essential Margaret Fuller,* ed. Jeffrey Steele (New Brunswick, N.J.: Rutgers Univ. Press, 1992), 379–85.

35. Horace Greeley, *Recollections of a Busy Life* (New York: J. B. Ford, 1868), 175–76.

2

FROM PERIODICAL WRITER TO POET
Whitman's Journey through
Popular Culture

DAVID S. REYNOLDS

•

T HE twenty-one poems, twenty-two short stories, and one novel that
Walt Whitman wrote before the 1855 *Leaves of Grass* have, over the
years, gotten bad press, and understandably so. Taken individually, none
of these works possess anything close to the stylistic distinction of an
1855 poem like "Song of Myself." But taken as a whole, the apprentice
work can be viewed as a testing ground for several ideas and stylistic
devices that appeared in his mature poetry—several, but not all. There
are themes and devices that are indeed distinctive to the major poetry,
and they arose between 1847 and 1855 largely in response to social and
political conditions that Whitman was observing closely.

My aim is to sort out the extent to which Whitman's "long foreground," as Ralph Waldo Emerson called it, was indeed such and to what
extent it was not. Which of his central themes had he been mulling over
for a long while, and which ones exploded almost spontaneously as a
result of the changed social conditions of the 1850s?

Whitman's early works have never been categorized or placed in their
popular cultural context. Most of his early works fit into well-established
popular categories, each with its own history. Among his pre-1855 imaginative writings, fourteen (nine poems and five tales) were dark works
about death or haunted minds; seven (five stories and two poems) were
sensational or adventurous; six others (a poem, three stories, a novel,
and a tale fragment) endorsed reform, particularly temperance; four
(two poems and two tales) were visionary works about angels or angelic
visitations; four (two poems and two tales) were patriotic or nationalistic;
four poems were political; three tales and one poem were moral; one
tale was biblical.[1]

The fact that nearly two-thirds of his early writings were dark or sensational accords with the preponderance of these kinds of works in ante-

bellum America. Contrary to the once-held view that the antebellum literary scene was dominated by sentimental, so-called feminized writings, my research has revealed that about 60 percent of all fiction volumes by Americans between 1831 and 1860 were adventurous, sensational, or satirical, while just over 20 percent were domestic or religious. About 70 percent of the fiction volumes written in these three decades were by men, 23 percent by women (7 percent were published anonymously).[2] As a man writing predominantly dark or adventurous works, then, Whitman was in keeping with the times.

He was atypical, however, in his extraordinary eclecticism, even at this early phase. These early writings show him reaching out in many directions, confining himself to no single style or theme. His readiness to test different popular modes distinguished him from other popular authors of the day, most of whom stayed in fairly narrow ruts. Some, like Timothy Shay Arthur, stuck to reformist or moral fiction; others, like Susan Warner, to domestic novels; others, like William Ware, to biblical and historical fiction; and others, like George Thompson, to sensational fiction. True, a few authors made dramatic changes in their careers. Joseph Holt Ingraham, for instance, began as a prolific author of blood-curdling sensational novels and then turned to pious biblical fiction. Later, Louisa May Alcott would turn from Gothic sensational thrillers to the writing of domestic and children's literature.

But no one, to my knowledge, explored as many different popular genres simultaneously as did Whitman. Whitman may not have distinguished himself in any individual work, but he did distinguish himself in his remarkable reach. His capacious imagination was already surveying the entire cultural landscape and testing some themes that would be developed more fully in his mature poetry. Among these specific themes were sensationalism, death, religion, reform, and politics. Each of them is, of course, a big topic in itself, and this essay cannot be exhaustive. Instead, I will point out some general ways in which Whitman's treatment of these themes changed between his early writings and his major poetry.

With respect to sensationalism, Whitman always had a tricky time positioning himself with regard to the increasing thirst for blood and gore that accompanied the rise of mass print culture in the United States. On the one hand, he knew full well the broad appeal that sensational writings had for the American masses. He was weaned in the cut-and-thrust world of penny-press urban journalism, and he noted the extreme popularity of what he called "blood and thunder romances with alliterative titles and plots of startling interest." "The public for whom these tales are written," he noted, "require strong contrasts, broad effects and the fiercest kind of intense writing."[3]

As chief editor of the *Brooklyn Daily Eagle* and later the *Brooklyn Daily Times,* he accommodated popular taste by printing horrid stories of crime and violence. Before that, he had reported murders for the *New York Tattler* and had written police and coroner's stories for the *New York Sun.* On the other hand, he would become outspoken in his opposition to excesses in such sensational literature. In his major poems he would make a studied effort to represent the sensational, as an important element of the cultural scene, while rechanneling it and combining it with uplifting images derived from other cultural arenas.

In the early 1840s, however, he had not yet developed such reservations about sensational literature. Nearly all the periodicals he wrote for were riding the wave of sensationalism. Several of his early poems and stories were sensational in a straightforward way, like the plotty, action-driven yellow-covered novels of the day. One of his poems, "The Inca's Daughter," portrays an Inca maid who, after remaining stoically silent while being tortured on the rack by Spaniards, stabs herself with a poisoned arrow and dies. Another, "The Spanish Lady," pictures the lovely Lady Inez, who is sleeping in her castle room when suddenly she is stabbed by "one whose trade is blood and crime."[4] Five short sketches Whitman wrote for the *Aristidean* in 1845, published as "Some Fact-Romances," lean toward the sensational. In one, a Long Island man tries to save his drowning sister but fails and thereafter is haunted by the vision of her dying face; he wastes away and dies. In another, a French emigrant whose wife has died becomes a helpless maniac and is committed to an asylum. Another, which Whitman called "a disgusting story of villainy and deceit," involves an imprisoned forger, and another gives a comic twist to sensationalism by describing a woman terrified at night by a thumping sound that turns out to be a fallen basket of peaches (*WEP,* 324).

Although his exercises in sensationalism were never as bloody as those of his popular contemporaries, he did not shy away from gory scenes. Two of his other tales in the *Aristidean,* "Richard Parker's Widow" and "The Half-Breed: A Tale of the Western Frontier," show him catering to the popular appetite for the grisly. The former tales recounts the aftermath of the 1797 *Nore* mutiny, whose leader, Richard Parker, was hanged from a yardarm. In a scene suggestive of necrophilia, Parker's maddened widow disinters his coffin, opens it, and embraces the corpse. "She clasped the cold neck," Whitman writes, "and kissed the clammy lips of the object of her search!" (*WEP,* 299). She later gets his body reburied at Whitechapel, but she is eventually reduced to wretched beggary. "The Half-Breed" is a darkly adventurous story with an improbable cast of characters, including a monk, a hunchback, a half-breed, and a black-smith. The plot, typical of sensational narratives of the day, is too tangled to be summarized: suffice it to say that the blacksmith, Peter Brown, is apparently murdered but is really not, and the hunchback is the true villain but the wrongly accused half-breed is tragically hanged and dies just before the frenzied Brown can rescue him. As the Indian's corpse swings on the rope, Brown dashes through the woods "with wild and ghastly visage, and the phrenzied contortions of a madman in his worst paroxysm" until "his blood-shot eyes were fixed upon a hideous object dangling in the air" (*WEP,* 290).

A certain amount of sensationalism runs through *Leaves of Grass,* sug-gesting that on some level Whitman was trying to appeal to the predomi-nantly working-class readers who consumed such literature. One thinks particularly of the bloody adventure narratives at the heart of "Song of Myself," describing the massacre of the 412 young men at Goliad and then the bloody sea battle between the *Serapis* and the *Bon Homme Rich-ard,* with gore dribbling from the ships' masts. One also thinks of the graphic images scattered throughout his poems, such as the amputated leg that falls horribly into the pail, the mashed fireman, or the suicide sprawled on the bloody bedroom floor. Still, there is something to be said for Whitman's remark that *Leaves of Grass* "yields nothing for the seeker of sensations."[5] He makes every effort in his major poetry to sub-sume sensationalism to some larger philosophical purpose. The gory im-ages in his poems are juxtaposed with life-affirming ones, as though tragic occurrences are a natural part of an ongoing cycle of life and death.

His revised treatment of sensationalism was linked to a revised treat-ment of death. It is not generally known that Whitman started out pri-marily as a writer of gloom and skepticism. Metaphysical angst character-izes many of his early writings. Here again, he corresponded to popular tastes. It is sometimes said that antebellum popular literature was com-fortingly pious and that dark authors like Nathaniel Hawthorne and Herman Melville stood in opposition to an easily optimistic culture. Ac-tually, though, much popular fiction and poetry of the time was riddled with doubt and sadness.

Several early Whitman pieces were typical. Life is full of "useless, vex-ing strife," Whitman wrote in the poem "The Love That Is Hereafter"; all dreams are invalidated by "hope dissatisfied," and since on each there is "Nought but wo," the heart "must look above / Or die in dull despair"

(*WEP,* 9). "Time levels all," he reflects in "The End of All"; the brilliant, rich, and gay "Live out their brief and brilliant day" and then "unheeded pass away" (*WEP,* 14). "All, all know care," he points out in "Each Has His Grief," and since death ends human agony, none should fear "The coffin, and the pall's dark gloom" (*WEP,* 17). Hopes for immortality through earthly renown are foolish, he says in "Ambition," for most who desire fame don't get it, and even those who do "must sleep the endless sleep" and will soon be forgotten (*WEP,* 23). A real fear of annihilation lurks behind the poem "Time to Come," in which he notes that "This brain, and heart, and wondrous form / Must all alike decay," and, as for the soul, "Will it e'en live?" (*WEP,* 27)

None of these thoughts were original or originally expressed. This kind of morbid writing filled the popular periodicals of the time. The popular obsession with death was variously visible in the fad of photographing the corpses of loved ones and in the thirst for death-obsessed verse later satirized by Mark Twain in his portrait of Emmeline Grangerford, the poet who always reached a corpse before the undertaker.

What distinguished Whitman was that over time he came to change his position on death. His almost nihilistic fear of death was largely alleviated by his exposure to two developments of the late 1840s: chemical science and spiritualism. The scientist who most strongly influenced him in this regard was the Stockholm chemist Justus Liebig. Liebig introduced a chemical explanation for the eternal recombination of atoms in an eternal cycle of decay and regeneration. When the American edition of Liebig's *Chemistry in Its Application to Physiology and Agriculture* appeared in 1847, Whitman raved about Liebig in the *Brooklyn Daily Eagle,* declaring that Liebig's fame was "as wide as the civilized world—a fame nobler than that of generals, or of many bright geniuses (28 June 1847). Liebig gave validity to the idea of the cyclical quality of all things by arguing that when an organism decomposed, its atoms were chemically recombined, giving rise, in his words, "to another arrangement of the atoms of a body, that is, to the production of a compound which did not before exist."[6]

There seemed, then, to be an ongoing resurrection and a democratic exchange of substances inherent in nature. Just as Liebig wrote that "the active state of the atoms of one body had an influence upon the atoms of a body in contact with it," so Whitman announced in the second line of "Song of Myself" that "every atom belonging to me as good belongs to you."[7] As Liebig said that after death humans are changed into other things, so Whitman could write:

We are Nature . . .
We become plants, trunks, foliage, roots, bark,
We are bedded in the ground, we are rocks,
We are oaks.

(*WCP,* 264)

If Liebig envisaged an exchange of life forms through decomposition and regrowth, so Whitman fashioned metaphors that vivified the idea of the ceaseless springing of life from death, such as the curling grass that he says transpires from the breasts of young men or the polished breasts of melons that grow from the "good manure" of the corpse (*WCP,* 86). Liebig wrote that "the miasms and certain contagious matters [that] produce diseases in the human organism" become "*not contagious*" when the organism is absorbed into the earth.[8] This becomes the central point in Whitman's "This Compost." He asks the earth in amazement: "Are they not continually putting distemper'd corpses within you?" and then provides the Liebigian answer:

Behold this compost! behold it well!
Perhaps every mite has once form'd part of a sick person—yet
    behold! . . .
What chemistry!
That the winds are really not infectious,
That this is no cheat, this transparent green-wash of the sea which is so
    amorous after me . . .
That all is clean forever and forever.

(*WCP,* 495)

Whitman also felt the direct influence of spiritualism, which surfaced in 1848 and spread with amazing rapidity, gaining millions of adherents, including such notables as Sojourner Truth, William Lloyd Garrison, and Sarah and Angelina Grimké. Spiritualism was nineteenth-century America's most influential movement challenging the idea of the finality of death. By 1857 Whitman could note in the *Daily Times* that there were some three to five million spiritualists in America and that the movement was "blending itself in many ways with society, in theology, in the art of healing, in literature, and in the moral and mental character of the people of the United States (26 June 1857). One of the things with which it blended was his poetry. In the 1855 preface to *Leaves of Grass,* he includes the spiritualist among "the lawgivers of poets" (*WCP,* 15). Spiritualist images are scattered throughout his poems. His repeated assurances about immortality retain the optimism of the spiritualists. It is just as lucky to be born as it is to die, he tells us in "Song of Myself." "I am the mate and companion of people, all just as immortal and fathom-less as myself," he wrote. "They do not know how immortal, but I know" (*WCP,* 33). With the confidence of the spiritualist he announced, "I know I am deathless" and "I laugh at what you call dissolution" (*WCP,* 46). This was a spiritualism without gimmickry, what he called a true spiritualism. In an anonymously published self-review of the 1855 edi-tion, he said of himself: "He is the true spiritualist. He recognizes no annihilation, or death, or loss of identity."[9]

His interest in spiritualism increased with time. On some level, the poet became associated in his mind with the spiritualist medium. As he wrote in his notebook, "The poets are divine mediums—through them come spirits and materials to all the people, men and women."[10] In an 1860 poem entitled "Mediums," he says that a new race of mediums is arising that will "convey gospels" about nature, the body, oratory, death (*WCP,* 590). He used the vocabulary of spiritualism in other poems: "O mediums! O to teach! to convey the invisible faith!", and, "Something unproved! something in a trance!"[11] In a poem in the "Calamus" cluster he feels surrounded by "the spirits of dear friends dead or alive, thicker they come," and in another 1860 poem he describes "The rapt promises and luminè of seers, the spiritual world" (*WCP,* 273, 595).

To be sure, he never became a card-carrying spiritualist, and he looked with amused detachment on the spirit-rappings, table-liftings, and other manufactured miracles that won over many of his contempo-raries. Still, he did befriend spiritualists, including the famous medium Cora Hatch, who dedicated a collection of her poems to him. Also, dur-ing the Civil War he did attend seances led by the renowned medium Charles H. Foster, and in 1871 he could report in a letter of a recent evening with friends: "We had a capital good hour & a half—*talked Spiri-tualism*—I enjoyed it thoroughly."[12] By 1888 he could still write a poem, "Continuities," that he said was inspired by a conversation with a spiritu-alist. The language he used in the poem was one of spiritualist consola-tion, as he wrote that

> Nothing is ever really lost, or can be lost,
> No birth, identity, form—no object of the world.
> Nor life force, nor any visible thing.
>
> (*WCP,* 626)

To the end, then, his poetry reflected his interest in spiritualism.

Just as science and spiritualism helped him overcome his earlier fears of death, so certain religious developments of the late 1840s and early 1850s expanded and intensified his philosophical vision. The expressions of religion and morality in Whitman's early magazine writings were largely conventional. Visionary tales like "The Angel of Tears" and "The Love of Eris: A Spirit Record" and moral stories like "A Legend of Life and Love" and "The Shadow and the Light of a Young Man's Soul" were staidly pious works that accorded with the benign liberal Protestantism permeating much popular fiction and poetry of the time.

During the antebellum period, hundreds of popular writers launched a wholesale attack on Calvinistic religion, which was considered harsh and inflexible, and advocated a religion of benign feeling, good works, and divine benevolence. Among the most popular strategies in promoting the new liberal Christianity was the visionary mode, or the imaginary descriptions of comforting angels or the afterlife. The numerous writers who used the visionary mode were trying above all to suggest that God was not angry or distant but rather close and nurturing. Whitman often used the visionary mode in this way in his early works. In "The Child and the Profligate" a "gentle angel" appears to the repentant drunkard John Lankton and the boy with whom he is sleeping; the next day Lankton awakes a temperate man. Another Whitman tale, "The Angel of Tears," depicts an angel who consoles a sorrowful murderer, communicating the message, "There are a million million invisible eyes which keep constant watch over the earth—each Child of Light having his separate duty" (*WEP*, 120). In "The Love of Eris: A Spirit Record," which appeared in the *Columbian Magazine* in 1844, Whitman tells of another kindly angel and wrote, "Who says there are not angels or invisible spirits watching around us? O! the teeming regions of the air swarm with many a bodiless ghost—bodiless to human sight, because of their exceeding and too dazzling beauty!" (*WEP*, 245).

If in his visionary works Whitman joined popular writers in trying to picture God's benevolence, his moral tales followed them in dramatizing the efficacy of good works and cheer. As I have shown in *Faith in Fiction*, by the late 1830s, when Whitman began to write popular poems and tales, popular religious literature in America had become notably secularized—that is, it had turned away from mainly celestial themes to earthly ones.[13] If visionary tales were designed to subvert the notion of God's wrath, moral ones were often meant to oppose the Calvinist notion that good works had no place in salvation. Persevering in good works despite formidable odds became central in many religious poems and narratives, culminating in best-selling religious novels like Susan Warner's *The Wide, Wide World* and Maria Cummins's *The Lamplighter*. Whitman, too, wanted to affirm optimism and morality in opposition to gloom and misfortune. In "A Legend of Life and Love" he contrasts a cynical man whose dark views lead to depression with his cheerful brother, whose faith in God and human nature leads him to take a positive view of life. "The Shadow and Light of a Young Man's Soul" pictures a poor man who is roused from despondency by the example of a hard-working farmer's daughter who teaches him the power of self-help and cheerful faith in God. "With an iron will," Whitman wrote of the man, "he substituted action and cheerfulness for despondency and a fretful tongue" (*WEP*, 330). In "Lingave's Temptation" Whitman shows a writer who is offered good money to produce trashy material but refuses the offer, knowing how important it is for a writer to link genius and virtue.

One of Whitman's religious stories, "Shirval: A Tale of Jerusalem," showed him following in the wake of a number of American writers who were revolutionizing the literary treatment of the historical Jesus. Because of America's powerful heritage of Puritanism, it had long been considered sacrilegious to deal freely with biblical topics in fiction. Only in the opening decades of the nineteenth century did some liberal writers dare to picture the human Jesus in concretely described historical settings. The movement toward the humanization of Jesus would lead to daringly secular embellishments of the Bible in best-sellers like Joseph Holt Ingraham's *The Prince of the House of David* (1855) and Lew Wallace's *Ben-Hur* (1880).

Whitman's contribution to the genre, "Shirval," was daring in its own right. Set in ancient Judea, the story tells of a funeral procession for a recently deceased man. When the procession reaches the city gates, it is met by a man "of middle stature and fair proportions, in every motion whereof was easy grace" (*WEP*, 294). He commands the dead man to rise, and to everyone's amazement the command is obeyed. Today, this tale seems blandly conventional, but in a time when American writers were still escaping Puritan restrictions against fictionalizing the Bible, it was actually bold. The realistic description of Jesus was unusual for its day. It showed Whitman participating in the movement toward a relaxed, familiar treatment of sacrosanct topics, a movement that also lies behind some of his casual treatments of biblical themes in his poetry, as in "Song of Myself," where he imagines himself "Walking the old hills of Judea with the beautiful gentle god by my side" (*WCP*, 62).

Despite such connections between Whitman's early religious pieces and *Leaves of Grass*, it must be noted that his treatment of religion in his major poetry was far more adventurously mystical and more erotically charged than it had been previously. The change can be attributed in part to the rise of Harmonialism and Swedenborgianism.

Whitman's treatment of religion in his major poetry had precedent in the Harmonial movement led by the "Poughkeepsie Seer," Andrew Jackson Davis. Whitman discussed Davis at length with his friend John Arnold and doubtless was exposed to one or more of the best-selling Harmonial books that Davis wrote between 1846 and 1854. An unlearned cobbler's apprentice, Davis was first put in a trance by a traveling mesmerist in 1843 and within four years developed a remarkable capacity to slip in and out of trances at will, without the aid of an outside operator. While in a trance state, Davis could accomplish apparently miraculous things, such as reading books through walls and peering inside people's bodies to spot hidden diseases. In a typical trance state his mind roamed beyond the walls of his home, looked through the roofs of surrounding houses and through the clothes of their inhabitants, and even saw backward into history and outward to the distant expanses of the heavens. Between 1845 and 1847 Davis popularized this so-called traveling clairvoyance in more than 150 lectures he gave while in a trance sate. He initiated the craze for trance performers that swept the nation in the fifties. Several of the mystics that followed him became known for their feats of traveling clairvoyance.

Whether or not Whitman had a trance-like mystical experience, as his friend and biographer Richard Maurice Bucke claimed, he was a skilled cultural ventriloquist who gave expression to the mass interest in trances and time-space travel. The early fifties, when he produced his mystical poetry, was a kind of watershed moment for popular mysticism. Whitman participated in the popular trend. In his notebook he described being "in a trance, yet with all senses alert" and with "the objective world suspended or surmounted for a while, & the powers in exaltation, freedom, vision" (*NUP*, 4:1401). He wrote, "I am in a mystic trance exultation / Something wild and untamed—half savage" (*NUP*, 1:194).

The early editions of *Leaves of Grass* are filled with his versions of traveling clairvoyance. A prominent stylistic feature of his poems is their constant shuttling back and forth between different images, often different times and places. He outdid even Davis and others in his adventurous gamboling with time and space. In "Song of Myself" he wrote: "My ties and ballasts leaves me. . . . I travel . . . I sail . . . my elbows rest in seagaps, / I skirt the sierras . . . my palms cover continents, / I am afoot with my vision" (*WCP*, 59). If the trance writers mentally traversed history and space, so Whitman jumped rapidly between historical events (e.g., Jesus in Judea, George Washington after the Battle of Long Island) and distant places ("Speeding through space . . . speeding through heaven and the stars" (*WCP*, 63]).

Not surprisingly, such time-space leaps caught the eye of Whitman's contemporaries, several of whom associated him with the weird mystical movements of the time. An early reviewer commented that Whitman sometimes ran toward chaos in his time-space flights, "as in the rigma-role of the trance-speaking mediums, and we are threatened on every hand with a period of mere suggestion in poetry, mere protest against order, and kicking at the old limits of time, space, the horizon, and the sky" (*New York Saturday Press*, 30 June 1860). A British reviewer similarly pointed out that Whitman's straining of time-space limits was odd to the foreign sensibility, "but perhaps not so to a nation from which the spirit-rappers sprung."[14]

Readers inclined to accept the new mystical movements, on the other hand, felt comfortable with Whitman's religious vision. Small wonder that the 1855 edition of *Leaves of Grass* received a long, positive review in the Harmonial magazine *Christian Spiritualist*. The reviewer placed Whitman's poems among several forms of direct spiritual inspiration that had arisen in recent years and called *Leaves of Grass* "a sign of the times, written, as we perceive, under powerful influxes; a prophecy and promise of much that awaits all who are entering with us into the open-ing door of a new era" (*WCH*, 84).

Closely allied to Harmonialism was Swedenborgianism, another pop-ular movement that affected Whitman as he made the transition from periodical writer to poet. The advent of Swedenborgianism helps to ex-plain the erotic mysticism in his verse. One of the greatest differences between his earliest writings and his major poetry was the almost com-plete absence in the early works of a positive treatment of sex. Critics have made connections between the homoeroticism of the early story "The Child's Champion" and the homoerotic themes of the 1855 po-etry. Actually, though, the relation of the sexuality between the early and later works comes closer to being one of contrast than of similarity. In early stories like "The Child's Champion," "Death in the School-Room," and "Bervance," homoeroticism often takes a violent, even brutal form, as when a cruel schoolmaster beats a supine student on his back or when a one-eyed sailor kicks a boy on the rear. In contrast, Whitman's treat-ment of sex and the body in his major poems was closely linked to reli-gion and the spirit.

Swedenborgianism, which became widely diffused through American culture after 1846, was a religious movement that showed how the erotic and the mystical could be combined. Whitman once said, "I think [Emanuel] Swedenborg was right when he said there was a close connec-tion—a very close connection—between the state we call religious ec-stasy and the desire to copulate. I find Swedenborg confirmed in all my experience" (*WWC*, 5:376). He apparently had been introduced to Swedenborgianism in 1846 when he attended two lectures by Professor George Bush of New York University, and in the 1850s he befriended several people active in Swedenborgian circles, most notably John Arnold, with whom he had long philosophical discussions. He had a friend who was close to the Swedenborgian Henry James, Sr., and in his notebooks he discussed several other Swedenborgians, including Thomas Lake Harris and James John Garth Wilkinson. In an 1858 *Brooklyn Daily Times* article he reviewed the Swedenborgian movement in America and said that Swedenborg would have "the deepest and broadest mark upon the religions of future ages here, of any man that ever walked the earth" (*Brooklyn Daily Times*, 15 June 1858).

There was an eroticism, even a kind of homoeroticism, intrinsic to Swedenborgian worship. Swedenborg had called God the Divine Man, or *Homo Maximus,* with the so-called highest heaven extending from the Divine Man's head down to the neck, the middle heaven from the breast to the loins, the lowest from the feet to the soles and the shoulder to the fingers. Whitman echoed this body-specific view when he addressed God in a poem as follows:

> Thou Ideal Man,
> . . . Complete in body and dilate in spirit,
> Be thou my God,

or when he called God "a loving bedfellow [who] sleeps at my side all night and close at the break of day."[15] For American Swedenborgians, union with God through prayer was seen as union with a Divine Man, often in an act of penetration. At the church of Thomas Lake Harris, which Whitman attended in the early 1850s, speeches were given by influx from God, with faith entering through the left temple, love for God's creation through the head and extending to the heart and lungs, and the Word of God through the forehead. Whitman used the Swedenborgian words "influx," "efflux," and "afflatus" in *Leaves of Grass* several times. In "Song of Myself" the persona calls himself "Partaker of influx and efflux" and declares, "Through me the afflatus surging and surging . . . through me the current and index" (*WCP*, 50). In "Song of the Open Road" Whitman writes, "Here is the efflux of the soul, / The efflux of the soul comes from within through embowered gates, ever provoking questions" (*WCP*, 301).

More important, he fused intense religiosity with body-specific mysticism, as in the famous section 5 of "Song of Myself," where his persona is pictured lying with his soul on the transparent summer morning. If

Harris could describe union with God as reception of the divine breath through the head or chest, so Whitman could imagine the soul plunging its tongue to the "barestript heart" and spreading until it embraced the beard and the feet. The fact that this erotic moment is followed immediately by an intensely religious one is also in keeping with Swedenborgian belief. In Harris's 1854 poem *An Epic of the Starry Heaven,* the soul, in its flight to the divine world, encounters countless men and women bound in love and is told, "We are all lovers in these pure dominions—Love reigns in all—Love the glorified."[16] Likewise, Whitman's persona feels he is bonded eternally to all the men and women ever born and that the kelson of the creation is love.

As to Whitman's last two themes, reform and politics, I can make just a few generalizations. In his early magazine writings Whitman endorsed many popular reforms. His reform at this point was very much *anti:* anti-drinking, anti–capital punishment, antitobacco, and so forth. Alcoholism was his favorite target, as evidenced by his poem "Young Grimes," his stories "The Child and the Profligate" and "Reuben's Last Wish," and his temperance novel *Franklin Evans or the Inebriate.* Such protest against vice was a common theme in many American periodicals of the time. To some degree, this "anti" voice is heard even in his mature writing, as when he denounced in the 1855 preface the "putrid veins of gluttons or rumdrinkers" and the "the privacy of the onanist," or when he wrote in "Song of the Open Road," "No diseas'd person, no rum-drinker, or venereal taint is permitted here" (*WCP,* 21, 303).

More characteristically, though, his poetry made affirmative statements that reveal the influence of positive health reforms of the day, particularly those promoted by the publishing firm Fowler and Wells, distributor of the first edition of *Leaves of Grass* and the publisher of the second. In particular the brothers Lorenzo and Orson Fowler promoted popular versions of phrenology and physiology that contributed to his outlook. The Fowlers called for frank, open treatment of the body and sexuality. They also advised keeping the brain organs and other bodily functions in equilibrium. Theirs was a holistic outlook that emphasized maintaining balance in every aspect of physical and mental being. Anything that threatened this balance could cause insanity or disease. The healer persona of Whitman's poetry was directly linked to the Fowlers' idea of health. Whitman wrote that the poet was the one in perfect equilibrium, the one to whom the diseased or troubled could look to for help.

Indeed, Whitman wrote *Leaves of Grass* largely because he thought the nation itself lacked equilibrium and needed immediate help. Whitman's connection to politics has been discussed by critics like Betsy Erkkila, who links the poet's democratic themes and styles to the heritage of Jeffersonian and Jacksonian republicanism.[17] But it should be noted that the fervent egalitarianism, rabid individualism, and almost jingoistic Americanism Whitman manifested in the first edition of *Leaves of Grass* had not always been there. To the contrary, earlier on, Whitman had been something of a snob, as is seen in his earliest extant letters, from Woodbury, Long Island, in 1840, in which he repeatedly denigrated the humble village folk as provincial, stupid, and dirty.

It was precisely such common folk, of course, whom he would champion fifteen years later in *Leaves of Grass,* but he passed through several phases before he learned to appreciate them fully. In the early 1840s he thought the principles of the Democratic Party should supersede loyalty to any individual. In the late forties, the intensifying slavery controversy made him turn against party loyalty and bitterly castigate social rulers in his political protest poems of 1850, such as "Blood Money," "Wounded in the House of Friends," and "Resurgemus." The political crisis of the fifties, in which the Whig Party collapsed and the Democratic Party gave itself over to proslavery forces, made him embrace with extreme fervor those same common types he had once spurned. Social rulers now seemed corrupt beyond hope, and he now thought redemption could be found only in average Americans. His anti-authoritarian position was fueled by the intense individualism of the fifties, a kind of dropout decade that also produced Henry David Thoreau's *Walden* and the anarchist activities of Stephen Pearl Andrews and others. The intensity of his Americanism was fanned by the fastest rising political group of the mid-fifties, the Know-Nothings. The imminent unraveling of the United States after the passage in May 1854 of the Kansas-Nebraska Act drove him to create a unifying poetic document that brought together the varied images of antebellum culture. Of all nations, he wrote in the 1855 preface, the United States needed poets. He believed that he could fill that need for togetherness and union in the face of impending collapse.

Thus, the great single difference between *Leaves of Grass* and his earlier writings for magazines and periodicals was its radical inclusiveness, its bringing together of diverse, sometimes contradictory cultural images under one literary roof. It was a desperate, almost utopian response to the centrifugal forces that threatened to rip apart the nation. As his bitterly ironic prose tract "The Eighteenth Presidency!" reveals, no one recognized the dangers of fragmentation, corruption, and possible political collapse more clearly than he. He offered his poetry as a gesture of unity and healing to a nation on the brink of war. The proof of the poet, he wrote in 1855, is that his country absorbs him as affectionately as he has absorbed it.

This was, of course, a hopeless dream. His poems never came close to being absorbed by America to the degree he envisaged. It was a worthy dream nonetheless.

NOTES

1. The specific works in their various categories are as follows:

(1) dark works about death or haunted minds: "Our Future Lot" (poem, 1838); "My Departure" (poem, 1839; revised as "Death of the Nature-Lover," 1843); "The Love That Is Hereafter" (poem, 1840); "The End of All" (poem, 1840; reprinted in 1841 as "The Winding-Up"); "Bervance; or, Father and Son" (tale, 1841); "We Shall All Rest at Last" (poem, 1840; later reprinted as "Each Has His Grief," 1840); "Ambition" (poem, 1841—expanded version of an 1839 poem, "Fame's Vanity"); "The Death and Burial of McDonald Clarke" (poem, 1842); "Time to Come" (poem, 1842); "The Tomb Blossoms" (tale, 1842); "My Boys and Girls" (tale; 1844); "The Boy Lover" (tale, 1845); "Revenge and Requital: A Tale of a Murderer Escaped" (tale, 1845; revised as "One Wicked Impulse," 1845); "Sailing the Mississippi at Midnight" (poem, 1848).

(2) sensational or adventurous works: "The Inca's Daughter" (poem, 1840); "The Spanish Lady" (poem, 1840); "Death in the School-Room" (tale, 1841); "Dumb Kate" (tale, 1844); "The Half-Breed: A Tale of the Western Frontier" (tale, 1845); "Richard Parker's Widow" (tale, 1845); "Some Fact-Romances" (tale, 1845).

(3) reform works: "Young Grimes" (poem, 1840); "Wild Frank's Return" (tale, 1841); "The Child and the Profligate" (tale, 1841); "Reuben's Last Wish" (tale, 1842); *Franklin Evans or the Inebriate* (novel, 1842); "The Madman" (tale fragment, 1843).

(4) visionary works about angels or angelic visitations: "The Punishment of Pride" (poem, 1841); "The Angel of Tears" (tale, 1842); "The Love of Eris: A Spirit Record" (tale, 1844); "New Year's Day" (poem, 1848) (also, there are visionary scenes in "The Child and the Profligate" and "Reuben's Last Wish").

(5) patriotic or nationalistic works: "The Columbian's Song" (poem, 1840); "The Last of the Sacred Army" (tale, 1842); "The Child-Ghost" (tale, 1842; later revised as "The Last Loyalist"); "Ode" (poem, 1846).

(6) political: "The House of Friends" (poem, 1850); "Resurgemus!" (poem, 1850); "Dough-Face Song" (poem, 1850); "Blood-Money" (poem, 1850).

(7) moral works: "A Legend of Life and Love" (tale, 1842); "The Play-Ground" (poem, 1846); "The Shadow and Light of a Young Man's Soul" (tale, 1848); "Lingave's Temptation" (tale, 1848).

(8) biblical works: "Shirval: A Tale of Jerusalem" (tale, 1845).

2. For a discussion of the popular cultural background of Whitman's era, see David S. Reynolds, *Beneath the American Renaissance: The Subversive Imagination in the Age of Emerson and Melville* (New York: Knopf, 1988) and Reynolds, *Walt Whitman's America: A Cultural Biography* (New York: Knopf, 1995).

3. *The Uncollected Poetry and Prose of Walt Whitman*, ed. Emory Holloway (Gloucester, Mass.: Peter Smith, 1972), 2:20–21.

4. Walt Whitman, *The Early Poems and the Fiction*, ed. Thomas L. Brasher (New York: New York Univ. Press, 1963), 6:10. This volume is hereafter cited in the text as *WEP*.

5. Horace Traubel, *With Walt Whitman in Camden* (New York: Mitchell Kennerly, 1914), 3:316. This volume is hereafter cited in the text as *WWC*.

6. Justus Liebig, *Organic Chemistry in Its Application to Agriculture and Physiology* (London: Thayer and Walton, 1847), 227.

7. Ibid.; Whitman, *Complete Poetry and Collected Prose* (New York: Library of America, 1982), 27. This volume is hereafter cited in the text as *WCP*.

8. Liebig, *Organic Chemistry*, 366.

9. *In Re Walt Whitman*, ed. Horace L. Traubel, Richard Maurice Bucke, and Thomas B. Harned (Philadelphia: David McKay, 1893), 19.

10. Walt Whitman, *Notebooks and Unpublished Prose Manuscripts*, ed. Edward F. Grier (New York: New York Univ. Press, 1984). This volume is hereafter cited in the text as *NUP*.

11. Walt Whitman, *Leaves of Grass: A Textual Variorum of the Printed Poems*, ed. Sculley Bradley, et al. (New York: New York Univ. Press, 1980), 2:291, 337.

12. Walt Whitman, *The Correspondence*, ed. Edwin Haviland Miller (New York: New York Univ. Press, 1961), 1:304.

13. David S. Reynolds, *Faith in Fiction: The Emergence of Religious Literature in America* (Cambridge: Harvard Univ. Press, 1981).

14. *London Critic* (1 Apr. 1856), quoted in *Walt Whitman, the Critical Heritage*, ed. Milton Hindus (New York: Barnes and Noble, 1971), 59. This volume is hereafter cited in the text as *WCH*.

15. *Leaves of Grass, Comprehensive Reader's Edition*, ed. Harold Blodgett and Sculley Bradley (New York: New York Univ. Press, 1965), 372, 269.

16. Thomas Lake Harris, *An Epic of the Starry Heaven* (New York: Partridge and Brittan, 1854), 38.

17. Betsy Erkkila, *Whitman the Political Poet* (New York: Oxford Univ. Press, 1989).

3

UNCOMMON DISCOURSE
Fanny Fern and the *New York Ledger*

JOYCE W. WARREN

•

*From the depths of the Middle Ages, a man was mad if his speech could
not be said to form part of the common discourse of men.*
—Michel Foucault

FOUCAULDIAN analysis has made us aware of the many ways in
which society excludes and prohibits discordant or uncommon discourse that threatens the status quo. To protect itself, society maintains
certain methods of exclusion to prevent the dissemination of threatening discourse and establishes conditions to limit the identity of the
speaker. One of the paradoxes of Fanny Fern's career is that she wrote
what might be called uncommon discourse, yet she wrote for sixteen
years for a newspaper that was dedicated to the common people. If
Fanny Fern's work was published in a paper that was aimed at the common reader, why was she able to write uncommon discourse—discourse
that she wrote not only with impunity, but for which she was greatly rewarded?

Fern's writing was polemical, controversial, and, to many, outrageous;
yet it was immensely popular, so popular that Fern was the most highly
paid newspaper writer of her time. I believe that the paradox is itself the
explanation. It was because Fern's writing appeared in a nontraditional
paper with a mass circulation that she was able to write uncommon discourse that was not subject to the constraints that Foucault identifies:
discourse that questioned and critiqued the conventions of her time;
discourse that threatened the status quo; discourse that ran contrary to
that taught by institutions of the day; and discourse that defied the rules
of established criticism, did not fit into the established discipline, and
was written by someone who was outside the "fellowships of discourse"
that establish exclusivity and limitation.[1]

Fanny Fern (Sara Willis Parton) was born in 1811.[2] The first American woman newspaper columnist, Fern became successful, not because

51

she wrote from within the social institutions that determine discourse, but in spite of the fact that she began to write outside the system—excluded and prohibited by such determinant institutions as patriarchy, pedagogy, and publishing. Although she was ultimately successful, her success was the result of her own determination and talent and in spite of gender-based prejudice, ridicule, and exploitation. Unlike Ralph Waldo Emerson and Henry David Thoreau or her own brothers, she did not have the training of the educated "literary man"; as a woman, she was not permitted entrance into institutions like Harvard and Yale. At the same time, again because she was a woman, she was not "one of the roughs"; unlike Walt Whitman, Herman Melville, or Mark Twain, she could not participate in male activities centered in saloons, sailing ships, or mining camps.

The rules of publishing also excluded women. Although women were getting books published in the mid–nineteenth century, and although many women had become editors, women were expected to write within a certain feminine mode. As Mary Kyle Davis wrote in "Women in Literature" in 1871, the rules of publishing in America prevented women from writing frankly: "Women will never write the truth—or at least not publish it. . . . All scribbling women destroy those productions that have in them most true passion, . . . and only publish those trivialities which Madam Grundy accepts as proper, and which editors mean to pay for when they say, 'We shall strive to make these columns peculiarly acceptable to the ladies.' And we sign our names without a blush to skim-milk love stories, in which the latest fashions and the most poignant emotions are mixed up together, to poetry written on the principle that where every other line rhymes the production cannot be prose, . . . and scarcely ever to anything more. Not so much that we cannot, as that we do not dare. . . . And so an original woman's book, with real women in it, and with a woman's actual thoughts stamped upon the pages, is the rarest of all literary productions" (*New York Ledger,* 16 Sept. 1871).

Because Fern attempted to write the truth, she was called unwomanly and unfeminine. Her brother, editor-writer Nathaniel Parker Willis, called her writing vulgar and indecent, traditional reviewers were appalled at her overt portrayal of female self assertion, and conventional people were shocked at her frank discussion of taboo subjects like venereal disease, prostitution, birth control, and divorce.[3] But common readers—particularly the thousands of women who wrote letters of sympathy to Fern and who by their gender were themselves excluded from the fellowships of discourse that maintained the power structure—responded enthusiastically to Fern's work.[4]

Fern wrote openly on topics that the establishment would have censored. She could write uncommon discourse for common people, which she would not have been able to do within the literary establishment. This essay will examine two important questions. First, what was peculiar about Fern's career, and, similarly, what was peculiar about the *Ledger* that put her writing outside the common discourse? Second, how did the *Ledger* affect her writing (if it did), and what effect did she in turn have on the character and quality of the *Ledger*?

To begin to answer the first question, we need to look at the unusual circumstances under which Fern's career began. In January 1851 Sara Farrington left her abusive second husband, taking her children to a hotel. On 28 June 1851, she published her first newspaper article, and she adopted the pen name of Fanny Fern a few months later. Readers admired her frankness and her no-holds-barred attitude. But conventional reviewers were shocked: nineteenth-century women writers were supposed to write delicate, feminine pieces. Women's humor was supposed to be gentle, not aggressive; women writers were not supposed to wield the "scimitar blade of sarcasm."[5]

Why was Fanny Fern able to write in such an unconventional manner? Part of the reason is that she had always been a rebellious, spirited person—even as a child, in spite of lectures and the example of her peers, she refused to accept the sober Calvinism of her father. But before she began to write, her rebellion and high spirits were always within the limits of female propriety. By 1851 something had happened to make her write, not only with spirit, but with shocking frankness, or, as Nathaniel Hawthorne later said, "as if the devil was in her."[6]

Fern had been married for two years to Samuel Farrington, a petty tyrant who reviled the memory of her first husband, denied her money for herself or her children, forced himself on her sexually, and in other ways was vindictive and violently abusive. Yet, as he told her, the law gave him the right to own her and everything she possessed. When she rebelled against his treatment, he vowed to destroy her reputation, and he kept his promise. He and his brother spread scandalous stories about her, portraying her as immoral and sexually promiscuous. His brother later admitted that these stories were fabrications,[7] but, at the time, Sara Farrington was shunned and ostracized by family and friends. She was unable to obtain a teaching job in Boston—partly because of the scandal—and her father and her first husband's father refused to help support her and her children.

A pious man, Fern's first husband's father was indignant that she might have behaved in such a manner; he responded by demanding that she turn her two children over to him and his wife. When she refused, he rewrote his will disinheriting her and her children (his only grandchildren) if she did not agree to surrender the children. If she did so and agreed to have nothing more to do with them, they would inherit all of his property (and he was quite well to do); if she did not turn over her children, his money would go to charity.[8]

In the double shadow of this ultimatum and of Farrington's character assassination, Fanny Fern began to write. In 1851, a middle-class American woman about whom such stories were told might as well have had the plague. Isolated by scandal and poverty and desperate to keep her children, Fern must have felt that she had nothing to lose. And this, I think, is the principal reason why she could write so frankly. Her reputation could not have been more tarnished than it already was, and nothing was more terrible to her at the time than the threatened loss of her children. She wrote what she felt—without regard for propriety or femininity. It was her desperation and her nothing-to-lose mindset that enabled her to write uncommon discourse.

Of course, other people might have been motivated to write in this way, but not many would have been able to get their work published. Fern was also a talented writer who persevered despite the criticism, lack of encouragement, and the outright hostility of the literary establishment—including her father and bother, both editors. Driven by the fear that she would lose her children, she refused to give up.

At last she found an editor who was willing to buy an article. An obscure Boston weekly, the *Olive Branch,* agreed to pay her fifty cents for a satirical article entitled "The Model Husband." The article was published on 28 June 1851; by the next day it had been reprinted in one of the large city papers. Although she did not receive any remuneration for the pirated article, the fact that a big newspaper had copied it was encouraging. The *Olive Branch* agreed to buy other articles from her, and her articles were soon appearing all over the United States and in England, subscribers were writing enthusiastic letters to the editor about this new writer, and the circulation of the *Olive Branch* soared. Within a few months, Fanny Fern was writing for another Boston paper as well, the *True Flag,* which similarly profitted from her work. Because it was clear that Fern's work benefitted the paper in which it appeared, she was given a great deal of freedom in her writing. In a sense Fern's uncommon discourse, which initially would not have found an outlet in the literary establishment, entered the mainstream by the back water, through the consciousness of the common reader. She found a vast audience in the powerless, the men and women—particularly the women—

who admired her courage and her ability to "call things by their right names."[9]

Fern's celebrity caused Robert Bonner of the *New York Ledger* to seek her out in 1855. Her articles had been appearing in newspapers all over the country since 1851, and her name had become a household word. In 1853 a collection of her articles, *Fern Leaves*, became a best-seller, and publicity surrounding her autobiographical novel *Ruth Hall* (1855) made her what today we would call a hot commodity. However, Bonner was not only attracted by her celebrity; he also admired her and her work. On 27 January 1855, he had written an editorial praising Fern's controversial novel. *Ruth Hall*, he said, was "one of the most extraordinary and attractive works ever given to the public by an American author. Genius is manifested on every page." On 17 February Bonner had defended Fern against the criticism of a female writer who had attacked Fern's "unfeminine" self-reliance, sneering at Fern's ability to say, "I have made my fortune in the world, and taken care of myself, and thanks to nobody." Minnie Myrtle (Nancy Johnson) had piously asserted that this was "not a boast" that she would "care to make." Bonner responded: "What kind of boast *would* the lady like to make, we wonder! The boast she repudiates, and expresses contempt for, is one that everybody possessing . . . a proper share of self-esteem, would rejoice to be enabled to make. . . . That boast need not cause a blush upon any countenance, be the wearer man or woman."

Because of her celebrity, Fern was already in a position of power when she came to the *Ledger,* and she refused Bonner's original generous offer of twenty-five dollars a column. When Bonner first approached her in early 1855, she had decided that writing books was more profitable and less tedious than writing for newspapers. She did not want to write for the *Ledger,* and she did not need the money. Bonner's perseverance persuaded her, she later said, more than the money he offered her; she admired his pluck and his refusal to give up.[10] When she rejected his first offer, he returned with an offer of fifty dollars a column; when she rejected that, he returned with an offer of seventy-five; and when she again refused, he offered her the unprecedented sum of one hundred dollars a column.[11]

Fern was initially hired to write a serialized story for the *Ledger* in ten weekly installments. The story, "Fanny Ford," began running in June 1855. Throughout the month of May, the terms of the agreement were the subject of much speculation; editors and readers responded with amazement and disbelief. On 19 May 1855, Bonner announced his coup: "Fanny Fern is now engaged in writing a Tale for the *Ledger*. . . .

For this production we have to pay by far the highest price that has ever been paid by any newspaper publisher to any author." In the same issue, Bonner cited the *New York Evening Mirror*, which had stated that he had agreed to pay Fern one hundred dollars a column to write the story. Bonner would not confirm the price, but said that the *Mirror* had not "underrated it." Fanny Fern, he said, "is the biggest 'card' in this country, or indeed in any other, and we are always willing to pay well for a good article." He quoted the *Mirror*'s comment: "We certainly do not know which to admire most, the ability and perseverance of the lady in making a reputation that commands such unheard-of remuneration for the labors of her pen, or the enterprise of the publisher who pays it. Such a price for newspaper writing is certainly unprecedented." On 26 May, Bonner noted that his announcement that Fern would write for the *Ledger* had created a sensation, and he printed the names of some of the many newspapers that had commented on it and had speculated about the price. On 2 June Bonner responded to the rumor; he issued a notarized statement that he had, in fact, agreed to pay Fanny Fern one hundred dollars a column to write an original story for the *Ledger*.

Fern's story ran from 9 June through 11 August. The success of the story was reflected in the substantial increase in the number of *Ledger* subscribers. On 16 June, Bonner printed an editorial under the masthead on the front page of the paper announcing that Fern's story had already paid for itself in the great number of copies sold: "Fanny Fern's new story *has* proved a GOOD CARD. . . . Notwithstanding the immense outlay, we know enough of the success with which it has already met, to warrant us in expressing the belief that *it will pay us three times over!* What have the timid, old-fogy, behind-the-age editors, who thought we were 'insane' in making the costly arrangement with Fanny, to say now?" On 29 December 1855, Bonner announced that he had made a new arrangement with Fern "for a new series of her spirited, lively, dashing, unrivalled sketches. We will have a complete sketch from her brilliant and popular pen every week during the entire year. Her efforts will be devoted exclusively to the *Ledger, as she will write for no other paper!*" Impressed with what she regarded as Bonner's strength of character as well as his enterprise, Fern signed an exclusive contract with the *Ledger* and in January 1856 began writing a regular column, which continued until her death in 1872.

Throughout her sixteen-year career with the *Ledger*, the relationship between Fern and Bonner was one of mutual respect and admiration. Both privately and publicly Fern made it clear that she thought highly of Bonner and his paper. On 15 March 1856, after she had been associated with the *Ledger* for less than a year, Fern wrote that if anyone could show her a better paper "or an Editor more liberal, more enterprising, more indefatigable in his endeavors to please, or more ready on all occasions to shiver a lance for woman than Robert Bonner, I will agree to write an article for such a paper, and such an Editor, as I do this—for nothing!" A year later, on 14 March 1857, she wrote of Bonner: "The audacity of the man bridges over chasms, before which timidity and irresolution cower and shrink." Ten years later, Fern's high opinion of Bonner had not changed: "I like a man like him, who can look the future squarely in the eye. . . . Had I been a man, I trust I should have been the sort of man Mr. Bonner is . . . self-made, independent" (27 June 1868).

Bonner was equally impressed with Fern and her work. On 16 February 1856, a month after she had become a regular columnist for the *Ledger*, Bonner wrote that she had a "magnetic *something*" about her that "defies description—not only of her person, but of [her] soul." On 3 May 1856, he wrote that she "was worth her weight in gold," and the following year he said that if he had foreseen the "immense benefit" that the *Ledger* would derive from her work, he would have paid her two hundred dollars per column (17 October 1856). Bonner's esteem for Fern is reflected in the fact that during most of the sixteen years that she wrote a regular column for the *Ledger*, Bonner placed her articles on page four, the same page on which he printed his own editorials. In the obituary that he wrote for her on 9 November 1872, Bonner wrote of Fern: "Her success was assured, because she had something to say, and knew how to say it. . . . She was brave and true and honest and faithful to her very heart's core; and it was the influence of these personal qualities, expressed through her genius, which gave such an attractive flavor to her writings. With all her intellect and genius, had there not been added to these her courage, her honesty of purpose, and her faithfulness of heart, she would not have been Fanny Fern. . . . She was one of the most humorous and witty of writers, but her humor and wit were never wasted in purposeless display. She always took aim at something that deserved to be hit, and wrote on subjects in which the great masses of people were interested." Bonner's final tribute to Fern was to purchase the huge marble tombstone for her grave.

The next step in understanding Fern's ability to write uncommon discourse is to look at the character of Robert Bonner and the *New York Ledger*.[12] Characterized by those who knew him as hardworking and shrewd but honest and kind, Bonner's goal was to create a paper that was of vital interest to the widest possible reading public. In 1851 he bought a small businessman's paper and made several important and in some cases revolutionary decisions. First, he lowered the price of the weekly to three cents a copy, which made it available to working people. Second, he eliminated all advertisements because, he said, they took up too much room, and he did not want to prevent readers from fully enjoying the *Ledger*.[13] The great benefit of the omission of advertising, however, was that it freed Bonner and the *Ledger* from obligations: he could print what he wanted without worrying about offending his advertisers. Moreover, his paper would not be aimed at a particular class or interest group.

The third important decision was Bonner's determination that he would print material that would be interesting and provocative but would be suitable for the whole family; thus, he resisted the blandness imposed on other papers by conventional piety while refusing to pander to the public's taste in prurient violence and pornography.[14] The key was variety: the *Ledger* would have something for everyone—poetry, politics, social commentary, sensational novels, literature, commerce. Bonner wrote on 12 January 1856, "Some editors seem to imagine that the harmlessness of a paper is in exact ratio to its stupidity; but that is a mistake; a stupid paper is only less injurious than a vile one. Human nature is active, analytic, investigating, and it must have something vital to feed upon." Finally, the most important feature of the *Ledger* was that it printed only signed, original material. In the days before an international copyright law, most American papers were filled with anonymous reviews and pirated material from England. Bonner recognized the appeal of a famous name, and he was willing to pay for it. Just as he lured Fern to the *Ledger*, he also paid high prices to obtain the exclusive services of other writers, including E. D. E. N. Southworth and Sylvanus Cobb, Jr., two of the most popular adventure novelists of the day. In addition to the generous pay with which he acquired regular writers, Bonner also offered high prices to celebrity writers to provide him with copy. He paid Charles Dickens five thousand dollars for an original short story and Henry Wadsworth Longfellow three thousand dollars for a poem. In 1867 he offered Henry Ward Beecher $30,000 to write a serialized novel for the *Ledger*.

Not only did Bonner pay his contributors well, but he offered them friendship and encouragement—as well as tangible support when necessary. During the time that Fern was a regular contributor, for example, Bonner gave her bonus checks in addition to her regular salary at difficult times in her life.[15] Bonner was a trusted friend to other regular contributors as well. He helped Southworth financially and found employment for her son, Richmond. In 1869, after she had been writing for the *Ledger* for thirteen years, Southworth wrote to Bonner saying that her meeting with him had saved her life.[16]

By the end of 1856, after Fern had been an exclusive columnist for a year, the *Ledger*'s circulation, which had been 2,500 when Bonner bought the paper, had soared to 180,000, the highest ever reached by an American paper until that time. Swings in the economy did not dampen the *Ledger*'s success. As Bonner noted on 7 November 1857, during the Panic of 1857, it was "a matter of astonishment . . . that the circulation of the *Ledger* should go on steadily increasing during these hard times. But the fact is, the *Ledger* has become a necessity." By 1860 the circulation of the *Ledger* reached a peak of 400,000.

The *Ledger* cut across class boundaries and differences in gender, age, and education. Of particular interest today is the democratizing effect of the *Ledger*. Because it provided material for everyone, working-class readers were exposed to reading matter that ordinarily would have been seen only by upper-class readers; similarly, upper-class readers encountered material that would ordinarily have been seen only by lower-class readers. Bonner would not lower the level of writing of his more literate contributors and numbered among his contributors senators and college presidents. He included novels of passion and adventure that appealed to the common reader. Sylvanus Cobb's *Gunmaker of Moscow* appeared side by side with essays by Edward Everett, a former president of Harvard. Also significant was the fact that because of the variety of the material, the *Ledger* was read by both men and women, unusual in an age of gender-specific journalism. On 16 February 1861, Fern asked, "Why is it necessary to sexualize newspapers? Why cannot an intelligent woman appreciate a paper which commends itself to the perusal of intelligent men?" She preferred a paper that was intended for both sexes, she said, because it put her "on the same level as the men in the house." The *Ledger* was such a paper. The implicit feminism in Southworth's popular adventure novels like *The Hidden Hand* and the explicit feminism of Fanny Fern's articles were printed side by side in the *Ledger* with Cobb's masculine tales of murder and revenge and traditional male news stories on business and politics. Fanny Fern's 13 March 1858 article gives an idea of the widespread appeal of the *Ledger:* "It is read in ferry-boats, cars, and omnibuses. School-masters search their pupils' pockets for it. . . . Hackmen allow their horses to nibble at ladies' bonnets in passing, while they sit on the box, deep in the *Ledger*'s fascinating contents. Working-girls will carry it home, though they give a shilling less for their bonnet and ribbons. Wives search the tombs of their husband's pockets and spring at the delinquent with a reproachful—'No *Ledger!*'" Geographically also, the *Ledger* had a wide appeal. Bonner employed news agents in all the major cities in the United States.[17]

Bonner was well aware of the reasons for the appeal of his newspaper, and he highlighted four major features of the paper in his advertising: the cheapness of the paper, the variety of the material, the excellence of the writers, and the high prices he was willing to pay to obtain the most sought-after writers. On 16 June 1855 he wrote on page 1: "ALL FOR THREE CENTS! Dear reader, we give you in this number of the *Ledger* the second installment of FANNY FERN'S GREAT STORY, together with a host of other "good things"—all for *three cents*. Were it possible, we would like to be at the side of each reader, after he has perused his copy of the *Ledger,* and ask him if he ever received such a vast amount of excellent and seasonable reading for the small sum of *three cents!* We think we would hear one universal response—No! By its excellence and cheapness combined we mean to run the *Ledger* up to an unprecedented—much even beyond its present—circulation." On 2 August 1856 Bonner wrote, "We pay more for original matter for the *New York Ledger* than any *six* family papers in the country." Fourteen years later this was still his policy; on 31 December 1870 he wrote, "We have just one rule in the conduct of the *New York Ledger:* it is, without regard to money or price, to procure and publish the best matter that can be had in the world."

One might say that the great success of the *Ledger* resulted from the vast amounts of money that Bonner was willing to spend in two areas. On 9 August 1856 he wrote that the *Ledger* had succeeded primarily because "we have spared no expense in engaging the best writers in the country, and we have lavishly expended money in advertising in order to let the public know the sort of paper we make." Bonner's list of contributors included the most famous writers of the day. In addition to regular features by writers like Fern, Southworth, and Cobb, and material from celebrity writers like Dickens, Longfellow, Louisa May Alcott, and Harriet Beecher Stowe, Bonner also obtained material from statesmen, senators, educators, physicians, and clergymen. One of his greatest coups was to obtain the services of Edward Everett, who served at various times as secretary of state, governor of Massachusetts, and president of Harvard University. Bonner offered to contribute $10,000 to the fund to preserve Mount Vernon if Everett would write a series of weekly articles for a year. Although Everett initially did not want to write for a common paper like the *Ledger,* he had been working hard to raise money to preserve Washington's home and felt that he could not refuse the offer. After writing for Bonner for a year, he found that he, like Fern, had come to like and respect Bonner so much that he continued to write for the *Ledger* until his death.[18]

On 8 March 1856 Bonner announced that, beginning with the next issue, the *Ledger* would carry no advertising, "the whole space of our columns being devoted to the entertainment, instruction and amusement of our readers." Although Bonner accepted no advertising in the *Ledger,* he himself spent more money on advertising than any other editor. He inaugurated a new era in American advertising, spending thousands of dollars each year using outrageous and innovative methods to advertise his paper. At a time when advertisements were small and unimaginative, he bought a whole page in other newspapers to print over and over again one or two sentences, such as "Fanny Fern writes only for the *New York Ledger*" or the title of a new story. He bought advertising space in other papers to print the first installment of a new *Ledger* story, with a notation after the cliffhanger ending informing the readers that the following installments could be found only in the *New York Ledger.* His most outrageous advertising feat was the purchase of all eight pages of the *New York Herald* and the *New York Times* to advertise the *Ledger* on 6 May and 13 May 1858, respectively. One week in 1857 he spent $27,000 in advertising.

Bonner's principal credo as a publisher was to leave his writers alone. Although he was selective in choosing his writers, he claimed that he never censored those who worked for him, and in fact, Fanny Fern sometimes wrote on issues with which he disagreed. For example, she wrote in favor of women's suffrage, she praised Whitman's *Leaves of Grass,* and she wrote critically of narrow religious dogma. On all of these issues Bonner held an opposing opinion, but he let her write what she believed. On occasion, he commented on the editorial page or in a more subtle way indicated a contrary opinion. An example of his subtle disagreement appeared in the issue of 10 May 1856; when Fern wrote favorably about Whitman's *Leaves of Grass,* Bonner printed on the same page an early sentimental article of hers called "Little Benny" (a testament to maternal affection), thus indicating that although Fern praised the controversial Whitman, she herself was not unwomanly and his paper was not licentious. Bonner occasionally commented explicitly on Fern's articles. For example, on 10 February 1872, when Fern criticized clergymen who preached narrow religious dogma, Bonner wrote a long editorial answer on the same page, opposing the criticism of theologians and insisting that theological doctrines were important to a clergyman just as navigation was to a river pilot. On 16 March 1872 Fern answered Bonner in an article entitled "A Woman Will Have the Last Word." Perhaps theology is important, she said, but if a pilot was rescuing a drowning man, "he would not waste time asking him whether he had properly studied the science of navigation before he pulled him ashore." What is important, she said, is not a person's creed but how he or she lives.

The difference between Fern and Bonner is perhaps most evident in their opinions on women's issues. When Fern urged women's suffrage, Bonner let her write her opinion, although he did not agree with it. Her first strong article appeared on 29 May 1858: "All my life I have taken the liberty to say what I think, and I am not going to stop now. . . . I hold up both hands for a woman's ballot-box. . . . [Men do not want women to vote because] yielding this point would place in our hands a weapon of power which they are very unwilling we should wield." Although Bonner did not comment overtly on Fern's article, he printed immediately after her article on the same page his editorial "The Christian Woman," in which he stated that "Christianity has done much for woman." Suggesting that women did not need to be involved in politics, he said, "The New Testament is woman's *magna carta.*"

Two years later, on 9 June 1860, Bonner stated in an editorial that his objection to women voting was that a respectable woman would have to "mingle with the degraded of her sex at the polls." Fern explicitly answered this objection in her article of 30 June: "The principal objection made by conservatives to [women voting] . . . is on the score of their being thrown into rowdy company of both sexes." Such arguments are ridiculous, Fern insisted, because women see all types of people every day on the streets, in the stores, and in other public places. "Pshaw!" she scoffed, "all such talk is humbug, as the men themselves very well know. We are always 'dear—delicate fragile creatures,' who should be immediately gagged with this sugar plum whenever we talk about that of which it is their interest to keep us ignorant." In the same issue Bonner replied to a correspondent who had questioned his editorial of 9 June: "Our objection to women's going to the polls," he said, "was founded on the fact that, in so doing, they would have to *mingle closely* with the degraded of both sexes, and hear language and see conduct not fit for them to hear and see; which would be paying altogether too dear a price for the privilege of 'female suffrage'." That he was willing to print Fern's opinion, which directly contradicted the opinion that he expressed in the same issue of his paper, indicates just how liberal he was with respect to her writing.

To understand how freely Fern was able to write, even when her opinions diverged from Bonner's own views, let us juxtapose two of Bonner's editorials, "American Women" (3 December 1857) and "Woman's True

Sphere" (14 May 1859), against articles that Fern wrote in the same year that each of the editorials appeared. Bonner's 1857 editorial praised American women for their virtues as wives and mothers. They were, he said, more "the type of Penelope," domestic and virtuous, than the type of Cleopatra or Zenobia. In 1857, however, Fern's columns focused on women's independence: she supported women doctors (11 April, 17 October); she wrote in favor of divorce (24 October); she praised Rosa Bonheur and Harriet Hosmer because they were "sufficient unto themselves, both as it regards love and bread and butter; in the meantime, there are plenty of monosyllabic dolls left for those men who, being of small mental stature themselves, are desirous of finding a wife who will 'look up to them'" (19 December).

Bonner's 1859 editorial stated that women's "true sphere" was the nursery, the boudoir, and the kitchen. "What would woman gain of substantial good—what would she lose of innocence, of prestige, of peace, by mingling in the strife and turmoil of the business world? . . . Transplant her . . . to the arena of politics and the vortices of speculation— and what would you make of her? What but a compound monster, a *man-woman*." He went on to suggest that independent, strong-minded women were immoral and lacking in maternal affection, "self-condemned as infidels, as contemners of marriage and its obligations, as the advocates of the 'largest liberty' in the indulgence of the passions." Earlier that year, on 12 February, Fern had asserted that "the 'coming' woman's Alpha and Omega will not be matrimony." In an attempt to make clear that a strong-minded woman need not be an immoral man-woman, she went on to say, "Heaven forbid she should stamp round with a cigar in her mouth, elbowing her fellows, and puffing smoke in their faces; or stand on the free-love platform." But, said Fern, she shall be a "broad-shouldered, large-souled, intellectual being" who will be "happy, self-poised and serene" whether or not she is married.

On the same day that Bonner's editorial appeared, Fern wrote "How Frivolous Women Are Made," urging women to make the most of themselves and not to allow themselves to be taken in by the forces in their culture that would hold them back. Women, she said, are brought up to have "no higher aim in life than an eligible matrimonial establishment; no career, as have their brothers, to look forward to; but merely, like a pretty statue, to sit still and be admired." To counteract this influence, said Fern, a woman must turn "a deaf ear to those men who would flatter her into remaining a fool, lest she might have intelligence enough to become troublesome to them." On 2 July 1859 Fern responded indirectly to Bonner's association of strong-minded women with free love, urging women to be as "strong minded as you will if only you will be pure." On 30 July she wrote the essay "Independence," calling attention to the fact that although Americans were celebrating their independence on 4 July, women were not free. "Can I be a governor? Can I be a senator?" she asks. "Can I *even* be President? Bah—you know I can't. '*Free!*' Humph!" On 8 October Fern wrote about a woman who had been arrested for wearing men's clothes. Apparently, the woman had dressed like a man so that she could earn a better living. Fern says why not, when there are so few opportunities for women and those that exist command one-third the wages that men get for the same work.

On many issues, however, Fern and Bonner agreed. For example, when Fern wrote an essay strongly criticizing the exploitation of women workers, an article that the *Atlantic Monthly* wanted, Bonner printed it on the editorial page on 26 January 1867. They expressed the same views about school reform and concurred on such issues as slavery and the Civil War. Moreover, although Bonner did not agree with Fern's more radical views on women, he was more liberal than many of his contemporaries. He supported married women's property rights, encouraged women writers, and advocated fair treatment of wives by husbands. On 9 June 1855, he wrote a favorable review in the *Ledger* of Margaret Fuller's *Woman in the Nineteenth Century*, commenting that it was a "solid and substantial volume."

The *Ledger*'s policies had an important effect on Fern's writing. On 14 March 1857, Bonner wrote, "We never think of cutting down, or even altering a word in Fanny Fern's articles." Because of this policy, she had a forum in which she could say what she wanted. Although she came to the *Ledger* at the height of her popularity and her status as a profit-maker gave her the power to write more freely than a writer who had to answer to publishers and editors, she probably would not have been able to sustain this power if she had not joined with Bonner. Bonner was himself outside the common discourse. He was a maverick whose bold methods shocked and astounded editors and publishers and whose methods of doing business obligated him to no one. Because he did not believe in borrowing money, he was not in debt, and because he did not allow the *Ledger* to become dependent on anyone other than himself, he answered to no one. This independence allowed Bonner to take the risk of employing a controversial writer and allowing her to write as she pleased. Matthew Hale Smith described the response of Bonner's contemporaries to his methods: "His mode of advertising was new, and it excited both astonishment and ridicule. His ruin was predicted over and over again. . . . He was assailed in various ways. Men sneered at his writers, as well as at the method in which he made them known. He had no competition. . . . Men who had been predicting Bonner's ruin from the start were anxious to see it accomplished. . . . The book-men and newspaper-men, who were left out, were quite willing to have the *Ledger* go under."[19] But the *Ledger* did not go under; instead, it became the most powerful weekly in the country, and the enterprising Bonner, who had come to New York poor and friendless in 1844, left a fortune of $6 million when he died in 1899.

Not only did Bonner's independence enable Fern to write freely, but her association with Bonner provided her with protection and security. First, she had job security: she could write what she wanted and she did not have to worry that she would be censored, ridiculed, or fired. Second, her association with Bonner gave her protection in the world outside the paper. Bonner was a powerful figure to have in her corner. She noted once that women lecturers "have the nerve to witness the effect of their own words; while I watch mine at a safe distance on paper, with Mr. Bonner to back me in the *New York Ledger*." Moreover, because Bonner's paper did not contain advertising, she did not have to fear that advertisers' whims or qualms about a controversial point of view might alienate their potential customers. Consequently, she had greater freedom than most journalists at the time, particularly women writers.

But Fern was also aware that Bonner expected her to remain within certain unspoken boundaries, which she herself knew it would not be politic to overstep. On 6 November 1858 she wrote that she could not stand having to weigh her words when she was writing: "If there is anything I hate, it is writing that way; I won't do it for anybody except Mr. Bonner, who has too much good sense to ask it—who gives me a wide pasture to prance in because he is sure that I will not jump the fence, though the conservatives sometimes needlessly hold their breath for fear I will." In this essay Fern made clear that it was her own discretion and Bonner's confidence in that discretion rather than his censorship that kept her within bounds. Yet at times she longed to jump the fence. In an essay printed on 10 February 1866, she indicated that there were subjects about which she longed to write but did not do so: "People who visit a great city . . . generally overlook the most remarkable things in it. They 'do it up' in *Guide-Book* fashion, going the stereotyped rounds of custom-ridden predecessors. If *my* chains were a little longer, I would write you a book of travels that would at least have the merit of ignoring the usual finger-posts that challenge travellers. I promise you I would cross conservative lots, and climb over conservative fences, and leave the rags and tatters of custom fluttering on them, behind me, as I strode on to some unfrequented hunting ground. . . . Don't be alarmed—there's no chance of my doing it. I dream of it, though, sometimes—this deliciousness of 'speaking right out in meetin'' without fear of the bugbear of excommunication." There were certainly opinions that Bonner would not have tolerated. For example, he was very moralistic. When Henry Ward Beecher was accused of adultery in 1875, Bonner dropped him from his list of contributors. Fern wrote with sympathy and understanding about prostitutes—in itself a courageous thing for a nineteenth-century woman writer to do—but she did not advocate promiscuous sexuality. If Fern had advocated free love or adultery, Bonner undoubtedly would not have renewed her contract. However, since all of the evidence indicates that Fern herself shared Bonner's opinions on these matters, she would not have felt under restraint. Fern did chafe against Bonner's policy of not having books reviewed in his paper. As she noted in an article published in the *Ledger* on 26 November 1859, she would have liked to review books, but Bonner believed that book reviews consisted too much of the mutual scratch-my-back syndrome, and he did not want to be beholden to anyone.

Fern's writing affected the *Ledger* principally in two ways. First of all, and most obviously, she helped Bonner to create a phenomenally successful paper. She was famous for her wit and satire and her controversial opinions before she began to write for the *Ledger,* and readers regularly crowded into the *Ledger* office on the day the paper came out so that they could be the first to see what Fanny Fern had to say. Many people bought the *Ledger* because Fern wrote for it.

The second way that Fern affected the *Ledger* is less obvious. Bonner himself was known for his fairness and his love of justice. In her columns Fern always championed justice and fair play; she satirized pomposity and pretension, cruelty and exploitation. In a sense, she helped set a tone that was reflected throughout the *Ledger.* The criterion was not gentility or wealth, as it was in papers like her brother N. P. Willis's *Home Journal;* the criterion was truth and justice. Fern wrote about working women; she urged prison reform; she urged equal pay for equal work; she wrote about birth control, venereal disease, and divorce. Her topics and her style of writing were not genteel, but her message was an honest concern for other people, particularly those who had been overlooked or undervalued by society.

In *Ruth Hall,* the editor hired by Ruth's brother Hyacinth Ellet (who was based on Fern's brother, N. P. Willis) is disgusted with Ellet's toadyism and wishes that he had his own paper. "Wouldn't I call things by their right names?" he says, "Would I have my tongue or my pen tied in any way by policy, or interest, or clique-ism? No—sir!"[20] In writing for the *Ledger,* Fern found an editor who conducted his paper in the way that she has envisioned in her novel. Because she was writing for a maverick who made his own rules; because she and her publisher functioned outside the established disciplines and institutions by which, as Foucault noted, "discourse is at once controlled, selected, organized and redistributed . . . to avert its powers and dangers";[21] and because her vast and heterogeneous audience was composed of many who were themselves excluded from the common discourse, Fern was able to write without many of the prohibitions and exclusions that society imposes on common discourse. She profitted from Bonner's policy, and she reinforced it by the example of her own candid, no-nonsense writing.

NOTES

1. Michel Foucault, *The Archaeology of Knowledge and the Discourse on Language,* trans. A. M. Sheridan Smith (New York: Harper, 1972), 215–37.

2. For information on Fern's life, see Joyce W. Warren, *Fanny Fern: An Independent Woman* (New Brunswick, N.J.: Rutgers Univ. Press, 1992). Fern's papers are in the Sophia Smith Collection, Smith College, Northhampton, Mass. See also her columns in the *Boston Olive Branch* and *True Flag,* 1851–53, American Antiquarian Society, Worcester, Mass.; the *New York Musical World and Times,* 1852–54, New York Public Library; and the *New York Ledger,* 1856–72, in the Watkinson Library, Trinity College, Hartford, Conn.

3. The critics' responses to Fern's writing are discussed in Warren, *Fanny Fern,* 124–30 and 207–10. For her brother's response to her work, see the letter from Nathaniel Parker Willis to Sarah Farrington [Fanny Fern], n.d., Sophia Smith Collection, Smith College, Northhampton, Mass. Willis wrote, "Your humor runs into dreadful vulgarity sometimes. I am sorry that any editor knows that a sister of mine wrote some of these which you sent me. In one or two cases they trench very close on indecency."

4. For a discussion of the common readers' response to Fern's work and the hundreds of letters she received each week, the majority of which came from women who shared with her the tragedies of their lives, see Warren, *Fanny Fern,* 257–60.

5. This quotation is from Fern's mock review of her own book, *Fresh Leaves,* in the *New York Ledger,* 10 Oct. 1857. See Fanny Fern, *Ruth Hall and Other Writings* (New Brunswick, N.J.: Rutgers Univ. Press, 1986), 290–91.

6. Nathaniel Hawthorne, *Letters to William Ticknor, 1851–1869,* ed. C. E. Frazer-Clark, Jr., 2 vols. (Newark, N.J.: Carteret Book Club, 1972), 1:78.

7. See the Farrington Papers in the Sara Parton Collection, Sophia Smith Collection, Smith College, Northhampton, Mass. Letter from Thomas Farrington, 28 Jan. 1851, Sophia Smith Collection. The story of the Farrington mar-

riage is reflected in Fern's portrayal of the marriage of Gertrude Dean in her novel *Rose Clark* (1856).

8. See the will of Hezekiah Eldredge, 16 July 1851, Register of Probate Court, Boston, Mass. The contents and significance of this will are discussed in Warren, *Fanny Fern*, 106–8.

9. This is a quotation from Fern, *Ruth Hall*, 161.

10. See Matthew Hale Smith, *Twenty Years among the Bulls and Bears on Wall Street* (Hartford, Conn.: J. B. Burr, 1870), 217.

11. See Smith, *Twenty Years*, 217–18; James C. Derby, *Fifty Years among Authors, Books and Publishers* (New York: Harper and Brothers, 1873), 202–3; Mary Noel, *Villains Galore* (New York: Macmillan, 1954), 64.

12. For information about Robert Bonner and the *New York Ledger*, see Smith, *Twenty Years*, 214–30; Frederic Hudson, *Journalism in the United States* (New York: Harper and Brothers, 1873), 646–55; Derby, *Fifty Years*, 200–207; Ralph Admari, "Bonner and the *Ledger*," *American Book Collector* 6 (May–June 1935): 176–93; James Playstead Wood, *Magazines in the United States* (New York: Ronald Press, 1949), 86–89; Frank Luther Mott, *A History of American Magazines*, 5 vols. (Cambridge: Harvard Univ. Press, 1957), 2:23–24, 356–63.

13. See Admari, "Bonner and the *Ledger*," 193; *New York Ledger*, 8 Mar. 1856.

14. For a discussion of the prevalence of prurient sexuality and gore in nineteenth-century American popular literature, see David Reynolds, *Beneath the American Renaissance* (New York: Knopf, 1988), 211–24.

15. Fanny Fern to Robert Bonner, 25 Jan. 1870, in the *New York Ledger*, 9 Nov. 1872.

16. See the E. D. E. N. Southworth Papers, William R. Perkins Library, Duke University, Durham, N.C.

17. See, e.g., Smith, *Twenty Years*, 220.

18. Ibid., 221–22, 228; and Derby, *Fifty Years*, 203.

19. Smith, *Twenty Years*, 219–20.

20. Fern, *Ruth Hall*, 161.

21. Foucault, *Archaeology*, 216.

4

SERIALIZATION AND THE NATURE OF
UNCLE TOM'S CABIN

SUSAN BELASCO SMITH

•

I

ONE of the positive developments in the current interest in literary theory is a closer understanding of the agencies at work on the production of a literary text. The paradigm of a text as a well-wrought urn that lives apart from its time and (gendered) creator and is possessed of a unity and wholeness perceivable to an informed, objective reader has given way to other models. Today, we are more likely to perceive texts not only as the objects of aesthetic appreciation but also as the subjects of social and political entanglements of all varieties. The interpretation of these texts is consequently problematic, especially because interpreters themselves may indeed be informed but are never objective. At the same time, the feminist interest in expanding the canon has prompted a movement to recover, restore, and include forgotten texts written by women. As a consequence, of course, many works that were not considered a part of the canon now figure prominently in discussions of literature and theory.

The revival of interest in Harriet Beecher Stowe's *Uncle Tom's Cabin*, considered for most of the twentieth century as a book for children, a piece of propaganda, or a sentimental woman's novel, is directly related to the foregrounding of theory in discussions of literature. Most of the recent discussions of *Uncle Tom's Cabin* have focused attention on the book version of this novel.[1] But Stowe's work was published first as a newspaper serial. An exploration of this original context demonstrates how some social and political insights about the context—and about the production of the text within that context—clarifies crucial features of the work. This essay will discuss *Uncle Tom's Cabin* conceptually and materially, situated as it originally was in the midst of a series of national and international debates about slavery and oppression in the *National Era,* the antislavery newspaper edited by Gamaliel Bailey and John Greenleaf Whittier, where the novel appeared in forty-one installments between 5

June 1851 and 1 April 1852. I will suggest some of the ways in which that debate is reflected and revised in the installments of *Uncle Tom's Cabin* and the extent to which the novel is an intervention by a woman into the sphere of national and international politics. To do so, I will call attention to the variety of voices, an enlargement of the various exhortations, or relations of experience given by the members of Uncle Tom's extended family of slaves in their first appearance in the novel and give an account of the origins of at least some of these voices.

II

IN book form, *Uncle Tom's Cabin* ends with chapter 45, "Concluding Remarks," Stowe's commentary on the authentic nature of the events depicted in her story as well as her sermonic appeal to the citizens of the United States to end the slave trade. But the version in the *National Era* concluded with the following epilogue:

> The "Author of Uncle Tom's Cabin" must now take leave of a wide circle of friends, whose faces she has never seen, but whose sympathies, coming to her from afar, have stimulated and cheered her work.
>
> The thought of the pleasant family circles that she has been meeting in spirit weekly has been a constant refreshment to her, and she cannot leave them without a farewell.
>
> In particular, the dear little children who have followed her story have her warmest love. Dear children, you will one day be men and women; and she hopes that you will learn from this story always to remember and pity the poor and oppressed, and, when you grow up, show your pity by doing all you can for them. Never, if you can help it, let a colored child be kept out of school, or treated with neglect and contempt, because of his color. Remember the sweet example of little Eva, and try to feel the same regard for all that she did; and then, when you grow up, we hope that the foolish and unchristian prejudice against people, merely on account of their complexion, will be done away with.
>
> Farewell, dear children, till we meet again. (1 Apr. 1852, 1)

In his textual study of *Uncle Tom's Cabin,* E. Bruce Kirkham cites this passage as one of the ways in which the serialized version of the novel published in the *National Era* differs from the novel that was published by John P. Jewitt in March 1852.[2] The passage had, in Kirkham's view, "appropriately, been deleted" from the novel.[3] Kirkham interprets this deletion as a kind of marketing strategy, explaining that although Stowe may have felt that she had written a novel for children, her audience for the future would primarily be adults.

Although I do not disagree with Kirkham's assessment of the appropriateness of this deletion from the published, two-volume novel, I want to suggest an alternative interpretation of Stowe's decision that signals the formal differences between a novel that is serialized and one that is published as a whole. Such an interpretation raises the question of the impact of serialization on *Uncle Tom's Cabin* which Charles Dickens saw as having been written very much in his own style.[4] Serialization—the writing of a story in sections that appear over a period of time with interruptions for the author as well as for the reader—is a mode of literary production that creates within the text of the novel a web of relationships and experiences that closely approximates the complicated conversations and exchanges of false starts, distractions, and breaks that occur within the family circle of Stowe's imagination and her actual experience.[5] Such a mode of literary production contrasts with the progressive linearity of a novel envisioned, written, and published as a whole text. The material implications for this particular mode of literary production are significant for Stowe's literary intervention into the arguments about the place of slavery in the United States. Because the enslavement of blacks placed them outside the social and familial relationships of the dominant white culture, the work of an antislavery writer involved reintroducing blacks into those relationships. Serialization serves to subvert the prevailing proslavery discourse—the discourse that the *National Era* was specifically designed to overturn—as Stowe creates an increasingly complex web of relationships that demonstrates the complicated tangle of human relationships and the dependence of humans, both and black and white, on one another. More specifically, the serialization of *Uncle Tom's Cabin* in the *National Era* led Stowe to adopt diachronic rhetorical strategies that would prove extraordinarily effective in shaping the events that led to the emancipation of slaves. Finally, serial publication offered readers the opportunity to participate closely in the narrative, for example, by writing letters to the editor of the periodical, as many of Stowe's readers did. Bailey occasionally published letters from readers who were enthusiastic in their praise of the story; on 27 November 1851 a subscriber wrote to say that "we hope she will not be in a hurry to finish it," while another prayed "that she may keep it going all the winter" (2). These and other letters suggest the intimacy of serialized publication; as in no other literary form, literature became a part of the day-to-day lives of readers.[6]

There was, perhaps, another consideration for the deletion of the epilogue. In these brief paragraphs, Stowe directly and quite naturally addressed the audience that had been reading *Uncle Tom's Cabin* on an almost weekly basis for nearly a year. She envisioned her readers as a "wide circle of friends" with whom she had "been meeting in spirit weekly," a specific acknowledgment of her story as evolving periodically and appearing in the issues of the *National Era*. The depiction and acknowledgment of the circle of friends is one demonstration of the impact that serialization had on the composition and reception of *Uncle Tom's Cabin*. Stowe clearly envisioned her installments as a two-way communication between herself and her readers. She was conscious of them privately, as around her kitchen table, and publicly, as she saw the installments appear and observed the variety of texts that stood side by side with the columns of her novel. The readership of the *Era* was small and invited such intimacy. The epilogue offers the rather radical challenge of racial toleration and points toward the far more difficult issue of the integration of blacks into white society, a topic that many ardent abolitionists found difficult to consider. Deleting the epilogue may also have signaled the difference between what the family of *Era* readers would have found acceptable and what the much larger reading public of mid-nineteenth-century America was unwilling to contemplate.

Generally speaking, serialization rarely enters critical discussions of *Uncle Tom's Cabin*.[7] Reasons are not hard to find. Until recently, discussions of literature have tended to privilege unity and wholeness over multiplicity and disjunction. The serial form discourages a straightforward, linear story line; instead, it invites the creation of scenes, tableaus, and parallel organizations of plot.[8] Indeed, for most commentators, the publication of the novel as a serial—and the consequent attention to parts or sections—is barely worth noting. In fact the details of the serialization of the novel and the nature of the *National Era* as an antislavery newspaper have often been erroneously reported.[9] But Stowe wrote the novel in parts as a serial, and some of the problems and opportunities raised by that special means of literary production had a marked impact on her work. Most studies of serialization in literature are concerned with the works of British writers, especially Dickens, William Makepeace Thackeray, and George Eliot, and most deal as least briefly with the various constraints that serialization placed before a writer: set or uniform lengths for installments, rigid deadlines, the pressure to make each installment dramatic or compelling, an emphasis on vividly drawn characters and sensational plots to aid the audience's memory, interruptions from illness or quarrels with the publisher, censorship, and a variety of editorial interventions.[10] Other studies deal with the similarities between serial publication and oral narrative.[11] Repetition of actions and scenes, mnemonic devices to assist readers in recalling characters and events, standard themes (such as the death of a child), and techniques of verbal visualization all enable readers to relate easily to the continuing story. Stowe was certainly restricted by many if not all of these constraints and conventions.

For instance, like Dickens with most of his major works, Stowe was faced with the difficulty of beginning the publication of a novel without having a completed manuscript before her. In other words, she had to commit to a story line and a cast of characters that she could not revise in later chapters. When she wrote to Bailey on 9 March 1851, she explained that she was "occupied upon a story which will be a much longer one than any I have ever written, embracing a series of sketches which give the lights and shadows of the 'patriarchal institution.' "[12] In the same letter, Stowe explained that she expected the serial to extend for three or four numbers and the manuscript would be ready in two or three weeks. But Stowe was unable to keep to her projected timetable, and the first installment did not appear until June 5.[13] Although it is not known how much of the manuscript Bailey initially received, he certainly did not have all of it, and he did not know how long the novel would be.

From the beginning, length was a problem for Stowe. Her editor naturally wanted a sufficient sense of the structure and plan of the serial to manage space in the newspaper, and later, when Stowe sold the copyright of the novel to John P. Jewitt before the serial had completed its run, he urged her to conclude the novel quickly, concerned that it would be too long and therefore unprofitable to publish. But there was an opposing pressure as well, one that is unique to the serial format: readers did not want the story to end too quickly. The conflicting pressures on the length of the work constitute one of the important formal problems Stowe faced.

Such concern with the length of a narrative also gave rise to a series of structural concerns for nineteenth-century serial writers. Just as Dickens generally began a novel with a strong sense of a single character whose life he wanted to explore, such as David Copperfield or Paul Dombey, Stowe apparently envisioned her story as evolving from her central character, Uncle Tom.[14] It is important to remember that the original subtitle of the novel was "The Man that Was a Thing," which tends to focus our attention on one central character. Such a focus may work well for a short work, but for a longer, serialized story, the focus had to be broader. Like Dickens, who created multiple characters and plotlines in his serials, Stowe provided not just a story about the growth of a single character but a series of incidents in the lives of slaves and slaveholders. Her second subtitle, the one that she used throughout the serial and as the only subtitle in the published version of the novel, was "Life among the

Lowly," pointing to the ensemble of characters that make up the scenes of *Uncle Tom's Cabin*. Rather than following the linear progress of a single character, Stowe created a variety of memorable characters—Uncle Tom, Eliza, George, Mrs. Shelby, Augustine St. Clare, Little Eva, and Topsy—whom readers could recall in subsequent episodes, even if they did not appear for weeks at a time. The creation of striking characters was crucial to the serial novelist, who was more concerned with scenes that had to work as independent installments than with the direct linkage of plot lines. Indeed, the strategy is still used today in serialized television programs.

There were other, more mechanical problems for Stowe to solve. *Uncle Tom's Cabin* was published in the *National Era* in installments of roughly a chapter a week, apparently according to an agreement between Bailey and Stowe.[15] But variations of several kinds sometimes altered the publication schedule. One no doubt resulted from the difficulty of getting installments from Brunswick, Maine (where Stowe wrote most of the book), to Washington, D.C., in a timely fashion. On 21 August and 30 October, Bailey announced that Chapters 12 and 19 arrived too late for inclusion, and on 18 December Bailey announced that he had received no word from Stowe about chapter 27. At other times chapters were published together (as in the first installment, which includes chapters 1 and 2) or were split in parts and published as separate installments, as space in the *Era* dictated. These complications placed additional demands on both writer and reader and had the net effect of extending the time with which both were engaged in the production and reception of the text.

Serial publication also loosened the author's control over the material. As Max Nänny has observed, "Serial publication as a mode of communication recreated some of the conditions typical of oral narrative,"[16] and in the text of *Uncle Tom's Cabin* there are certainly a number of repetitions and parallels in scenes and plots as well as in detailed descriptions of settings and in lengthy depictions of clothing and other physical attribute of characters, all designed to help the readers remember characters and events. Moreover, Stowe uses analogy, commonly used in oral narrative to suggest correspondence or similarity with a known experience of the authors, throughout her novel. Stowe had initially told Bailey that her purpose was to "give the lights and shadows of the 'patriarchal institution,'" defining her vocation as that of a painter. "There is no arguing with *pictures,* and everybody is impressed by them, whether they mean to be or not," she said shrewdly.[17]

Creating resemblances through analogy was a particularly effective strategy for Stowe in her efforts to undermine the proslavery arguments. One analogy deployed generally in the *National Era* concerns the relationship between the tumultuous events in Europe and the potential for similar upheavals in the United States. The European revolutions of 1848 received full coverage not solely in the large city newspapers but also in small newspapers like the *National Era*. Its readers were consequently informed about the provisional government established by Lamartine after the abdication of King Louis Phillippe in February 1848; the repeal of the Corn Laws in England, which undoubtedly did much to check revolutionary fervor there; and the Italian revolt against Ferdinand II, as well as news of the dozens of rebellions that occurred in Austria, Prussia, Spain, and Hungary. The various revolutions captured the imagination of Americans, who often tended to see themselves as directly responsible for the uprising against Old World tyranny. John Greenleaf Whittier, associate editor of the *National Era,* wrote to Charles Sumner in March 1848: "What glorious changes in the Old World! I feel, almost like going myself, and would if I could do anything more than gratify my feelings by so doing."[18]

A less attractive implication of the European revolutions to most Americans was the possible parallel between the overthrow of tyranny in Europe and the overthrow of tyranny in the American South, which Bailey and countless other journalists were quick to exploit. Writing from the revolutionary scene in Europe, Margaret Fuller made the analogy explicit and dramatic: "Then there is this horrible cancer of Slavery, and this wicked War [the Mexican War], that has grown out of it. How dare I speak of these things here? I listen to the same arguments against the emancipation of Italy, that are used against the emancipation of our blacks; the same arguments in favor of the spollation of Poland as for the conquest of Mexico. I find the cause of tyranny and wrong everywhere the same—and lo! my Country the darkest offender, because with the least excuse, foresworn to the high calling with which she was called—no champion of the rights of men, but a robber and a jailer; the scourge hid behind her banner; her eyes fixed, not on the stars, but on the possessions of her men."[19] In *European Revolutions and the American Literary Renaissance,* Larry J. Reynolds suggests that Stowe exploits a similar analogy in *Uncle Tom's Cabin,* first implicitly in Augustine St. Clair's conversation in chapter 19 with Ophelia, in which he muses on the possibility of general slave rebellions similar to what is "working in Europe" and later in the argument between Alfred and Augustine.[20] As Reynolds notes, Stowe explicitly stated the analogy in the final installment, which appeared on 1 April 1852, when she told her readers, "This is an age of the world when nations are trembling and convulsed. A mighty influence is abroad surging and heaving the world, as with an earthquake. And is America safe: Every nation that carries in its bosom great and unredressed injustice has in it the elements of this last convulsion" (1). Readers of the *National Era* would have understood exactly the connection that Stowe was making. The relation of the slaveholders to the oppressors of Europe was a way of helping her readers understand the great danger to the safety of America. It was a memorable analogy that helped readers internalize the story that Stowe was telling. Indeed, coming a few paragraphs before Stowe's direct address to her "wide circle of friends" and the "dear children" of the epilogue, her warning inextricably merged international politics with family politics.

III

THE formal prerequisites of serialization are perhaps too easily seen merely as obstacles or constraints for the writer to overcome. But we should avoid reducing serialization to a set of requirements that present only problems for the author while ignoring the possibilities or opportunities for a writer engaged in a work that is both written and read over a period of time. Serialization, as a dominant mode in the production of literary discourse, offers a special form of communication for a writer, involving a complex negotiation by which a writer acts on as well as reacts to a particular and evolving publishing environment. Stowe obviously recognized that unique aspect of serialization, as she quite naturally ended the final installment of *Uncle Tom's Cabin* with a gracious farewell letter to her loyal readers on the front page of the *National Era*.

A model of this act of communication is presented in the text of *Uncle Tom's Cabin* itself. In the third installment (chapter 4 of the novel), "An Evening in Uncle Tom's Cabin," which appeared on 19 June 1851, the slaves gather in the cabin of Uncle Tom and Aunt Chloe. Stowe lingers over the description of the cabin, showing us the flowers and vegetables that Aunt Chloe carefully cultivated in front and guides us on a careful tour of the interior of the one-room cabin, including the details of the pictures hanging over the fireplace: "Some very bilious scriptural prints" and, in a pointed reminder of the analogy of revolution that Stowe uses throughout the work, "a portrait of General Washington" (1).[21] Numerous people are in the cabin talking and eating the supper that Aunt Chloe has prepared, including a baby learning to walk, Uncle Tom practicing his reading and writing, and a variety of children. They are later joined by a large group of neighbors and friends, a "motley assemblage," as Stowe says, and the slaves spend the evening gossiping, exchanging news, singing, and, of course, telling stories. Stowe explains that "various exhortations, or relations of experience, followed, and intermingled with the singing" (1). In this black slaves' parlor, there is no orderly progression of events and stories but rather a collage of diverse fragments of experience and ideas. It is, however, a collage with an underlying purpose—the reinforcement of what is today called—with its own political charge—family values. As much as possible in a condition of slavery, Uncle Tom and Aunt Chloe use the parlor as a forum of instruction, both moral and religious. Joan Hedrick has recently shown that Stowe's work is derived from a tradition of "parlor literature," the activity of ongoing sharing and reading of works in a domestic setting that was popular before the Civil War and prior to the professionalization of literary production.[22]

The publication of literature in serial form—especially a serial that appeared in an anti-slavery newspaper—is directly related to the sharing of exhortations and relations of experience that occurred in Stowe's own parlor and is reflected in the fictionalized cabin of Uncle Tom and Aunt Chloe. At the time that Stowe was writing the installments of *Uncle Tom's Cabin,* her own parlor was particularly full. She was a professor's wife, expected to entertain Calvin Stowe's colleagues and visitors to Bowdoin College; she was a mother of six small children; and she was a part-time journalist and teacher trying to make an extremely inadequate income cover many expenses in the Stowes' new home in Brunswick, Maine. According to Hedrick, Stowe took many opportunities to read her work to the family members, friends, and even her students in small private classes that she taught in her home.[23] In addition to sharing her work with her children and students, Stowe was, of course, a member of a very important family of writers and speakers in nineteenth-century America. While she was writing *Uncle Tom's Cabin,* the most famous woman in the United States, her sister, Catherine Beecher, was living in her home. Given the circumstances of composition, it is not surprising that *Uncle Tom's Cabin* is a profoundly domestic novel. Stowe's first auditors were these friends and family members who made up the Stowe household.

Stowe's second audience was the readership of the *National Era,* which was a forum for antislavery writers of all backgrounds and descriptions, and the domestic imagery of the novel has its roots in the pages of this newspaper as well. Established by the American and Foreign Anti-Slavery Society in Washington, D.C., the *National Era* was published from 7 January 1847 through 22 March 1860, shortly after Bailey's sudden death.[24] The declared purpose of the *Era* was "to represent the class of anti-slavery men . . . and to lay before the Southern men . . . such facts and arguments as may serve to throw further light upon the question of slavery, and its disposition."[25] To present "such facts and arguments," Bailey further announced that "The *National Era* would not be confined to the discussion of one subject. Political questions of general interest will be freely examined in its columns. The cause of Literature will receive a large share of attention; a record of current events will be carefully kept up and a full, though condensed report of Congressional proceedings will be given."[26] As diverse as the article, stories, and features in the paper were, the underlying purpose of all the coverage was nonetheless to promote the antislavery cause, often through the domestic imagery of the union as a house and the American citizens as a family.

To promote abolition, Bailey and his writers were engaged in the task of militating against a political system that accepted slavery and, with the passage of the Fugitive Slave Law in 1850, made all a party to it. It was necessary to challenge the discourse of the advocates of slavery—the antagonists of the *National Era*—and to make the antislavery argument persuasive and ultimately acceptable. Bailey had been specifically chosen for the editorship of the newspaper because of his reasonable, diplomatic personality as well as because of his moderate view that Southerners and southern slaveholders might be persuaded that slavery was more than a sectional issue. While William Lloyd Garrison and his followers called for disunion and cared little about offending Southern readers, Bailey's paper was directly addressed to Southerners. Bailey, according to his biographer, wanted to treat Southerners as reasonable beings whom he might involve in a "national campaign against a moral, social, political, and economic evil."[27] To that end, Bailey decided to shed further light on the question of slavery for a distinctly Southern audience. Steady persuasion in a variety of forms was the course chosen by Bailey, and one way of reading the hundreds of articles, essays, reviews, continuing stories, and poems in the *National Era* is to consider the many ways in which the argument against slavery is extended by analogy to a number of issues to subvert the ideology of slaveholding.

To understand how these subversions worked, it is necessary to look closely at the polyphonic nature of the *National Era*. The variety of voices that appeared on the pages of the newspaper exemplify the diversity of language itself. To read *Uncle Tom's Cabin* column by column in issue after issue is a very different experience from reading the novel in book form, in part because one is constantly reminded of the presence of the many voices and speakers. On a mechanical level, one is simply struck by the number of other texts that compete for attention on the pages of the newspaper. And in the case of the *National Era*, a newspaper specifically designed to include imaginative literature, aesthetic and political materials inhabit the same space. The interrelation of these texts, their languages and voices, their "various exhortations, or relations of experience," is suddenly clarified. For instance, the *National Era* for 5 June 1851 included not only the first installment of *Uncle Tom's Cabin* but also pointed letters from a variety of American citizens to the editor protesting the Fugitive Slave Law in which the writers linked Congress with civil despotism; "A Reminiscence," a sketch by a popular writer, Patty Lee, about the sad death of a young girl (with more than a passing resemblance to Little Eva); an account of the murder of a master by a slave girl in North Carolina (suggestive of the course of action Cassy decides not to take); an account of a disturbance at a festival involving several thousand German immigrants in Hoboken, New Jersey, that was widely reported in the Southern press as a riot; the text of a speech by Louis Kossuth, the Hungarian revolutionary, demanding his release from Kutahja; notices of articles appearing in other periodicals such as *Blackwood's* and *Harper's;* a blistering review of Daniel Webster's attitudes toward slavery; and pieces such as a "Letter from Cincinnati," detailing the population growth of this increasingly important city in the free state of Ohio. The presence of these other texts points up the extent to which *Uncle Tom's Cabin* was one part of a strong program undertaken by the *National Era* to expose the scandal of slavery in American society in a variety of ways.

IV

IMAGES of revolution and rebellion abound in *Uncle Tom's Cabin,* and they are closely linked with the analogy of the nation as a family under threat. Stowe's conservative warning of a "last convulsion" suggests that a refusal to deal with slavery would undermine the very fabric of American life—both elegant plantation houses and rustic cabins would crumble unless action was taken. Antislavery journalists and writers were quick to exploit the connection between the overthrow of tyranny in Europe and the overthrow of tyranny in the American South, and many of the scenes in *Uncle Tom's Cabin* also suggest this connection. In the installment entitled "The Freeman's Defence," published on 2 October 1851, George Harris argues that the Fugitive Slave law destroyed his family by returning them to a condition of brutality and slavery. In his defense of his right to protect his family, he disavows the law that the posse is intent on enforcing. Stowe remarks, "If it had been only a Hungarian youth, now bravely defending in some mountain fastness the retreat of fugitives escaping from Austria into America, this would have been sublime heroism; but as it was a youth of African descent, defending the retreat of fugitives through America into Canada, of course we are too well instructed and patriotic to see any heroism in it; and if any of our readers do, they must do it on their own private responsibility. When despairing Hungarian fugitives make their way, against all the search-warrants and authorities of their lawful government, to America, press and political cabinet ring with applause and welcome. When despairing African fugitives do the same thing,—its—what *is* it?" (1). Readers of the *National Era* would have recognized the allusion to Louis Kossuth, a youth among the Hungarian rebels who had unsuccessfully attempted to free his country from the Austrian monarchy in 1848–49.[28] In 1850–51, Kossuth was a virtual prisoner in Turkey; he accepted an invitation to visit the United States and arrived in December 1851. The American political situation was highly charged in the aftermath of the passage of the Fugitive Slave Law, which generated ongoing debates about the expansion of slave territories, and both proslavery and antislavery forces had high expectations about his visit. In the *Era* throughout 1850–51, Bailey published dozens of articles and reports about Kossuth's life and impending arrival in the United States; he saw in Kossuth's visit an opportunity to overcome the major obstacle—slavery—that obscured his vision of what America could be: a fully democratic example "for other nations of the world as they struggled to overthrow despotic rule."[29]

Bailey appears to have favored American intervention in foreign affairs in two ways. First, he believed in a symbolic intervention, conducted largely in the columns of his newspaper as he published accounts and editorials in which he repeatedly appealed to Americans to serve an example to Europe in their efforts to overthrow despotism by the abolition of the tyranny of slavery. Second, Bailey supported a direct intervention by making a champion of Kossuth and offering financial aid to the Hungarian and the remnants of his rebel forces. To oppose intervention in Europe, in Bailey's mind, was to oppose intervention in the institution of slavery in the American south.

Stowe's brother, Henry Ward Beecher, who played a major role in the increasingly bitter discussions, was also a strong supporter of Kossuth. On 23 October 1851, Beecher published a lengthy essay, "Liberal Meditations—Kossuth and Cotton" in *The Independent*. Bailey published about half of that piece in the *Era* on 6 November 1851, when it appeared with chapter 19, 'Topsy," of *Uncle Tom's Cabin*. "Kossuth and Cotton" is primarily an imaginary dialogue between several American clergymen and Kossuth. Bailey introduced the extract that ran in the *Era* by explaining that Beecher "caustically depicts the absurdity if not hypocrisy of pretending to honor the champions of Liberty in other lands while upholding Slavery and such acts as the Fugitive Slave Law in our own" (1). In the dialogue, the American clergymen speak the conventional discourse noted by Stowe in an earlier installment of *Uncle Tom's Cabin*, chapter 12, "Select Incidents of Lawful Trade," published on 28 August 1851. In this installment, Stowe depicted Uncle Tom watching Haley, the slave trader, sell Lucy's baby from a riverboat without her knowledge. Stowe describes Tom watching the transaction with "a perfect understanding of its results. To him, it looked like something unutterably horrible and cruel, because, poor, ignorant black soul! he had not learned to generalize, and to take enlarged views. If he had only been instructed by a certain minister of Christianity, he might have thought better of it, and seen in it an every-day incident of a lawful trade; a trade which is the vital support of an institution which an American divine tells us has 'no evils but such as are inseparably from any other relations in social and domestic life'" (1).[30] Here Stowe mimes conventional discourse, which in *Uncle Tom's Cabin* she subverts with numerous examples of Tom's simplicity and clear obedience to higher, religious laws, as opposed to the civic laws that permitted slavery. In Beecher's dialogue, Kossuth assumes the role of Uncle Tom; he is examined by the clergymen about his "notions of law and government, patriotism and treason." Like Uncle Tom, Kossuth is presented as a simple man who affirms that his allegiance to his Hungarian rebels and the righteousness of their cause is more important than blind obedience to civil laws. The clergymen attempt to educate Kossuth but turn away in disappointment, believing that the Hungarian is "inclined to fanaticism." Like Uncle Tom, Kossuth is a man whose "limited knowledge of Republican Governments" has curtailed his understanding of the greater good of American law, as Beecher ironically put it. In Stowe's installment and in Beecher's dialogue, the clergymen are presented as blind and insensitive adherents to man-made laws who are finally un-christian, while Uncle Tom and Kossuth are presented as fundamentally Christian men who eschew civil law for a higher one. Ironically, those who disobey civil law become heroic advocates of the moral opposition to slavery. To Stowe, busily writing the middle chapters of *Uncle Tom's Cabin,* the Hungarian revolution could thus serve as a convenient analogy to the situation in the United States.[31]

Stowe uses a number of individual acts of rebellion, such as George's "Freeman's Defence," as well as a few on a somewhat larger scale to demonstrate the destructive effects of a system that, as she observed in her "Concluding Remarks," made every slaveholder "an irresponsible despot" and America a nation that would consequently be subject to the same "convulsion" currently shaking Europe. The united efforts of the slaves on the Shelby farm to hinder the progress of Haley in capturing Eliza represent one kind of rebellion portrayed in the novel. This rebellion against the authority of the slave trader, which is supported by Mrs. Shelby, actually represents one of the few comic episodes in the novel. A considerably more serious rebellion, however, was dramatized in the final installments of the novel, when Stowe moved the action to the farm of Simon Legree.

In chapter 32, published in two parts on 29 January and 5 February 1852, Stowe specifically compared Legree to a "potentate . . . who governed his plantation by a sort of resolution of forces" (29 January 1852, 3). A contemporary reader would have instantly recognized this as the pattern by which various European monarchs divided and conquered numerous principalities in Europe. And in the *Era* of 5 February, readers would have noted the "Ode to Republican Rome," by Augustine Duganne, just three columns away. In this poem, the working men of Rome are congratulated for having broken their "shackles, and hurled back in proud defiance / The gauntlet of your faith at slavery's blow!" The working men are further urged to greater defiance of the "crownless tyrant of France, Louis Napoleon, who was busily trying to undermine and destroy what was left of the revolutionary impulse in Italy to a "resolution of force" (1).

Stowe portrays similar divisions on Legree's farm. The black overseers, Sambo and Quimbo, who "cordially hated each other," vie with one another and with Legree for favor and control. The plantation hands hate the overseers and of course Legree and perpetuate all manner of cruelties in an elaborate perversion of household unity and accord. Although initially divided, Cassy and Emmeline come to represent yet another faction in this battle for control, and ultimately it is Tom, through his Christianizing of the other slaves and humanizing of Cassy, who is responsible for the successful overthrow of Legree's power. Tom's intervention into Legree's complex power base serves as an analogy for the ways in which both the text of *Uncle Tom's Cabin* and *Era* operate as interventions into the proslavery discourse espoused by Southern slaveholders.

Many critics of *Uncle Tom's Cabin* have pointed to the centrality of the debate in chapter 23 (which appeared on 20 November 1851) between Augustine and Alfred St. Clair to the more general implications for the institution of slavery in the United States.[32] In the debate, Alfred—whose very name connotes an Anglo-Saxon sense of hierarchy—denigrates Augustine's view that the downtrodden masses may rise and overthrow their tyrannical masters. Alfred speaks in the conventional idiom of the slaveholder; his voice is the one that Stowe counters with Augustine, who pointedly reminds Alfred of the contemporary possibilities for revolution by oppressed people: "They took *their* turn once, in France" (1). And Augustine clearly understands that such action includes the possibility of rebellion among American slaves. Alfred interrupts Augustine's warning about potential insurrections by exclaiming, "As if we hadn't had enough of that abominable, contemptible Hayti!" (1). Readers of *Uncle Tom's Cabin* would have immediately understood the reference and implications: the figure of Toussaint L'Ouverture, the black leader who rose from slavery to organize a successful 1791 revolution in Haiti that all but destroyed the white master class, represented a fearful prospect for slaveholders.

For many abolitionists, Toussaint had become the model for blacks in the United States. Emphasizing his virtues of wisdom, dedication, humanity, and Christianity, abolitionists invoked Toussaint in their arguments for the virtues of peaceful emancipation, calling attention to his reluctance to engage in the more violent aspects of the revolution and his loyalty to his white master. Like her abolitionist friends—Harriet Martineau in her biography of Toussaint, *The Hour and the Man;* Whittier in his poem, "Toussaint L'Ouverture"; and Wendell Phillips in his often-delivered lecture on Toussaint—as well as other writers in the *National Era,* Stowe used Toussaint to promote the idea that slavery as an institution demeaned the black race. In the final chapter of *Uncle Tom's Cabin,* Stowe lists examples of black men and women who had achieved a variety of accomplishments in a "state of freedom." Like those who invoked Toussaint as the model for what black slaves might become, Stowe also reminded her readers of the consequences for the American family if peaceful emancipation did not take place.

In the pages of the *National Era,* Bailey sought to counter the position of many slaveholders that slavery was necessary to control an inferior, unruly race. As Alfred insists to Augustine, "Never you fear for us; possession is our nine points. We've got the power. This subject race . . . is down and shall stay down! We have energy enough to manage our own power" (20 November 1851, 1). For several years, Bailey had responded to such arguments by contending that slavery was the cause of the need to exert such power and asking if it would not be wiser to end the threat through peaceful emancipation, thus aligning former slaves "with law and order, instead of against it."[33] Echoing such a position, Stowe situates the debate between Alfred and Augustine in a chapter called "Henrique"—the name of Alfred's oldest son. The immediate context for the debate between the brothers is actually the behavior of Henrique, who has just viciously whipped his slave, Dodo, and threatened Uncle Tom. Augustine asks Alfred if this is what "we may call republican education" and suggests that Henrique's impatience and hot-headedness would threaten his race's ability to govern effectively. Alfred admits that the system of slavery "is a difficult one to train children under" and thinks that he will send Henrique north for a time. Augustine's response is ominous: "Since training children is the staple work of the human race, I should think it something of a consideration that our system does not work well there" (1).

V

FOR Stowe there was no clearer exposure of the scandal of slavery. The epilogue for her serialized novel was, after all, addressed especially to the children who had been following her story. The potential for the destruction of the family when the complex relationships among human beings are ignored was for Stowe the most powerful argument she knew for abolition. As we have seen, this argument takes a variety of shapes within the text and is emphasized in a variety of ways. Chapter 9, "In Which It Appears That a Senator Is but a man," was published in two parts, on 24 and 31 July 1851. In yet another of the parlors that are described in *Uncle Tom's Cabin,* a senator and his wife are preparing for an evening at home. Just as Aunt Chloe had been busy superintending dinner and children in her cabin earlier in the novel, the senator's wife is employed in a strikingly similar fashion. In the novel, the senator and his wife are the Birds; in the serial, their name is Burr; no reason is known for the name change.

The name of Burr, of course, carried a significant and controversial political edge. To Stowe, who would later use the historical figure of Aaron Burr as a minor character in *The Minister's Wooing* (1859), the name may have merely suggested the ambiguity of a "treasonous" act. When the Burrs have a quiet moment to talk, Mrs. Burr challenges the senator to explain to her the rationale for the passage of the Fugitive Slave Law. In these two installments, Mrs. Burr literally becomes a burr in the side of the senator in her persistent questioning about the law. Calling her his "fair politician," the Senator is overwhelmed not by the arguments that Mrs. Burr offers in opposition to the law but rather by her outraged demeanor and by the domestic terms in which she develops the implications of the passage of the law. When Eliza appears in the kitchen and the Burrs are confronted with a real mother and her child, the senator finds himself subverting the law and aiding the fugitive slave. Stowe's account of the senator's thoughts capitalizes on the word *fugitive* made flesh: "His idea of a fugitive was only an idea of the letters that spell the word,—or at the most, the image of a little newspaper picture of a man with a stick and a bundle. . . . The magic of the real presence of distress,—the imploring human eye, the frail, trembling human hand, the despairing appeal of helpless agony,—these he had never tried. He had never thought that a fugitive might be a hapless mother, a defenceless child,—like that one which was now wearing his lost boy's little well-known cap,—as he was a man, and a downright noble-hearted one, too,—he was, as everybody must see, in a sad case for his patriotism" (1).

In this passage, Stowe deploys what Jane Tompkins has termed "sentimental power" in a stinging critique of the political institutions that permitted and upheld slavery.[34] To Stowe, the preservation of the family and the responsibility of a society for the upbringing of children was all important. The presentation of this argument—that slavery destroys families both black and white—in a novel that was written and read over a period of time is in itself a significant part of the power of *Uncle Tom's Cabin*. By participating with the other editors and writers of the *National Era*, Stowe assisted in the creation of the counterdiscourse of abolition, which was designed to undermine and subvert the ideology that produced the proslavery discourse of the day. Stowe's argument against slavery, offered through the graphic images of the domestic implications of slaveholding, gained considerable power by unfolding from week to week in the pages of a family newspaper.

NOTES

I am grateful to Donald E. Pease, the members of his National Endowment for the Humanities 1990 Summer Seminar, "Reconstructing America's Civil Imagination: 1845–1900," and Lloyd Michaels, David C. Miller, and Kenneth M. Price for helpful comments on an early version of this essay. I am especially indebted to Linck C. Johnson for his thoughtful response to a subsequent draft.

1. See, for example, Elizabeth Ammons, "Stowe's Dream of the Mother Savior: *Uncle Tom's Cabin* and American Women Writers before the 1920s," in *New Essays on Uncle Tom's Cabin*, ed. Eric J. Sundquist (New York: Cambridge Univ. Press, 1986), 155–95; Joshua D. Bellin, "Up to Heaven's Gate, Down in Earth's Dust: The Politics of Judgment in *Uncle Tom's Cabin*," *American Literature* 65 (1993): 275–95; Ann Douglas, introduction to *Uncle Tom's Cabin, or Life among the Lowly*, by Harriet Beecher Stowe, ed. Ann Douglas (New York: Penguin,

1981); Myra Jehlen, "The Family Militant: Domesticity versus Slavery in *Uncle Tom's Cabin*," *Criticism* 31 (1989): 383–400; Karen Halttunen, "Gothic Imagination and Social Reform: The Haunted Houses of Lyman Beecher, Henry Ward Beecher, and Harriet Beecher Stowe," in *New Essays on Uncle Tom's Cabin*, 107–34; Hortense Spillers, "Changing the Letter: The Yokes, the Jokes of Discourse, or, Mrs. Stowe, Mr. Reed," in *Slavery and the Literary Imagination*, ed. Deborah E. McDowell and Arnold Rampersad (Baltimore: Johns Hopkins Univ. Press, 1989), 25–61; Robert B. Stepto, "Sharing the Thunder: The Literary Exchanges of Harriet Beecher Stowe, Henry Bibb, and Frederick Douglass," in *New Essays on Uncle Tom's Cabin*, 135–53; Jane Tompkins, *Sensational Designs: The Cultural Work of American Fiction: 1790–1860* (New York: Oxford University Press, 1985), 122–46; Eric J. Sundquist, introduction to *New Essays on Uncle Tom's Cabin*, 1–44; Richard Yarborough, "Strategies of Black Characterization in *Uncle Tom's Cabin* and the Early Afro-American Novel," in *New Essays on Uncle Tom's Cabin*, 45–84; and Jean Fagan Yellin, "Doing It Herself: *Uncle Tom's Cabin* and Woman's Role in the Slavery Crisis," in *New Essays on Uncle Tom's Cabin*, 85–106.

2. The standard study of the writing, serialization, and publication of *Uncle Tom's Cabin* is E. Bruce Kirkham, *The Building of Uncle Tom's Cabin* (Knoxville: Univ. of Tennessee Press, 1977), especially 61–149. See also Thomas G. Gossett, *Uncle Tom's Cabin and American Culture* (Dallas: Southern Methodist Univ. Press, 1985), 88 ff.

3. Kirkham, *Building*, 183.

4. Dickens made several observations about *Uncle Tom's Cabin*. To a friend on 22 November 1852, he wrote: "In the matter of 'Uncle Tom's Cabin,' I partly though not entirely agree with Mr. James. No doubt a much lower art will serve for the handling of such a subject in fiction, than for a launch on the sea of imagination without such a powerful bark; but there are many points in the book very admirably done. There is a certain St. Clair, New Orleans gentleman, who seems to me to be conceived with great power and originality. If he had not 'a Grecian outline of face,' which I began to be a little tired of in my earliest infancy—I should think him unexceptionable. He has a sister too, a maiden lady from New England, in whose person the besetting weaknesses and prejudices of the abolitionists themselves, on the subject of the Blacks, are set forth in the liveliest and truest colors and with the greatest boldness. She (I mean Mrs. Stowe) is a leetle unscrupulous in the appropriation way. I seem to see a writer with who I am very intimate (and whom nobody can possibly admire more than myself) peeking very often through the thinness of the paper. Further I descry the Ghost of Mary Barton, and the very palpable mirage of a scene in the children of the Mist; but in spite of this, I consider the book a fine one with a great and gallant purpose in it, and worthy of its reputation" (Graham Story, Kathleen Tillotson, and Nina Burgis, eds., *The Letters of Charles Dickens* (Oxford: Clarendon, 1988) 6:807–8. See also Dickens's comment in his essay "North American Slavery" in Harry Stone, ed., *Charles Dickens' Uncollected Writings from Household Words, 1850–1859* (Bloomington: Indiana Univ. Press, 1968), 2:436; as well as com-

ments on Stowe in his recollections of Grace Greenwood in Philip Collins, ed., *Dickens: Interviews and Recollections* (Totawa, N.J.: Barnes and Noble, 1981), 2:236.

5. I am following Linda K. Hughes and Michael Lund in my definition of a serial: "a continuing story over an extended time with enforced interruptions," *The Victorian Serial* (Charlottesville: Univ. Press of Virginia, 1991), 2. This important study as well as their other work has greatly informed my examination of *Uncle Tom's Cabin*. See Hughes and Lund, "Studying Victorian Serials," *Literary Research* 11 (1986): 235–52; and their "Linear Stories and Circular Vision: The Decline of the Victorian Serial," in *Chaos and Order: Complex Dynamics in Literature and Science,* ed. N. Katherine Hayles (Chicago: Univ. of Chicago Press, 1991), 167–94.

6. Students of British serializations often point out that the lengthy process of publication led to "an enfolding and merging of literature and life," as the readers of a serial followed the events throughout a year or more in real time (Hughes and Lund, "Studying Victorian Serials," 237).

7. In *Harriet Beecher Stowe,* (New York: Twayne, 1989), John R. Adams suggestively comments that "of all the sources of *Uncle Tom's Cabin,* the most decisive is the one least considered: the periodical for which it was written, whose policies were implicit in the shaping of the story. Here as always, Mrs. Stowe was writing for an editor and a public whose expectations she could not afford to disregard. More than the author knew, her story was nourished, during its long period of serial publications, on the spirit of the *National Era* itself" (36).

8. For useful discussion of the impact of serial publication on narrative and plot, see Peter Hughes, "Narrative, Scene, and the Fictions of History," and Max Nänny, "Narrative and Modes of Communication," in *Contemporary Approaches to Narrative,* ed. Anthony Mortimer (Tübingen: Gunter Warr Verlag, 1984), 73–87, 51–62.

9. For instance, both Jehlen ("The Family Militant," 386) and Sundquist (introduction, 9) give incorrect information about the subtitle: *Uncle Tom's Cabin: Life among the Lowly* was the full title that appeared in the *National Era* on 5 June 1851. *Uncle Tom's Cabin: or the Man that Was a Thing,* was the title announced by Bailey in the *National Era* on 8 May 1851. The subtitle was changed prior to the publication of the first installment of the novel. The dates of serialization are often given incorrectly: for example, Yellin gives the dates as 3 June 1851 through 2 Apr. 1852 ("Doing It Herself," 147) (the correct dates are 5 June 1851 through 1 Apr. 1852). In addition, the nature of the *National Era* is frequently mischaracterized; occasionally it is referred to as a magazine when it was, in fact, an antislavery weekly newspaper, like many others, including the *Liberator.* In the afterword of an edition of *Uncle Tom's Cabin* (New York: New American Library, 1981), widely used in classrooms, John William Ward increases the length of the *Era* from four standard sheets (which it was from its inception on 7 Jan. 1847) to eight (478). Accounts of the content of the installments that appeared in the *Era* are occasionally mistaken. Kirkham writes that George Harris is introduced in the second episode of the serial; George appears

in chapter 2, which appeared with chapter 1 as a single installment on 5 June 1851 (*The Building of Uncle Tom's Cabin*, 8). This list of errors underscores the relative unimportance accorded the details of the serialization by contemporary commentators on *Uncle Tom's Cabin*.

10. For studies of the methods by which Dickens composed and published his novels, see John R. Butt and Kathleen Tillotson, *Dickens at Work* (London: Methuen, 1957), and Archibald C. Coolidge, *Charles Dickens as a Serial Novelist* Ames: Iowa State Univ. Press, 1967). Other useful studies of serialization in general are Hughes and Lund, *The Victorian Serial*, as well as J. Don Vann, *Victorian Novels in Serial* (New York: MLA, 1985).

11. See especially Nänny, "Narrative," 61.

12. Joseph S. Van Why and Earl French, eds., *Nook Farm* (Hartford, Conn.: Stowe-Day Foundation, 1975), 17.

13. See Kirkham, *Building*, 69–149, for a detailed summary of the extant materials relating to Stowe's preparation of the manuscript for the *National Era*.

14. For a summary of the various, conflicting accounts of Stowe's conception of Uncle Tom, see Kirkham, *Building*, 72–75.

15. See Stanley Harrold, *Gamaliel Bailey and Antislavery Union* (Kent, Ohio: Kent State Univ. Press, 1986), 142–43; Kirkham, *Building*, 69–72; and Forrest Wilson, *Crusader in Crinoline: The Life of Harriet Beecher Stowe* (Westport, Conn.: Greenwood, 1941), 259–63.

16. Nänny, "Narrative," 61.

17. Van Why and French, *Nook Farm*, 18.

18. John B. Pickard, ed., *The Letters of John Greenleaf Whittier* (Cambridge: Harvard Univ. Press, 1975) 2:537.

19. Margaret Fuller, *"These Sad But Glorious Days": Dispatches from Europe, 1846–1850*, ed. Larry J. Reynolds and Susan Belasco Smith (New Haven: Yale Univ. Press, 1991), 165.

20. Larry J. Reynolds, *European Revolutions and the American Literary Renaissance* (New Haven: Yale Univ. Press, 1988), 52–53.

21. In the two-volume edition of *Uncle Tom's Cabin*, the "scriptural prints" are described as "brilliant" instead of "bilious," with its connotations of melancholy (see Douglas, introduction, 68).

22. Hedrick's documentation is an important background for an understanding of how serialization followed naturally from the sharing of stories within the family circle. See Joan Hedrick, "Parlor Literature: Harriet Beecher Stowe and the Question of 'Great Women Artists,'" *SIGNS* 17 (1992): 275–303.

23. Joan Hedrick, *Harriet Beecher Stowe: A Life* (New York: Oxford Univ. Press, 1994), 218–23; see also Wilson, *Crusader in Crinoline*, 271.

24. Details about Bailey, his background, and the *National Era* are taken from Harrold, *Gamaliel Bailey*, 81–107, 139.

25. Quoted in ibid., 87.

26. Quoted in ibid., 88–89.

27. Ibid., 85.

28. For another view of this scene, see Reynolds, *European Revolutions,* 154–56. See also his detailed discussion of Kossuth and his impact on the American literary imagination, especially 153–61; an excellent additional source is Donald S. Spencer, *Louis Kossuth and Young America: A Study of Sectionalism and Foreign Policy, 1848–1852* (Columbia: Univ. of Missouri Press, 1977), 22–23; 66–68.

29. Harrold, *Gamaliel Bailey,* 157.

30. In the text of the *Era* and in the novel, Stowe footnoted this passage to identify the "divine" as Dr. Joel Parker of Philadelphia. For the controversy that ensued over this note, see Kirkham, 188–90; Wilson, *Crusader in Crinoline,* 266, 281, 285–87, 303–22.

31. After Kossuth's arrival in the United States in December 1851, Beecher actively campaigned to aid the Hungarian rebel. By charging admissions to talks, he raised $10,000 at his Plymouth Church of Brooklyn. But as historians of Kossuth's time in America have noted, the actual appearance of the Hungarian on American soil at once began to dilute the enthusiasm for him and for his revolutionary cause. Garrisonian abolitionists were almost immediately angered when Kossuth refused to take a stand on slavery, feeling that such an intervention into American domestic policy would hurt his efforts to raise funds for his cause. Of course, he was right, but the refusal to take a stand cost him dearly on both sides. Garrison was moved to publish a nearly one hundred–page letter protesting Kossuth's position, while Southerners protested his scheduled tour of American cities. See Spencer, *Louis Kossuth,* 66–68. Stowe's personal interest in Kossuth is not well documented, but she did take time to visit him on her first trip to Europe, shortly after the publication of the novel *Uncle Tom's Cabin* (Charles Edward Stowe, *Life of Harriet Beecher Stowe* [Boston: Houghton Mifflin, 1889], 237). On 23 May 1853 Charles Beecher recorded in his journal the following comments about the visit: "We drove a little further out from the center to the residence of Kossuth, whom we found at home. He received us gladly and conversed with point on slavery and on Harry's reception. He lives very plainly, no show, no luxury. Everything is even poor about him. He seems worn. He is constantly at work. He 'trusts in God and in the people and keeps working,' he said. He alluded to Harry's great reception in a way that showed both his feelings and his insight. How much of all this enthusiasm is *curiosity,* superficiality; how much is genuine benevolence? By some tones, words, gestures I saw he felt deeply the *neglect* of the English aristocracy. Bidding him Godspeed, we left" (Joseph S. Van Why and Earl French, eds., *Harriet Beecher Stowe in Europe: The Journal of Charles Beecher* [Hartford, Conn.: Stowe-Day Foundation, 1986], 119).

32. See especially Reynolds, *European Revolutions,* 52, and Sundquist, introduction, 27–28.

33. Harrold, *Gamaliel Bailey,* 87–88.

34. See Tompkins, *Sensational Designs,* 122–46. Tompkins's focus in this chapter is on the centrality of women in "domestic" novels and the "story of salvation through motherly love" (125).

5

LYDIA MARIA CHILD AND THE
JUVENILE MISCELLANY
The Creation of an American
Children's Literature

CAROLYN L. KARCHER

•

"I know what that shout means among the children," said Miss Amy; "the Miscellany has come."

So I ran down stairs and saw Papa with the book in his hand, stooping down to Mary, who was stretching up her neck, and Emily, who was standing tip-toe to get a look at it; while little black Dinah showed her white teeth for joy. Fortunately, there were two numbers, and as soon as they had been ex-am-in-ed by the elder members of the family, Mary took one copy, and Emily the other. I soon heard dear little Emily spelling Ju-ve-*line*. Then I begged Mary to find Emily an easy place to read; and Mary was good-na-tur-ed enough to stop in the midst of a pretty story, and show her the "Sailor's Dog." Then little Emily looked very earnest, and spelt almost a page, until the bell rang for eight o'clock. (*Juvenile Miscellany,* Nov. 1829, 215–16)

THIS lively description of "A Family Scene" in Charleston, South Carolina, re-creates the excitement with which the entire household greeted each bimonthly issue of Lydia Maria Child's *Juvenile Miscellany*. This vignette, written by one of the *Miscellany*'s chief contributors, the transplanted Bostonian Caroline Howard Gilman, also captures the spirit of a magazine that served as primer, storybook, "library of entertaining knowledge," and purveyor of moral values. The relations it pictures between parents and children, older and younger siblings, masters and servants, suggest the social mission of nineteenth-century children's literature: to promote domestic harmony, provide behavioral models for parents and children, foster a desire for education, and bridge the gap between the privileged classes and their subordinates.[1]

The presence of the slave child, "little black Dinah," and, even more tellingly, the silence about her actual status (Gilman would soon become an apologist for her adopted region's "peculiar institution") indicates the conservative nature of this mission.[2] The cultural establishment that sponsored the *Juvenile Miscellany* conceived of children's literature as a buttress for the dominant society's hierarchies of race, class, and gender, not as a site for challenging them.[3]

When Child founded the *Juvenile Miscellany* in 1826, however, she did not perceive the contradiction between promulgating the moral, social, and political ideology of America's white middle class and furthering a vision of racial equality that threatened white hegemony. For most of its eight-year existence, the magazine successfully combined aims whose incompatibility would not become apparent to either its editor or its audience until controversy over slavery polarized the country in the 1830s.

The reminiscences of readers brought up on the *Miscellany* testify to how skillfully Child packaged her dual message and how imaginatively she fused didacticism with entertainment. "No child who read the *Juvenile Miscellany* . . . will ever forget the excitement that the appearance of each number caused," wrote the abolitionist and woman's rights advocate Caroline Healcy Dall in 1883, three years after Child's death (*Unitarian Review,* June 1883, 525–26). The tableau Dall sketched of the neighborhood hubbub on delivery day confirms that Gilman was not simply puffing the magazine in "A Family Scene."

"The children sat on the stone steps of their house doors all the way up and down Chestnut Street in Boston, waiting for the carrier," recalled Dall. "He used to cross the street, going from door to door in a zigzag fashion; and the fortunate possessor of the first copy found a crowd of little ones hanging over her shoulder from the steps above. . . . How forlorn we were if the carrier was late!" Half a century later, Dall fondly remembered her favorite stories; their mere titles—"Garafelia," "Ferdinand and Zoe," "The Easter Eggs"—still conjured up "vivid pictures of past delight."

Though the *Miscellany* had long been eclipsed by vastly more sophisticated children's magazines, Dall pronounced it superior to its successors "in simplicity, directness, and moral influence." She went on to pay Child the tribute of ranking her above all the children's writers who had inherited her mantle, including Louisa May Alcott, whose popularity has endured into our own day. "Never did any one cater so wisely and so well for the unfolding mind," she asserted.

Alcott herself indirectly acknowledged Child's influence by borrowing a famous episode in *Little Women*—Jo March's decision to help raise money for the family by selling her hair—from a *Juvenile Miscellany* story, "The Orphans" (July 1828, 314–26).[4] Her contemporary, Lucy Larcom, an editor of the post–Civil War children's magazine *Our Young Folks,* credited the *Juvenile Miscellany* with inspiring the founding of the millworkers' periodical in which she made her literary debut, the *Lowell Offering.*[5]

Yet another New England writer molded by "that delightful pioneer among children's magazines in America" was the abolitionist Thomas Wentworth Higginson. His 1868 biography of the woman to whom he attributed his conversion to antislavery opened with his "earliest recollections" of the persona she assumed in so many of the *Miscellany*'s dialogues and sketches: "She came before us . . . as some kindly and omnipresent aunt, beloved forever by the heart of childhood,—some one gifted with all lore, and furnished with unfathomable resources,—some one discoursing equal delight to all members of the household."[6]

I

WHAT accounts for the delight Child's juvenile readers took in the magazine, and why did it leave such a lasting impression on them? A prime factor was the novelty of the entertainment and instruction the *Miscellany* offered. Dall, Alcott, Larcom, and Higginson belonged to the first generation of American children to enjoy a magazine and a body of literature produced especially for them.

The birth of a genre self-consciously aimed at socializing children occurred at a historical moment when several related developments were interacting to create a need for such a medium: first, the shift of economic production from the home to factories and the accompanying transmutation of homemaking and child rearing into full-time activities for married women of the middle class; second, the emergence of a new concept of childhood and a new concern for the moral edification of children; and third, the formation of a middle-class value system stressing hard work, productivity, usefulness, frugality, self-denial, sobriety, orderliness, and punctuality—a value system that the middle class wished to transmit both to its own youth and to other classes.[7]

Although children's literature was created for that purpose by late eighteenth-century British writers, Child was the first to adapt the genre to the needs of American youth. She made children's literature a vehicle for inculcating the principles she held most vital to a democratic republic (as opposed to a monarchy)—principles that included a commitment to equal rights for all and the courage to stand by one's inner convictions, as well as the internalization of the middle-class work ethic. The enthusiastic reception of her 1824 children's book, *Evenings in New Eng-*

land, with its mixture of diverting stories, informative articles, and moral precepts, gave publishers the idea of asking her to design and edit a magazine on the same model.[8]

With the inventiveness she showed so often in her career, Child quickly turned the *Juvenile Miscellany* into a sophisticated professional enterprise. She enlisted a network of contributors that included most of the leading women writers of the day: Lydia Huntley Sigourney, Catharine Maria Sedgwick, Eliza Leslie, Sarah Josepha Hale, Caroline Howard Gilman, Hannah Flagg Gould, Anna Maria Wells, and a host of others who can no longer be identified. (Contributors typically published under pseudonyms or initials, while Child left her pieces unsigned.) Each produced works commissioned especially for the *Miscellany* and tailored to fit the regular series it featured. Sigourney, Gilman, Gould, Hale, and Wells supplied poems and occasional sketches. Sedgwick, Leslie, "F." of Stockbridge, "Mater," and Child herself provided domestic fiction. "A.B.F." authored moral dialogues between "Mother and Eliza" and "Botanical" dialogues between Mother and Harry. "D**" detailed the habits of insects, and "X.Y.Z." the wonders of "Conchology." "F." (possibly Child's brother, Convers Francis) devoted the column "Scripture Illustrations" to explicating obscure biblical references by drawing on travelers' accounts of Middle Eastern customs. Child, who wrote from a quarter to a third of every 108-page number and practiced all these genres, specialized in biographical sketches of American heroes, dialogues on American history, translations of European fairy tales, and stories of Indians, blacks, and ethnic groups from other continents.[9]

The wide range of selections, enhanced with illustrations and supplemented with riddles, ensured that the *Miscellany* would appeal to children of both sexes and various ages. Every issue opened with an engraved frontispiece accompanying the lead story and closed with verses, puzzles, and the answers to the preceding issue's "conundrums." Fusing "amusement" with "instruction," as the magazine's subtitle proclaimed, fiction served to inculcate moral principles, and whimsical sketches ("Letter from Summer to Winter," "Complaint of the Letter H, to His Brother K") conveyed lessons in geography and spelling.

Any modern reader would of course find the magazine oppressively didactic. Nevertheless, its nonsectarian approach toward forming youthful minds was both liberal and innovative for its day. To appreciate the *Miscellany*'s pioneering character, one need only glance at its chief competitor, the *Youth's Companion,* which began publication seven months later, in April 1827, under the editorship of Nathaniel Willis.[10] Willis's "Prospectus" clearly distinguished his aim from Child's. Unlike extant

"Literary Magazines for youth, which exclude[d] religious topics" or emphasized "mere amusement," the *Youth's Companion* would give priority to "articles of a religious character." Accordingly, Willis's four-page weekly consisted almost entirely of brief anecdotes centering on children's conversion experiences or exemplary deaths. The titles speak for themselves: "Death Bed Scene of a Child Six Years Old," "A Child's Prayer for His Minister," "Force of Conscience." Moreover, despite Willis's claim that the *Companion* would be broader in scope than "Tract and Sabbath School Magazines," he borrowed the preponderance of his selections from those sources.

Willis's narrow religious focus left no room for educational articles, like the natural history essays and dialogues that occupied such a prominent place in the *Miscellany*. Even when Willis introduced a natural history department in the *Companion* (perhaps in response to the popularity of the *Miscellany*'s) he gave it a biblical stamp. A brief article on "The Elephant," for example, assembled biblical references to the animal and speculated about whether to identify it with Job's behemoth. In contrast, Child and her contributors were using natural history in the spirit of the Deist Thomas Paine and the Unitarian scientist Joseph Priestley—to exemplify the workings of an "All-Wise Providence" that had fashioned all creatures for the "necessities of their situation."[11]

Further, because the *Companion* eschewed anything that smacked of levity, riddles and conundrums were out of the question. Willis did eventually bow to the public taste for illustrations, but the tiny engravings he squeezed sideways into the upper left-hand corner of the *Companion* betrayed the reluctance with which he must have followed Child's lead.

Indeed, nothing could testify more eloquently to the *Miscellany*'s role as a trendsetter in the field it inaugurated than its gradual infiltration of its conservative rival. Within a few months of its founding, the *Youth's Companion* was already reprinting poems, didactic dialogues, and moral sketches from the *Miscellany*. At first, Willis confined himself to borrowings compatible with the *Companion*'s religious orientation, such as the poem "Mother, What is Death?" by Caroline Howard Gilman and the pious account of "The Deaf, Dumb, and Blind Girl" by Lydia Huntley Sigourney. Yet before long he began reprinting Child's biographical sketches of William Penn, Tadeusz Kosciusko, and Baron de Kalb (Lafayette's Polish and German analogues). By September 1828 he was even reprinting Child's celebrated stories "The Cottage Girl" and "Garafelia"—material he had formerly stigmatized as "frivolous."[12]

Revealingly, the only items Willis never borrowed from the *Miscellany* were Child's stories about Indians and blacks. The *Miscellany*'s most original feature, they also mark the limits of the influence Child exerted on the development of the fledgling genre. Willis realized what the young woman from whom he learned his craft refused to admit—that children's literature could not fulfill its socializing mission if it defied the prejudices of the dominant society. Hence, he contented himself with accounts of converted Indians and pious slaves.[13]

II

ALTHOUGH the *Youth's Companion* and the *Juvenile Miscellany* represented opposite poles in the spectrum of early-nineteenth-century American children's literature, which ranged from Calvinist orthodoxy to Unitarian liberalism, they shared a commitment to inculcating the middle-class value system. American children's literature of the 1820s, like its British prototype of the 1790s, had a critical role to perform while the nation was shifting to an industrial capitalist economy. Along with schools, churches, and the myriad societies for the promotion of industry, frugality, and temperance that sprang up in the mid-1820s, children's literature served to disseminate the bourgeois work ethic so essential to capitalist production. As one historian has explained, these cultural agencies sought to create "an orderly society" in which "citizens would be self-reliant, hard-working, and sober; obedient to their superiors; attentive to their labors; and self-disciplined in all their pursuits."[14]

Indoctrination in the bourgeois virtues is ubiquitous in the *Miscellany*. "Industry conquers everything," reads the motto on the opening volume's frontispiece, which pictures a man tilling fields against a symbolic backdrop of paired beehives. Through sermons, dialogues, biographical sketches of bourgeois heroes, and stories of children whose industry, frugality, and perseverance overcome all obstacles, Child and her contributors drive home the message that sound work habits and austere living will earn their rightful reward.

Symptomatically, Benjamin Franklin appears often in early issues of the *Miscellany*. A recurrent figure even in British classics of children's literature, Franklin personified the conjunction of the Protestant ethic and the spirit of capitalism.[15] In fact, Max Weber illustrates the hallmarks of the capitalist ethos—obsessive concern with making and saving money as ends in themselves, and "strict avoidance of all spontaneous enjoyment of life"—by quoting copiously from the famous passage in Franklin's *Advice to a Young Tradesman* beginning, "Remember, that *time* is money."[16]

Child's first New Year's message to *Miscellany* readers, entitled "Value of Time," invokes Franklin's authority. "It is your duty—a solemn, and serious duty—to make good use of the time God has given you," she exhorts children. Assuring them that it is vital to their happiness to be "always employed," she advises, "Make a regular arrangement of your time. Devote some hours to study, some to walking, some to work, and some to play." Significantly, however, when Child quotes Franklin's dictum "Time is money," she amends it to reflect what she values most highly: "Time is learning too. That is, a diligent use of it, will procure both wealth and knowledge."[17]

Child similarly adapts Franklin's message to her own ends in her biographical sketch of him, which singles out three causes for his "rise in the world": the "spirit of enterprise" he manifested, the "habits of close observation" he cultivated, and the "economy" he developed into a fine art. Franklin was "frugal in his own expenses; frugal in his system of politics; and frugal even in his words," comments Child pithily, foreshadowing her appropriation of his role in her domestic advice book, *The Frugal Housewife* (1829), two years later.[18] The qualification she immediately adds—"Yet his economy seems to have had no touch of meanness"—is characteristic of a woman repeatedly portrayed by her contemporaries as "denying herself every luxury and many common comforts, in order to compass the power to relieve or to prevent suffering."[19] Child proceeds to credit Franklin with a style of generosity she herself would practice to the end of her life: "He was always willing to lend money to those who were entering life destitute; and when these people were able and willing to pay him, he would often say, 'Lend it to the first poor tradesman you find, who is industrious and honest; and tell him to lend it to another, as soon as he is able to spare it. In this way, with a small sum of money, I shall do good to the end of time'" (*JM*, Mar. 1827, 18–23).[20] Summarizing the lessons of Franklin's career, Child holds it up as a model of middle-class virtue that the idle rich would do well to imitate—a pervasive theme in children's literature.[21] "If the laugh of the gay and fashionable, should ever make industry and economy appear like contemptible virtues," she admonishes her readers, "let them remember that Benjamin Franklin, a poor, hard-working mechanic, became, by means of these very virtues, a philosopher, whose discoveries were useful and celebrated throughout Europe" (22–23).

Franklin, of course, is only the best known of the exemplars Child enlists to school her juvenile readers in the values they must internalize if they are to become the hardworking, enterprising citizens the American republic needs. Like Franklin, two of the other paragons she cites—the traveler John Ledyard and the painter Benjamin West—demonstrate that by resolutely adhering to these values, Americans can win recognition for their country as well as for themselves.[22] Ledyard teaches "the important lesson of *perseverance*" by braving the snows of Lapland and Siberia and the "burning sands" of the African desert and by pursuing his voyages of discovery, even when reduced to "utter poverty" (*JM*, Sept. 1826, 14–20). West shows how much "industry, ingenuity, and perseverance" can accomplish when he becomes "an artist of first rate eminence—admired and respected by the nobility of London, Paris, and Rome—" after fabricating a paintbrush with a black cat's tail and learning from the Indians how to make red and yellow paint (*JM*, Jan. 1827, 19–25).

Although all of the bourgeois heroes the *Miscellany* celebrates in its biographical sketches are men, Child preaches the same values to girls in her didactic dialogues and stories. A particularly interesting instance is "Mother and Eliza" in the first issue of the *Miscellany*. Markedly different from the mother-daughter dialogues later contributed by "A.B.F.," it seems to reflect Child's feminist and antiracist concerns.[23]

In response to Eliza's complaint that the composition her teacher has assigned is beyond her capacity, Mother tells a story contrasting a little girl who gives up too easily with her brother who perseveres. The little girl, Mother suggests, has never learned to persevere because her thoughts have been occupied by dress and other "trifling amusements," and "trifles always tend to weaken the character, and excuse exertion." Her brother, meanwhile, has "thought more of the necessity of studying and improving himself," because he has been "fitting for college" and preparing "to become a man." Implying that girls ought to be given the same training and opportunities as boys, Mother reiterates "the necessity of being interested in something important, solid and useful" (Sept. 1826, 40–47).[24]

Mother realizes, however, that sermons on perseverance are not enough and that little girls must be given confidence in their abilities. Thus, she suggests a composition based on an account Eliza heard of a sea captain's visit to China. Once Eliza has recalled the details of that account, she sees that she has more than enough material for a composition. At the same time, the captain's description of the Chinese serves to amplify Mother's lesson on perseverance by compelling respect for a foreign people who exhibit the prime bourgeois virtues. The Chinese are so "industrious" and "ingenious," Eliza remembers, that they contrive to perform several tasks simultaneously. The women, for example, iron clothes by sitting on them, which leaves their hands and feet free for other work! Such a people, comments Mother, would not say "because a thing was difficult, that *they could not do it*."

If Child preaches perseverance and industry to girls and boys alike, her fiction nevertheless reveals inadvertently that the rewards of practicing those virtues are far greater for boys. The story "The Industrious Family" (1831) illustrates the constraints of gender even as it seeks to transcend them. Its competent, responsible heroine, Ellen Temple, may well be Child's answer to Charlotte Temple, the fallen woman who gave her name to Susanna Rowson's best-selling novel of seduction ("few works do so much harm to girls of fourteen or fifteen," Child warns in *The Mother's Book,* published the same year as "The Industrious Family"). The eldest in a family of orphans, Ellen dutifully raises her brothers and sisters: "She was a good Latin, Italian, and French scholar, painted beautifully, and played with great taste on the harp and guitar. But for all she was so accomplished, she thought it no shame to work with her own hands for the support of her orphan brothers and sisters. For several years after her father's death, she was too poor to pay a domestic; and the noble-minded girl, without a murmur, made the butter, cooked the food, and kept the little swarm of children as neat and busy as so many bees."[25] Ellen's industry, frugality, and self-denial shield the family against starvation and inspire her brothers and sisters to emulate her.

Child's point is that they must emulate her for the family to survive. This is not a story of female self-sacrifice but of socialization into the bourgeois virtues that ensure individual and collective prosperity, among them respect for manual labor. Hence, it is as important for Ellen's brother, John, to exercise self-denial as it is for Ellen to "work with her own hands." John has a passion for books, and "if he had cared only about pleasing himself, he would have read from morning till night; but he knew this would be selfish; and he cheerfully worked in the garden and about the house, without allowing himself an hour a day for his favorite occupation."[26]

Ultimately, a fairy godfather shows up in the person of a sea captain uncle who rewards the children for their assiduity. The moral that God helps those who help themselves is explicit: "God always provides a way for such industrious, kind-hearted little ones." Child's insistence on male self-denial is equally explicit—because John has shown himself to be "a good, hard-working boy, willing to deny [himself] for the sake of others," his uncle enables him to fulfill his dream of attending college.

The disparity between the rewards the male and female siblings earn, however, drastically undercuts Child's efforts to establish a single standard of virtue for both sexes. While John becomes "a lawyer of great reputation" and his brother, William, also helped by their uncle to pursue his studies, makes "a large fortune by his success in machines," what of Ellen and her sisters? The best to which they can aspire is to marry men like their brothers—a clergyman in Ellen's case and wealthy manufacturers in the cases of her sisters.

This gender inequality is all the more conspicuous in a magazine that marks such an advance beyond the strict sexual stereotyping of early British children's literature, with its unrelieved subordination of women to men.[27] Yet it is also symptomatic of the contradictions that pervade nineteenth-century children's literature and the bourgeois ideology it promulgates. Again and again, the egalitarian claims of bourgeois ideology conflict with the patently inferior position it accords women, the poor, and people of color.

"The Industrious Family," like most stories in the *Miscellany*, presents poverty as a temporary reverse that hard work and frugality can always overcome. As "F. of Stockbridge" puts it in a similar story, "In this favored land, no one, who is blessed with health, and willing to be industrious and economical, need be destitute of the comforts of life" (July 1828, 276–93). Child specifically attributes her young protagonists' good fortune to their industry and self-denial. "I am sure you need not ask if they prospered in the world," she writes in an aside to readers (221). "The prudent and industrious generally contrive to accomplish their purposes, in one way or another," agrees "F. of Stockbridge." The children's status as orphans underscores the message that they have had nothing to rely on but themselves. Commenting on the ubiquity of orphans in children's literature, the historian Isaac Kramnick explains, "Orphans allow a personalization of the basic bourgeois assumption that the individual is on his or her own, free from the weight of the past, from tradition, from family." By definition, orphans are responsible "for their own fate," forced back on "their own hard work, self-reliance, merit, and talent."[28]

How ironic, then, that Child must resort to a deus ex machina—the proverbial rich uncle—to rescue the children from poverty. This device, so frequent in *Miscellany* stories, implicitly acknowledges that hard work and frugality do not suffice, that the poor cannot be left to rely on themselves but must instead be helped out of poverty and given financial support if they are to acquire the education needed for upward mobility. As a vehicle for solving the problem of poverty, the deus ex machina also masks the reality of class conflict. Usually, this figure is not a relative but a rich person who expects some deference in return for charity. Needless to say, neither giver nor recipient ever questions the social structure or suggests that charity may be a right, not a privilege to be earned by good behavior. The traditional happy ending of such stories—a marriage between the poor person and the rich patron's son or daughter—neatly averts class conflict by promising selective upward mobility.

The story "Louisa Preston" (Mar. 1828, 56–81) is typical. Its heroine, a poor washerwoman's daughter, is almost thwarted in her attempts to educate herself for a career as a primary school teacher: "It took so much of her time to assist her mother in washing, to mend her brother's clothes, and to tend the baby, that it seemed to be almost impossible for her to get her lessons." (58). In addition to the heavy workload she must carry in a household too poor to allow her the leisure for studying, Louisa faces the obstacle of class snobbery, as her rich schoolmates taunt her for her patched clothes. Predictably, Child moralizes, "But to the industrious and persevering, nothing is impossible; and Louisa Preston, with all her discouragements, was always the best scholar in school."

The opportunity for Louisa to achieve her goal arises when it is announced that the student who demonstrates the most thorough command of ancient and modern geography will earn "a handsome copy of Miss Edgeworth's 'Moral Tales,' and one year's education at the best school in the city" (64). Twice, however, Louisa is forced to drop out of school for weeks at a time to nurse her mother and sister through serious illnesses. Thus, her rich classmate Hannah White ends up winning the prize.

Realistically, the story recognizes that poor students cannot compete on equal terms with their rich classmates and that the odds against them are overwhelming. What finally allows Louisa to fulfill her ambition is the charity she earns through her virtuous behavior. First the mothers of her classmates, hearing of Louisa's "good character," present her with "plain, neat suits of clothes" and give her mother "constant employment" (69). Then her rival, Hannah, who had formerly made fun of her, publicly admits that Louisa would have earned the prize had she not been obliged to nurse her mother and sister. As a result, the school examiners give both girls prizes. In the end, Louisa not only succeeds in becoming a teacher but manages to send her brother to college. Consummating her advancement to middle-class status, she marries Hannah White's brother.

The threat of class conflict is very much on the surface of this story, which honestly acknowledges the enormous gulf between rich and poor. Yet Child defuses that threat by showing how the barriers of class can be transcended. Louisa's virtuous behavior literally reconciles class conflicts: it elicits the charity of the rich, sets a standard of morality they come to emulate, and culminates in a marriage of classes (paralleling the recurrent interracial marriages in Child's fiction for adults). The fact Child overlooks is that such a solution puts the burden of reconciliation on the poor and obfuscates the causes of poverty.

If adopting bourgeois habits of industry, perseverance, and self-denial opens the door to upward mobility, by implication the reverse is also true—the poverty of those who fail to achieve upward mobility can be blamed on their stubborn persistence in lower-class habits of sloth, improvidence, and drunkenness (the epitome of self-indulgence). "The Brothers, or . . . The Influence of Example" (Nov. 1827, 209–26) takes precisely this line. The story contrasts two pairs of poor brothers who respond differently to upper-class programs for the socialization and uplift of the working class. The first pair, Charles and George, work during the week to help their widowed mother support the family, and they attend the Sunday school provided for the village poor. The second pair, Lying Harry and Skulking Dick, waste their time playing truant in the woods and getting drunk. Worse, they exert a pernicious influence over all the poor boys of the village by denouncing the Sunday school as a sop for poor folk, about which "the Squire and the Parson feel mighty grand" (211). George temporarily falls under their sway and nearly forfeits the respect of the other villagers, but thanks to his brother Charles's virtuous example, he repents in time.

Here, as in "Louisa Preston" and "The Industrious Family," hard work and sobriety earn Charles and George the charity they need to further their education; education, in turn, allows them to rise in the world. Charles obtains a post in "one of the best schools in the state—the income of which made him much richer than he ever expected to be," and George invents a machine and becomes a wealthy manufacturer. In "The Brothers," however, Child meets the threat of class conflict head on, explicitly drawing a social rather than an individual moral: "New England is a blessed land. In every corner of it there are people willing and able to assist those who are anxious to gain knowledge" (219). That is, Charles and George owe their good fortune not merely to their own efforts, but also to a society that deals justly with the poor and rewards the well-deserving. Such a society obviously needs no redistribution of wealth to eliminate poverty.

Because they reject this ideological premise, Lying Harry and Skulking Dick come to bad ends—if they accepted it, they would realize that it is in their interests to conform to their superiors' ethic of hard work and sobriety. Growing so dissolute that no one will employ them, they sink even deeper into poverty until they are finally imprisoned for robbery. Although he learns his lesson too late, Skulking Dick endorses the story's moral with his dying breath. His fate, he admits, is due to Harry's bad example; had he followed Charles's path, he, too, might have become a prosperous middle-class citizen.

Interestingly, recent historical studies tend to support the contention that workers who adopted their employers' burgeois ethic did actually enjoy greater upward mobility than the "traditionalists" who "clung to customs and habits inherited from the loose . . . morality" of the preindustrial era. Often, however, these "model workers" were "bound by ties of kinship, religion, or neighborhood" to their employers and were thus more prone to embrace an ideology that blamed poverty on "idleness and self-indulgence rather than [on] exploitation."[29]

Stories like "The Brothers" naturally minimize such factors. Even more significantly, they omit an alternative represented by a third group of workers that Paul Faler calls "rebel mechanics"—those who adopt the bourgeois moral code while rejecting bourgeois ideology. The rebels articulated what the Lying Harrys and Skulking Dicks inchoately felt—that their employers' wealth was the product not just of "hard work, self-reliance, and shrewdness," but also of "petty fraud and heartless extortion." "The most vigorous opponents of capitalist exploitation," they used bourgeois work discipline "in their own class interest" to struggle for higher wages, and they refused to be bought off by the promise of selective upward mobility.[30] In short, they embodied the specter of class conflict that nineteenth-century children's literature sought to exorcise.

Paradoxically, children's literature looked ahead to the future and harked back to the past at the same time. As an instrument for creating the disciplined labor force required by the developing industrial capitalist economy, children's literature helped propel nineteenth-century America into a new era. Yet when confronting the terrible urban poverty produced by industrial capitalism, the genre offered a solution rooted in the communal ethic of the preindustrial village.

None of Child's *Miscellany* stories dramatizes the contradiction more poignantly than "The Cottage Girl" (Sept. 1828, 3–19). What makes this tale of urban poverty particularly revealing is that Child rewrote it in 1856, after three decades of mushrooming urbanization and accelerating immigration had completely transformed the America of her youth. Titling the new version "Rosy O'Ryan,"[31] she registered the changes: the replacement of the native-born American poor by still poorer Irish immigrants; the widening gap between them and the rich in cities that intensified the anonymity of the destitute; the diminishing opportunities for upward mobility. She also noted the elements of a future solution—solidarity among the poor themselves. Nevertheless, she ended the story as she had in 1828 by symbolically restoring the rural community of the past.

The two versions of "The Cottage Girl" are revealing in another respect as well. Issues of class and gender intersect in both, but "Rosy O'Ryan" expresses the heightened feminist consciousness fostered by the women's rights movement of the 1830s and 1840s. In addition, it exhibits increased familiarity with the lives of urban working-class women as a result of Child's 1841–50 sojourn in New York, during which she frequently visited slums, asylums, and prisons.

Set in Boston (though its oddly incongruous title foreshadows the rural haven the story offers its heroine), "The Cottage Girl" can no longer assume a village community like that of "Louisa Preston" in which the plight of a deserving poor family comes naturally to the attention of prosperous neighbors, whose charity can be relied on. Instead, the wealthy seem unaware of the misery around them and unconcerned about the welfare of the washerwomen and scullions they hire to do their menial labor. "The rich people, for whom [Mrs. Wood] worked with patient drudgery, paid her wages, and thought nothing more about her," writes Child ("Rosy O'Ryan," 159). To dispel this callous indifference, she brings home to her readers what poverty means. "It is harder work than many rich little girls imagine, to earn enough to eat, and coarse clothes to wear," she points out, explaining why Mrs. Wood, "a poor woman, whose husband had left her with two little children, to support herself as she could," ends up dying of overwork ("Cottage Girl," 3).

In the 1856 version, which fleshes out the hardships such a woman faces, Child turns the deserted Mrs. Wood of "The Cottage Girl" into a battered wife, whom she renames Mrs. O'Ryan: "Mary O'Ryan was a poor Irish woman, whose husband spent all his wages for strong drink. She went out to do washing and scouring, and left her little ones at home for some kind neighbour to look after; as many a poor woman is obliged to do. When she returned after a day of hard work, she often found her husband intoxicated, and he would beat her cruelly, to make her give him the money she had earned" (158). Of course, the portrayal of the Irish husband as a drunkard and wife-beater falls into ethnic stereotyping. Now, however, Child recognizes that lower-class women must work—and leave their children in the care of neighbors—whether or not they have husbands. In fact the death of her husband at least gives Mrs. O'Ryan "control of her own wages" (160). The problem is the inadequacy of those wages and the severance of the bonds that had once prompted rich people to relieve the distress of their poor neighbors, as they do in the village of "Louisa Preston."

In both "The Cottage Girl" and "Rosy O'Ryan," the only person who comes to the help of the distressed mother is a "poor washer-woman" (named Mrs. Kinsley in the former, Mrs. Wood in the latter). "A great many people in Boston would have helped . . . if they had known" of the family's need, Child concedes in "The Cottage Girl," yet she implies that their ignorance is almost willful. After all, those who see the hearse go by know that it contains the body of "some poor person, because no carriages, and very few people" follow it. Still, they do not think to inquire about the circumstances. Child contrasts their heedlessness with the washerwoman's kindness: "Every night, after she had finished her hard day's work, she used to go in and ask how neighbor Wood did, and give the children a portion of her own supper" ("Cottage Girl," 5). In "Rosy O'Ryan" Child sharpens her social criticism, pointedly commenting, "Benevolence is commendable in the rich, who can give away ten dollars without depriving themselves of any thing they need; but in the sight of God and angels it is less beautiful and holy than the generosity of the poor. No one knew how often Mrs. Wood was obliged to deny herself a cup of tea, or a morsel of meat, because she had used up her small funds to feed Mary O'Ryan's famishing children" (159).

Child develops the bonding of the two women into a major theme of "Rosy O'Ryan," where Mrs. Wood shelters Mary O'Ryan and her children during Mr. O'Ryan's drunken sprees and the two women enjoy a "rivalry of mutual kindness" for a year before Mrs. O'Ryan takes ill (160–61). Another new element Child adds to "Rosy O'Ryan" is the transformation of the friendship into a cross-ethnic alliance. By making Mrs. Wood English and Mrs. O'Ryan Irish, Child suggests that feminist sisterhood and class solidarity can transcend ethnic divisions.

Yet Child never perceives the sisterhood and solidarity of the poor as alternatives to the charity of the rich. If the poor can alleviate each other's suffering, they cannot help each other to achieve upward mobility. And upward mobility remains the only solution Child can envision to the problem of poverty. Thus, despite having shown that the urban rich are utterly oblivious to poverty, Child must find a way of eliciting their charity to save the washerwomen and her adopted children from the fate of the dead mother. Suddenly, employers and landlords who have hitherto failed to manifest the slightest curiosity about the struggling family learn of the washerwoman's generosity and resolve to assist her.

That assistance inevitably takes the form of transplanting the family to a rural environment and providing the children with opportunities for advancement. Adopted by a wealthy family, the son becomes a "prosperous" manufacturer in the 1828 text, and a "civil engineer . . . profitably employed in the construction of railroads" in the 1856 text, where his adopted family suffers financial reverses obliging him to make "his own way in the world" ("Rosy O'Ryan," 188). His sister can only improve her status through marriage. She grows up with the washerwoman, refusing to abandon her even when invited to join her brother's family some years later, but ultimately "marrie[s] a sensible, industrious man, who own[s] a good farm" ("Cottage Girl," 18–19; "Rosy O'Ryan," 188–89).

The divergence of the children's paths raises several issues that the story attempts to address but fails to resolve satisfactorily. First, it foregrounds a major disadvantage of upward mobility—the gulf created between successful individuals and the families and class they leave behind. Second, it suggests the unnaturalness of class distinctions, which literally subvert the principle of human brotherhood by dividing brother from sister. Third, it reflects the limitations that gender places on upward mobility.

Child's response to all three issues is to bridge differences. Although the sister initially finds it "strange" that *"her own brother — her twin brother, too . . .* should be dressed so much better" than she is, she tells herself she is glad he is "so well off" and philosophizes, "After all, I don't believe he is a bit happier than I am" ("Cottage Girl," 15–16). For his part, her brother has an impulse to "put on a frock, and come to work in [his sister's] garden." (In "Rosy O'Ryan" he has the opposite impulse of wanting to support his sister and her adopted mother, "so that they need not work so hard," but the washerwoman, speaking for Child, admonishes him, "Work is a good thing; and nobody can be happy without it" [183]). The irony Child confronts here is basic to bourgeois ideology: once attained, the bourgeois goal of acquiring wealth and bettering one's condition threatens the ethic of hard work and frugality that distinguishes the virtuous middle class from the idle rich.[32] Hence, the upwardly mobile individual must relearn the necessity of hard work from the poor.

Also serving to bridge the class differences between brother and sister in "The Cottage Girl" is charity. The brother's wealthy adopted parents send his sister "to a good school" and make her frequent "presents of neat, suitable clothing" (18). Not only has Child reconstituted the village environment of "Louisa Preston," with its communal ethic binding rich and poor, but she has actually converted the two classes into one big family in which all have their proper places. Significantly, she cements the union of rich and poor through the ritual that had epitomized the communal ethic in the Medford of her childhood. Every Thanksgiving brother and sister sit down together at her "plain, but plentiful table," which symbolizes their reciprocal relations (19).

The story does not succeed in bridging the difference of gender. As in "The Industrious Family," Child cannot realistically provide male and female siblings with the same opportunities for advancement. No amount of schooling can permit a girl to become an engineer or manufacturer. By taking her urban orphan out of the city and marrying her off to a farmer, Child implies what a number of feminist historians have argued—that most women were better off under the domestic economy of the past, in which they controlled many remunerative activities, than they were under industrial capitalism.[33] Child's solution to the problem of urban working women's immiseration is thus to restore them to their previous status as productive members of self-sufficient rural households. This becomes especially obvious in "Rosy O'Ryan," which ends with a catalog of the productive occupations in which Mrs. Wood and her adopted daughter, Rosy, engage on the farm: "[Mrs. Wood] made many hundred pounds of butter for the market; and when she was too old to do that, she sat in her rocking-chair, sewing woolen mats, or knitting stockings for all the family. . . . Rosy was too busy to attend much to a flower garden; but she *would* find time to put a few seed in the ground" so as to enjoy the sight of flowers "while she was skimming milk in her pantry" (189).

In their very celebration of bourgeois ideology, stories like "The Cottage Girl," "Rosy O'Ryan," "Louisa Preston," "The Brothers," and "The Industrious Family" repeatedly betray its contradictions. Promising all citizens equal opportunity to enjoy the benefits of American democracy, they distribute opportunities and benefits unequally among men and women, rich and poor. Serving to socialize children into an industrial capitalist society, they repudiate the consequences of capitalist development and resurrect the rural past. Extolling individualism and self-reliance, they re-create class relations of mutual dependency. Blaming poverty on idleness and hymning the rewards of hard work and self-denial, they depict a world in which the poor die of overwork and the rich pay others a pittance to do their cleaning, washing, and sewing. Yet these stories also convey the power and persuasiveness of the ideology they promulgate. It is easy to understand why Child's juvenile readers and their parents found the magazine so compelling.

The organs of the cultural establishment provide ample evidence of how highly Child's contemporaries valued the ideological work the *Juvenile Miscellany* performed. The prestigious *North American Review*, while admitting that children's literature lay "beyond our jurisdiction," made a special point of recommending the *Miscellany* and expressing "respect for an accomplished lady, to whom we have been indebted for entertainment in former times." Sarah Hale's *Ladies' Magazine* reviewed several numbers and urged "every family where there are children" to subscribe. Indeed, wrote Hale, "grown people would not find their time misspent while perusing its pages, which is more than we would be willing to say in favor of, at least, one half of the new publications that are thronging us." Perhaps the most telling index of the *Miscellany*'s cultural significance is the amount of exposure it received in the *American Traveller,* a gossipy, widely circulated Boston newspaper with an attractive literary page. The *Traveller* greeted each issue of the *Miscellany* as it appeared, occasionally reprinted selections from it, and singled out "The Cottage Girl" for special praise as a story set in "this city" and "calculated to rivet the attention, please the fancy and improve the mind." This newspaper's many enthusiastic reviews best sum up the achievement of the magazine it hailed as the "Children's North American": "The fair editor . . . has a peculiar tact for extracting the pith from subjects, dry and obscure in themselves, though important and useful, and presenting it to her youthful readers in the most pleasing and attractive forms." "Miss Francis, with the aid of several lady contributors of high literary attainments, succeeds, beyond the anticipations of her friends, in sustaining the popular character of the Juvenile Miscellany; and each successive number . . . presents us with something new, something palatable, and something to gratify and instruct the tender juvenile mind"; and "The whole [is] adapted to the juvenile capacity, and eminently calculated to give a proper direction to the expanding passions and sympathies of the heart. . . . The useful lessons and valuable principles of '*Aunt Maria,*' will hereafter, we are confident, in many instances, be remembered as the first incentives to distinction and usefulness."[34]

Despite the enormous popularity it enjoyed, the *Juvenile Miscellany* fell out of favor almost as soon as Child espoused the antislavery cause. In the summer of 1830, a pivotal meeting with the young abolitionist William Lloyd Garrison persuaded Child to devote her literary talents to promoting emancipation. That September, she published her first antislavery story in the *Miscellany*, "The St. Domingo Orphans." Nearly every subsequent number of the *Miscellany* carried some reference to slavery, be it a story, an article, an anecdote, or a bit of information tucked away in an unlikely context. The sudden rash of antislavery commentary in a magazine that had preserved an all but total silence on this controversial issue for the first four years of its existence did not escape the notice of parents and sponsors. As the new orientation of the magazine became increasingly apparent, subscriptions started dwindling, and the *Traveller* ceased reviewing it. By January 1833, persistent rumors had begun to circulate that "Mrs. Child . . . is about to give up the editorship" of the magazine (*JM*, Jan. 1833, 323). The run of canceled subscriptions turned into a stampede after August 1833, when Child's *Appeal in Favor of That Class of Americans Called Africans* came off the press. In May 1834 Child finally had to announce that the *Miscellany* was "about to be discontinued, for want of sufficient patronage."[35]

The *Miscellany's* adult sponsors had clearly indicated that their support of the magazine depended on its conformity to the dominant ideology. As long as the *Miscellany* propounded values that met the needs of the capitalist ruling class, the magazine won approbation. Once Child began threatening the economic and political interests of her elite subscribers by advocating the abolition of slavery and preaching against racial prejudice, they withdrew their patronage.

The children who read the *Miscellany* so avidly did not always share their parents' reactions, however—witness the fond reminiscences of Caroline Healey Dall and Thomas Wentworth Higginson, both from conservative families opposed to antislavery agitation. These juvenile fans seem rather to have prized the magazine because it appealed to their idealistic impulses and elicited their sympathy for the oppressed, regardless of race. A sizable cadre of them grew up to share the passionate identification with slaves and the determination to fight for a multiracial egalitarian America that inspired the editor of their beloved *Miscellany*. Canceled subscriptions and parental anathemas could not stifle the humanitarian sentiments awakened in them by stories in which charitable neighbors help smooth the path of industrious poor folk; like Child herself, they extended the ethic of human brother- and-sisterhood beyond the bounds of race.

Whatever contradictions we may find between the conservative socializing mission of children's literature and the radical message of racial equality the *Miscellany* preached alongside paeans to the bourgeois virtues, the readers who credited the magazine with having taught them the values they later applied as abolitionists saw none. The final word on the *Miscellany's* political impact rightly belongs to its young fans. Nothing can better sum up what the magazine meant to them than this personal tribute to Child by a former "schoolgirl" abolitionist and lifelong reformer, written thirty years after the *Miscellany's* demise: "Although I am altogether unknown—to you, you have been my friend from an early day, ever so long ago as when the Juvenile Miscellany was the delight of my childish heart. . . . Your influence over me has always been ennobling, & purifying, & elevating, & stimulating to benevolence and charity."[36]

NOTES

This essay is extracted from chs. 3 and 7 of my book, *The First Woman in the Republic: A Cultural Biography of Lydia Maria Child* (Durham: Duke Univ. Press, 1994).

1. The Library of Entertaining Knowledge was one of Lydia Maria Child's principal sources for informational articles in the *Miscellany*. For excellent studies of nineteenth-century American children's literature and its cultural mission, see Anne Scott MacLeod, *A Moral Tale: Children's Fiction and American Culture. 1820–1860* (Hamden, Conn.: Archon, 1975), and R. Gordon Kelly, *Mother Was a Lady: Self and Society in Selected American Children's Periodicals, 1865–1890* (Westport, Conn.: Greenwood, 1974). I am indebted to Kelly for stimulating my interest in the *Juvenile Miscellany* and children's literature and to both books for teaching me to read this literature with sensitivity to its cultural implications.

2. In 1820 Caroline Howard Gilman's husband, Samuel, a clergyman, had taken a Unitarian pulpit in Charleston. An ardent Southern sympathizer by the 1830s, when she and Child broke with each other, Gilman actually sided with the Confederacy during the Civil War.

3. See John C. Crandall, "Patriotism and Humanitarian Reform in Children's Literature, 1825–1860," *American Quarterly* 21 (Spring 1969): 3–22.

4. The heroine, Lucy Mann, like Jo March, has "long, thick, and glossy" hair of "an uncommon colour" (though "golden brown," rather than chestnut, as in Jo's case). Lucy, too, gets the idea of selling her hair from a story she reads (about an English girl). After an agonizing conflict between her desire to "make her [grandmother] comfortable" and her attachment to her "pretty hair," she performs the sacrifice. Child moralizes that Lucy's hair is not important for its own sake, because it might have been cut if Lucy had become ill and would eventually turn gray anyway, "but it was a great thing for her own character, whether she allowed vanity, to overcome her sense of duty. . . . If she had indulged her vanity in this particular, it would have grown stronger, and been harder to overcome, the next time she was tempted; and perhaps, when she became a young lady, she would be tempted to do some very wicked thing, to gratify her vanity" (314–16). In *A Hunger for Home: Louisa May Alcott and "Little Women"* (Philadelphia: Temple Univ. Press, 1984), 32, Sarah Elbert has also pointed out an episode in *Little Men* where Alcott dramatizes a method of punishment Child had suggested in *The Mother's Book* (1831). Alcott's mother, Abba, an intimate friend of Child's, had applied it to Louisa when she was six years old. For Child's reminiscenes of Abba May Alcott and assessment of Louisa, see Child to Sarah Shaw, 18 June 1876, *Lydia Maria Child: Selected Letters, 1817–1880*, ed. Milton Meltzer, Patricia G. Holland, and Francine Krasno (Amherst: Univ. of

Massachusetts Press, 1982), 534–35; and Child to Louisa May Alcott, 19 June 1878, *Collected Correspondence of Lydia Maria Child, 1817–1880,* ed. Patricia G. Holland, Milton Meltzer, and Francine Krasno (Millwood, N.Y.: Kraus Microform, 1980), microfiche card 90, letter 2398. Hereafter cited as *CC,* followed by microfiche card number and letter number.

5. Lucy Larcom, *A New England Girlhood, Outlined from Memory* (1889; New York: Corinth, 1961), 169–75. Child was one of the first writers Larcom solicited for contributions to *Our Young Folks* on its inauguration. See "Freddy's New-Year's Dinner," "Grandfather's Chestnut-Tree," and "The Two Christmas Evenings," which Larcom featured as lead stories in the July and October 1865 and January 1866 issues of *Our Young Folks.*

6. Thomas Wentworth Higginson, "Lydia Maria Child" (1868), *Contemporaries,* vol. 2 of *The Writings of Thomas Wentworth Higginson* (Boston: Houghton, Mifflin, 1900), 108.

7. The best summary of these developments is Isaac Kramnick's "Children's Literature and Bourgeois Ideology: Observations on Culture and Industrial Capitalism in the Later Eighteenth Century," *Culture and Politics: From Puritanism to the Enlightenment,* ed. Perez Zagorin (Berkeley: Univ. of California Press, 1980), 203–40. See also Philippe Ariès's classic study, *Centuries of Childhood: A Social History of Family Life,* trans. Robert Baldick (New York: Random House, 1962); the essays by Mary Lynn Stevens Heininger, Karin Calvert, and Harvey Green in *A Century of Childhood, 1820–1920* (Rochester, N.Y.: Margaret Woodbury Strong Museum, 1984); Jacqueline S. Reiner, "Rearing the Republican Child: Attitudes and Practices in Post-Revolutionary Philadelphia," *William and Mary Quarterly* 39 (Jan. 1982): 150–63; the early chapters of Carl N. Degler's *At Odds: Women and the Family in America from the Revolution to the Present* (New York: Oxford Univ. Press, 1980); Louise A. Tilly and Joan Scott, *Women, Work, and Family* (New York: Holt, Rinehart, and Winston, 1978), especially chapters 4 and 6; Heidi Hartmann, "Capitalism, Patriarchy, and Job Segregation by Sex," *The SIGNS Reader: Women, Gender, and Scholarship,* ed. Elizabeth Abel and Emily K. Abel (Chicago: Univ. of Chicago Press, 1983), 193–226, especially 203–10; Mary Lynn McDougall, "Working-Class Women during the Industrial Revolution, 1780–1914," and Theresa M. McBride, "The Long Road Home: Women's Work and Industrialization," both in *Becoming Visible: Women in European History,* ed. Renate Bridenthal and Claudia Koonz (Boston: Houghton Mifflin, 1977), 255–79, 280–95; Gerda Lerner, "The Lady and the Mill Girl: Changes in the Status of Women in the Age of Jackson," *Midcontinent American Studies Journal* 10 (Spring 1969): 5–15; Nancy F. Cott, *The Bonds of Womanhood: "Woman's Sphere" in New England, 1780–1835* (New Haven: Yale Univ. Press, 1977), especially chapters 1–3; and Alice Kessler-Harris, *Out to Work: A History of Wage-Earning Women in the United States* (New York: Oxford Univ. Press, 1982), especially chapter 3, on "Industrial Wage Earners and the Domestic Ideology." On the middle-class value system, Max Weber's classic study, *The Protestant Ethic and the Spirit of Capitalism,* trans. Talcott Parsons (1905, 1920; New York: Scribner's, 1958), remains extremely useful.

8. On the reception of *Evenings in New England* and the beginnings of the *Juvenile Miscellany*, see Child to Mary Francis Preston, undated and 28 Aug. 1826, *CC*, 1/15–16, as quoted in Anna D. Hallowell, "Lydia Maria Child," *Medford Historical Register* 3 (July 1900): 100; and review of *Evenings in New England, North American Review* 20 (Jan. 1825): 231. For an analytical description of *Evenings in New England*, see "*The First Woman in the Republic,*" chapter 3.

9. For other overviews of the *Juvenile Miscellany*, see Alice M. Jordan, "The Juvenile Miscellany and Its Literary Ladies," in *From Rollo to Tom Sawyer and Other Papers* (Boston: Horn Book, 1948), 46–60; and Ruth K. MacDonald, "*The Juvenile Miscellany: For the Instruction and Amusement of Youth,*" in *Children's Periodicals of the United States*, ed. R. Gordon Kelly (Westport, Conn.: Greenwood, 1984), 258–62.

10. Willis launched a "Prospectus" of the magazine, consisting of a sample number, on 16 Apr. 1827, but the *Youth's Companion* (hereafter cited as *YC*) did not actually begin appearing on a regular basis until 6 June. For an overview, see David L. Greene, "*The Youth's Companion,*" in *Children's Periodicals of the United States*, ed. Kelly, 507–14.

11. Compare "The Elephant," *YC* 1 (31 Aug. 1827): 55, with "Wonders of the Deep," *Juvenile Miscellany* 1 (January 1827): 66–80; quotation, 73. See the section "Defining the True Revelation" in Thomas Paine's *The Age of Reason*, ed. Philip S. Foner (1794; Secaucus, N.J.: Citadel, 1974), 68–70.

12. The earliest borrowing I have found is the poem "Ellen's May Day," signed W., *YC* 1 (14 Sept. 1827): 64. Gilman's and Sigourney's selections appear in the *Companion*, 11 Jan. 1828 (132) and 6 June 1828 (5–6) respectively. The three biographical sketches appear in the 18 July and 1 and 8 Aug. 1828 numbers (29–30, 39, 43), and the two stories cited appear in the 19 Sept. and 31 Oct. 1828 numbers (65–77, 89–90). In the issue containing "The Cottage Girl," Willis reviewed the *Miscellany*, describing it as "well worthy of the attention of our young friends" (68). All borrowings are attributed to the *Miscellany*. Initially sporadic, borrowings become regular by March 1828. They are most frequent right after the publication of each bimonthly issue of the *Miscellany* and seem to taper off as Willis runs out of material he considers worth reprinting. In his "Prospectus," Willis had pledged to avoid "every thing frivolous." He had also objected to magazines of "mere amusement, whose influence is unfavorable to religion and morals" (1).

13. A typical example is "Pious Negro," *YC* (27 July 1827): 34, reprinted from the Scottish *Children's Friend*. It tells of a young girl who must refuse an old black man's pleas for charity because she has "nothing with her that could be of use to him" but who reads him an extract from the New Testament instead and prays for his conversion. The anecdote ends with his pious death. See also "Seneca Mission," *YC* 7 (22 Feb. 1834): 157, on the achievements of Indian converts and the need for greater efforts to spread the gospel among Indian tribes. For a discussion of the *Miscellany*'s stories about Indians and blacks, see *The First Woman in the Republic*, chapter 7. The first issue of the *Miscellany* opened with a story about Indians, "Adventure in the Woods," and many other such tales ap-

peared in the early volumes. The magazine also featured a multitude of selections about foreign peoples of color. Child began including stories about blacks in September 1830.

14. Paul Faler, "Cultural Aspects of the Industrial Revolution: Lynn, Massachusetts, Shoemakers and Industrial Morality, 1826–1860," *Labor History* 15 (Summer 1974): 367–94; quotation, 367, describes the campaign of shoe manufacturers to disseminate the new industrial morality among their workers. I am grateful to Dorothy Ross for bringing this article to my attention. The Lynn Society for the Promotion of Industry, Frugality, and Temperance was founded in 1826, the same year as the *Juvenile Miscellany*. In *A Shopkeepers' Millennium: Society and Revivals in Rochester, New York, 1815–1837*, Paul E. Johnson describes a similar campaign. On the British precedent, see Kramnick, "Children's Literature and Bourgeois Ideology."

15. Kramnick, "Children's Literature and Bourgeois Ideology," 230. The instance he cites is from [Anna Letitia Barbauld], *Evenings at Home; or, The Juvenile Budget Opened. Consisting of a Variety of Miscellaneous Pieces, for the Instruction and Amusement of Young Persons*, 6 vols. (London: J. Johnson, 1792), 6:250.

16. Max Weber, *Protestant Ethic*, 48–53.

17. "Value of Time," *Juvenile Miscellany* 1 (Jan. 1827): 103–5. This publication will be hereafter cited as *JM*. See also the dialogue "Time and Money," by "Mater," *JM* (July 1829): 218–26. To explain the dictum "time is money" to her daughter, Mother uses the example of bees, who "spend their time in making honey; which is sold for money" (224). She, too, goes on to say, "If time is money, time is knowledge, too; and knowledge in connexion with virtue, is the best means of happiness, as well as usefulness." The biblical metaphor she cites evaluates knowledge in monetary terms as well: "It is among the treasures 'that neither moth nor rust corrupt, nor thieves break through and steal'" (225).

18. For a discussion of Child's domestic advice book, *The Frugal Housewife*, see *The First Woman in the Republic*, chapter 6.

19. Elizabeth Stuart Phelps, *Chapters from a Life* (Boston: Houghton Mifflin, 1896), 182–83.

20. Child adopted a similar strategy when she used the proceeds from *The Freedmen's Book* to buy more copies for free distribution to former slaves. For reminiscences of Child that describe her self-sacrificing charity, see Hallowell, "Lydia Maria Child," 115; and James Russell Lowell, "A Fable for Critics," quoted in Higginson, "Lydia Maria Child," 129–30.

21. Kramnick, "Children's Literature and Bourgeois Ideology," 224, 232.

22. The biographical sketches obviously serve patriotic purposes as well. Thus, except for foreign heroes of the American Revolution, their subjects are all Americans. In 1831, however, Child introduced a new biographical series, "Remarkable Boys," which featured a number of European child prodigies. The sketches of Isaac Newton and James Ferguson are typical in attributing their scientific achievements to the "habits of thought and attention," "industry and perseverance" that each developed at a young age (n.s. 6 [Apr. 1831]: 32, 34).

23. No selections in the first issue are signed, suggesting that Child may have written all or most of them and then solicited contributors who could follow the models she provided. At the end of the second issue, she apologizes in a note for not printing a contribution from an "anonymous correspondent" because it was too similar to a selection that had already been included (1 [Nov. 1826]: 108). And in the third issue, she apologizes for errors "to be attributed to the carelessness of the editor—not to the writer of the article on botany" (1 [Jan. 1827]: 108). These apologies would seem to indicate that she initially rewrote unsigned articles contributed by others. By the third issue, the series "Mother and Eliza" is signed by "A.B.F.," and the initials of other regular contributors begin to appear. And by the fourth, a note "To Correspondents" announces that "the editor of the Juvenile Miscellany has, as usual, received a number of excellent communications. That they are so numerous, must be an excuse for deferring some which deserve immediate notice" (2 [Mar. 1827]: 108).

24. Eleven years later, the women's rights advocate Sarah Grimké would translate this critique of girls' upbringing into explicit feminist terms. See her *Letters on the Equality of the Sexes, and the Condition of Woman* (1837–38), especially letter 8.

25. "The Industrious Family," *JM* n.s. 6 (July–Aug. 1831): 217–30; Lydia Maria Child, *The Mother's Book* (Boston: Carter, Hendee, and Babcock, 1831), 91.

26. Child had been emphasizing the importance of manual labor in her "Hints to Persons of Moderate Fortune," appended to the second edition (1830) of *The Frugal Housewife*.

27. Kramnick points out that books like Maria Edgeworth's *Harry and Lucy* and Anna Letitia Barbauld's *Evenings at Home* were "important vehicle[s] in transmitting the sexual stereotypes emergent in the new notion of the family— the superiority and usefulness of men." He adds: "Things were much more exciting . . . for the young boy readers" of Edgeworth and Barbauld, because these authors were "concerned with providing new heroes for the young male reader"—inventors, manufacturers, and engineers rather than "kings, lords, generals, prime ministers" ("Children's Literature and Bourgeois Ideology," 225, 229).

28. Kramnick, "Children's Literature and Bourgeois Ideology," 217.

29. Faler, "Cultural Aspects of the Industrial Revolution," 390–91; see also Johnson, *A Shopkeepers' Millennium,* 120–26.

30. Faler, "Cultural Aspects of the Industrial Revolution," 391–92.

31. "Rosy O'Ryan," in *A New Flower for Children (For Children from Eight to Twelve Years Old)* (New York: C. S. Francis, 1856), 158–89.

32. See Weber, *Protestant Ethic,* 174–75.

33. See, for example, Hartmann, "Capitalism, Patriarchy, and Job Segregation by Sex," 193–225, especially 203–7.

34. W. B. O. Peabody, "Origin and Progress of the Useful Arts," review of *The Frugal Housewife, North American Review* 33 (July 1831): 81; reviews of the *Juvenile Souvenir* and *Juvenile Miscellany, Ladies' Magazine* 1 (Jan. and July 1828): 47–48,

336; 2 (Sept. 1829): 440; reviews of *Juvenile Miscellany, American Traveller* (29 Dec. 1826), 2, (11 July 1828), 2, (5 Sept. 1828), 2. A dialogue on "Coral Reefs" from the *Miscellany* of November 1826 is reprinted in the *Traveller* of 7 Dec. 1826, 4. I am grateful to Deborah Clifford for directing my attention to the *American Traveller.*

35. For a fuller discussion, see *The First Woman in the Republic,* chapter 7.
36. Sarah Van Vechten Brown to Child, 2 Mar. 1869, *CC,* 71/1887.

6

MAGAZINE PRACTICES AND MELVILLE'S *ISRAEL POTTER*

SHEILA POST-LAURIA

•

THE designation "classic writer" has long been equated in American literary scholarship with cultural isolation.[1] Literary historians of the marketplace in antebellum America frequently suggest that classic fiction writers—intolerant and disdainful of "popular" practice—employed subversive tactics that largely escaped the notice of their publishers, editors, and even readers. Perhaps no classic writer has sustained a reputation as one who resisted popular practice more than Herman Melville, whom a variety of critics accused of revolting against his readers, quarreling with fiction, digging beneath and going under forms dictated by a marketplace necessity.[2]

Several problems emerge in the formulation of Melville as a culturally alienated genius. Though celebrated for an originality understood as independence from popular literary practices, Melville's fiction in fact exhibits considerable engagement with popular forms, genres, and themes of his day.[3] Indeed, Melville's own formulation of the interactive nature of artistry stresses the importance of a creative reliance upon popular sources: "Whereas, great geniuses are parts of the times, they themselves are the times, and possess a correspondent coloring."[4] With this understanding of masterworks as a necessary mixture of cultural forms and personal insight, Melville, like Nathaniel Hawthorne and Edgar Allan Poe before him, not only endorsed existing practices but aligned his periodical fiction with specific magazine practices (see Poe, "Magazine Writing: Peter Snook," *Broadway Journal,* 7 June 1845; Hawthorne, preface to *Mosses from the Old Manse* [New York: 1851]).

Formulations of classic writers as cultural isolates project a bifurcated view of mid-nineteenth-century literary culture, a perspective that reflects the stratification of modern culture more than it recovers the historical and cultural circumstances of the time. Although the majority of journals from this period catered to middle-class readers, the contrasting styles found in these magazines demonstrate the necessity for acknowledging the diversity that marked middle-class antebellum writing and reading. The heterogeneity of periodical production, in turn, enabled writers to choose which magazines most closely fit their own interests. Magazinists, therefore, could either find ready outlets that paralleled their own perspectives or tailor their works to reflect editorial policies and readers expectations of chosen magazine environments.

When Melville turned to magazine writing in 1853, he participated in the distinct literary environments of *Harper's Magazine* and *Putnam's Monthly*. Writing for these two major monthlies of the 1850s that differed significantly in ideological perspectives and literary styles required, on Melville's part, a stylistic heterogeneity and creativity that modern readers have associated with Melville but have disassociated from the cultural sources with which the author engaged. Melville's magazine writing, together with his novels of the fifties, exhibit the author's deep concern over a wide range of social issues, including poverty, homelessness, industrialization, slavery, and sexism. While both magazines published some of the author's most sophisticated formulations of political, social, and aesthetic themes, the particular articulation of these themes reflects Melville's consideration of their publishing contexts, the stylistic conventions that distinguish *Harper's* from *Putnam's*.

Magazine writing offered Melville the opportunity to earn a prescribed and steady income, a reason commonly cited for his switch from the novel form. Both magazines paid a high rate per page, five dollars: as a result, Melville enhanced his earnings by publishing simultaneously in both journals, and consequently more tales appeared than if he had published solely in one magazine. However, more than financial gain was at stake. For the first time in his career, Melville discovered large audiences receptive to his literary interests, which have been largely overlooked by modern readers who do not place Melville's fiction within the context of these magazines. Indeed, scrutiny of the stylistic conventions and publishing contexts of Melville's tales in *Harper's Magazine* and *Putnam's Monthly* reveals a direct link between the author's particular articulations of political, social, and literary themes and magazine practice.[5]

The unusual compositional history of *Israel Potter; or, Fifty Years of Exile: A Fourth of July Story,* which appeared in serial form in *Putnam's* from July 1854 through March 1855, illustrates how Melville adapted his style to the different politics and practices of *Harper's* and of *Putnam's*. Of all the author's periodical fiction, this narrative of a Revolutionary War "hero" remains the only work by Melville that—upon rejection from one magazine—was reconceived to meet the editorial policies of the other.[6] These noticeably different environments provide clear contexts for the author's orientation, methods, and his own treatment of historical canonization in *Israel Potter.*

I

STARTED in 1850, *Harper's Magazine* became one of the century's most widely read magazines, with a circulation surpassing 100,000 by 1860. Its overwhelming popularity stemmed largely from its editorial policy of aiming to please all segments of the middle class—to reach "the great mass of the American people" ("A Word at the Start," *Harper's,* June 1850). Because the "great mass" of middle-class readers held different— at times opposing—political views, the monthly discouraged controversy: "The Magazine . . . will provide . . . the most perfect freedom from prejudice and partiality of every kind" (June 1851). It accomplished this feat by strictly maintaining a noncritical stance on politics, social issues, and religious topics. *Harper's* catered to the taste of a mixed reading public through a stylistic mode that hoped to assuage more than it criticized.

With their determination to remain a magazine of light literature aimed at parlor readers, the editors favored a sentimental style.[7] This narrative mode, while employed in thematic treatments of an array of topics, including domestic, social, and even political issues, subordinated analysis of events to an emphasis on the emotional responses of narrators, characters, and readers. Sentimental fiction in *Harper's* cast the motifs of suffering, abuse, poverty, and exploitation—very real social problems that plagued American society in the 1850s—into stylized portraits of moral fortitude. This sentimental style was employed to emphasize the abilities of characters to find contentment through the hardships they encountered by transforming social problems as literary issues into a celebration of the moralistic principles of toleration and acquiescence. Such thematized messages attempted to demonstrate that "difficulties are the tutors and monitors of men placed in their path for their best discipline and development" (Jan. 1852, 212) rather than to focus on the issues themselves. In this light, the fiction of *Harper's* loosely corresponds to the genre that David S. Reynolds has called conventional reform literature, a genre popular with the middle-class antebellum readers who constituted the audience for the monthly.[8]

The emphasis on class in *Harper's* fiction reflects the larger social distancing that was occurring between working-class people and the burgeoning new middle classes. Celebrating the economic success of middle-class readers, *Harper's* tales relegate the stance of acquiescence and toleration to the lower classes, who are the subjects, rather than the narrators. Aloof, spectator narrators representing the privileged middle class (who were themselves aspiring to an elite status) isolate themselves from the events they relate and use their status to observe less fortunate characters from above on the ladder of success. Although narrators allude to the misery of poverty and alienation, they deflect the reader's empathy by disengaging themselves from the environments of their unfortunate characters. This abstract representation of social issues coupled with emphasis on the emotions, philanthropy, or simply the good fortune of the narrator enabled writers to support *Harper's* commitment to a perspective that supports raising timely issues but stops at implication.

Forerunner of the Saturday night radio programs listened to by American families a century later, the parlor literature of *Harper's Magazine* catered to a family-oriented, entertaining, moralistic—what Melville called family-circle—reading. This emphasis on entertainment and nonpartisanship, in turn, provided a needed outlet for a more critically oriented journal that would provide analysis for those interested more in social issues than in family entertainment.

II

PUTNAM'S Monthly started in 1853 as a critical commentary on the times and as a direct contrast to the political conservatism of *Harper's Magazine*. Rigorously analytical, *Putnam's* appealed to a more intellectual, politically liberal, and thus smaller stratum of an essentially middle-class audience that ranged from ten thousand to twenty thousand subscribers, averaging around sixteen thousand readers monthly.

Putnam's promised commentary on both national and international affairs. In the first editorial, Charles Briggs asked readers, "In what paper or periodical do you now look to find the criticism of American thought upon the times?" (Jan. 1853, 2). Answering his own question, Briggs promised to collect "the results of the acutest observations, and the most trenchant thought, illustrated by whatever wealth of erudition, of imagination, and of experience" that American writers possess (2). By emphasizing trenchant thought and erudition, the editors conveyed the nature of the rhetorical style and thematic orientation to which they aspired.

The monthly treated social, political, and literary themes from a perspective markedly different from the nonpartisan, nonanalytical stance of *Harper's*. *Putnam's* strongly condemned sentimentalized writing, rejecting this mode as a tool for representing the times because it glossed over reality and "paints only the gentle, the grieving, the beautiful" (Feb.

1854, 223). Articles, essays, and stories in *Putnam's* analyzed—and eval-
uated—the variety of perspectives on a particular issue. Briggs contributed tales that directly confronted inequalities resulting from industrialization and slavery. George William Curtis, who as assistant editor put
into practice the editorial policies and politics of the monthly by contributing more than fifteen pieces and two serialized novels within a three-
year period, provided social criticism by highlighting what he deemed
hypocritical and limited viewpoints.

Melville's thorough understanding of writing as well as his creative
reasons for doing so within these different environments contributed to
the ease with which he could move from one set of conventions to another. That he continued to submit works to both monthlies indicates
his interest in working within the different magazine environments. Em-
powering the sentimental style with potentially different levels of significance while reflecting a nonconfrontational stance on the social and
political issues raised in the tales provided an artistic goal for Melville, as
his stories for *Harper's* demonstrate. At the same time, *Putnam's* provided
Melville with an alternative representational style that directly criticized
the appropriateness of the sentimental mode for analyzing the times.

Throughout his previous works, Melville had targeted disparate read-
erships with often different and frequently contradictory expectations,
ideological perspectives, and stylistic preferences.[9] The author's reliance
on a compositional strategy of stylistic tailoring goes far in explaining
textual ambiguities as well as contextual similarities in Melville's magazine fiction.

III

ON 25 May 1854 Melville wrote to *Harper's* in an attempt to solicit
interest in a "Serial in your Magazine, supposing you had one, in prospect, that suited you."[10] The proposed serial—presumably *Israel Potter*—
received either no response or a rejection from the editor at *Harper's*.[11]
Turning to the politically progressive *Putnam's* on 7 June, Melville submitted his "sixty and odd" pages of manuscript originally intended for
Harper's.

The periodical context can help to clarify what has appeared to be
compositional and textual ambiguities in *Israel Potter*. The "sixty and odd"
paged manuscript corresponds roughly to chapters 1–6. Of those chapters, all but chapter 1 (a geographical description of the Berkshire region) represent what Walter Bezanson, (the editor of the historical notes
to the Northwest-Newberry edition of *Israel Potter*) has called "a virtual
paraphrase" of Henry Trumbull's *Life and Remarkable Adventures of Israel*

R. Potter (1824). While these early chapters—and presumably the manuscript—parallel their historical source, the remainder of the finished serial (and book) diverge markedly from the source, calling into question the practice of paraphrased biography, which the early chapters—and narrative style—appear to endorse.

Overlooking the periodical context as an explanatory source for textual discrepancies or at least what looks like changing intentions of the author, some Melville scholars have attributed the very different stylistic modes of narration employed in the early chapters (and manuscript) and later chapters to a lack of compositional planning on the part of the author.[12] But placed within the conflicting stylistic practices of *Harper's* and *Putnam's,* the shift in stylistic modes in *Israel Potter* suggests an awareness on Melville's part of the different magazine environments.

A surviving but incomplete transcription of a letter to George Palmer Putnam that accompanied the submitted sample offers insight into the composition of *Israel Potter.* In this letter Melville attempts to clarify the purpose of his enclosed manuscript: "The manuscript is part of a story called 'Israel Potter,' concerning which a more particular understanding need be had."[13] This letter represents the only known clarification or "understanding" of one of his magazine works. Why would Melville have needed to explain his manuscript to the editors at *Putnam's* unless the writing sample did not appear to reflect the interests of the editor, general editorial tastes, or magazine practices?

The subject of an American Revolution hero would easily have spurred interest from a magazine that consistently displayed a keen preference for politically charged material. *Putnam's* had not only published several politically oriented articles and sketches per issue, but it had also carried a short serial on the history of one Founding Father, George Washington. Since *Israel Potter* was to contain its own treatment of a Founding Father, Benjamin Franklin, something other than the actual subject matter of the proposed serial required clarification. In other words, perhaps there was something that Melville thought *Putnam's* might find questionable regarding the treatment of his subject.

One hypothesis suggests that Melville tried to demonstrate that his sample would not challenge what he called the "tender consciences of the public" or "shock the fastidious."[14] Melville scholars have long thought that this letter represents the author's reaction to the magazine's rejection of "The Two Temples," a tale that the author had submitted the previous month. And indeed, the letter of 7 June employs language that recalls Melville's references to the rejected story in a letter of 16 May.[15] Some weeks prior to the submission of the *Israel Potter* manuscript, Melville had overestimated the editorial claim to "criticize the times." The editors regretfully rejected Melville's theologically critical story, "The Two Temples," because, "editorial experience compels me to be very cautious in offending the religious sensibilities of the public, and the moral of the Two Temples would array against us the whole power of the pulpit, to say nothing of Brown, and the congregation of Grace Church."[16] While the editors were willing to "lose one thousand Southern subscribers" by publishing Melville's probing study of a slave revolt in "Benito Cereno," they stopped at challenging religious beliefs.[17] The fact that Putnam, the publisher of the monthly, took it upon himself to write an additional letter to Melville to reassure him of the monthly's interest in and strong support of his ideologically challenging fiction indicates the high regard that the editors of *Putnam's* held for Melville's tales.

However, Melville ended his letter by claiming that his new work would not breach the monthly's commitment to silence on the subject of religion: "I engage that the story shall contain nothing of any sort to shock the fastidious. There will be very little reflective writing in it; nothing weighty. It is adventure."[18] This promise certainly refers to criticizing religious attitudes and practices, issues raised in his previous correspondence with *Putnam's,* because the magazine's editors had not expressed shock over the idea of the homelessness and the starvation of Bartleby or over the violent slave revolt and the grotesque image of Babo's decapitated head impaled upon a pole, both of which were published in its pages. But such a promise strongly implies that the submitted sample did not contain any "weighty" material.

If the submitted sample corresponds to chapters 2–6, the only portion of *Israel Potter* that closely paraphrases Trumbull's biographical narrative of Israel Potter, and in doing so challanges few if any social or political attitudes, then why did Melville feel the need to explain his manuscript? Because the "particular understanding" that Melville had provided has been deleted from the transcript, we can only surmise its contents. Thought to be an explanation of the proposed book as a "virtual paraphrase" of Trumbull's *Life and Remarkable Adventures of Israel R. Potter,* this supposition supports only the contents of the submitted manuscript—material originally written for *Harper's.*[19]

From reading and writing for *Putnam's,* Melville could easily have discerned editorial disapproval of "paraphrased" biographies, a policy followed by *Harper's.* Since the author had consistently displayed through his magazine submissions a clear understanding of the differences in literary conventions and styles between *Harper's* and *Putnam's,* it seems at least questionable that the author "did not yet know that he would abandon sustained use of the *Life* in the next batch of manuscript," as Walter E. Bezanson has suggested.[20]

On the contrary, Melville's need to explain a manuscript that paraphrased an existing biography must have required, on the author's part, a commitment—and thus a conscious decision—to move rapidly away from this narrative mode to a nonsentimentalized, critical treatment of a historical subject. Melville would have needed to sell his *Harper's* tale to the editors at *Putnam's* by explaining how he would develop his proposed serial. Melville's letter to Putnam suggests that the author tried to interest *Putnam's* in his serial by proposing a more detailed account of the novel than the sample indicated, as the excerpt of his letter implies—in other words by proposing that he would go beyond the sample. Biographical stories in *Harper's* differed considerably from those published in *Putnam's*. To understand the extent to which Melville would come to shape his *Israel Potter* serial, we must examine the practices of the competing monthlies.

IV

TWO articles on the same topic that appeared within one month of each other in *Harper's* and *Putnam's* indicate the different orientations and styles of these magazines. In March 1853 *Harper's* published excerpts from J. Ross Browne's "Crusoe-Life; A Narrative of Adventures in the Island of Juan Fernandez." In this account, Browne exploits the associations of the island with Daniel Defoe's famous character and recounts in a sentimental style his exploration of the reputed home of Robinson Crusoe: "Never shall I forget the strange delight with which I gazed upon that isle of romance. . . . Think then, without a smile of disdain, what a thrill of delight ran through my blood, as I pressed my feet for the first time upon the fresh sod of Juan Fernandez! Think of it, too, as the realization of hopes which I had never ceased to cherish from early boyhood; for this was the abiding place, which I now at last beheld, of a wondrous adventurer, whose history had filled my soul years ago with indefinite longings for sea-life, shipwreck, and solitude! Yes, here was verily the land of Robinson Crusoe" (*Harper's,* Mar. 1853, 306). The story is dotted with illustrations of scenes from Defoe's novel, and Browne recounts his exploration of all the popular events and characters from the tale with whom he met in his imagination and in his ramblings over the island.

It is central to understanding *Harper's* practice to note that Browne both emphasized his narrator's emotional response to the scenes described and appealed to the emotions of sentiment and melancholy so popular in the magazine's stories. Adapting the style of Donald Mitchell's famous *Reveries of a Bachelor*, well known to *Harper's* readers because it was serialized for over a year in the pages of the monthly, Browne employs the sentimental mode as he murmurs to his readers, "What pleasant sadness was it that weighed upon my heart?" Browne's account contains references to the past, to childhood, dreams, visions, fancy, adventure, and longings, all motifs characteristically found in *Harper's* sentimental fiction.

The emphasis on melancholic emotions and reveries parallels *Putnam's* characterization of this leading conventional style. In a note in the February 1854 issue of *Putnam's*, Briggs recalled the beginning of what he referred to as the "sentimental school." Reviewing the success of *Reveries of a Bachelor*, he listed the conventional topics of sentimental writing: "much sentimentality, and a little thought about nature and the poetic side of every-day life, expressed in the form of the soliloquy, although occasionally breaking into the colloquial, the author addressing his words to some imaginary hearer. . . . Reveries, thinkings, memories, mysteries, shadows, and death—old times, voices from the past, stars, moonlight, night winds, old homesteads, flowing rivers, and primeval forests, filled the pages of the new books, and the columns of the daily papers. Ik Marvel delighted the readers of the morning paper with a deer, a dog, and a dead girl, served up in every conceivable style of sorrow, sadness and sighs, for a whole year, at least once a week (*Putnam's*, Feb. 1854, 223). Another article augmented the list of conventional motifs written in the sentimental mode: "A mother weeping over the grave of her son of fifteen summers; a husband stealing with soft step, modulated voice, and imprisoned agony, round the death-bed of his young wife; a love scene between a youth and a maiden, where passion exhales itself into a dreamy mist, enveloping them both and softening their outlines to our vision til they melt away in a cloud of splendor, and leave us pleased but unsatisfied" (*Putnam's*, Feb. 1853, 77). This sense of disconnected emotion dissatisfied *Putnam's*. In a series of exposés, the editors argued that the sentimental style of *Harper's* fiction severed the link between social problems and the teller's emotional response to them by highlighting abstracted sentiment rather than the actual subject. The antisentimental stance implies a dissatisfaction with the consistently "clear, true, and transparent" prose of sentimental writing.

Browne was certainly capable of writing more realistic narratives, as his 1846 *Etchings of a Whale Cruise* testifies. Indeed, the sentimental narrative style of his contributions to *Harper's* suggests an understanding of the particular practices that marked the literary environment of the magazine.

A travel article on the same topic that appeared in the March 1853 issue of *Putnam's* reflects the different approach used by its writers. Entitled "Robinson Crusoe's Island," this anonymous (as all works were in *Putnam's*) piece does not exploit the conventional views of Defoe's character for sentimental effects as Browne does so effectively in the *Harper's* story; rather, the story problematizes the question of historical accuracy: "It is a remarkable fact in literary history, or, perhaps, we should rather say, in literary criticism, that for more than a hundred years an unquestioned connection has been maintained in popular opinion between Robinson Crusoe and Juan Fernandez . . . while yet the slightest examination of an unabridged copy of *Robinson Crusoe* will show that it contains no references whatever to Juan Fernandez, but that, on the contrary, a very well-defined locality in another part of the Western Hemisphere, is assigned to the imaginary island" (*Putnam's*, Mar. 1853, 275–76). "Robinson Crusoe's Island" compares the story of Selkirk, Defoe's reputed source for island information, to that of the narrative of Peter Serrano and argues that the latter's experience on a Caribbean island provided Defoe with the material for the island home of Robinson Crusoe. Through this critical approach, the author deconstructs the sentimentalized myth popularized by Defoe. This attempt to challenge conventional attitudes and folkloric knowledge can be found throughout the pages of *Putnam's* and represents the orientation and policies of the analytical monthly.

Perhaps the most marked difference between the practices of the two magazines can be seen in their biographical stories. With the flexible boundaries between historical and literary narratives that existed in mid-nineteenth-century American writing, biographical tales in both magazines adhered to Aristotelian dictates for narrative structure (the most revered mode at midcentury).[21] That is, the narrator does not stop at reciting facts but rather incorporates the biographical facts, incidents, and stereotypes into a plot-driven, dramatic narrative.

Harper's biographical stories reiterate previous biographical and autobiographical accounts of a famous life. Jacob Abbot, among others, supplied *Harper's* with fictionalized accounts of the lives of Franklin and Napoleon (Jan.–Feb. 1852, 145–65, 289–309; June 1853, 50–70). Factual in orientation, these pieces supported popular views of such cultural heroes. After briefly mentioning in the introductory paragraphs that the account was based on Franklin's autobiography, Abbot writes as if he were the actual informational source.

The factual recounting of incidents in *Harper's* creates the tone of the biography as history. But as in most stories published in this magazine, biographies are exploited for their sentimental and moralistic value. The biographical story is told not for its own intrinsic values but rather for "the picturesque and almost romantic interest which attaches itself to the incidents of his personal history," Abbot mentions in "Benjamin Franklin" (Jan. 1852, 145). *Harper's* supported popular romantic pictures of life, love, and history, and writers employed a sentimental style that served to celebrate and emphasize popular knowledge and folklore surrounding a famous life. By glossing over disconcerting facts and realities, this approach underscored the predictable and represents the more conservative use of the sentimental mode. In this context, *Harper's* practice reinforced conventional views rather than providing direct critiques, analyses, and insights, which often appear as subtexts in sentimental works.

The facts of a life in the pages of *Harper's* do not speak for themselves as biographical facts but serve to emphasize morality: "A Quaker lady came to [Franklin] one day, on board the vessel in which he was sailing to New York, and began to caution him against two young women who had come on board the vessel at Newport, and who were very forward and familiar in their manners. . . . When they arrived at New York the young women told him where they lived, and invited him to come and see them. But he avoided doing so, and it was well that he did, for a few days afterward he learned that they were both arrested as thieves. If Franklin had been found in their company he might have been arrested as their accomplice" (Jan. 1852, 153). Like their more literary counterparts in *Harper's*, biographical stories come to represent ultimately an ideological principle fundamental to the middle classes. They act as ideological metaphors: "His public life, in fact, began and ended with the beginning and the end of that great protracted struggle by which the American nation was ushered into being. His history is then simply the history of the establishment of American independence (Feb. 1852, 309). Perhaps because this orientation reflected the larger tradition of *Harper's* writing, biographies occupied a disproportionately large space as well as the front matter of the monthly's pages and seem to have been a genre quite popular with readers.

In contrast to the all-knowing, omniscient tone of the *Harper's* narrator, who appropriated a biography and retold it as his own, the biographical narrator in *Putnam's* adopts the role of an interpreter and evaluator of the reputed facts of a life. In the opening paragraph of "Washington's Early Days," the narrator introduces his method and approach: "We shall make use of all authorities within our reach, not even rejecting tradition, which is often the vehicle of important truth where character is to be estimated" (*Putnam's,* Jan. 1854, 1). Narrators refer openly and throughout the magazine to the various biographical sources on which they rely. Known biographical "facts" were not exploited for their thematic potential but were analyzed, questioned, and probed in keeping with the overall policies of the management.

Conventional views of heroes, such as George Washington's reputed powers of self-control, are challenged: "For the temperament of Washington was impetuous, and his passions were fiery, though we are little accustomed to think so" (Jan. 1854, 6). Through this approach, *Putnam's* writers challenge the truth of "facts" and treat them as literary embellishments: "We must allow Mr. Weems the praise of a good narrator, and his generous enthusiasm makes him an inspiring one. As to the facts, we must first accept them as honestly believed by a gentleman and a clergyman; and many of them can claim the benefit of internal evidence. If not literally true, '*Ils meritent bien de l'etre*'" (Jan. 1854, 4). In this manner, writers of these more analytical and critical biographical tales highlight the fictional elements of the genre and thus call to attention the difficulty of absolute truth in the historical narrative.

V

AS a potential serial for the pages of *Harper's, Israel Potter* would have needed to seem as factual as possible to conform with the styles of the biographies of Franklin and Napoleon. As Bezanson has pointed out, Melville's early chapters closely resemble the factual tone of Trumbull's text.[22] More than 50 percent of Melville's manuscript contains transcribed words and phrases from Trumbull. This appropriation of the material of a previous biographer exactly reflects *Harper's* tradition, but it is central to understanding Melville's reliance on magazine practice that the majority of these appropriations are found in chapters 2–6, most likely the portion of the manuscript originally intended for *Harper's*. In chronicling the life and loves of a historical figure, chapters 2–6 belong to the genre of biographical stories popular with *Harper's* readers. Melville's interest in preserving this established tradition contextualizes the close paraphrasing in the chapters representing the submitted manuscript.

But *Harper's* biographical stories, as we have seen, underscored sentiment, and the early chapters of *Israel Potter* follow this pattern. Israel's doomed love for a neighborhood girl frames chapter 2, which concludes in a manner closely aligned to the sentimental style in *Harper's* stories:

"But if hopes of his sweetheart winged his returning flight, such hopes were not destined to be crowned with fruition. The dear, false girl, was another's" (*IP*, 11). The short-lived romance of Israel Potter is only referred to once after chapter 6. While this abrupt drop of the romance supports Bezanson's conjecture that chapters 2–6 represent the original manuscript sent to the magazines, it also demonstrates Melville's changes to make the story suitable for *Putnam's*. Because this antisentimental magazine would have had little interest in a sentimentalized biographical romance, it seems logical that Melville dropped the episode.

Why did he not omit it altogether? Though including such material seems more in line with the policies of *Harper's*, Melville exploits the possibility of simultaneously representing and criticizing a sentimental style. *Putnam's* prided itself on criticizing sentimental topics for their limited insight, and Melville had employed this strategy in both "Bartleby, the Scrivener" and "Benito Cereno," stories published in *Putnam's* prior to the serialization of *Israel Potter*.[23]

While closing chapter 2 with the sentimental exclamation about lost love, Melville begins chapter 3 by dashing all hopes for a sentimental biography. Mentioning various romantic exploits, the omniscient narrator clearly warns the reader of the antiromantic and mostly realistic nature of this narrative: "But if wandering in the wilderness; and wandering upon the waters; if felling trees; and hunting, and shipwreck; and fighting with whales, and all his other strange adventures, had not as yet cured Israel of his hopeless passion; events were at hand for ever to drown it" (*IP*, 12). This move from sentimentalized response to its critique exemplifies Melville's ability to make conventional forms more complex and multitextual as well as suggests a conscious attempt to follow *Putnam's* practice.

But *Putnam's* did not rest in evaluating popular use of the sentimental mode. Indeed, the larger orientation of the magazine could be said to have been political. Melville's additions and changes reflect his attempt to gear his *Harper's*-oriented manuscript to the conventions of *Putnam's*. One significant parallel between the ideological orientation of *Putnam's* and Melville's tale rests in the nationalism inherent in celebrating the Yankee character—in chapter 3, for example, at the expense of the English. Because *Putnam's* prided itself on being a strictly American magazine that rebuffed all English influence, these additions would have been lauded by the editors of *Putnam's*. *Harper's*, which sought to model itself after English literary tastes and contained a large proportion of English literature, would clearly have found Israel's rebellious attitude toward English culture antithetical to their orientation. The American national pride pervading these early chapters represented the hallmark of *Putnam's*.

The political analysis that dominates *Israel Potter* reflects most precisely Melville's use of *Putnam's* policies. The author introduces in his prefatory lines the theme of political rebellion, which complements his exploitation of the Yankee theme dominating the remainder of the submitted manuscript pages. He dramatizes the politically rebellious spirit of Yankees in chapters 5 and 6, where he significantly lengthens Trumbull's description of the encounter between Israel and the British king. Melville's departure from the Trumbull manuscript may indeed suggest the nature of the modifications he ultimately made when tailoring his tale for the pages of *Putnam's*, for it goes directly against the practice of *Harper's*. Without the manuscript this remains conjecture; however, in light of Melville's treatment of political institutions and themes of rebellion in other stories for the monthly, *Israel Potter* reflects the author's style in *Putnam's*.[24] Transforming the manuscript and plans for *Israel Potter* into *Putnam's* piece required major stylistic revision. At a deeper level, chapters 2–6 differ markedly from Trumbull's text and *Harper's* practice.[25] One of the most significant changes is in the point of view. The biographical stories in *Harper's* were narrated in first person (as was Trumbull's narrative) to enhance the authenticity of the narrator-author. Melville shifts from first- to third-person narration, thereby altering the nature of biographical narrator to reflect the tone of *Putnam's*, where the specific use of third person constantly highlights the genre as a tale told by someone of questionable authenticity. Melville's own prefatory discussion in *Israel Potter* concerning the nature of biography, the narrative method used, and the adoption of the role of editor reflects the general practices in *Putnam's* of problematizing narrative representation.

Because *Putnam's* did not share *Harper's* interest in publishing serialized biographical accounts of historical figures, it seems logical that Melville would supplement his submitted sample with a description and promise of analysis, travels, and characterizations more in keeping with *Putnam's* conventions. His changes to the Trumbull narrative in chapters 2–6, coupled with his reputed "restlessness" and conscious move to "elaborate free fiction" after chapter 6, indicate his commitment to a fictionalized, literary treatment of political anomalies in keeping with *Putnam's* editorial policies.[26] The investigation into the nature of a hero and the ambivalence of a government that allows soldiers to die in poverty reflects this journal's commitment to questioning, analyzing, and criticizing destructive political policies and institutions.

Putnam's American commentary on European culture provided un-flinching analyses of the differences between the politically powerful and weak. "How They Manage in Europe," an article in the April 1853 issue, concluded with this devastating opinion of political conditions in Europe: "This, then, is the way they manage to govern the people in Europe. By the skillful use of patronage, of the church, and of educa-tion; by the denial of the press, of free-locomotion, and the rights of the trade; and by the distribution of standing armies, they bamboozle, de-lude, suppress, and constrain, until the wretched people, impoverished, ignorant, separated and set at enmity with each other, are reduced to a slavery from which it seems almost madness for them to hope to escape" (436). Melville reflects these attitudes not only in condemning the tyr-anny of the English king but also in equating poverty with slavery. In "Israel in Egypt," Israel Potter considers his miserable situation and reit-erates themes presented in "How They Manage in Europe": "Sometimes, ladling out his dough, Israel could not but bethink him of what seemed enigmatic in his fate. . . . Here he was at last, serving that very people as a slave, better succeeding in making their bricks than firing their ships. To think that he should be thus helping, with all his strength, to extend the walls of the Thames of the oppressor, made him half mad. Poor Is-rael! well-named—bondsman in English Egypt" (*IP,* 157).

Melville also provided more complex portraits of famous heroes than found in *Harper's.* "Seeking here to depict him in less exalted lights," he offered the readers of *Putnam's* a less sentimentalized and more analyti-cal depiction (48). The undercutting of idealized portraits of American heroes—as in Melville's treatments of Franklin, Ethan Allen, and John Paul Jones—locates this work as a distinctively *Putnam's* production.

Perhaps the most *Putnam*-like characteristic of *Israel Potter* was its American spirit. Throughout the serialization, reviewers in various pa-pers and magazines commented upon this quality. Praising the first issue in July, a New York paper declared *Israel Potter* "an original American romance," and indeed, its original subtitle, "A Fourth of July Story," in-vited such a response (*New York Commercial Advertiser,* 3 July 1854). This American spirit was formulated as a direct, honest style, something that Melville's characterization of Israel continually exemplified. The au-thor's writing style complemented the characterization of his American hero. Reviewers of the serialization praised *Israel Potter* for its "manly, direct, and clear" style (*Morning Courier and New York Enquirer,* 29 July 1854). The *Boston Post* (15 Mar. 1855) praised *Israel Potter* for its "curt, manly, and independent tone." These reviews imply a contrast between a manly tone and political ideology.

Putnam's editors hoped for precisely such independent and direct writing from their contributors. Melville's story of a rebellious hero whose life dramatized the contradictions inherent in commonly held ideologies of the Founding Fathers reflected magazine policies perfectly. Through his innovative manipulations of magazine conventions in *Israel Potter,* Melville displayed his mastery of form as well as his geniality toward editorial policy and toward politics.[27]

NOTES

1. The term *classic* is borrowed from F. O. Matthiessen, *American Renaissance: Art and Expression in the Age of Emerson* (New York: Oxford Univ. Press, 1942). David S. Reynolds sketches the critical formulations associated with the term *classic writers* in *Beneath the American Renaissance: The Subversive Imagination in the Age of Emerson and Melville* (1988); reprint, Cambridge: Harvard Univ. Press, 1989). Some of the most noted studies on the subversive practices of classic writers include Marvin Fisher, *Going Under: Melville's Short Fiction and the American 1850s* (Baton Rouge: Louisiana State Univ. Press, 1977); Michael Paul Rogin, *Subversive Genealogy: The Politics and Art of Herman Melville* (New York: Knopf, 1983); Henry Nash Smith, *Democracy and the Novel: Popular Resistance to Classic American Writers* (New York: Oxford Univ. Press, 1978); and Michael T. Gilmore, *American Romanticism and the Marketplace* (Chicago: Univ. of Chicago Press, 1985).

2. Ann Douglas, *The Feminization of American Culture* (New York: Knopf, 1977), 319; Nina Baym, Melville's Quarrel with Fiction," *PMLA* 94 (1979): 903–23; Reynolds, *Beneath the American Renaissance,* and Fisher, *Going Under.*

3. See Johannes Deitrich Bergmann, "'Bartleby' and *The Lawyers's Story,"* *American Literature* (1975): 432–36. Mary K. Bercaw, *Melville's Sources* (Evanston: Northwestern Univ. Press, 1987); Edwin M. Eigner, *The Metaphysical Novel in England and America* (Berkeley: Univ. of California Press, 1972); Carolyn L. Karcher, *Shadow over the Promised Land: Slavery, Race, and Violence in Melville's America* (Baton Rouge: Louisiana State Univ. Press, 1983); Reynolds, *Beneath the American Renaissance;* Sheila Post-Lauria, "Genre and Ideology: The French Sensational Romance and Melville's *Pierre," Journal of American Culture* (1992): 1–9; and Sheila Post-Lauria, *Correspondent Colorings: Melville in the Marketplace* (Amherst: Univ. of Massachusetts Press, 1995).

4. Herman Melville, "Hawthorne and His Mosses," *Literary World* (August 1850); reprinted in *The Piazza Tales and Other Prose Pieces, 1839–1860,* ed. Harrison Hayford, Alma A. MacDougall, and Thomas Tanselle (Evanston and Chicago: Northwestern Univ. Press and Newberry Library, 1987), 239–53.

5. See Post-Lauria, *Melville in the Marketplace.*

6. No evidence indicates that Melville revised "The Apple-Tree Table," a tale rejected by *Harper's* and sent immediately to *Putnam's.* By 1856 when Melville wrote this tale, the editorial management of *Putnam's* had changed so drastically

as to seem a carbon copy of *Harper's*. By this time, *Putnam's* had published several tales on the subject of superstitious beliefs, so Melville's tale fit easily into both magazine environments.

7. For discussions of the tastes of a readership Melville called "fireside readers" and what Joan Hedrick has labeled "parlor" literature, see Hedrick, "Parlor Literature: Harriet Beecher Stowe and the Question of 'Great Women Artists,'" *SIGNS* (1992): 275–303; Ronald J. Zboray, *A Fictive People: Antebellum Economic Development and the American Reading Public* (New York: Oxford Univ. Press, 1993), and Post-Lauria, *Correspondent Colorings,* chapter 1.

8. Reynolds, *Beneath the American Renaissance,* 57–58.

9. See my study of Melville's writing strategies in "'Philosophy in Whales . . . Poetry in Blubber': Mixed Form in *Moby-Dick*," *Nineteenth Century Literature* (1990): 300–316.

10. Melville to *Harper's,* 25 May 1854, in Herman Melville, *Correspondence,* ed. Lynn Horth (Evanston and Chicago: Northwestern Univ. Press and Newberry Library, 1993), 263–64.

11. No letter from *Harper's* to Melville concerning this serial has been located. See *Correspondence,* 263.

12. See Walter E. Bezanson, "Historical Note," in Herman Melville, *Israel Potter: His Fifty Years of Exile,* ed. Harrison Hayford, Hershel Parker, and G. Thomas Tanselle (Evanston and Chicago: Northwestern Univ. Press and the Newberry Library, 1982), 184. This edition of *Israel Potter* is hereafter cited in the text as *IP.*

13. Melville to *Putnam's,* 7 June 1854, in Melville, *Correspondence,* 265. While others have suggested 12 June as a more probable date for this letter (see Bezanson, "Historical Note," 181–82), Horth in *Correspondence* refutes this claim decisively by providing the actual letter dated 12 June.

14. Melville to George P. Putnam, 16 May 1854, *Correspondence,* 261; 7 June 1854, *Correspondence,* 265.

15. The 16 May letter concerns Melville's attempt to solicit continued support from the editors at *Putnam's* despite their rejection of "The Two Temples": "I have your note about the 'Two Temples.' . . . Ere long I will send down some other things, to which, I think, no objections will be made on the score of the tender consciences of the public" (*Correspondence,* 261).

16. Charles Briggs to Melville, 12 May 1854, in *Correspondence,* 636.

17. See Sheila Post-Lauria, "Editorial Politics in Melville's 'Benito Cereno,'" *American Periodicals,* forthcoming.

18. Melville to Putnam, 7 June 1854, *Correspondence,* 265.

19. Henry Trumbull, *Life and Remarkable Adventures of Israel Potter* (Providence: Henry Trumbull, 1824); Bezanson, "Historical Note," 182.

20. Bezanson, "Historical Note," 184.

21. For a discussion of midcentury debates on genre, see Post-Lauria, "'Philosophy in Wales,'" 300–316.

22. Bezanson, "Historical Note," 188.

23. See Sheila Post-Lauria, "Canonical Texts and Context: The Example of Herman Melville's 'Bartleby, the Scrivener: A Story of Wall Street,'" *College Literature* 20 (1993): 206–305.

24. See Post-Lauria, "Editorial Politics in Melville's 'Benito Cereno.'"

25. Bezanson, "Historical Note," 187–91.

26. Ibid., 194.

27. Some Melville scholars have pointed out that *Putnam's* itself seems to have criticized Melville for not following Trumbull's biographical tale more closely. It is important to remember that *Putnam's* changed hands in the spring 1855, just before Melville's serial finished. Thus, the editorial that criticized *Israel Potter* reflected the views of a new editor and a new management. This changed perspective would soon drastically alter the editorial policies and politics of *Putnam's* and transform the once-analytical monthly into a mirror image of *Harper's*. This example underscores the necessity for acknowledging the complexities inherent in given magazine environments, contexts frequently altered through changes in management policies, reader expectations, literary shifts, and cultural developments.

7

ADDRESSING OR REDRESSING THE MAGAZINE AUDIENCE
Edmund Quincy's *Wensley*

EZRA GREENSPAN

•

E DMUND Quincy is today largely an unknown figure. Whatever recognition his name brings is more likely than not linked to his family name, the city with which the family was associated, and the history attaching to his city and family in the annals of colonial and early national Massachusetts. Even he might have seen a certain justice in this attribution, since one of the best known of his works was his respectful biography of his father, Josiah Quincy, and some of his most important associations were with local social, educational, and cultural institutions. To the extent that he is remembered today in his own individuality, it is probably for the role he played as an activist in the antislavery movement during the several decades preceding the Civil War. Far less well known is the fact that Quincy also occasionally wrote fiction and that the most sustained of his fictions, *Wensley: A Story without a Moral,* was one of the finer periodical serials published in the 1850s.

Quincy was born in 1808 in Boston, the second son to one of the city's and the region's leading families. The family had been prominent in Massachusetts since the arrival of the first Quincy (also Edmund) with John Cotton in 1633 and had remained active in civil affairs. Edmund's father led a distinguished life in service to city, state, and nation as mayor of Boston, member of Congress, and president of Harvard. His own early years shadowed by the legacy of a Brahmin heritage, Edmund followed family lines as he moved toward manhood. He was educated at Andover Academy and then completed his formal studies at Harvard, from which he graduated with a B.A. (received with high honors) in 1827 and an M.A. in 1830. Although trained in the law, he was independently wealthy and consequently was under no obligation to practice that or any other profession. His good friend James Russell Lowell was to remark that the young Quincy devoted himself instead to "the somewhat arduous profession of gentleman."[1] Though "arduous" may strike a later age as obtuse, Quincy clearly struggled to find himself and his identity during the decade following his studies. While his older brother devoted himself to the affairs of the railroad and the Whig Party, Quincy struck off gradually in the mid-1830s in a different—and un-Quincylike—direction. Energized by the social, political, and religious forces transforming the stable Unitarian, upper-class world into which he was born, Quincy gave himself over to various new reform movements, especially radical antislavery. In 1835, he witnessed the mob attack on the office of William Lloyd Garrison's *Liberator,* one of a series of events and encounters in the mid-1830s that culminated in the November 1837 murder of the abolitionist Elijah Parish Lovejoy by a mob. This event drove Quincy into antislavery circles and to a personal commitment to political action.

His work for the antislavery movement drew on perhaps his chief skill, his ability with his pen. Over the following years, he wrote for a number of the movements' partisan journals and also edited several of them, including the *Non-Resistant,* the *National Anti-Slavery Standard,* and, in Garrison's absences, the *Liberator.* A smooth and polished writer, he also frequently contributed journalistic pieces, some belletristic, to mainstream organs, such as the *New York Tribune* and the *New York Independent.* But his work on behalf of the antislavery movement and other reforms, such as female suffrage, never completely monopolized his time or attention, and it did not negate his attraction to belles lettres. So it is not surprising that a convergence of circumstances brought about the publication during the second half of 1853 of his short novel *Wensley* in *Putnam's Monthly,* a new monthly first published that January and overseen by George Palmer Putnam in conjunction with Charles Frederick Briggs, George William Curtis, and Parke Godwin.

The initiative for the serial publication of *Wensley* in *Putnam's* came from the magazine's chief editor, Briggs. A New Englander himself, Briggs was on friendly terms with many of the region's leading writers, including several of Quincy's closest friends.[2] Recognizing the depths of the talent pools dotting the New England landscape, Briggs moved quickly to tap into them for contributions to the new monthly. Through their common friend Sidney Howard Gay, he first learned that Quincy, whose reputation as a polemicist journalist was already well known to him, also dabbled in fiction.[3] Briggs then lost no time in trying to secure Quincy's pen for the magazine, though he initially left open the possibility that Quincy contribute both fiction and nonfiction articles. First addressing him in February 1853 in a warm, encouraging letter, he urged

Quincy to send him either an article on Mormonism or the fiction manuscript mentioned by their friend as being "either finished, or nearly so." Though he assured Quincy that he had "hardly a doubt that it would be most acceptable," Briggs made it clear that final acceptance of the story would necessarily be conditional on editorial approval. If it proved acceptable, the "publishers" (his standard euphemism for Putnam) would offer three dollars a page payment, the magazine's standard rate for prose contributions, and would put it into print as soon as possible. As further inducements to Quincy, Briggs also mentioned that the current number of *Putnam's* had sold twenty-five thousand copies and that his editorial policy for the magazine rigorously excluded all "oldfogyisms of a proslavery" position.[4]

Negotiations soon followed between the two over the choice of acceptable contributions, which continued along the two-track line of fiction and nonfiction. Perhaps Briggs's own assessment of Mormonism as likely "to be the predominant religion of this Continent" impelled him to persuade Quincy to address that subject in the magazine.[5] At the same time, Briggs continued to voice his enthusiasm for a fictional contribution, making clear his preference for a story free from didacticism. The tendency to preach was, in his opinion, the most serious flaw of popular letters, a view that may have influenced Quincy in his choice of subtitle. By the beginning of June, Briggs and Quincy had reached a general agreement about the publication of *Wensley* in the magazine, with its first installment to be printed in the July issue, which Briggs expected to equal the previous month's printing of thirty-five thousand copies.[6] When that first number appeared, however, it issued under the name of its subtitle, "A Story without a Moral." Briggs, it seems, had never been enthusiastic about Quincy's initial title for the work, *The Tory's Daughter,* which struck him as too similar to many other such titles already in print circulation; therefore, he had taken an editor's prerogative in substituting the subtitle for the title in that July issue of the magazine. In explaining this ex post facto reasoning to Quincy, he urged him to consider the alternate title of *Wensley,* a fictionalized place-name in the story.[7]

The appearance of *Wensley* in *Putnam's Monthly* created a curious intersection between the lives of the story's author and publisher. The direct paternal ancestors of Putnam and Quincy, General Joseph Palmer and Josiah Quincy, had been associated back in the mid–eighteenth century in the first glass manufactory established in the British colonies.[8] The families were neighbors living in the vicinity of the town later named Quincy and were well known to each other, the Quincys being occasional visitors at Palmer's estate overlooking the ocean. Following the death of General Palmer and the dispersal of his family, the ties between the two families relaxed and eventually came undone until the reunion of their descendants through *Putnam's*. That reunion, it can be claimed, was one as rich in the sociocultural terms of the mid–nineteenth century as had been the association of their ancestors in the mid–eighteenth century.

The magazine had only just been launched when Quincy was first solicited for possible contributions. With a shrewd mixture of ideological altruism and publishing acumen, Putnam had established the magazine and publicized its character under the banner of cultural nationalism as the first American journal open exclusively to American authors. Its intended audience was to be the same one addressed by the parent publishing house of G. P. Putnam and Company: the expanding middle-class readership of the United States, centered in New York City but embracing all regions of the country. At the same time that the publishing house was issuing such works as *Homes of American Authors* and the catalog of the first World's Fair held in North America, *Putnam's Monthly* was printing articles by dozens of the leading nonfiction writers in the country on a wide range of social, political, economic, and cultural issues, more often than not of a specifically American nature. Meanwhile, Briggs, who was largely of one mind with Putnam and his fellow editors on such matters, continually searched for fictions that likewise addressed the concerns of his nationalistically minded readership. Seen against this ideological publishing priority, *Wensley* was virtually a made-to-order creation for Putnam and Briggs's magazine: it told a story of young Anglo-American love and shifting American identities with verve and set against the double context of early-nineteenth-century, small-town New England and the era of the American Revolution. Had the story been available to them earlier, it is not hard to imagine that Putnam and Briggs would have wished to print it as the magazine's inaugural serial.

The novel proved immediately popular with its audience, as Briggs and Putnam had foreseen. To Briggs, the story was "capital" from its first installment, and his response, as he read the contributions as they came in one by one, was the kind of deepening interest that he hoped to see registered by the broad *Putnam's* readership for the full range of the magazine's serials.[9] By the time he had read the final installment, Briggs was completely won over and wrote back to Quincy to state his admiration for the overall work. He also made clear his appreciation of Quincy's talent generally, expressing himself with the candor for which he was well known: "You will allow me, therefore, to remark, entre nous, that I could not help thinking that Fortune did you an ill turn when she thrust a silver spoon in your mouth; a wooden ladle or a steel pen, I imagine, would have resulted in an American novelist of whom we might have been proud."[10] At the same time, Briggs was able to report back to Quincy on the overwhelmingly positive reaction that the serial was receiving both from *Putnam's* correspondents and through word of mouth, as it passed monthly through the press. Capitalizing on the magazine's official policy of authorial anonymity, Briggs played along with the guessing game about the writer's identity that began soon after the publication of the first issue and delighted in passing on word to Quincy that his fiction had been attributed to, among others, James Russell Lowell and Charles Francis Adams.[11] Of all contemporary responses, the best known was that attributed to John Greenleaf Whittier, for whom the novel was said to be "the most readable book of the kind since Hawthorne's Blithedale Romance."[12] Precisely what kind of book Whittier had in mind is not easy to say, although he probably meant a regionally based (or specifically New England–based) fiction of manners. That his high opinion was not unrepresentative can be seen by the fact that the year following its serial publication the novel was brought out in book form by Ticknor and Fields of Boston, the leading literary publishing house of the country and the publishers of the works of many of Quincy's friends.[13] But in the decades following its initial popularity, the novel—and Quincy's reputation as a fiction writer—fell out of the public spotlight, and in the twentieth century the novel has been all but entirely neglected.

That neglect is undeserved. Compelling as an early instance of American regionalism and fascinating as a study in periodical literature, *Wensley* seems to me simultaneously a candidate for inclusion in the expanding canon of American literature and a model for a case study of authorship, readership, and discourse—two possibilities of which Quincy himself was not unaware. For the purposes of this essay, though, I will concentrate on the latter topic, which, despite all the attention it has gotten generally in studies of fiction, has gone relatively unexamined in the specific cultural setting of antebellum periodicals.

Though its author was a literary amateur in every sense of the term and was Brahmin enough to have looked down on any other form of authorship, *Wensley* was written with a degree of narrative sophistication, not to mention wit and charm, unusual by the standards of even the best fiction of the day. As a narrative text, *Wensley* presents an unusually interesting case study in the art of composition, whether viewed internally or externally. To judge from the correspondence between Briggs and Quincy that continued through the six-month period of its publication in *Putnam's,* the inscription of the story proceeded only shortly ahead of each month's publication date. The report that Briggs had heard back in February 1853 that the story was "either finished, or nearly so" was clearly erroneous. Briggs received each new installment only shortly before it was due to go to press, sometimes having had to prod Quincy to meet deadlines and once or twice having had to read proof when time was insufficient to allow mailing it to Quincy's home in Dedham, Massachusetts. With regard to the October installment, he was obliged to print only part of the copy due to the unexpected length of another contribution.[14] And with the concluding installment, Briggs went so far—reluctantly, he explained to Quincy—as to cut a page and a half of the story to compensate for the printer's mistaken estimate of its length in laying out that month's magazine.[15] Although this kind of interactive editorial license and authorial improvisation was not at all atypical in nineteenth-century serial publication, it is particularly intriguing in the case of a work such as *Wensley,* which is itself a tale of unstable and shifting identities subjected to outside pressures beyond the control of the characters, though not beyond that of the author. One may even speculate that the story's sometimes improvised composition and publication imposed additional pressure on its already internally unstable relationships, although to what degree external factors affected the plot must remain a matter of debate.

The story is the creation—and a highly self-conscious one, at that—of its first-person narrator, Frank Osborne, who looks back on an era of his life already a generation or more in the past.[16] As the story opens, eighteen-year-old Frank has been farmed out by the authorities of Harvard to the village of Wensley, Massachusetts, as punishment for a sophomoric prank committed by him and his circle of college friends. His host during the months of his recuperation is the town's elderly minister, Adrian Bulkley, the pastor of the Congregational church in this one-congregational town. Bulkley, it turns out, is the last of the Puritans in Wensley and, since the town has preserved the traditions and practices of the region long after they have disappeared elsewhere, a symbol of a vanishing way of life in New England. Disappointed in love early in life, Bulkley has lived a bachelor's existence in town for decades with only Jasper, his black serving man and all-purpose majordomo, as a companion. In offering his house in loco parentis to Frank, he is doing what he has periodically done in the past for other students suspended from Harvard. In this case, though, the arrangement turns out to be based on an unanticipated mutuality, because Frank is an orphan with no siblings whose closest claim to family is a rather emotionally remote guardian, Mr. Moulton, who lives in Boston and oversees Frank's finances. Far from finding Bulkley the bore he had expected, Frank quickly comes to see him as a trustworthy adviser and eventually comes to regard him, though he never uses the term, as a kind of foster father.[17]

Though of an age and a disposition to question authority and generally inclined at the outset of the story to do so, Frank quickly learns to overcome the initial skepticism that he brings with him to his place of exile. From his first meeting with Bulkley, he is taken with the man's genial spirits and broad humanity. That quick liking is enhanced by Bulkley's revelation that he had been well acquainted with Frank's father, a relationship that began during their student days at Harvard and that was strong enough to cause the senior Osborne to visit occasionally at Wensley (and it is also Bulkley who reveals to Frank that the town beauty, Eleanor Allerton, is his distant cousin). At the same time, Frank, an urban dweller by background and experience, is also quickly charmed by the town's pastoral character, which in fact serves as setting for several of the key scenes in the novel, particularly the impressively staged confrontation scene witnessed by Frank between the Allertons and their accuser, Ferguson, that takes place at the "Sachem's Seat" deep in the primordial forest. To a large degree, Frank's attraction to Bulkley and his fondness for the town are different aspects of the same phenomenon: for him, Bulkley really is Wensley and Wensley, Bulkley. This is one reason why he is surprised to hear that Bulkley served in the Continental army from Lexington to Yorktown; he cannot readily identify Bulkley with any other place or set of circumstances.

Frank most readily identifies Bulkley with his parsonage and church, as does the reader. Though Bulkley is called out of town to Boston and to a nearby town during the course of the novel, the reader never sees him anywhere but in Wensley. This plotting is presumably deliberate, because the worldliness for which Frank admires him is purely regionally centered and is set off nicely against the cosmopolitanism of the novel's various Anglo-American characters, especially Colonel Allerton and Harry Markham, Frank's friend and romantic rival. As much as the text identifies Bulkley with the town, it also identifies him with a way of life that the older Osborne nostalgically sees as lost. The text makes that point most effectively in the sabbath scene at church, as the minister, followed by his young guest of honor enters the building to the silent respect of his standing congregation and, after his long orthodox sermon (for Bulkley "was none of your twenty minute men"), exits it again, trailed by Frank, to a community that awaits his departure before filing out itself. Though forced by social circumstances to play his dutiful role in the ceremony, Frank is plainly uncomfortable to be situated within the official order. A Unitarian by background and latitudinarian by character, he has followed the ceremony and the tough sermon from a point of detached involvement. Unmoved by the logic of the sermon at the time, he is even more detached in maturity as he remembers that earlier era and formulates the thesis that Bulkley's uncontested monopolization of religious discourse in Wensley may actually have compromised his hold on the faith of the congregation, which collapsed as wholly after his death as did the "one-hoss shay" of Oliver Wendell Holmes.

The authority underlying Bulkley's faith proving barely as long lived as he, what alone survives the parson is his memory, as preserved in and through the telling of his story. Though a paterfamilias to the community, the childless Bulkley passes on his memory to posterity primarily through Osborne, his unlikely successor, whose first thought in the story is to indicate the historical injustice should Bulkley's name not pass beyond "the narrow bounds" of Wensley and clerical circles. In his capacity as narrator, then, Osborne becomes Bulkley's only surviving kin in a fast-changing world. Meanwhile, their parent-child relationship is surrounded by and played out through similarly posed relationships in the story, which can easily be read as a story of parents and children. The most important such relationship is that between Eleanor and Colonel Allerton, who have only each other for family and live set off from the rest of the community, a mysterious Anglo-American couple recently settled in town who provide the nearest social and intellectual company Wensley has to offer to Bulkley and, not surprisingly, the love interest for young, romantic Frank. While the plot is built upon the developing relationships between the characters of these two houses, the parent-child motif carries through the story in other ways, complicating the relationships between the major characters. For example, the villain Ferguson, who threatens to destroy the reputation and estate of Colonel Allerton unless Eleanor agrees to marry him, turns out to be the son of Bulkley's one and only love; and the Jewish agent, Abrahams, who helps Ferguson to steal from a fund overseen by Allerton, the Crown's agent in America responsible for compensating Loyalists for their confiscated property, flees to his parents' protection in New Jersey when Frank and Markham come to arrest him near the story's end. Much as these relationships provide an interlocking set of relationships to fill out the plot, they also provide Quincy with a family-centered construct through which to express the essential issue of the story: the relationship between past and present.

Quincy has Osborne tell his story in such a way and with such a mind-set as to keep the cross-generational perspective of past and present—or more precisely, of present looking back on past—continuously before his readers' eyes.[18] "Then" and "now" is, in fact, the most powerful oppo-sitional construct in the narrative, structuring not only the manner of telling but also the implied reception of the telling. "Then" was a slower, simpler age than "now," which Osborne thinks of as "the fast age," an age of horses and stagecoaches versus an age of trains. Wensley, an in-land town, was farther removed from Boston "in those days" than "in these days," and Massachusetts from the rest of the country, a point that figures in the long-distance workings of the plot, in which limitations of transportation and communications—and the human relations man-aged through their agencies—leave crucial matters (such as the state of Colonel Allerton's reputation and property back in England and the nature of Eleanor's affections) confused or uncertain.

On the other hand, relations in that earlier era were more personal and localized than Osborne can claim they are in the narrative present. Had they not been, Markham and Frank would never have been able to track down Abrahams to South Jersey by following a trail of clues initi-ated by Jasper's knowledge of local individuals and places. The same local quality flavors life in Wensley, where people know one another well and life adheres more closely than "now" to the rhythms and cycle of nature. If the present age is one of trains, the story characterizes the earlier era repeatedly as an age of horses. In fact, one of the central genre scenes depicting small-town life in Wensley concerns the relative merits of horseflesh and of their owners' knowledge of their value, a scene played humorously in ways quickly reminiscent of Augustus Bald-win Longstreet's "The Horse Swap." Such scenes, juxtaposed against the faster-paced, more geographically dispersed society of the narrative pres-ent, naturally lead Osborne to wonder about the relative merits of past and present. Rather predictably, Osborne looks back on the vanished past with regret, even a measure of nostalgia (although nostalgia more complicated than he is aware).[19] Not only do individual faces and places change, but so do types. He wonders, for example, whether any of the local characters he had come to know and enjoy have survived into the present age: "I am afraid that they have had all their sharpness ground down by the mill-wheels, and that they are all reduced to undistinguish-able particles; or that their originality has been all crushed out of them by the locomotives that fly, screaming like so many devils, all over the country (Aug. 1853, 163). Of all the disappearing types, naturally the one he misses most is the figure of Bulkley.

This fact may explain the motivation behind his telling the story, but it does not entirely account for the manner of its telling, a rhetorically foregrounded mode of presentation that openly negotiates a collaboration between its author/narrator and its readers. The partners to this narrative collaboration are Osborne, a man now in his fifties who speaks of himself as being well informed about a wide variety of matters and acquainted with a wide circle of life experiences and people, including most of the leading writers of the time; and his readers, whom he expects also to be well versed in the ways of life. He can therefore assume that they will be available for questions he considers rhetorical, such as "Who does not remember, that is old enough, the morning of a journey to New-York, in those days, before railways?" and that they will recognize the changes of terminology occurring during the last generation. Similarly, he can assume that they will be interested generally in the quaint character of the past as manifested by Wensley, an assumption operative both anterior to and coterminous with the telling of the narrative.

More importantly from his vantage point as a narrator addressing an audience, he can assume that his readers are well versed in the literature and the accompanying literary conventions of the day. That is, he knows that he can operate with his audience narratively on the basis of a literarily based peer relationship. Assuming therefore that his readership is literate in the polite belles lettres of the day and possesses a common fund of literary sources, Osborne draws on that fund throughout the narrative, making allusions to characters or lines from such texts as Henry Wadsworth Longfellow's "The Village Blacksmith" and Harriet Beecher Stowe's *Uncle Tom's Cabin* and referring to the narrative talents of Nathaniel Hawthorne, Charles Lamb, and Thomas De Quincey. Particularly powerful in his reading of his readers' literary sensibilities is his estimation of Sir Walter Scott as an influence on contemporary reading habits and expectations, a factor he outspokenly respects but from which he also deviates. Furthermore, he handles these writers and texts in such a way as to make clear his belief that they are a matter of shared familiarity with his audience. This does not mean that author/narrator and audience are smoothly equal in function or identical in interests. For example, Osborne's description of Eleanor Allerton, his golden-haired love interest in the story (and his wife, we learn only at its end, during the three intervening decades between the time of the story and its narration) becomes a point of negotiation between author (unwilling to give too many physical details) and reader (eager for these and more). But even when one yearns and the other withholds, the conflict is joined between like-minded friends rather than adversaries. If there is a rift between them, it lies along common territory—namely, the space occupied by conventional middle-class fiction. Likewise, the narrator is often solicitous of his readers' interest and character, as when he defers to their sensibility in omitting "an expletive 'now better far removed'" in referring to Ferguson's malicious behavior (Nov. 1853, 520).[20] The twists and turns of the plot get played out in the conventional ways that mid-nineteenth-century readers—as the narrator well knows—expect they will: in the end (for such a story must have an end, and a strong one, at that) heroes and villains are revealed for who they truly are, and Eleanor chooses Frank over Markham (for, as a young woman come of age, her supreme choice in life is to choose between possible mates). In the specific textual space of this narrative, though, these things do not work themselves out against a blank wall; they work themselves out against the prior and ongoing agreement between author and readers that these matters must be resolved for true reader satisfaction to be achieved. And this author is intent on giving his readers precisely that kind of satisfaction.

The assumed literacy and taste of his audience are more than a matter of education or breeding, however important these qualities may have been to Quincy outside (and perhaps also inside) the construction of his fiction. To a large extent, they are important elements determining the external structure cohabited by author and reader, whose actual address in the world, they both outwardly know, is *Putnam's Monthly*. In naming his audience at one point as the "Putnam public" (Sept. 1853, 297), he makes explicit the fact not only that he and they are of the same time and society but that they meet through the literary mediumship of that magazine.[21] The very discourse on which the novel is founded, one consistent with the contemporary world as envisioned by the story, is a magazine-based mode of expression that, like *Putnam's* itself, necessarily speaks a translocalized language addressed to a large number of people scattered over a large, undefined area. Such a discourse would not have been necessary under the conditions of life dominant in Wensley a generation before, but, following the disappearance of characters like Bulkley and of a society like early-nineteenth-century Wensley, it is in the historical present.[22] In a similar way, *Wensley* itself, as a work of fiction, exists in an era of quickly and manifoldly reproducible texts. Quincy as author (and, for that matter, Briggs as editor) was self-consciously playing on the reproducibility of the specific, the homely, and the regional in his depiction of Wensley and its central character. In fact, Quincy well knew (as, of course, did Briggs) that through the print-based medium of *Putnam's* he had the power to make singular, old-time figures like

Adrian Bulkley and Colonel Allerton reproducible and available to thousands of mid-nineteenth-century families all over America—a power of dissemination of which no American writer living in the aftermath of *Uncle Tom's Cabin* could have been unaware. This insight underlies the opening thought of the narrative, which is to lift the figure of Bulkley out of the "homely annals of the Parish Records" and the "Triennial Catalogue of Harvard College" and elevate it to a higher level of timelessness. Never unaware from its opening paragraph of its power or status as popular narrative, *Wensley* locates itself and its function on a level alongside the contemporaneous *Times* of London, to whose files Osborne sends the curious reader intent on learning all the details concerning the accusation against and the eventual acquittal of Colonel Allerton.

In short, *Wensley* is a profoundly magazinish fiction, as its editor was aware all along; the novel simultaneously occupies and encodes within itself the specific cultural space of midcentury periodical literature. Little wonder that Briggs took so fully to Quincy and his story, which he could readily see as impressing the *Putnam's* readership as a work of art both genial and congenial. By the time *Wensley* was halfway through its serialization, Briggs was ready to accord Quincy the magazine's highest honor, offering to include him—voluntarily or not, he joked—in a group daguerreotype of a "party of Putnamites" tentatively scheduled to be printed in the January issue.[23] Friendly though Briggs may have been in his intentions, one can detect more than a bit of cynicism surrounding his handling of texts such as *Wensley*. While he took pride in his ability as editor of *Putnam's* to read public taste and to issue a magazine designed to please it, Briggs was hardly at peace with the public he dutifully served, which he sometimes thought of as a monster guided by capricious taste. He experienced this lesson during the run of *Wensley* when, he confidentially noted in a letter to Quincy, the "Putnam public" approved enthusiastically of such popularized fare as *Evangeline* and Martin Farquhar Tupper's *Proverbial Philosophy* but rejected a poem written by Lowell for the magazine that he personally thought "superlatively good."[24] Early on he warned Quincy, himself no novice at contemporary journalism, "It is a capricious public, and manifests, at times, a mortifying lack of taste," a valuation particularly ironic when applied to a novel, such as *Wensley,* that inscribed friendly author-reader relations into its text.[25] Fortunately for his own peace of mind, that fickle public liked *Wensley*.

For Quincy, though, one may reasonably expect that there should have been no such easy rationalization between desire and actuality.

Briggs might not have been in the business of reforming his middle-class audience, but Quincy was, at least in much of his other writing. Calling himself in a letter to the *National Anti-Slavery Standard* "the Nestor of Correspondents to New York papers," he had devoted a good deal, if not all, of his time through the antebellum generation to the causes of the day.[26] Unlike his cousin, Wendell Phillips, however, he seldom did so without a cultivated self-irony and gentlemanly sense of detachment, traits clearly present in the telling of *Wensley*, which may fairly be called "a story without a moral"—or, at least, "moral" in Quincy's sense of the term.

To readers today, though, the story may seem to have a moral, and if so, that moral is likely to be read as a deeply conservative one that justifies both the literary and the extraliterary status quo. It would be difficult to know whether Quincy actually saw characters such as Jasper, the black servant stiffly loyal to Bulkley and to American patriotism who surprises Frank by his literacy (an act, the narrator makes a point of noting, typically guided by his finger), and Eleanor, the exemplary daughter loyal to her father but somewhat independent of mind who occupies a slim territory hemmed in on all sides by males, as figures harmonious with his reformist sentiment toward blacks and women in his society. To readers a century and a half removed from that society, they will hardly seem such. Then again, even Quincy's status as the author of *Wensley* has its own unintended irony, when one realizes that Quincy, who was immortalizing Bulkley by lifting his figure above the level of the *Harvard Triennial Catalogue* to that of *Putnam's*, kept the former on his desk next to his copy of the Bible and consulted it as an authoritative source for determining an individual's standing in society. When an unfamiliar name came to his attention, one commentator noted, Quincy turned to the *Triennial* to identify it. "If a man was in it," the commentator reported Quincy as saying, "that's who he was; if he wasn't in it, who was he?"[27] That question can also fairly be asked about the author of *Wensley*, who may have been well known to a coterie of others whose names appeared with his in the *Triennial* but who as man and author is little known to us today.

NOTES

1. Quoted in M. A. DeWolfe Howe, "Biographer's Bait: A Reminder of Edmund Quincy," *Proceedings of the Massachusetts Historical Society* 68 (Oct. 1944–May 1947): 377.

2. In fact, that autumn, right in the middle of the run of *Wensley*, Briggs

printed "A Moosehead Journal" by their mutual friend James Russell Lowell.

3. Gay moved in the same social and antislavery circles as Lowell and Quincy, the latter his coeditor of the *National Anti-Slavery Standard*. For a general discussion of various intersections among the lives of these three men, see Martin Duberman's fine biography, *James Russell Lowell* (Boston: Houghton Mifflin, 1966).

4. Briggs to Quincy, 20 Feb. 1853. This letter and those that followed from Briggs to Quincy during the next year are used by permission of the Massachusetts Historical Society.

5. Ibid., 8 Mar. 1853.

6. Ibid.

7. Ibid., 13 June 1853.

8. Edmund Quincy at least was aware of this partnership, which he mentioned in his biography of his father, *Life of Josiah Quincy of Massachusetts* (Boston: Ticknor and Fields, 1868), 7–8.

9. Briggs to Quincy, 1 June 1853.

10. Ibid., 15 Nov. 1853.

11. Ibid., 4 Aug. 1853. Briggs hoped that Quincy, too, was enjoying the guessing: "It will be a good joke to 'confound your enemies' by announcing you as the author when they shall have all praised it. It may lead them to think there is something more in Abolitionism than they had dreamed of."

12. Although the words are generally assigned in modern reference works directly to Whittier, they were actually an attribution to him by Robert C. Winthrop, the president of the Massachusetts Historical Society and Quincy's lifelong friend (*Proceedings of the Massachusetts Historical Society* 15 [June 1887]: 283).

13. Quincy apparently raised the possibility of the publication of *Wensley* in book form by G. P. Putnam and Company as the final installment of the serial was going to press. Briggs wrote back to call the prospect of book publication "a splendid idea" but thought that its regional content dictated Boston, not New York, as the appropriate place of publication. He suggested that city's leading publishing house, Ticknor and Fields, who specialized in the belles lettres, as the best address for the book and offered his services as intermediary (Briggs to Quincy, 22 Nov. 1853). Half a year later, he was able to congratulate Quincy on his agreement with the firm's senior partner: "I was very glad to hear that Ticknor had taken Wensley in hand, and I have no doubt it will be a success, although it is too good to run off like the Lamplighter" (Briggs to Quincy, 24 Apr. 1854). Although Briggs's judgment may have been debatable, his prediction turned out to be accurate. The book was issued the following month in a fairly standard first printing of two thousand copies (Warren S. Tryon and William Charvat, eds., *The Cost Books of Ticknor and Fields and Their Predecessors, 1832–1858* ([New York: Bibliographical Society of America, 1949], 285).

Once that book appeared, Quincy found himself even in its own end pages in the immediate company of his New England friends and peers. In the copy of the novel I have seen, Ticknor and Fields, who often tipped advertising sheets listing the names and works of their authors into various other works of the firm, associated Quincy's novel with works by Nathaniel Hawthorne, Lowell, Edwin Percy Whipple, John Greenleaf Whittier, George Hillard, Grace Greenwood, and others.

14. Briggs to Quincy, undated (but presumably Sept. 1853).

15. The possibility of the editor's need to change the text arose first the previous month, when Briggs wrote to inform Quincy about that possibility: "I think it will be better to let me have the copy, and, if it should need cutting down, perhaps I might do it" (Briggs to Quincy, 2 Oct. 1853).

When he did make cuts the following month, Quincy apparently wrote back to demand an explanation. In response, Briggs tried to assure Quincy that "the excisions were so discretely done that you would not have missed them" (Briggs to Quincy, 15 Nov. 1853). A week later, probably in response to Quincy's request, Briggs sent him proofs of the excised parts of the story and assured him that they in no way detracted from the story line (Briggs to Quincy, 22 Nov. 1853).

Briggs's unilateral decision to make cuts to the story was not unusual. As an overworked editor operating under severe time and space constraints and often finding his room for maneuvering limited by slow or unreliable mail service, he sometimes had to make hasty decisions to cut, alter, or even table manuscripts that today may seem imperious or arbitrary. His high-handed treatment of Quincy had numerous parallels. During his two-year editorship of the magazine, for instance, Briggs also laid a heavy hand on the work of other authors whom he admired, such as Herman Melville and Lowell.

16. To avoid confusion between the young man in the story and the middle-aged narrator engaged in reminiscing about his youth, I will call the former Frank and the latter Osborne. In a work self-consciously conceived as a narrative discourse existing in a historical context of narrative discourse, this distinction becomes a matter of primary interpretive importance.

17. The text raises this issue early on. The first question Frank is asked by the townspeople upon his arrival at Wensley and his request for directions to Bulkley's house is whether he is a "relation" of the minister, to which he responds, "None whatever, that I know of" (July 1853, 82). The novel was serialized in six monthly installments running through the second half of the year. Its final installment ended right before the concluding part of Melville's "Bartleby, the Scrivener" in the December 1853 issue of the magazine, a story to which Briggs called Quincy's specific attention, presumably with pride, in his letter of 2 October 1853. All citations from *Wensley* will be drawn from the original text as published in *Putnam's Monthly*.

18. To judge from another of Quincy's stories, "An Octogenary Fifty Years Since," Quincy favored the subject of the older man looking back on an event in his youth and narrating it in his own voice against the background of a historically interesting era. That story resembles *Wensley* in obvious ways: an older man remembers how, during his days as a Harvard undergraduate, he made the acquaintance of a distinguished man now advanced in years who had lived through

the events of the Revolutionary War. That man becomes the source of his admiration and a model of behavior that he carries into his own maturity.

In the context of this discussion, what is most striking about "An Octogenary" is the fact that Quincy chooses not to foreground one of the issues central to *Wensley:* narrative discourse and its relation to the norms of discourse in sociohistorical context. Although no less aware than *Wensley* of the gap between past and present, "An Octogenary" is nearly entirely lacking in the rhetorical strategy of reader involvement and the related internal literary discourse with which *Wensley* is inscribed. "An Octogenary Fifty Years Since" was published in the posthumous edition of Quincy's short works compiled and edited by his son, also Edmund Quincy, *The Haunted Adjutant and Other Stories* (Boston: Ticknor and Company, 1885).

19. One may be tempted to read Osborne's narrative as an act of nostalgia, a reading frequently invited by Realistic fiction of its century as well as more broadly by cultural re-creations of vanishing folkways. But, as I will argue, *Wensley* juxtaposes not only past and present but past and present modes of discourse in ways that complicate any simple interpretation of the novel as an act of nostalgic preference of past to present.

20. Behind this omitted "damned" may have been an unspoken agreement, communicated perhaps with a wink, between author and editor, Briggs having earlier urged Quincy to "be so good as to avoid all the devils and damns you can, because they offend the nerves of some of our pious readers, who remonstrate against such wickedness" (Briggs to Quincy, no date, but endorsed by Quincy on back as July 1853).

21. A similar point gets made when the narrator declares at the end of his story, "I was determined when asked to write for this periodical, that it should be something not in the remotest degree edifying or instructive" (Dec. 1853, 608).

In the Ticknor and Fields book edition of *Wensley,* the term the "Putnam public" naturally gets reduced simply to "the public," and the term "this periodical" in the above quote to "press." In most important respects, the magazine and book texts are nearly identical. The primary difference between them is a preface that was written specifically for the book edition whose most notable characteristic is its continued participation in the central fictional device of *Wensley,* the attribution of the authorship of the novel to Frank Osborne (Quincy's name not appearing on the title page and the author's address given at the end of the preface as Osborne's novelistically established one in Pennsylvania rather than Quincy's in Massachusetts).

22. For a good general overview of changes overtaking the terms of literacy and print discourse during the era fictionalized in *Wensley,* see David D. Hall's "The Uses of Literacy in New England, 1600–1850," in *Printing and Society in Early America,* ed. William L. Joyce, David D. Hall, Richard D. Brown, and John B. Hench (Worcester, Mass.: American Antiquarian Society, 1983), 1–47; and William J. Gilmore, *Reading Becomes a Necessity of Life: Material and Cultural Life in Rural New England, 1780–1835* (Knoxville: Univ. of Tennessee, 1989).

23. Briggs to Quincy, 2 Oct. 1853. No such daguerreotype was ever printed.
24. Ibid., undated (but presumably Sept. 1853).
25. Ibid., 13 June 1853.
26. Quoted in Howe, "Biographer's Bait," 380.
27. Ibid., 391.

8

SERIAL POLITICS IN WILLIAM
GILMORE SIMMS'S *WOODCRAFT*

PATRICIA OKKER

•

IN 1842 William Gilmore Simms, the editor of *Magnolia: or Southern Appalachian,* reversed his predecessor's practice of publishing novels serially, urging contributors to send "as few articles as possible which require *serial* publication." As Simms explained, "We shall always give place and preference to those performances, which are unique and *publishable* entire (*Magnolia: or Southern Appalachian,* Aug. 1842, 128). Despite such proclamations, however, Simms had already made considerable use of serials, as both an editor and writer. When in 1825 he founded, along with several other young men, a weekly literary miscellany, the *Album,* Simms's own contributions included a series of letters and two novellas, "The Robber—An Eastern Tale" and "Moonshine," issued in seven and thirteen installments, respectively. Similarly, while editing the *Southern Literary Gazette* in 1828, Simms published his six "Chronicles of Ashley River," and as editor of Charleston's *City Gazette* in the early 1830s, Simms contributed a series of ten travel letters based on a visit to Louisiana and Mississippi and published in serial form James Lawson's *Tales and Sketches, by a Cosmopolite.* In the 1840s and early 1850s, other work by Simms appeared as serials, including "Caloya: or, The Loves of the Driver," "The Moral Character of Hamlet," "The Hermytte of Drowsiehedde," "The Maroon: A Legend of the Caribbees," "Maize in Milk: A Christmas Story of the South," *Father Abbot, Norman Maurice, Michael Bonham,* and "Marie de Berniere."[1] Given this long-standing use of serialization for essays and shorter fiction, it is hardly surprising that in 1850 Simms ignored his earlier editorial advice and published for the first time a full-length novel, *Katharine Walton,* in serial form in *Godey's Lady's Book.*

When writing his next full-length novel, Simms turned again to serialization. *The Sword and the Distaff* (later issued under the now-familiar title *Woodcraft*) appeared in semimonthly literary supplements of Charleston's *Southern Literary Gazette* from 28 February through 6 November

1852. These literary supplements were part of an ambitious campaign by the magazine's publishers. Hoping to establish a publishing house that would encourage southern authors, William C. Richards and Joseph Walker planned to publish fiction in the *Gazette*'s literary supplements and then issue the works in book form, as they did with Simms's *Sword and the Distaff* in September 1852.

Though not his first serial novel, *The Sword and the Distaff* represents an important development in Simms's thinking on the serial form. As his first attempt at publishing a novel in a southern magazine, *The Sword and the Distaff* is the first demonstration of what would become Simms's lifelong support for such periodicals. Himself an editor of numerous magazines,[2] Simms often asserted the importance of successful southern periodicals for the development of southern literature. In May 1845, for example, he asked the subscribers of the *Southern and Western Monthly Magazine and Review* to support southern periodicals: "Give them good countenance, encourage them with proper hopes to proper enterprise, and, our life upon it, you will soon create a literature which not only the South and West, but which the whole American world, 'will not willingly let die'" (364). In publishing *The Sword and the Distaff* serially in the *Gazette* rather than pursuing the more lucrative New York–Philadelphia market, in which he had already enjoyed success, Simms renewed his commitment to southern periodicals, and his actions suggest that he now understood the power of serial fiction in making a periodical succeed. The importance of such fiction was openly acknowledged by the magazine's management. In announcing the publication of *The Sword and the Distaff*, the publishers promised that the newly revised *Gazette* would "surpass its former series, in variety, quality, and brilliance of material, and they confidently appeal[ed] to the people of the whole South to sustain them in their purpose and endeavours" (3 Jan. 1852). Given Simms's own commitment to southern periodicals and literature, this arrangement, though somewhat risky, must have been appealing. Here, Simms was able to write directly to a southern audience, and he did so with the hope that his efforts would help establish a southern publishing company.[3]

Though he did not begin thinking of the work as a novel to be published in a southern serial, Simms's own letters suggest that he composed a significant part of the novel with this specific audience in mind.[4] In his attempt to engage this audience, Simms did more than simply set his novel in a southern locale. Indeed, Simms used this opportunity to speak directly to a southern audience as a forum for discussing the nation's political crisis of the early 1850s, in which South Carolina particularly was embroiled. Certainly, throughout the early 1850s, much of South Carolina continued the debate over secession fueled by the passage of the Compromise of 1850. While in many Southern states this legislation was viewed as an acceptable compromise that eased, at least temporarily, the growing secession movement, South Carolina maintained its radical position. Indeed, the debate within Simms's state focused primarily on when and how—not whether—secession should take place. Simms himself was a strong supporter of the so-called cooperationists, who urged South Carolina to seek support from other states before seceding. Nevertheless, Simms's commitment to secession never wavered. As early as January 1850 he wrote to Nathaniel Beverley Tucker that secession was a "now inevitable necessity," and he denounced any compromises as "originat[ing] in cowardice and a mean spirit of evasion on the part of the South,—and in a spirit of fraud and deliberately purposed wrong on that of the North." By August of the same year, Simms declared in another letter to Tucker that it "must be clear enough to every Southron & man of sense, that there is no living with a people so utterly hostile & reckless as those of the North." Simms's commitment to secession and sense of outrage only increased as he watched other southern states "surrender" to what he and many other South Carolinians called the Submissionists. However distraught over the rise of union sentiments in Georgia and Virginia in particular, Simms continued to urge patience, and he insisted that without a strong Southern alliance, secession was doomed. As he told Tucker in March 1851, "My fear is that premature action of S. C. will retard the event & discourage the proper action when the moment really arrives."[5]

Simms expressed similar views as editor of the politically oriented *Southern Quarterly Review* from 1849 until 1854. He regularly published pieces supporting slavery, state's rights, Southern economic development, and Southern history. As Jon L. Wakelyn has described, Simms emphasized "the concept of a cooperating South, searching for common bonds of political relations and needs."[6] Much of these same political themes about secession and Southern unity emerge as well within *The Sword and the Distaff*, itself composed in 1851 and 1852 in the aftermath of the compromise. Indeed, through the novel's two primary metaphors—marriage (or union) and war (or independence)—Simms explored southern political issues of secession, submission, and cooperation. Simms's experimentation with the by-then familiar structure of the marriage plot is particularly relevant here. In choosing to leave all his major characters unmarried at the novel's closing, Simms was able to suggest both the need for Southern independence from the North and, simultaneously, his ideal of Southern cooperation.

In his presentation of Sergeant Millhouse's view of courting, Simms examines the violent nature of forced unions—here implicitly connected with the federal government's insistence on a compromise that was, at least in the case of South Carolina, unwanted. Indeed, Millhouse's comparison of courting to "storming an inimy's batteries" and his insistence that Porgy show the widow that he is "determined to conquer" parallel Simms's political concerns about the federal government's threat of force if South Carolina were to secede—were to refuse, in other words, a union with the North.[7] In both the personal and political contexts, union is presented as something violently imposed. Though the narrator and Simms clearly reject Millhouse's utilitarian notion of love and marriage, his image of courting as an act of aggression is itself enhanced by Porgy's own dress as he first visits the widow Eveleigh. With nothing but tattered clothes that no longer fit him, Porgy is forced to wear his military uniform, complete with sword and pistols. Although Simms's primary aim here is humor, Porgy's appearance suggests, as do Millhouse's comments, the possibility of aggressively pursued unions.

Ironically, although Millhouse imagines Porgy as the conqueror, Simms's portrayal of Porgy's visit to the widow casts Porgy, not the widow, as particularly vulnerable. With his clothes so tight and so threadbare that he can hardly move for fear he will, as Tom says, "bu'st dem breeches" (354), Porgy's physical appearance highlights his precarious economic position. Significantly, Porgy's financial weaknesses emerge as a primary focus of this meeting. Throughout chapter 48 ("Porgy Finds a Banker"), in fact, the two assume roles opposite to those in which Millhouse imagined them. Hardly the victim of a conqueror, Mrs. Eveleigh— whom Porgy describes as having "the soul of a man" (372)—becomes the "banker," controlling Porgy's fate and establishing their entire financial arrangement. Thus, while Millhouse envisions the widow as Porgy's victim, Simms highlights the risk of forced unions by portraying the supposed conqueror as victim as well.

If Millhouse's speeches and Porgy's actions suggest that courting, like national political compromises, can be acts of violent aggression, Porgy's own indecision about which widow to marry suggests another political issue in South Carolina's political climate of the early 1850s—namely the idea that national union involves considerable risk of personal liberty. As in the ever-popular Southern rhetoric about the importance of protecting its "peculiar" traditions and institutions from the threat of Northern aggression—rhetoric in which Simms frequently engaged—Porgy risks losing his identity in any union, regardless of whom he marries.[8] When considering a union with Mrs. Eveleigh, Porgy fears a "feeling of constraint": "There was no doubt, indeed, that the superior social position of Mrs. Eveleigh, her equal grace and dignity of bearing, the calm, natural manner with which she met his approaches, all joined, in some degree, to restrain our hero—to lessen, somewhat, his own ease; to make him less assured on the subject of his own dignity" (394). To emphasize the risk to Porgy, Simms portrays the features with which Porgy has been most identified as the most threatened by a potential marriage with Mrs. Eveleigh. Indeed, the narrator describes Porgy as feeling that he must watch "the *brusquerie* of his army habits" and "check his involuntary *escapades*" and even avoid swearing and smoking—all features of Porgy's character well established by this point in the novel (394).

Even though Porgy is more comfortable in her presence, Porgy's concern about marrying Mrs. Griffin suggests a similar loss of individual identity. As he explains to himself, "She is not wise; not learned; is really very ignorant; has no manners, no eloquence; is simply humble and adhesive; . . . she has still a face of exquisite sweetness, but she is no associate for me;—she has no resources, no thoughts, no information; has seen nothing, knows nothing!" (392–93). Though Porgy's use of the term *resources* makes clear that his hesitation is prompted at least partly by Mrs. Griffin's lack of wealth, his comments about her intellectual inferiority also suggest that an aspect of his personality would be lost if he were to marry her. By this point in the novel, Porgy has certainly shown himself to be someone with a penchant for witty dialogue and philosophical discussions. To lose them would represent at least as much of a loss of self as if he were required to abide by Mrs. Eveleigh's standard of proper behavior.

While Millhouse's and Porgy's views of courting allow Simms to suggest the threat of forced unions, Simms inversely implies the glories of independence in Mrs. Eveleigh's view of marriage. Like South Carolina's political leaders, who rejected advice from so-called submissionists that they accept a compromise with abolitionists, Mrs. Eveleigh voices South Carolina's pride in independence. Once again, the metaphor used to suggest that independence is marriage. When her son begins to meddle in her personal affairs, she angrily responds, "I will submit to no dictation. I shall be the mistress of my own thoughts, feelings, and sympathies, as far as it lies in my power to be so. I shall account to you in no respect, unless I am pleased and prefer to do so. . . . If it should seem to me wise, and right, and grateful to take another husband, it shall be my own will that I shall consult in the matter" (435). Here again, although Simms makes no direct political statements, the language itself heightens the political implications. Mrs. Eveleigh's refusal to capitulate to her son— to "submit"—and her insistence that her decisions will be based on what she decides is "wise, and right" parallel South Carolina's, and more specifically Simms's, response to the political compromises of the early 1850s. Indeed, Simms believed that submission and compromise were unacceptable precisely because he insisted on the wisdom and morality of slavery. As he told John Pendleton Kennedy, "We believe also that Negro Slavery is one of the greatest of moral goods & blessings, and that slavery in all ages has been found the greatest and most admirable agent of Civilization."[9]

In the context of Southern politics in the early 1850s, calls for independence inevitably carried overtones of resistance and even of war. Significantly, Simms integrated this military context into his novel's endorsements of independence. Mrs. Eveleigh is repeatedly characterized as willing and able to fight for her rights and her independence. The novel opens, of course, as the "brave widow" appeals to Colonel Moncrieff for the restoration of her "property," and this exchange is presented as a battle in which she has a distinct advantage (38–39). While the colonel fails to realize that he is engaged in battle because he assumes the widow will abide by genteel traditions, Mrs. Eveleigh acts the part of the warrior. She turns to Moncrieff only after she has secured the slaves herself, and she responds to his lax security by stealing the document from his desk. As if to highlight even further the association of the widow with a willingness to fight for her rights, Simms describes her love of weapons—the pistols, swords, and sabers in Moncrieff's office—and he portrays her as someone not content to admire weapons from afar. When she sees a Turkish scimitar, she waves the "bright steel upward, with a somewhat gladiatorial air" (47). This image of the widow as an independence-loving gladiator is, moreover, reinforced in the ways other characters in the novel describe her. M'Kewn, the novel's most notorious fighter himself, for example, insists, "She has the eye of a hawk! She would fight too! Sword or pistols, five paces even, and never wink an eye! She should have been a man!" (413).

This association of independence with a willingness to fight is developed even more fully within the characterization of Porgy.[10] As a leader among Revolutionary War forces, Porgy is clearly identified as someone willing to fight for independence. That characterization is reinforced during the elaborate interchange with the sheriff. Though Simms again uses humor within these scenes, they have a political implication as well. Specifically, the sheriff's reliance on the "decrees, and judgments" of the law as a means of confiscating Porgy's plantation—itself a representation of Southern culture—parallels what many South Carolina leaders saw as the North's aggressive prohibition of their rights and traditions (426). Like the state's political leaders, Porgy remains committed to his position, unwilling to compromise. Quite the contrary, he understands that "Life, after all, is a constant warfare," and he stands willing to resist his enemies: "I know them! I defy them!" (455).

Porgy's defense of his own illegal behaviors helps explain how the metaphors of war and marriage work together in the novel to suggest its political reading. Specifically, Porgy is able to fight as aggressively as he does precisely because he is single. As he explains, "I can die without a grunt to-morrow. I have neither wife, nor child, nor mother, nor sister, to deplore my fate, or to profit by my departure" (455). In this way, personal ties are seen as restricting one's ability to resist oppression. The validation of independence, in other words, can only be achieved by resisting the expected conclusion of the marriage plot.

Though marriage is presented as anithetical to independence, the novel does suggest that other ties—not governed by the law—provide appropriate grounds for alliances. In chapter 48, for instance, in which Millhouse wants Porgy to "conquer" Mrs. Eveleigh, Porgy and the widow themselves decide upon other alliances. At first, Mrs. Eveleigh suggests that their financial arrangement be a "business transaction simply" (370), but the generous terms of her offer quickly reveal her more altruistic motives. For his part, Porgy, too, demonstrates a commitment to an alliance stronger than any legal and business code, for he willingly trusts her "with all [his] property, without any security." As Porgy explains, they have rejected an adversarial relationship in favor of one bound by sympathy: "The pleasurable feeling of sweet faith and confidence, and generous unreserve, and liberal sympathy, which you have this day shown me, is more grateful to me than any amount of wealth or money. I now know where I can confide. I feel, too, that there is one, at least, who can confide in me. We do not watch each other as victims, or as birds of prey; seeking to devour, fearing to be devoured. Madam, if you will permit me, I will be your friend—your friend" (372–73). Porgy's language here is instructive, for in contrasting bonds of "sweet faith and confidence" with those in which two parties "watch each other as victims," Porgy implies that some bonds are destructive and that he favors loose bonds of friendship. Mrs. Eveleigh confirms their commitment to bonds of sympathy rather than legally-binding contracts when she later declines his marriage proposal: "My dear captain, why is it that men and women can not maintain an intercourse, as friends, without seeking any other relation. Is it not astonishing that such a thing should seem impossible to everybody? Now, why should not you and I be true friends, loving friends, trusting each other with the utmost confidence, coming and going when we please—welcomed when we come, regretted when we have to depart—and never perilling the intimacy of friendship by the fetters of matrimony." Thus, though she offers the captain her hand, she does so as a pledge of "good faith" and "friendship," preferring that there be "never a word more of marriage" (531–32).

Simms's preference for loose bonds of sympathy rather than legally imposed ties certainly contradicts the novel's pervasive defense of slavery. Ironically, however, Simms uses the idea of sympathetic bonds to support his view of slavery. In his portrayal of Tom and Porgy as mutually devoted to each other, for example, Simms tries to portray slavery as a desired—rather than forced—relationship upon the slave. The most elaborate depiction of this vision of slavery is, of course, the scene in which Tom refuses Porgy's offer of freedom: "'No! No! maussa,' he cried, with a sly shake of the head, 'I kain't t'ink ob letting you off dis way. Ef *I* doesn't b'long to *you, you* b'long to *me!* You hab for keep dis nigger long as he lib; and him for keep you. You hab for fin' he dinner, and Tom hab for cook 'em. . . . I no guine to be free no way you kin fix it; so, maussa, don't you bodder me wid dis nonsense t'ing 'bout free paper any more. I's well off whar' I is I tell you'" (528). However preposterous, Tom's insistence that he is not owned but that the two men belong to each other and his image of their shared meals together—their supposedly mutual nurturing—demonstrates Simms's willingness to extend his notion of sympathetic bonds even to a system as coercive as slavery. Indeed, given Simms's support of slavery and his rejection of enforced legal ties, such an extension was virtually inevitable.[11]

These images within the characterizations of Porgy, Mrs. Eveleigh, and Tom of alliances based on independence and sympathy rather than legally binding unions matched Simms's own view of proper political relationships. In a letter to John Pendleton Kennedy in May 1851, Simms bemoaned the fact that abolitionists had destroyed "the only bond (that of sympathy) by which the people of our separate sections were ever truly held together. Common cause, common necessities, and the belief in a common feeling—these were the true articles of confederation."[12]

In the same way that it proved the solution to the captain's and the widow's personal situations, common "sympathy" represented, for Simms, an acceptable solution to the nation's political crisis. If the North and South could, like the captain and the widow, be "unfettered" by legal matrimony, each section could renew those connections that were mutually beneficial (such as trade, perhaps). With "common" causes the only bond, the nation would not have to agree on issues like slavery, which for many Southerners and abolitionists alike could not be negotiated. Thus, while distancing himself from marriage plots, which suggest a united position, Simms favored alliances depicted as nonbinding friendships, precisely because the latter allowed for considerably more dissent. For Simms and for many other white Southerners in the antebellum period, this right to dissent—the right to maintain traditions and beliefs considered untenable in other parts of the nation—remained absolutely essential.

In addition to suggesting Simms's vision of an appropriate relationship between the North and South, this focus on bonds of sympathy, commonality, but independence relates as well to his ideal of Southern unity. Throughout his editorial career, Simms urged Southern states to recognize what he described in this letter as "common cause" and "common necessities." Significantly, the image of the South with which he ends *The Sword and the Distaff* features both commonality and independence. Certainly, the two adjoining plantations—the widow's estate and Porgy's own Glen-Eberly—match the image of Porgy's and Mrs. Eveleigh's relationship. People visit frequently between the two plantations, they offer neighborly aid, but they remain independent from each other, as is highlighted by Porgy's paying off his debt to Mrs. Eveleigh. Thus, although Simms does not use the term here, the two plantations are an ideal image of Southern cooperation.

The balance between commonalities and independence is also explored in the novel's final scene, as Porgy accepts his "defeat" in finding a wife. Here, the primary metaphor is again marriage, with a special emphasis on gender differences. As Porgy tells his "companions" that he had "thought of deserting" them by "taking a wife," he apologizes: "I sometimes meditated bringing in upon you a fearful influence, which might have lessened your happiness, and destroyed the harmony which prevails among us." Continuing, he asserts his allegiance to his "comrades": "I shall live for you only. You could not well do without me; I will not suffer myself to do without you. You shall be mine always—I shall be yours. To woman, except as friend or companion, I say depart! I renounce ye! . . . For your sakes, dear comrades, there shall be no mistress, while I live, at Glen-Eberley" (536–37). Again, as with so many of

Simms's portraits of domestic life, Porgy's image here of a united, harmonious group carries strong political connotations. Certainly, in imagining this group as an idyllic bond that includes both Porgy and Tom, Simms reveals his belief that slavery was a beneficent system, agreeable to slave and plantation owner alike. Less obviously, however, this image of domestic bliss around the "cheerful fires . . . blazing on the hearth" also suggests Simms's interest in southern unity against northern oppression. Here, Porgy rejects the idea of submitting to a "fearful influence" originating outside his own group, and he vows loyalty to what he imagines to be a like-minded group. Such, indeed, was precisely Simms's vision of Southern cooperation.

These political implications within the novel were themselves reinforced by the conditions under which the novel was initially published. Although the *Southern Literary Gazette* was by no means as political as Simms's own *Southern Quarterly Review,* the *Gazette* did not ignore the political crisis of the early 1850s, and during the serialization of *The Sword and the Distaff,* numerous pieces expressed political ideas similar to those in Simms's novel. For example, just as Simms used a historical setting— post–Revolutionary War South Carolina—to comment on contemporary issues, an essay, "The Progress of Fanaticism," published in the *Gazette* on 21 August 1852, made explicit connections between Europe's early religious persecutions and northern abolitionists, whom the writer attacked for their "indignant ravings." Continuing, the writer offered this description of the "Emancipationists": "Having wilfully blinded themselves to Truth and Reason, and systematically smothered the last spark of common judgement and experience, they conduct their mad Crusade against the extension or existence of Institutions, which their desperate folly cannot at once destroy, but which it is calculated to convulse in bitterness and blood." Recalling the bloody result of Europe's Crusades, the writer pointedly asked, "Have we any reason to suppose that the fanaticisms of modern days, will in their results be less disastrous than those that have preceded them?" (79–80).

Though the political implications are less explicit, another series of essays, entitled "The Huguenot Refugees," which also appeared in the *Gazette* during the serialization of *The Sword and the Distaff,* suggests connections between early European history and the U.S. political crisis of the early 1850s. The first installment of "The Huguenot Refugees" explored the religious group's persecution in fifteenth-century France. Significantly, the writer—identified only as a "descendant of the Huguenots"—opened with a vision of civil war: "France is, in truth, a nation of revolutions, of civil commotions, of kindred strifes, and barbarous massacres. No other civilized nation has the pages of its history so stained with the blood of its citizens, shed by the hands of brothers, as this. No other has so cruelly pierced its own bosom with the sword" (*Southern Literary Gazette*, 22 May 1852, 241). The series of essays continued to trace the nature of the massacres, continued persecution, and the resulting immigration of the Huguenots to South Carolina.

While it is obviously inaccurate to read this series in the context of the Civil War—still at this point, a decade away—these essays unquestionably raise many of the political issues at the center of North-South political divisions. Certainly, the image of the Huguenot debate as a civil war parallels Simms's—and much of the South's—view of the federal government as willing to harm its own people because of a fanatic desire to rid the nation of slavery. Consider, for instance, this description of Francis I, offered in the second chapter of "The Huguenot Refugees": "[He] declared, in the spirit of impassioned bigotry and fanaticism—if his very arm were corrupted with a taint of heresy, he would tear it from his body; and if his own children were found guilty of such execrable blasphemy, he would at once yield them up as an acceptable sacrifice to God." The nature of the fanaticism also parallels escalating tensions between the North and South in 1850s politics. Certainly, one of the major themes of "The Huguenot Refugees" was the tension between tolerance for difference and national unity. Here, not unlike the Southern depiction of the North, the French government is portrayed as pursuing a "policy, to extirpate the Huguenot heresy, and to establish unity of religion in the nation." As in many Southern portrayals, national unity is the result of a despotic government, a "bigoted and tyrannical monarch," that oppressed its own "unoffending and industrious subjects" and refused to tolerate any political and cultural differences (*Southern Literary Gazette*, 29 May 1852, 253). Significantly, the author repeatedly emphasized political rather than theological differences, explaining that while the Huguenots maintained a presbyterial form of government, French officials insisted upon episcopal organization. At times, the author of "The Huguenot Refugees" used even the rhetoric of the antebellum debate about slavery, repeatedly describing the Huguenots' independent organization, for instance, as "peculiar." Though the author never made the connection explicit, the Huguenots' tenacious insistence on the value of their "peculiar worship" and "peculiar organization" certainly parallels the South's own refusal to abandon its own "peculiar institution" (*Southern Literary Gazette*, 3 July 1852, 317–19).

Of all the political contexts of the *Gazette* during the serialization of

The Sword and the Distaff, nothing was more pervasive than Harriet Beecher Stowe's *Uncle Tom's Cabin,* which was still being serialized in the *National Era* during part of the initial publication of Simms's *The Sword and the Distaff.*[13] Indeed, the numerous references to Stowe's novel during the serialization of *The Sword and the Distaff* (especially during the novel's second half) highlight the political implications of Simms's novel. One editorial, for example, announced a new volume "in favour of the policy and morality of 'the peculiar institution'" and denounced "our Northern antagonists," who were "entrenching themselves in and behind 'Uncle Tom's Cabin,' and hurling pretty fictions at our cause." A week later the editors described the "*broad, beaming, happy, universal outgushing of contentment*" at a racially integrated local church service and expressed a desire to have a daguerreotype of the scene issued as a frontispiece of Stowe's novel. Another announcement in the same issue sarcastically suggested that Stowe use her "extraordinary profits" to "buy up a whole Colony of Negroes for Liberia" (*Southern Literary Gazette,* 17 July 1852, 20; 24 July 1852, 32, 34). Similarly, the magazine included repeated advertisements for and a review of Mary Eastman's *Aunt Phillis' Cabin: Or, Southern Life as It Is.* Further suggesting their confidence that Stowe's novel was very much on their own readers' minds, in October the *Gazette*'s editors abandoned their usual practice of opening the magazine with "lighter literature" to reprint John R. Thompson's review of *Uncle Tom's Cabin,* originally published in the *Southern Literary Messenger.* As the *Gazette* editors themselves declared, the review would be "*more* interesting to the majority of readers, at the present time, than the most brilliant tale we could furnish" (23 Oct. 1852, 181). This long review, which included attacks on Stowe's personal character, was issued in three installments in the *Gazette*—again, all during the serialization of *The Sword and the Distaff.*

It is impossible to do anything but speculate about whether these reminders about northern "fanaticism," especially Stowe's novel, had any influence on the first readers of *The Sword and the Distaff.* But the context in which the novel first appeared does suggest another possible interpretation for Simms's oft-quoted remark that the novel was "probably as good an answer to Mrs. Stowe as has been published."[14] Though scholars have long argued about whether Simms's comment accurately describes the novel, the debate has centered on whether or not Simms's novel was written in response to *Uncle Tom's Cabin.*[15] The political themes of the novel and its serial publication suggest, however, that *The Sword and the Distaff* may have been an "answer" to Stowe not because one was written as a reaction to the other but because both were written in response to the

Compromise of 1850. Such an interpretation allows for a much richer political reading of the novel because it highlights the fact that for many white Southerners the debate in the early 1850s was not simply about whether slavery was moral but rather about issues of Southern cooperationism, secession, and resistance to northern aggression and fanaticism. If read in the context of both these complex political issues and the explicit and implicit references to those issues within the *Southern Literary Gazette, The Sword and the Distaff* is an answer to *Uncle Tom's Cabin,* but it is not simply a "propagandistic device" for slavery.[16] Indeed, in addition to presenting slavery as moral and beneficent, the novel explores questions of states' rights and Southern identity.

Though it is beyond the scope of this essay to offer an extended comparison of *The Sword and the Distaff* and *Uncle Tom's Cabin,* a brief exploration of how these novels address the issue of national union can suggest their different political perspectives. As I have shown, Simms's decision not to have any of his major characters marry even while devoting considerable attention to courting suggests his political commitment to the principle of sectional independence rather than national union. Significantly, Stowe's novel argues the opposite political point with somewhat similar plot devices. While Simms's major characters favor friendships rather than family ties, Stowe's novel reveals a strong impulse toward building and strengthening family alliances. No doubt, Tom's family is shattered by his sale and subsequent death, and numerous other families within the novel are threatened and devastated by slavery. But Stowe's vision of a moral, unified nation—one that has abolished slavery—is depicted as beginning with a strong, moral family. This impulse toward unity and family building rather than independence is best demonstrated by the elaborate plot manipulations at the end of the novel, in which, for example, Cassy is revealed as Eliza's mother and Madame de Thoux as George Harris's brother. These images of family ties parallel her presentation in the final chapter of a unified nation—composed of both North and South—ready to repent and rectify the nation's sin.

As I have suggested throughout my reading of *The Sword and the Distaff,* Simms did not endorse this vision of a unified nation. Though he certainly advocated cooperation among Southerners, his novel balances that trait with independence. This balance between cooperation and independence is itself suggested by the novel's original title. Not content to be solely a peacemaker in the post-Compromise crisis, Simms sought to balance images of peace—the distaff—with those of outright, even armed, resistance, in this case, the sword. The difference between these two novelists in this regard can be seen in Simms's portrayal of Mrs. Eveleigh. Unlike Stowe's strongly maternal women, who consistently fight to maintain family unity, Mrs. Eveleigh is repeatedly presented as independent, a wealthy widow who refuses marriage and who risks her relationship with her son to defend her individual choices and rights.

Simms's serial publication of *The Sword and the Distaff* strongly enhanced his political perspective. By publishing the novel about southern history in a southern periodical, Simms encouraged his audience to identify themselves as citizens first and foremost of the South. Inevitably, such identification yielded political implications as well, for even magazines as literary as the *Southern Literary Gazette* carried strong political overtones in the aftermath of the Compromise of 1850. Indeed, the very act of endorsing southern identity and unity was itself political, as Simms, the longtime southern editor, well knew. The political associations of serial publication in a southern periodical were not, however, a burden for the novelist. Quite the contrary, he used the opportunity to explore questions of southern unity and independence—issues of great personal concern to him. Though a political resolution to the post-Compromise crisis proved far more illusive, Simms found a literary solution in his dramatic re-visioning of the marriage plot. By resisting the movement of the marriage plot toward concluding unions and by highlighting, instead, the importance of personal autonomy, Simms found the balance between independence and cooperation for which he sought.

NOTES

I am grateful to the University of Missouri Research Board for its support of this project.

1. "Caloya" was published in *Magnolia: or Southern Monthly* in 1841; "The Moral Character of Hamlet" and "The Hermytte of Drowsiehedde" both appeared in *Orion* in 1844; "The Maroon: A Legend of the Caribbees" was published in the *New York Illustrated Magazine of Literature and Art* in 1847 and then again in the *Southern Literary Gazette* in 1850; and "Maize in Milk: A Christmas Story of the South" first appeared in *Godey's Lady's Book* in 1847. Simms's series of essays titled "The Home Tourist," which eventually became *Father Abbot*, was published serially in the *Charleston Mercury* in 1849. Simms's dramas, *Norman Maurice* and *Michael Bonham*, first appeared in the *Southern Literary Messenger* in 1851 and 1852, respectively. "Marie de Berniere: A Tale of the Crescent City" was published in *Arthur's Home Gazette* in 1852.

2. Although he often complained of the difficulties of managing periodicals, Simms's editorships included the *Album* (1825–26), the *Southern Literary Gazette*

(1828–29), the *Charleston City Gazette* (1830–32), the *Magnolia: or Southern Appalachian* (1842–43), the *Southern and Western Monthly Magazine and Review* (1845), the *Southern Quarterly Review* (1849–54), and the *Columbia Phoenix* (1865). In 1865–66 Simms also served as associate editor of the *Charleston Daily South Carolinian.*

3. For a brief overview of the magazine and the publishing house, see Rayburn S. Moore, "*The Southern Literary Gazette,*" in *American Literary Magazines: The Eighteenth and Nineteenth Centuries,* ed. Edward E. Chielens (New York: Greenwood, 1986), 380–85.

4. Simms had initially planned *The Sword and the Distaff* as a novelette for Philadelphia's *Arthur's Home Gazette,* and in September 1851 he offered what he described as a half finished novel to another Philadelphia book publisher. Simms soon altered his plans, for the *Gazette* announced the novel's serialization in December 1851, with publication beginning in February. Simms did not complete the novel until August 1852. On the composition of the novel, see John Caldwell Guilds, *Simms: A Literary Life* (Fayetteville: Univ. of Arkansas Press, 1992), 206.

5. *The Letters of William Gilmore Simms,* ed. Mary C. Simms Oliphant, Alfred Taylor Odell, and T. C. Duncan Eaves, 5 vols. (Columbia: Univ. of South Carolina Press, 1952–56), 3:8, 54, 76, 99.

6. Jon L. Wakelyn, *The Politics of a Literary Man: William Gilmore Simms* (Westport, Conn.: Greenwood, 1973), 202. For a brief overview of the *Southern Quarterly Review,* see Janice L. Edens, "*The Southern Quarterly Review,*" in *American Literary Magazines,* 399–404.

7. See William Gilmore Simms, *Woodcraft; or Hawks about the Dovecote,* ed. Charles S. Watson (Albany, N.Y.: New College and Univ. Press, 1983), 321. Because the revised version of *The Sword and the Distaff* (under the title *Woodcraft*) is far more accessible to today's readers, all references will be to this version and will be cited within the text.

8. Simms's defense of slavery is pervasive in his published and private writings. One of his most well-known discussions is his 1837 essay "Miss Martineau on Slavery," originally published in the *Southern Literary Messenger,* later reissued in pamphlet form, and then revised as "The Morals of Slavery" and published in *The Pro-Slavery Argument* (1852).

9. *Letters,* 3:174.

10. On Porgy's characterization as a military man, see Mary Ann Wimsatt, *The Major Fiction of William Gilmore Simms: Cultural Traditions and Literary Form* (Baton Rouge and London: Louisiana State Univ. Press, 1989), 166–72.

11. For a discussion of how proslavery arguments, including Simms's, portrayed slavery as a charitable system arising from the mutual interests and needs of all parties, see Drew Gilpin Faust, *A Sacred Circle: The Dilemma of the Intellectual in the Old South, 1840–1860* (Baltimore: Johns Hopkins Univ. Press, 1977), 112–31.

12. *Letters,* 3:122–23.

13. On the serial publication of Stowe's novel, see Susan Belasco Smith's "Serialization and the Nature of *Uncle Tom's Cabin*" in this volume.

14. *Letters*, 3:222.

15. See Joseph V. Ridgely, "*Woodcraft*: Simms's First Answer to *Uncle Tom's Cabin*," *American Literature* 31 (1960): 421–33; Hugh W. Hetherington, *Cavalier of Old South Carolina: William Gilmore Simms's Captain Porgy* (Chapel Hill: Univ. of North Carolina Press, 1966), 38–50; Charles S. Watson, "Simms's Answer to *Uncle Tom's Cabin:* Criticism of the South in *Woodcraft*," *Southern Literary Journal* 9 (1976): 78–90; James B. Meriwether, "The Theme of Freedom in Simms's *Woodcraft*," in *"Long Years of Neglect": The Work and Reputation of William Gilmore Simms*, ed. John Caldwell Guilds (Fayetteville: Univ. of Arkansas Press, 1988), 29–30; Guilds, *Simms: A Literary Life*, 208; and Charles S. Watson, *From Nationalism to Secessionism: The Changing Fiction of William Gilmore Simms* (Westport, Conn.: Greenwood, 1993) 94–104. In addition to exploring Simms's response to Stowe's *Uncle Tom's Cabin*, Watson's *From Nationalism to Secessionism* reads the novel in the context of the Compromise of 1850, especially the Fugitive Slave Act.

16. Guilds, *Simms: A Literary Life*, 208. Guilds opposes efforts to read *The Sword and the Distaff* as a response to *Uncle Tom's Cabin* because he views such interpretations as denying the literary merits of Simms's novel.

9

"DON'T TELL! THEY'D ADVERTISE"
EMILY DICKINSON IN
THE *ROUND TABLE*

ROBERT J. SCHOLNICK

•

EMILY Dickinson is not a writer one would expect to see included in a collection entitled "Periodical Literature in Nineteenth-Century America." This private, fiercely independent, and reclusive writer refused to participate in the literary marketplace. Unlike other significant poets from the nineteenth century, she did not print her work in periodicals and books. She wrote out her poems in her idiosyncratic system of punctuation and then filed them neatly away in bound fascicles.[1] That is not to say that she wrote in isolation; she sent at least a third of her approximately 1,775 poems in letters to a large circle of friends.[2] To one of her regular correspondents, the prominent Boston critic Thomas Wentworth Higginson, she wrote on 7 June 1862, "I smile when you suggest that I delay 'to publish'—that being foreign to my thought, as Firmament to Fin."[3] Only some ten poems by Dickinson appeared in print during her lifetime, and even with that handful, we have no documentary evidence that Dickinson initiated publication.

Of these ten poems, nine appeared first in newspapers, including the *Springfield Republican,* the *Brooklyn Daily Union,* and *Drum Beat,* a paper published during the Civil War to raise money for the U.S. Sanitary Commission.[4] She allowed her friend Helen Hunt Jackson, who repeatedly urged her to publish, to submit "Success is Counted Sweetest" for inclusion in an anonymous collection, *A Masque of Poets,* published by Roberts Brothers in 1878. Only one poem, "Some keep the Sabbath going to Church," appeared first in a magazine. On 12 March 1864 a New York weekly, the *Round Table* (1863–69), included the poem under the title "My Sabbath." A wide-ranging journal of opinion and analysis, the *Round Table* was just then mounting an attack on the corrupting conditions of publishing and literary reviewing. To examine Dickinson's appearance in the *Round Table* is both to see her relationship to the literary market-place in a new light and to understand the role of this pioneering weekly in helping to create a space in American culture in which such a critical journal could flourish.

In the context of the contemporary marketplace, Dickinson is an example of what William Charvat has described as the private poet: "The verse of both private and the public poet originates from the unique privacies of the poet as a person. The private poet is concerned not only to preserve that uniqueness but to intensify it through the writing of verse—even at the cost of being rejected for unintelligibility. But the public poet progressively subordinates or submerges his uniqueness. Representativeness *in his time,* then, is the differentiating quality of the public poet, and it is the quality that makes the fundamental difference between his verse and that of the private poet."[5] Because Dickinson did not need the financial returns of publication, there was little incentive for her to enter a commercial marketplace that threatened her integrity. A fundamental concern for the young literary critics who rallied to the *Round Table* was exploring the relation between popularity and intrinsic literary value, between reputation in one's time and lasting fame. As Dickinson wrote to Higginson, "If fame belonged to me, I could not escape her—if she did not, the longest day would pass me on the chase—and the approbation of my Dog, would forsake me—then—My Barefoot-Rank is better."[6]

I

TWO cousins, Charles Humphreys Sweetser (1841–71) and Henry Edward Sweetser (1837–70), founded the *Round Table* in New York in December 1863. An orphan, Charles Sweetser moved to Amherst in 1847 to be raised by his uncle and aunt, the Luke Sweetsers, friends and neighbors of Emily Dickinson. After his graduation from Amherst College in 1862, where he was class poet, he served an internship on the *Springfield Daily Republican* before coming to New York. Henry Sweetser, after graduating from Yale in 1858, became a journalist, working on the *New York Times* and then the *New York World*. His mother was Emily Dickinson's aunt, Catherine, her father's sister; his father, Joseph H. Sweetser, was a successful New York merchant. Although there is no evidence about exactly how "My Sabbath" came to the *Round Table,* without these family connections the poem clearly would not have appeared in the magazine. Yet, as we will see, the Sweetsers' weekly articulated many of the reservations about the literary marketplace that we find in Dickinson's poetry, and in criticizing the moralism, sentimentality, and deadening metrical conventions of American poetry, it called for new departures.

Established in the midst of the Civil War—its first issue appeared on 19 December 1863—the *Round Table* from the outset faced the most uncertain prospects. In fact, a sharp increase in costs during the first half of 1864 forced the Sweetsers to suspend publication after the 23 July 1864 issue. Remarkably, on 9 September 1865 the cousins were able to revive the *Round Table*. Less than a year later, in April 1866, Henry Sweetser withdrew, and Charles left the following November to found the *Evening Gazette*.[7] Their places were taken by Dorsey Gardner and then Henry Sedley, who from December 1868 through the magazine's final number, 3 July 1869, had sole responsibility. During the magazine's last year, Sedley moved the *Round Table* sharply to the right.[8]

Modeled after England's *Saturday Review*, the Sweetsers' weekly proudly proclaimed its independence from political, ideological, or economic interests. Taking all of American life, including politics, society, religion, finance, art, and literature, as its subject matter, the *Round Table* introduced a new vision of periodical literature in America. Not least among its subjects was the industry in which it was a small, vulnerable participant: publishing.

By 1866 the Sweetsers had come to realize that their magazine could never support itself with subscription revenues alone: "It is perhaps an unpleasant fact, but nevertheless one that cannot be blinked, that journals of the character of the *Round Table* are everywhere dependent upon their advertising patrons for support. . . . It is notorious with [the best English weeklies] that their circulation is but a small item of their support. But the class of people to which they appeal makes them exceedingly valuable for advertisers, and hence they go forth every week full freighted with advertisements." This statement served to justify the editors' decision "to devote the first and last pages . . . to advertisements." They had to admit that the quality of the publication—the amount of "reading matter" that could be included—directly depended on the amount of advertising that could be booked. Conceding that "American readers, who do not thoroughly understand the science and necessity of advertising, are apt to be repelled by advertising on the covers of their periodicals," they asked their readers to recognize that "there can never be well sustained weeklies in our midst without resort to our plan" (2 June 1866, 344).

Ironically, the Sweetsers had begun life by satirizing excessive advertising claims by publishers and by forthrightly attacking the larger system in which periodicals were all too willing to puff a publisher's products in return for advertising dollars. For instance, on 30 January 1864 the *Round Table* asked "Is Newspaper Influence Marketable?" The answer was clear: "The fact is notorious that our public journals do not hold their opinions, to a greater or less extent, subject to business patronage. The whole practice of newspaper puffery is in fact another name for a sale of newspaper influence. A quack doctor wants a 'first-rate' notice of his nostrum; an inventor of his patent; a manager of his new play; a publisher of his last novel; it is secured to all of them by giving a few dollars—in advertising" (99). Such practices made impossible that on which the magazine had staked its existence: an unbiased, critical discussion of public policy and ideas. The Sweetsers argued that this subversion of critical integrity was the more serious because it took place during a war that daily tested the moral fabric of the republic.

In "I'm nobody," poem 288, Dickinson anticipates just such a criticism of the publishing industry. After beginning by thankfully acknowledging her own anonymity—"I'm nobody"—the speaker advises other similarly anonymous nobodies not to blow their covers: "Don't tell," she warns. If the instruments of fame and public recognition should find "a pair of us," then "they'd advertise—you know!" The resulting fate would be

> dreary—to be—Somebody!
> How public—like a Frog—
> To tell one's name—the livelong June—
> To an admiring Bog![9]

The penalty for publication went far beyond the late twentieth century's allotted fifteen minutes of fame to include at least a month of making meaningless sounds to other self-admiring nobodies.

When Dickinson wrote the poem in 1861, advertising had long since become an inescapable part of periodical publishing. Such prominent periodicals as *Harper's Magazine* (1850), *Putnam's* (1853), *Appleton's Journal* (1869), and *Scribner's Monthly* (1870) had been—or shortly would be—established by publishers to advertise the house, not least by keeping the firm's name before the public. The pioneers in this practice were the Harpers, who established their monthly as a "tender to our business."[10] A main purpose of *Harper's* would be to interest readers in the British fiction that it serialized in the magazine and later brought out in separate volumes. Among the many subscribers was Lavinia Dickinson, Emily's sister, who considered the arrival of the magazine each month important enough to note in her diary, as on 21 January 1851: "Received my usual magazine."[11] Ezra Greenspan has summarized the firm's goals: "Despite their claims of serving the general public with the magazine, the Harpers were clearly also serving themselves, using the magazine as a convenient forum for printing serials which could later be profitably reprinted by the house as books, for giving additional publishing opportunities to Harper's authors as well as for enticing other writers into the house, and for publicizing the merits of the works and achievements of the house. The profitability of the magazine and its many-sided utility to the house inspired numerous other American publishers to go a similar route."[12]

Their literary contents conceived as implicit advertisements for the firms that owned them, these periodicals also carried advertising of the firm's current list. Further, even while advertising reading materials, periodicals increasingly carried ads for all manner of nonliterary products as well: the *Round Table* advertised patent medicines, sewing machines, jewelry, fireplace implements, and a host of other products of an expanding industrial capitalism. Advertisements for books appeared side by side with those for mundane commercial products, and the same language was used to sell both. For an author, appearance in a prominent periodical served as a means to earn money, become better known, and build a relationship with its publisher. Similarly, publishers could entice potentially lucrative writers to the firm by offering significant payments for periodical appearance.

From the perspective of the explosive growth of publishing as an industry, the new focus on advertising may well have been inevitable. During the 1840s and '50s, publishers combined new, efficient methods of distributing printed matter throughout the country with automated production processes to create huge, integrated firms capable of meeting a growing demand for reading materials from a rapidly expanding audience and increasingly literate population.[13] After a fire in 1853 destroyed their New York factory, the Harpers invested large sums to create a plant that was a wonder of mechanization and the division of labor. Such a factory needed a constant supply of "product," which in turn required a steady national demand as well as a carefully worked out national advertising campaign.

Further, the new printing techniques of electroplating and stereotyping, which meant that all of a writer's works now could be kept in print, changed not only the way books were manufactured but also the public persona of the writer. Ronald Zboray put the matter succinctly: "Stereotyping and electrotyping encouraged publishers to boost not only the sales of the particular work but also the author's celebrity, in the hopes of pushing his or her previous works. Writers more than ever came before the public eye, and publishers gave substantial emoluments to reviewers in numerous periodicals for selling notices—puffs used extensively in advertising copy."[14] It was precisely this system of paying off the reviewers and periodicals that drew the ire of the *Round Table*.

Emily Dickinson's 1863 poem "Publication—is the Auction" (709) condemns this process:

> Publication—is the Auction
> Of the Mind of Man—
> Poverty—be justifying
> For so foul a thing
>
> Possibly—but We—would rather
> From Our Garret go
> White—Unto the White Creator—
> Than invest—Our Snow—
>
> Thought belong to Him who gave it—
> Then—to Him Who bear
> Its Corporeal illustration—Sell
> The Royal Air—
>
> In the Parcel—Be the Merchant
> Of the Heavenly Grace—
> But reduce no Human spirit
> To Disgrace of Price—[15]

The term *auction* accurately describes a literary marketplace where authors were in fact bought and sold. For instance, in 1852 *Graham's* offered fifty dollars per poem to the two most popular American poets, William Cullen Bryant and Henry Wadsworth Longfellow, but it insisted on dictating the length of the poems, their subject matter and treatment, and the frequency of composition. William Charvat explained the terms offered to Bryant: "(1) To get the maximum magazine rate, he had to turn out poems at the editor's pace, not the poet's (he sent in only two a year). (2) To maintain the contract, he would have had to continue to produce the kind of poems that *Graham's* wanted. (3) The poems in *Graham's* were instantly reprinted, without payment, by half the magazines in the country."[16] As the literary marketplace expanded, the "auction" grew more heated. *Graham's* advertised in 1853 that it had "spent as high as $1,500 on a single number *for authorship* alone . . . which is more than twice the sum that has ever been paid by any other magazine in America."[17] One can understand why Dickinson wrote that only poverty could justify the selling of that which has no price. Or is she saying that poverty is a fitting punishment for so "foul a thing?"

While it is hard to imagine Dickinson submitting her work to general-interest magazines, apparently she had invitations elsewhere. She wrote to Higginson on 25 April 1862 that "Two editors of Journals came to my Father's House, this winter—and asked me for my Mind—and when I asked them 'Why,' they said I was penurious—and they, would use it for the World."[18] Thomas H. Johnson suggests that the editors may have been Samuel Bowles and J. G. Holland, both then of the *Springfield Republican*. Dickinson enjoyed long friendships with both and included them and their families in the circle to which she sent poems.

Poet, novelist, moralistic essayist, and founding editor of the profitable *Scribner's Monthly Magazine*, Holland was arguably the most successful American writer in the 1860s and '70s. So perfectly at one with his readers was he that the postwar years became known as the "Holland age of letters."[19] Dickinson and Holland enjoyed a long, unbroken friendship, and yet it is hard to imagine more dissimilar writers. Dickinson was the great private poet of her generation, while Holland was the public writer, a man whose rise from poverty to social prominence and prosperity in New York served to confirm the immense appeal of his maxims.[20]

Although Dickinson elected not to publish in literary periodicals, they constitute an essential component of her development, as reflected in the 1862 letter she wrote to Higginson after reading his "Letter to a Contributor" in the *Atlantic Monthly*. The resulting correspondence lasted for the rest of her life. Higginson's continuing interest in her poetry must have served Dickinson as one indication of its potential significance. Further, as David Higgins has written, "For a shy spinster in a small town, Emily Dickinson knew a surprising number of notable contemporaries. Her regular correspondents, all but a few, were known to the public of the day."[21] And since not all of Dickinson's letters have survived, we may not know of other possible correspondents. Jay Leyda suspects that she maintained a correspondence with Charles H. Sweetser, since the publication of "My Sabbath" in the *Round Table* "must have required some exchange.... There is a reward waiting for the student who searches *all* the newspapers that employed C. H. Sweetser."[22]

Dickinson may well have been disingenuous, then, in poem 441, "This is my letter to the World," in which she claims that "the world" "never wrote to Me." The poem itself suggests some of the ways that she developed her conception of poetry in response to contemporary periodical practices. Assuming the stance of a journalist reporting to a national audience, she tells not of sensational events, but

> The simple News that Nature told—
> With Tender Majesty
>
> Her Message is committed
> To Hands I cannot see—
> For love of Her—Sweet—countrymen—
> Judge tenderly—of me[23]

Contemporary periodicals and books were filled with public "letters," analogues of the private communications that kept highly mobile Americans in touch with one another wherever they might travel.[24] Higginson's use of the convention of the letter enabled him to write "intimately" to the many potential contributors to the *Atlantic.* Dickinson's unsent "letter to the world," then, comments ironically on this convention. With similar irony, Henry David Thoreau reports in *Walden* that his dispatches from the environs of Concord would be "published" only in the most select of "journals," his own notebooks. Sharing such reservations, the young proprietors of the *Round Table* set out to practice a form of journalism that could never be popular. Nevertheless, they were willing to invest large sums to create a periodical that, as part of its wide-ranging criticism of the national life, would take the measure of the literary marketplace.

II

REMARKABLY, the Sweetsers were not in the least afraid to begin life by biting the hands that fed them advertising revenues. The first issue of the *Round Table* attacked publishers for falling to the level of the most crass commercial advertisers:

> And what concerns us of the *Round Table* more nearly, the publishers are fast falling into the van of this clamorous crusade. Books go through their half dozen of editions (in the advertisements) before we can take breath through our race through the first chapter, and before we can fairly sharpen our pen to prick through any full-blown maggot which has skipped from the brain of some "favorite author," the town is forestalled with the snap-judgments of some half score of country journals, that fill up half a column of the *Tribune.* Parton's Butler (a work of tender affection for all that we know) is sandwiched about among advertisements like a new liver pill, or a wonderful preparation of Bachu (with no odor attaching). Mr. Carelton, with his cabalistic signal, is as fecund of supreme excitements, "startling novelties," and "rare flow of humors," as ever old

Ephesian Diana with the three tier of breasts. Indeed, if we might be allowed to suggest an appropriate heading for the more vehement of the later advertisements, conveying at once an imitation of the intellectual food afforded as well as a graceful compliment to the consumers—it would be this:—SUCK FOR THE WISE.

Lamenting that even the "stately old *North American Review*" had gotten into "the advertising arena with the clumsy agility of some superannuated aerobat," the *Round Table* remarked that since the subject was "too wide for present discussion," it planned to "return to it some day with illustrative annotations" (19 Dec. 1863, 6).

Return to it the weekly did during the course of its short life. With both moral fervor and humor, the *Round Table* revealed both the crassness of the publishers' advertising and the more serious matter of the corruption of criticism through the use of advertising dollars as bribes. In "What American Literature Needs," 25 June 1864, the *Round Table* insisted that if there were to arise a "rougher, stronger race of literary athletes," then the "one great requisite is trenchant, unsparing, vigorous criticism." The essay, which has the marks of Eugene Benson,[25] the self-styled literary frondeur, painter, and art critic, denounces the press: "Look at the periodicals of the country, and with the exception of a few quarterlies which nobody reads, observe how few there are that dare to offer criticism with perfect impartiality. Friendship for the author, or, what is more common, a pecuniary regard for advertisers, too often smooth the critic's pen, which should be hard and pointed. Of course, criticism is not fault-finding. . . . The first sign of a renovated literature . . . will be a higher style of criticism than has been current, and the development of a class of critics who will deal fairly with all books committed to their consideration, regardless of authors or publishers" (18).

As we have seen, the *Round Table* began life at a most uncertain time. Given the extreme vulnerability of such an enterprise, the willingness of the Sweetsers to confront publishers, the group on whom they most depended for survival, was remarkable. But they argue in the first issue that the very tragedy of a fratricidal war provided the strongest possible evidence for precisely what it was that their journal set out to accomplish: "It is our purpose to condense within its columns whatever, in the crowded and varied life of each passing week, most merits or demands the thoughtful attention which it is impossible men should give to the facts of each day as they fly past them on the wings of the morning journal. While the dark cloud of trial and endurance which now rests upon the land throws its shadow upon us, it is well that we should learn to think. Our American life has heretofore been so full of sunshine and action, so buoyant and untrammeled, that the most serious problems of national existence have come upon us like a thief in the night. We are beginning, however, to make the truth real to ourselves" (19 Dec. 1863, 4). In creating a cultural space for itself, the *Round Table* would have to educate readers to understand the purpose of such criticism, which in turn demanded a willingness to think in new ways about the meaning of America itself. The blind optimism of the prewar years, the editors claimed, left no room for the sort of frank analysis of the nation's failings that might have prevented the war.

The Sweetsers predicted, then, that "the weekly journal, which has become so powerful a lever of public opinion in England, is destined, therefore, to exert an influence not less important in this country, offering as it does both to the writer and to the reader the opportunity of reconsidering under all their aspects the questions which must necessarily be passed upon by the daily press, as it were, at full gallop" (19 Dec. 1863, 4). The challenge for such a weekly would be to identify the salient issues of the times and, drawing from the best minds from around the country, promote the thoughtful analysis of national issues that a complex, modern society demanded. Although the *Round Table* itself would not realize these goals, its prediction that the critical weekly would play an essential role in the national life of the United States was no less valid. The Sweetsers' weekly helped to open the way for the wide-ranging criticism that can be found today in such successors as the *Nation* and the *New Republic*.

In spite of the need to treat the great issues of politics, finance, war, and peace, the Sweetsers expected that their paper would take its essential character from their own literary and artistic interests. Pointing to the connection between artistic expression and the public culture, they argued in the opening issue that the Civil War made possible a new seriousness in American literature by opening the way for the tragic: "It used to be pleaded in explanation of the poverty of American literature in all that relates to the painting of the passions, that the contrasts and compressions of European life were wanting here. There was force in the plea. The dramatic element is evolved by the conflict of man with his accidents, with the powers beyond and about himself, which men call destiny and chance. Individual life was so free with us that the conflict rarely attained to dramatic proportions. Lovelace could never have thrown such force of conviction into his song to Althea, if he had not actually been imprisoned. The reality of 'stone walls' was needed to make him feel that 'stone walls do not a prison make.' We are in a fair way to have our stone walls set up about us now" (19 Dec. 1863, 4). The *Round Table* challenged writers, then, to confront the tragic reality of America. Dickinson's most intensely creative period coincided precisely with the Civil War, when she produced approximately a poem a day. Her inner sense of tragedy now had a public face. The weekly jointly edited by her cousin and her former Amherst townsman provided an opportunity to consider the significance of that transformation for literature.[26]

On the assumption that its readers would be able to reflect on the important questions if they were not distracted by personalities, the *Round Table* subscribed to the principle of anonymous journalism. But how to promote the magazine—and tout its roster of writers—without revealing their identities? In concluding the first volume, on 11 June 1864, the Sweetsers could not resist presenting a list of sixty-seven regular contributors. Inviting the reader to "surmise what articles came from their pens," they listed such younger New York–based writers as Thomas Bailey Aldrich, George Arnold, Edmund Clarence Stedman, Richard Henry Stoddard, and William Winter, all opposed to the didacticism represented by Henry Wadsworth Longfellow. The name of Eugene Benson identified its regular art critic. Other New Yorkers included Gaylord Clark, the Crolys, George Curtis, and Kate Field; Bostonians included George Hillard, Justin Windsor, and R. C. Winthrop; Yale professors were G. P. Fisher, Daniel Coit Gilman, and Noah Porter. The prominent transcendentalist Moncure Conway sent long literary letters from London and the poet Frederick Goddard Tuckerman contributed from Greenfield, Massachusetts. Harriet Prescott wrote from Newburyport, Massachusetts. The most prominent political name was that of General George McClellan.

Whatever the theoretical arguments for anonymous journalism, in practice it served as a disincentive for authors who had no choice but to play by the rules of the game. As I have written elsewhere, E. C. Stedman, for instance, decided that he would not send his best poems to the *Round Table* because its "impersonal" rule "hides its author's name." Further, Stedman observed that such a journal of opinion "can reach but a limited audience."[27]

The magazine's adherence to the principle of anonymous journalism was, however, consistent with the Sweetsers' avowedly disinterested approach to public life. The lead article in the opening number, for instance, "A Word for Candor in Politics," urges Northerners of both parties to put "away . . . all this false and malevolent partisanship. Let us respect each other's rights and opinions, and estimate the patriotism of men by what they do and suffer for their country, not by our own opinions and prejudices. So shall our politics acquire purity, breadth, and manliness, and politician and knave no longer be synonymous." It asked the reader to assume the perspective of some "disinterested observer" just landed in the North from another planet who, witnessing senseless partisan strife, would "conclude that, if what these two divisions of the American people say about each other and the government is but half true, there can be no hope for the nation; there is not enough integrity left anywhere to save it; and it must perish in madness and guilt" (19 Dec. 1863, 3). Similarly, the magazine took the high ground in recommending that in place of heavy war borrowing, the government should raise taxes. That there was surplus money floating around was clear from the conspicuous consumption of war profiteers.

At the end of the first volume, the Sweetsers renewed their promise to make the weekly "a worthy exponent of American life, American literature, and America itself" (6 Nov. 1864, 401). But how did the Sweetsers and those associated with them see "America itself?" While the *Round Table* proceeded on the assumption that the Civil War demonstrated the need for fundamental improvement in America, it was unable to articulate a specific social policy agenda to bring about change. It assumed the posture of the wise, disinterested observer, but the Sweetsers did express a strong interest in preserving certain well-established features of the social order. That was the case in matters of gender, where it resisted female suffrage (24 Feb. 1866), and in religion, where it denounced the pantheism of Theodore Parker and Ralph Waldo Emerson (20 Feb. 1864). Even in the area of race, where it saw the need "for protection, kindness, and sympathy" for blacks, it subscribed to the established principles of racial hierarchies: "That the white man is the highest of the three races is hardly a more unquestionable fact than that the negro is the lowest" (13 Feb. 1864, 181).

The *Round Table* best articulated a criticism of contemporary practices in literature and the arts. In the second issue it turned its critical guns on none other than Charles Sweetser's former employer on the *Springfield Republican*, J. G. Holland. The magazine used a review of *Letters to the Joneses*, the last of three volumes of advice that Holland had written under the pseudonym of Timothy Titcomb, as an opportunity to take issue with a pervasive moralism in American letters. Holland's book is "simply another proof of the oft-repeated assertion that the didactic and personal style of writing will in time force itself into failure and almost disgust." To "catch the ear of the masses" may well be "a very fascinating employment," but "it is not the best development of literary taste and

culture." Popular writers like Holland did little more than reflect back
to their readers what they picked up from them. "We have an abundance
of didactic writing in this country. It was already become too prolific for
its success. Those writers who have adopted it have many of them injured
their literary reputations and fame. The pulpit is the true field of
preacher, and not the printed page." Literature should be "suggestive
rather than expostulatory. . . . The new class of authors who are throw-
ing about so lavishly the products of their experience do not really advance literary interests, which are confined to no country and no class
of men" (26 Dec. 1863, 27). The reviewer pointed out that literature is
not a direct transcription of the author's own experience, but a reflection on it; successful writers do something different than merely reflect
back to the readers what they have absorbed. Dickinson, in explaining
her literary procedure in a July 1862 letter to Higginson, wrote that
"When I state myself, as the Representative of the Verse—it does not
mean—me—but a supposed person." [28]

In the same number, in a long review of Longfellow's *Tales of a Wayside
Inn*, the *Round Table* considered another question of immediate interest
to Dickinson: the difference between the contemporary popularity of a
writer's work and its enduring significance. The unidentified reviewer
begins by scornfully attacking the notion, advanced by the *Atlantic*, that
Longfellow was the "New England Chaucer." After patiently enumerat-
ing the inconsistencies of the tales and the patent contrivance in the
use of setting, the reviewer offers a more appropriate comparison, that
between Robert Browning and Longfellow, as a way of defining "the difference between a great poet and a pretty one."

This leads to a concluding paragraph, which offers an excellent explanation of what it meant to be a public poet at midcentury:

> The impression left upon our minds by this last volume of Mr. Longfel-
> low's (the tenth . . . he has published in twenty-five years) is, that the popu-
> larity which he enjoys is considerably above that which his talents entitle
> him to. Not gifted with genius in the highest sense, and possessing no
> unusual qualities of intellect, he has succeeded in winning a large circle
> of intelligent readers. This he has done by never writing above their com-
> prehension. His themes, even those which are the furthest removed from
> their knowledge, are still within the range of their sympathies, and so man-
> aged by him as not to cost the majority too much effort to understand
> them. The common and familiar in real life—the pretty and pathetic in
> books—picturesque aspects of the past—gentle trains of sentiment and
> reflection, colored by a practicable morality—of such stuff the tissue of

his songs is woven. His diction is simple and direct, with a kind of freshness about it, a certain sweetness and elegance natural to him; and his measures generally plastic and melodious. He has done many things well. But the things which authenticate the great poet, who, by virtue of his divine office, is a cosmical thinker as well as a profound artist, he has not done and cannot do. What rank he will hold in the future is a problem with which he does not appear to trouble himself, and wisely, since no man can foresee or control the world's fluctuations of opinion. John Cleveland was for years a more popular poet than John Milton; and Pope than Goldsmith and Cowper; and Tom Moore than Shelley; even poor Tupper had, and we dare say has, multitudes of admirers. But the whirligig of Time will bring its revenges. How the grim old graybeard will deal with Mr. Longfellow, we can only conjecture; he honors him as the most popular of living poets. (26 Dec. 1863, 27)

Dickinson, in her letter of 7 June 1862 to Higginson, had remarked that she had no intention of publishing: "If fame belonged to me, I could not escape her—if she did not, the longest day would pass me on the chase."[29] This implicit argument in the *Round Table* that to the extent that Longfellow moved in the direction of popularity he moved away from the real work of poetry, is entirely consistent with Dickinson's decision not to seek contemporary popularity. Lasting fame was quite another matter.

Just as the *Round Table* was willing to take issue with the didacticism of Holland and the mediocrity of Longfellow, so too did it treat the limitations of contemporary metrical conventions. In a review published on 6 February 1864 of a book on Civil War poetry, it complained that "the soul cannot be awakened to enthusiasm, nor can the eye grow dim over such twaddle. It is the quintessence of mediocrity, whose smooth and sapless iambics flow with exasperating faultlessness over subjects that should have set the wildest and most wondrous fancies ringing out." The *Round Table* here encourages poets to break out of deadening metrical conventions.

The *Round Table* argued in "Individuality in American Art and Literature," published on 19 March 1864, that the great need in American art was for distinctive personal expression. Charvat's distinction between public and private poets, cited earlier, is apposite. For the *Round Table* insisted on individuality, on a personal vision, as a precondition of artistic expression: "We are created individual souls, charged with the necessity of making that individuality act in the world, using it as a light to reveal and make good what others have neglected. He who is false to his individuality is false to his most sacred and special possession. For we are endowed with a special genius for a special purpose. . . . To yourself be true, and according to the force of your individuality you will be cherished by the world. We act on the world, and are remembered, not through the fulness of our intellectual equipment, but by means of the force of our nature. Byron used his individuality and impressed two continents with his genius, but his intellectual culture was meagre" (211).

Just the week before this defense of individuality, on 19 March 1864, the *Round Table* published Dickinson's "My Sabbath," poem 324:

> Some keep the Sabbath going to church,
>   I keep it staying home,
> With a bobolink for a chorister,
>   And an orchard for a dome.
>
> Some keep the Sabbath in surplice,
>   I just wear my wings,
> And instead of tolling the bell for church,
>   Our little sexton sings.
> God preaches—a noted clergyman,
>   And the sermon is never long;
> So instead of going to heaven at last,
>   I'm going all along.

In publishing in the *Round Table* Dickinson did not have to worry about being the victim of advertising; here was one periodical that did not print contributors' names. And in view of her close family connections to the Sweetsers, no doubt she did not have to worry about entering the literary marketplace and auctioning her work to the highest bidder. Hers was precisely the sort of individual voice for which the magazine had called. The *Round Table,* in questioning the real significance of popularity and contemporary fame, provided for its readers a critical lens through which to examine the "admiring Bog" of the contemporary literary marketplace.

NOTES

1. For a discussion of Dickinson's composition habits, see Ralph William Franklin, ed., *The Manuscript Books of Emily Dickinson* (Cambridge: Harvard Univ. Press, 1981).

2. Martha Nell Smith, *Rowing in Eden: Reading Emily Dickinson* (Austin: Univ. of Texas Press, 1991), 2.

3. *The Letters of Emily Dickinson,* ed. Thomas H. Johnson, 3 vols. (Cambridge: Harvard Univ. Press, 1958), 2:408.

4. Karen Dandurand, "New Dickinson Civil War Poems," *American Literature* 56 (1984): 17–27.

5. William Charvat, *The Profession of Authorship in America* (New York: Columbia Univ. Press, 1992), 109. Similarly, after his appointment to the New York Customhouse, Herman Melville in effect withdrew from the literary marketplace that had caused him so much trouble. He focused on poetry, publishing such volumes as *John Marr and Other Sailors* privately, in editions limited to twenty-five copies. He had become a private poet.

6. *Letters,* 2:408.

7. Biographical information on the Sweetser cousins is from *Appleton's Encyclopedia* and Jay Leyda, *The Years and Hours of Emily Dickinson,* 2 vols (New Haven: Yale Univ. Press, 1960), 1:72–73.

8. See my entry on the *Round Table* in *American Literary Magazines: The Eighteenth and Nineteenth Centuries,* ed. Edward E. Chielens (New York: Greenwood, 1986), 394–443. Another source of information is Frank Luther Mott, *A History of American Magazines,* 4 vols. (Cambridge: Harvard Univ. Press, 1957), 3:319–24.

9. *The Complete Poems of Emily Dickinson,* ed. Thomas H. Johnson (Cambridge: Harvard Univ. Press, 1960), 133.

10. Eugene Exman, *The Brothers Harper* (New York: Harper and Row, 1965), 304; quoted by Barbara M. Perkins, "*Harper's Monthly Magazine,*" in *American Literary Magazines,* 167.

11. Jay Leyda, *The Years and Hours of Emily Dickinson,* 2 vols. (New Haven: Yale Univ. Press, 1960), 1:191.

12. Ezra Greenspan, *Walt Whitman and the American Reader* (Cambridge: Cambridge Univ. Press, 1990), 34.

13. The most recent study is Ronald Zboray, *A Fictive People* (New York: Oxford Univ. Press, 1992).

14. Ibid., 10.

15. *Complete Poems,* 348–49.

16. Charvat, *Profession of Authorship,* 109.

17. Arthur Wrobel, "*Graham's Lady's and Gentleman's Magazine,*" in *American Literary Magazines,* 158.

18. *Letters,* 2:261–62.

19. Benjamin T. Spencer, *The Quest for Nationality* (Syracuse, N.Y.: Syracuse Univ. Press, 1957), 295.

20. For a discussion of the shape of Holland's career, see my "J. G. Holland and the 'Religion of Civilization' in Mid–Nineteenth Century America," *American Studies* 27 (1986): 55–79.

21. David Higgins, *Portrait of Emily Dickinson: The Poet and Her Prose* (New Brunswick, N.J.: Rutgers Univ. Press, 1967), 12.

22. Leyda, *Years and Hours,* 1:72–73.

23. *Complete Poems,* 211.

24. See Zboray, *A Fictive People,* chapter 8, "The Letter and the Reading Public."

25. See "Between Realism and Romanticism: The Curious Career of Eugene Benson," *American Literary Realism* 14 (1981): 242–61.

26. Daniel Aaron, *The Unwritten War: American Writers and the Civil War* (New York: Knopf, 1973), 355–56.

27. Scholnick, "*The Round Table,*" in *American Literary Magazines,* 341.

28. *Letters,* 2:410.

29. Ibid., 2:408.

10

HOME FROM THE THEATRE OF WAR
The *Southern Magazine* and
Recollections of the Civil War

KATHLEEN DIFFLEY

•

T O this day, the white mile markers once laid out by Charles Mason
and Jeremiah Dixon carry the traces of an *M* on one side and a *P*
on the other. Every fifth mile along the Mason-Dixon line still sometimes
reveals an aging "crown" stone, which displays the Baltimore coat of
arms on its southern front and William Penn's family crest facing north.
Across more than two hundred miles, the two British astronomers laid
these markers due west in the 1760s and thus settled at last the border
dispute that had chafed the colonies of Maryland and Pennsylvania for
more than eighty years. The line they surveyed a bare fifteen miles from
Philadelphia later became the designated boundary between slave and
free states in 1820, when Congress hammered out the Missouri Compromise holding the Union together for a time. So in 1861, when an ill-
fated troop train left Philadelphia carrying the Sixth Massachusetts, the
first regiment to march after Sumter fell and President Abraham Lincoln called for volunteers, the boys from Lowell and Worcester who
passed the stone markers were loading their muskets as they headed for
Baltimore and rebellion to the south.

The first blood of the war was drawn when those Massachusetts re-
cruits tried to make their way across Baltimore's streets, a provocation
that turned to tumult and that brought the city under martial law.[1] For
the next four years, Maryland remained a border state, tied to the South
by sympathy and tobacco but bound to the North by the Union and
trade. Equally a crossroads after hostilities ended, Maryland surged with
postwar capital, and Baltimore proved a haven for both southern refugees and German immigrants. Many of the immigrants went west to farm
the prairies, however, while many of the refugees remained to tug at the
city's political compass and fortify its culture. They were among the first
to bolster the magazine trade outside eastern publishing centers and

thus to welcome a distinctly regional literature that would challenge the cultural ascendancy of the Northeast, consolidate interest in the local, and ultimately transform the "real" war that got into literary magazines. With informal copyright agreements newly in place to step up royalty payments and thereby curtail transatlantic piracy, the firmer professional standing of American authors by the 1870s also helped to create an appetite for regional contributions and a market for new periodicals like Baltimore's *Southern Magazine*. Journal of choice for ex-Confederates looking ahead to recovery, Baltimore's preeminent literary forum was instrumental in sustaining the postwar shift in storytelling from the open battlefields and pitched fealties of Virginia to the border territory of Louisiana parishes, where hearts and minds were considerably harder to read and the principle of loyalty itself was in doubt. Relocating the "waw," especially in new regional magazines, in turn jimmied the familiar paradigm of fixed spheres, as both public and private domains were enlisted in competing regional designs on the nation's future.

Curiously, the guns that boomed across Charleston harbor in the spring of 1861 have rarely echoed for literary critics, who have customarily raised the flag of American literary nationalism over the likes of Ralph Waldo Emerson, Nathaniel Hawthorne, and Mark Twain. As a result, few scholars have caught the Civil War's narrative recoils in the contemporary popular press. Yet between the fall of Fort Sumter in 1861 and the Centennial celebrations in 1876, some sixteen literary magazines circulated more than three hundred stories of the war, many of these journals from the South and West as well as the culturally dominant Northeast. By turns domestic, romantic, and adventurous, these stories represent some of the first and most public efforts to give shape to civil cataclysm, even at its most private and even away down south in Dixie. Before the war ended in 1865, the principal southern challenge to the memories guiding Boston's *Atlantic Monthly* or New York's *Harper's Weekly* came from Richmond, where the wartime *Southern Illustrated News* quickened the pace and galvanized the politics of the baronial *Southern Literary Messenger.* Thereafter, once shortages, siege, and surrender had throttled the Confederate capital, Baltimore would emerge as the North's best if fleeting antagonist in setting the rhetorical terms upon which "the South" might arise from Reconstruction to enter the national lexicon.

Baltimore may seem a ramshackle site for a literary capital, but it was in this Chesapeake harbor that Francis Scott Key wrote the "Star-Spangled Banner" more than a decade before the arrival of Edgar Allan Poe. During the euphoric days after the War of 1812, Baltimore stood poised to become the nation's leading port: its mills processed western grain and southern cotton, and its tall ships made the city the best purveyor of notions and dry goods, coffee and fertilizer, for hundreds of miles.[2] In the 1790s, when the town was chartered, population doubled, and it doubled again during the next decade, while Boston fell behind. Just a few years after the war that produced an anthem, Baltimore's imports exceeded $5 million, and the city's trade reached Europe, South America, India, and China. By the 1820s Baltimore was laying tracks for the first railroad west and, as Colonel F. Schaller would later note in the *Southern Magazine*'s "Immigration of Capital and of Population to the South" (Apr. 1872), local importers were monopolizing the sale of Peruvian guano. So intermeshed were the city's industrial concerns that Baltimore began manufacturing quantities of cotton duck for the long, high masts that gave its distinctive clippers an exceptional canvas spread and extraordinary speed.

Greater prosperity bred the money for leisure, which in turn provoked a demand for books, booksellers, and magazines that led Baltimore to crowd out Annapolis on Maryland's cultural stage. If Philadelphia was the Athens of America for newly minted patriots, Baltimore was fast becoming the young nation's Rome. As early as 1795, the city's circulating libraries were augmented by the more august Library Company, whose fifty-nine original shareholders grew to more than three hundred in less than five years. By 1802 Baltimore could claim a typographical society and by 1806 its own type foundry; only Philadelphia at the turn of the century could boast as much. Where Annapolis echoed Britain's eighteenth-century coffee houses in founding the Tuesday Club of literary wags, Baltimore cut in with a Monday Club that first met on Wednesday and then a Wednesday Club as the city's taste for music and drama grew. Francis Scott Key was associated with the Delphian Club, which was so distinguished that only nine men could join at any one time, each partner to a muse. John Neal, said to be James Fenimore Cooper's closest American rival, was a prominent member and the mercurial editor of the *Portico,* a monthly magazine published as early as 1816 with the help of Delphian friends like lawyer William Wirt, artist Rembrandt Peale, and novelist John Pendleton Kennedy. In the 1830s Kennedy's success with plantation fiction would insinuate a disquieting southern edge to previously nationalistic fare; but even then, border tension dissipated when northern readers made a novelist like Kennedy popular and when the writer himself was more urban than the landed masters he described. Besides, in the teens and twenties when the Delphians were active, the cultural adversary was British, the *Portico*'s aim was a native literature in an obstreperous American lingo, and the most unwanted praise came when the *Edinburgh Review* called Baltimore's magazine one of the best in the United States.[3]

During the years of civil war, the Yankees never took Baltimore as they did Savannah, Columbia, and Richmond because they never lost it. In 1865, after Sherman had marched to the sea and Grant had besieged the Confederate capital, Baltimore was still making umbrellas and pianos and elliptic yoke shirts, was running new steamer lines to Havana and Liverpool, and was about to throw open the doors of the Peabody Institute. No city south of the Mason-Dixon line was better positioned to sponsor a literary resurgence or better able to shore up a southern alternative to Yankee boosterism and a cultural alternative to the "New South" that would bring consumerism and Atlanta to the fore. Certainly no more southerly city after Appomattox could grab hold with Baltimore's aplomb of the communications network that magazines promised. At a time when the periodical trade was burgeoning in the Northeast and commencing nationwide, postwar Baltimore generated at least twenty-three literary journals, what Ray Atchison in his study of southern magazines has called "the largest number published in any city during the Reconstruction era." Leading this phalanx, the *New Eclectic* gradually abandoned its miscellaneous reprints from British periodicals to become the self-proclaimed "exponent of the best thoughts and feelings of our Southern people" and thus, in 1871, the *Southern Magazine*.[4]

Through merger, relocation, and shifts in title, the journal had already established an enviable reputation. Founded as the *Richmond Eclectic* in 1866 by two Presbyterian ministers, the largely pirated magazine moved to Baltimore two years later, drawn by what editor Moses Drury Hoge called "energy, fine literary culture, practical acquaintance with business, and, what I never possessed—capital" (Dec. 1867, 191). Despite the loss of about five thousand dollars, the *New Eclectic* was solvent enough in 1869 to absorb Charlotte's *Land We Love* and to become the official organ of the Southern Historical Society. Under the ultraconservative William Hand Browne, who joined Fridge Murdoch from the previous staff and General Daniel Harvey Hill from the *Land We Love*, the journal was rechristened in January 1871, when original contributions from southern writers like Paul Hamilton Hayne, John Esten Cooke, and William Gilmore Simms had come to replace the reprints from abroad. By then, the magazine was already claiming a circulation larger than that of all other southern magazines combined. As a creation of the postwar era, the *Southern Magazine* had more verve and less erudition than the *Southern Literary Messenger* (now defunct), but it came closest to the same honorable success until contributors found that they were better paid for their work in the North and the magazine folded at the end of 1875.

Largely responsible for the journal's southern orientation, editor William Hand Browne was no more tolerant of scalawags than editors further south and no less outspoken than volatile wartime columnists. By the 1870s, however, the fate of the Confederacy had been decided, northern troops were occupying the military districts of the South, and the best cause not yet lost lay for many in encouraging a distinctly Southern literature. For Browne and the *Southern Magazine,* the catechism of despair that preoccupied other journals was considerably less insistent than the literature of protest, especially when the Civil War was remembered in the magazine's seventeen stories. In place of the sagging homesteads and failed romances of earlier southern magazines, thirteen of these stories were adventurous tales of the ones who got away—from northern prisons, from Petersburg under siege, from Federal troops, or from naval engagements on the Atlantic. They were thus stories of a second chance, narratively as protean as Baltimore itself, verbally as obstreperous as peculiar regional settings allowed, thematically as rebellious as Jefferson Davis without the bombast, and historically as far from the war stories in the *Galaxy* or *Putnam's* as a failed revolution would permit. Unexpected and diverse, these war stories helped to confirm a profound shift in national recollection toward border warfare, a shift that would push the previously neglected trope of the "house divided" toward the central position it occupies today.

Wholly southern stories like Confederate Gray's "T. J.'s Cavalry Charge" (Apr. 1870) or Max Marrowfat's "Seeking Dixie" (Dec. 1872) never appeared in the years of the war or the magazines of the East. That a literature of resistance coalesced somewhat later and in places like Baltimore is a consequence, at least in part, of the agitation for an international copyright law that was reinvigorated after the war. Stretching back to 1790, when the First Congress passed a law protecting American authors for fourteen years before their work became public property, the pressure to respect the rights of authors at home and abroad was brought to bear yet again in Washington after the International Copyright Association was founded by men like publisher George Palmer Putnam and author James Parton in 1868. Failing in their attempt to secure immediate legislation, they continued their campaign into the 1870s, when congressional representatives mounted spirited debates on a series of proposed bills that fretted the distinction between what was private and what was public. The issue that emerged for the Forty-second Congress (1871–72), when the *Southern Magazine* was taking hold, rhetorically pitted the "absolute right" of authors against the "grant of monopoly privileges," and thus the "indiscriminate and disgraceful pillaging" of "literary pirates, virtually armed with letters of marque from their Governments" against the public's right to cheap books, wide circulation, and free trade in knowledge. In popular magazines, too, the copyright issue turned on the friction between private ownership and public need, specifically on the author's right to the fruits of labor as opposed to the public's right to ideas and their free access.[5]

The solution that James Parton urged in the *Atlantic Monthly* was to integrate the private and the public by couching private recompense as public benefit, a solution he initiated by appealing to the interests of publishing houses as middlemen who could themselves secure good work through good wages. The result would be a fostering of native production, a leap in readership, and a spurt in markets that publishers could tap once they left off the overproduction of cheap books and bad translations of European literature that were sapping native fare. "It was the intention of the founders of this Republic," Parton wrote, "to give complete protection to intellectual property, and this intention is clearly expressed in the Constitution. Justified by the authority given in that instrument, Congress has passed patent laws which have called into exercise an amount of triumphant ingenuity that is one of the great wonders of the modern world; but under the copyright laws, enacted with the same good intentions, our infant literature pines and dwindles" (Oct. 1867, 451). Pass the international copyright law, Parton reasoned, and personal recompense would redound to the public's benefit by ending the "blight" on "immature genius" and creating a nation of readers.

Congress did not, in fact, pass an act granting foreign authors copyright protection in the United States until 1891. But the energy with which the case was argued in the halls of Congress and on the pages of literary magazines did result in postwar royalty agreements of an informal nature that curtailed foreign imports, spurred the expansion of the American magazine trade, and shifted dramatically the way that the war would be remembered. In San Francisco, the *Overland Monthly* was founded under Bret Harte's aegis in 1868 and, like the *Southern Magazine,* began almost immediately to publish Civil War stories that skewed the norms set by Eastern journals. When black soldiers stood watch in "A Dark Night on Picket" (July 1870) or Kansas abolitionists defied the mob in "The Cabin at Pharaoh's Ford" (Oct. 1874), readers were reminded that along the border of what they knew best were soldiers who were not white and preachers who could be strung up for what they believed. In Chicago, the *Lakeside Monthly* began appearing in 1869, when editor Francis Fisher Browne discovered in the Midwest a peculiar zeal and regional ability that matched the offbeat vigor of the *Southern Magazine*. Subsequent *Lakeside Monthly* stories about a more western war in "Two Only Sons" (Dec. 1870), "Our Adjutant" (May 1873), or "In the Palmy Days of Slaveholding" (July 1870) strikingly complicated the glory of enlistment and the privilege of plantation households or the ease of their dismantlement when such stories were set in Ohio, Georgia, or Florida. Much closer to border skirmishing than to clear lines of attack, these regional journals focused more often on the thickets and backwaters of war through the lens of their reconstructive moments, which suddenly brought these out-of-the-way places into public view.

The careers of the *Southern Magazine* and William Hand Browne might best be understood in such irregular Western company. A useful barometer of Baltimore's energy and political temper, Browne published his first story—a translation from the German—in 1861, when Baltimore gave rise to an interested and insurgent newspaper called the *South*. After the Civil War, he joined Albert Taylor Bledsoe in 1866 to found the *Southern Review,* a journal of literature, science, philosophy, and education that quarreled relentlessly with the North until Bledsoe made the review into a church mouthpiece in 1871 and thereafter quarreled relentlessly with northern Methodists. Meanwhile, Browne had gone on to edit a Baltimore weekly that kept up with politics, literature, and art in the late 1860s. A scholar of decided opinions, he would become one of the first university librarians at Johns Hopkins, one of the editors of the *Maryland Historical Magazine,* and one of the state's most ardent historians. He eventually retired as a professor of English literature. Browne's purpose, as he saw it, was to resurrect southern culture; immediately after the war, his forum was the literary journal, which was peculiarly well situated in the later nineteenth century to begin codifying American memories of civil conflict and spurring the future that readers would help to construct. To poet and frequent magazine contributor Paul Hamilton Hayne, Browne declared in 1870, "I want the new South, so far as it may be new, to be distinctly and especially the *South,* and not a bastard New England." Nowhere was he more successful in mounting sectional resistance to what he called "Yankeeisation" than in the reconstructive pages of the *Southern Magazine*.[6]

Railing against the spirit of "centralism and consolidation" or, as he insisted, the "club-law" imposed by the despotic North, Browne advanced instead a vision of Southern cum American civilization that scorned paramount national citizenship to promote local and white interests, equally bound to a revolutionary past and an industrial future.

"The true policy of Conservatism," he wrote in his monthly column "The Green Table," "is not (if that were possible) to blot out the past, but to lead the country, which has gone widely astray, back to the true paths, and to go forward in them." What the Baltimore editor valued in his uninterrupted campaign for states' rights was the principle of "local self-government," whose guarantee of personal liberties thwarted the reach of federal bayonets. "Every step towards empire on the part of the government," he further wrote, "is a step toward the enslavement of the citizens" (Dec. 1874, 647). Dead set against Reconstruction legislatures, which he dismissed as "the domination of negroes and carpetbaggers" (Apr. 1873, 509), Browne feared not only the radical elevation of ex-slaves but the "taint of blood" that unification would encourage and the "mongrel race" that would cost the South its future by "fixing the savage element indelibly in the nerves and brain" (Aug. 1873, 254). Even the bedroom thus seemed vulnerable to the congressional imposition of change, as public policy obliterated individual rights.

To combat these malignancies, Browne joined contributing writers like Henry Ewbank, Edward V. Valentine, and G. W. Archer in fighting to preserve the heritage of Robert E. Lee and P. G. T. Beauregard, not only in the pages of the *Southern Magazine* but through the offices of the newborn Southern Historical Society that took as its purpose "the vindication of Southern history from misrepresentation" (Jan. 1874, 105). With one hand on the society's "Transactions," published as monthly addenda to the magazine beginning in July 1874, Browne reached with his free hand for a southern future conceived out of Baltimore's steady reliance on immigration and trade. "The South needs development," he had declared. "She requires railways, canals and public improvements of all sorts, which she has neither money nor credit to pay for, and without which she must languish and may die" (Apr. 1873, 510). Not at all the agrarian model that southern apologists would consecrate after the frenetic urban ascendancy following World War I, Browne's conservative program looked instead to industrial development, foreign capital and labor, and a coalition with Western interests to resist Eastern monopolies and invite prosperity's return. "We must descend from the spectators' benches," he wrote, "come down into the arena, and take our part in the world's great struggle" (Jan. 1874, 105), a typically Baltimorean maneuver for transforming the legacy of the country's forefathers into the coin of the realm.

Browne's agenda for the South and his sense of the role that the defeated Confederacy might play in the national drama to come were deftly underscored by the peculiar function of setting in the war stories his magazine published. With surprising regularity, these seventeen narratives echoed Baltimore's border status by opening between places: at a window, on a ferry, in a harbor. Their characters, more often than not, seem poised for flight, on the Cumberland River in B. R. Forman's "A Confederate Prisoner's Experience" (Apr. 1870), in a railroad car in G. J. A. Coulson's "Mrs. Spriggins, the Neutral" (Feb. 1871), from a federal prison on Lake Erie in "An Escape from Johnston's Island" (Nov. 1872), or down the road out of town in R.S.R.'s "The Last Confederate Flag on the Atlantic" (July–Aug. 1875). While confederate prisoners and wartime nurses like Mrs. Spriggins are ready to jump on the railroads that served both their best interests and Browne's agenda, they are more nearly the Southerners Browne celebrated for resisting federal authority through artful dodging. Almost every Civil War story in the *Southern Magazine* was and is a narrative of escape, as though reciting episodes in the southern epic of national defeat meant exploring the territory under federal surveillance for avenues of resistance. Of course, when those avenues ran home for Confederate prisoners and wartime nurses, "home" was itself transformed from cloister to crossroads, as private refuge was charged in Browne's magazine with public purpose.

Snatching the "old homestead" from its apparent rhetorical serenity outside the sphere of war and loss suggests the regularity with which seemingly ordinary places, even the most private, were infused with political urgency when stories of the war were told. Especially in occupied territory, homes were no longer depicted as sacred to family but as open to all comers. Like other public sites during Reconstruction, they could therefore be cast as the imaginative spaces in which national identity was forged and might then be called heterotopias, Michel Foucault's term for everyday places that are charged with ideal purpose as private citizens are publicly bound to people they scarcely know. Reaching for such politically vested territory the way that Browne once reached for southern turf, Foucault writes, "The space in which we live, which draws us out of ourselves, in which the erosion of our lives, our time, and our history occurs, the space that claws and gnaws at us, is also, in itself, a heterogeneous space."[7] On streets and in trains, as Foucault points out, people are bound to a set of peculiar and irreducible relations that make real places shimmer, imbued as such places are with the mythic function of orienting personal desire to public civility. If utopias invert the real and are therefore "nowhere" in every sense, Foucault's heterotopias counter the real outside of ordinarily trafficked intersections and are therefore "not here" but along the border of the familiar. By way of example, Foucault points to military barracks, boarding schools, prisons, and gardens, all places on the outside of quotidian life even as it was represented in journals like the *Southern Magazine.*

Before and after Appomattox, almost any war story in almost any magazine served to buttress some version of the nation's legacy and some vision of its future, even the tentative future of the Confederacy. Mise-en-scène thus generally involved claiming ordinary space for patriotic purposes, and war stories generally culminated in lessons that citizens would recognize. In principle, at least, heterotopias abounded when warring nations told their tales. But Foucault's keen sense of exclusivity is best realized in those narrative sites that share his emphasis on an enforced break with traditional time and a compulsory or necessarily privileged rite of entry. So his museums or libraries suspended in time might be compared with the camp routines of boredom and drill or the shock of battlefield concussion, just as his saunas or motels might narratively become military inductions or hospitals stays. For Foucault, the ultimate heterotopian goal is the purging of resistance through illusion or compensation that he finds in boats or brothels, which might be seen by narrative analogy as the illusory freedom of a midnight canter through enemy territory or the compensatory appeal of federal camps for fugitive slaves. In short, heterotopias function for Foucault as countersites, territories of covert negotiation designed to transform crassly social spaces into the utopias we would supposedly like them to become. Speaking from the *Southern Magazine,* Browne might have added that the shape of the American utopia and thus of postwar nationalism was up for grabs.

In Civil War stories, the heterotopian role of setting was to insinuate public need into personal space and thereby to recast local households as public thoroughfares, to promote public households that could absorb wartime traffic, and to thwart the distinction between private property and public space. Domestic space was narratively reconceived in literary magazines nationwide so that private bedrooms, for instance, were on the decline as Reconstruction continued, while slave quarters (which had never once appeared in stories written while the war was fought) were showing up in literary magazines with greater frequency by the 1870s. Parlors were declining, but porches were holding their own; ballrooms were down, but gardens were more numerous and docks were on the rise. Wartime sites like prisons, hospitals, and battlefields were much less often invoked as the narrative itinerancy of the 1860s diminished, but in their place hotels, boarding houses, and offices gained a hold on narrative priorities to become more permanent and more public homes of a sort.

On a grander scale, too, Civil War stories slipped more frequently out of settled spaces and into border territory by moving west, a move that complicated heterotopian guarantees. As the Centennial approached, the Virginia locales that had characterized stories from the *Southern Literary Messenger* during the war and the *Land We Love* shortly thereafter, as well as from the Northern press to date, gave way to more Louisiana settings in magazines published on both sides of the Mason-Dixon line. Specifically, the open confrontation between North and South that was seen to spark the batteries and artillery blasts at Big Bethel in the *Southern Literary Messenger*'s "Peninsular Sketches" (Nov.–Dec. 1862; July 1863) or "the rattle of musketry, the heavy boom of cannon, and the fierce cry of onset" at the battle of Ball's Bluff in *Harper's Weekly*'s "The Revenge of a Goddess" (24 Sept. 1864, 622) almost entirely disappeared; in place of battle lines, heterotopian maneuvers and domestic relations wobbled strangely when a New Orleans family thought lost and a childhood sweetheart thought dead suddenly reappeared in *Lippincott*'s "The Young Priest" (Dec. 1868) or a Creole heiress turned servant was unmasked as a spy in "Mrs. F's Waiting Maid," published in *Harper's Monthly* (June 1867). In Louisiana, a different and internecine war was fought, a war in which Virginia's open wheat fields and purple cockles, clear enemies and abolitionist lessons, pitched battles and thus distant heterotopias for turning brothers into soldiers and husbands into citizens, were nowhere to be found.

The distinct functions of Virginia and Louisiana as narrative locales for rendering the personal more public, as the shiver of wartime clash and pain of national reconstruction were destined to do, is clearest in two roughly contemporary stories about discontent in the ranks, one published in the North and one published along the western border. "The Story of a Mutiny," which was circulated in 1870 by both the *Galaxy* (Aug.) in New York and Frederick Douglass's *New National Era* (11 Aug.) in the nation's capital, is set before Yorktown during George McClellan's siege of the city in April and May 1862, while the Peninsular Campaign was underway. The narrative centers on the army's failure to clothe and pay a regiment that then refuses to take arms, at least until the presiding general summons a firing squad. An editorial note reveals that the story is "undoubtedly true" since it came from an assistant surgeon who served in one of the regiments of General William H. Emory, here praised as a "distinguished" commander and a "stern, faithful soldier" (*Galaxy*, Aug. 1870, 224). The story's Foucauldian purpose, then, is to transform homeboys into citizens, citizens into soldiers, and soldiers into a disciplined regiment, and it is a telling sign of this Virginia bivouac cum heterotopia that the distant trenches around the city have been replaced for these resting troops by the more orderly rows of an infantry encampment, here described as "a canvas village with ten streets, each bounded by a row of tents on either side, and the parade-ground directly in front" (224). Eventually, the mutiny collapses, the men take arms, and the general leaves the parade ground with the hearts and minds of the soldiers in his pocket, ready confirmation that this Virginia home away from home will run with military precision on the nation's behalf. No wonder the story was published twice, both times in the North and both times in 1870, on the heels of Reconstruction's sternest legislative dictates.

More unsettling is a similar turn of events and a different set of pockets in "Sentenced and Shot," a story that appeared in Chicago's *Lakeside Monthly* (Nov. 1870) and was set near Shreveport, Louisiana, in 1865. In this story, the issue is the questionable execution of a well-liked sergeant at the hands of a despised General Custer, later to die at Little Bighorn and here vilified as a "yellow-haired circus-rider from the Shenandoah" come to teach "Army of the Potomac notions" (271) to the Military Department of the Gulf after Lee at Appomattox and even Kirby Smith in Galveston had surrendered. Once again bivouacking troops form a hollow square, a fitting image of the heterotopian alacrity with which private individuals support public ends by filling holes with meaning. This time, however, the soldiers face onto a vacant sugar field edged round by "long festoons of Spanish moss," a "shallow" and "murky" river, a "dreary old tumble-down village" and a "dilapidated levee," the "long-haired, swarthy, ill-clad remnants of the late Confederate army," a host of "distrustful, impoverished citizens moving about disconsolately," and the "*debris* of two armies scattered in every direction" (274) amid the stifling heat. Once again the general prevails, this time by rescuing the offending sergeant within seconds of the execution volley that the blindfolded man hears as fatal and that the general means as instructive, especially on the periphery of the Virginia discipline he knew best.

But it is a sign of this corrosive heterotopia that its transformative mission nearly fails; across the devastated sugar plantations of Louisiana, the sergeant's regiment has carried to the execution loaded carbines and forty rounds in stored cartridge boxes. As the narrator observes, "To be shot by a rebel at Alexandria, Virginia, in 1861, is not at all like being shot by your friends at Alexandria, Louisiana, in 1865" (270). Assigned to occupy a defeated country while Virginia regiments were packing up and going home, the Second Cavalry resists the general's eastern authority and the camp's heterotopian design and thus frays the national purpose that the soldiers were enlisted to serve. Particularly as the reconstructing states moved away from the war, stories set in Louisiana like "Sentenced and Shot" revealed bayous of deception and chapels of foreign ritual, the iron gates of decrepitude and the moss-drapery of madness, where things were seldom what they seemed and never what they seemed in Virginia.

Even in the *Southern Magazine*, whose stories were almost always in transit, the distinction between Virginia and Louisiana as settings was pronounced. On the whole, Browne's journal associated Virginia with the older country of revolutionary days and Louisiana with the more tempestuous union that would emerge from Reconstruction. Richmond, in particular, stood for tidewater aspirations and what the Confederacy might have been, while Red River parishes suggested backwater truculence and what the South might become. As a comparison of representative stories reveals, Virginia and Louisiana could be used as spatial markers for a ragged nation whose military districts were struggling toward the Centennial. With renegade insistence, the *Southern Magazine* thereby charted the difference between Confederate nationalism and Yankee occupation, established order and ad hoc resistance, straight roads and mud.

How much was once riding on the orderly triumph of Richmond is perhaps clearest in a Southern story that rides readers out of the besieged capital. "A Midnight Ride from Petersburg" (Dec. 1871) follows a late-night carriage quietly requisitioned by the quartermaster general for friends, a carriage that takes readers past surprisingly settled turf —civilian tent camps on the city's edge, Confederate breastworks, Beauregard's headquarters and Lee's distant flag, the "lonely, silent streets" of the shelled city, houses like "huge sentinels" (705–6) and a railroad sitting room turned barracks—before arriving at the iron rails upon which the last train waits to depart. Aboard the carriage and then the train, characters become fugitives looking for a way out of a Confederate heterotopia gone wrong, here described as the "citadel of a young nation's hope" (703) that the fugitives and the journal's readers relinquish.

If Virginia became thereby the site of hope and loss in the *Southern Magazine*, Louisiana was more readily the site of loss and hope, however sly. Loss is initially foremost in "A Trying Journey" (Nov. 1872) when a wagon loaded with cotton bales to be sold in Baton Rouge leaves the ill-supplied hospitals of New Orleans. Almost immediately, the wagon slips into ruts and a quagmire of mud; after prying the vehicle loose, the story's heroines further endure three rainswept miles in the woods and then a trudge into town so the wagon will not be confiscated, only to lose the cotton while the Yankees pocket the proceeds. This misfortune is the last in a narrative series of transactions that begins in New Orleans, a city occupied by Northern troops early in the war and thus a place where exploding shells were less a reality than business deals. The story's protagonists are repeatedly taken in, most importantly by the federal authorities in New Orleans who do not honor their bargain to meet hospital needs when the cotton is sold. Along the road, the ladies subsequently stay in a chamber that is infested ("the beds, sheets, walls, floors were alive, a marching army" [624]), in a plantation manor that has been sacked, and in a hotel that fronts on the daily maneuvers of a black U.S. regiment. Amid occupied territory, there seem to be no tent cities with bedroom furniture, no silent streets with houses standing guard, no waiting trains on iron roads.

Nevertheless, these resourceful Louisiana ladies are taken in by their friends as well as by their enemies. Along the road to market, they are repeatedly offered assistance and lodging by other Southerners who resent the Northern interlopers. The ladies are thereby portrayed less as fugitives finding a way out than as temporary refugees finding a way in, however meager, to a relocated "home." Robbed of their "citadel" when the Yankees take New Orleans, they opt for the trade in cotton that Browne himself might have recommended and the home among strangers that, at least for them and for a while, replaces Northern occupation in New Orleans with Southern solidarity along the road west. In the chamber, the plantation manor, and then the hotel, they discover progressively more public homes away from home along the border of the familiar road, homes that thereby become sites of covert Southern negotiation outside the trafficked intersections of occupied territory. Of course, such local countersites function differently from the Yankee heterotopia par excellence in New Orleans, where General Benjamin F. Butler's "Woman Order" midwar sought to bring even belligerent ladies to heel by declaring them prostitutes when they insulted Northern troops. In the *Southern Magazine* a decade later, New Orleans disappears almost immediately in the "trying journey" from public orders to private escape in a competing public cause, a journey that would transform private homes into way stations charged with unifying purpose.

Enlisted in the cause of Southern resistance, home as setting in Browne's journal began itself to shimmer, imbued as it became with the mythic function of orienting the private intransigence of characters to the public education of readers. More than other journals after the Civil War, the *Southern Magazine* undertook the public task of binding private citizens to others they scarcely knew through the process of reading and thus through narrative encounter and the charged political function of southern hospitality. Specifically, Browne's readers could grasp the appeal of a national homecoming and the transformative potential of border settings in the verve and idiosyncrasy of Caroline Marsdale's stories of the mid-1870s. Two of these tales were Civil War narratives that can be read for the unusual domestic space they carve out, not only as adventures when earlier southern magazines had been steeped in doom but also as exercises in countering Northern rhetorical designs on "the South." In every sense, Marsdale's stories arise out of border territory, even in getting published at all. Because Baltimore never deserted the Union in defending the South, the city could sponsor the postwar forum that would insist on defining national reconstruction as the adventure of returning home to founding fathers. Because Marsdale's stories banish the level battlefields of Virginia for the darker pine forests and mysterious bayous of the deeper South, her settings complicate the supposed obeisance of the late Confederate states and, in local details worth a closer look, frustrate the imposition of Northern hegemony. Because southern magazines like Browne's could circulate such stories to thousands of readers, whereas the antebellum *Portico* could only reach hundreds, the booming magazine trade could help negotiate the cultural space in which boys from Boston and boys from Baltimore would suddenly become national citizens.

One of Marsdale's stories is worth examining because it relies on the skedaddle of the western war to mediate the upheaval inside the house of the Union. Entitled "Cousin Jack," the story was published in December 1873 and set a decade earlier in the bayou country north of New Orleans. It tells the tale of a wounded Confederate scout who escapes federal troops in Unionist strongholds to make his way back home, a tale employing shifting narrators and events to weigh marriage against respite, the dilapidated log cabin of Jack Harrington's cousins in Sabine Parish against the manor of the Union-loving Miss Calline up country. Where the Harrington family home along the Bayou Teche is located outside New Orleans, the wartime removal of the cousins to the more northern Sabine Parish is a relocation to true border country, and Miss Calline's stately home and Unionist sympathies are on the border of a border war. In 1863, after one eggnog too many, Cousin Jack throws off his stolen Yankee overcoat to display his Confederate jacket and then successfully escapes the Yankee soldiers Miss Calline summons by hightailing it through woods and clearings, over fences, and across ditches before flinging himself into the river that delivers him to his own picket line. If Jack Harrington were a sort of midwar text for the body politic,

it would be hard to read his book by its jacket and harder still to block-
ade the channels that allow him to slip away from Yankee reconnais-
sance. Over the river and through the woods, Cousin Jack could still be
headed in 1863 for his Confederate home and the independence secured by revolutionary war.

But in 1873, when Marsdale's story appeared, Reconstruction had
already been imposed on the South, federal troops had returned to occupy Louisiana, and Republican congressmen were already representing
the state in the nation's capital. So it is revealing that Captain Harrington escapes from the deceptive Miss Calline as though on the edge of
an unwelcome heterotopia—that is, he bolts from a spiral staircase out
a second-story window across the roof of the front piazza and down the
prickly trunk of a holly tree. The "ten thousand separate and distinct
scratches" (717) he suffers suggest the price a recalcitrant South would
pay for past dereliction and the initiatory rite that would bring even
erring Louisiana back to the household of the Union and the demands
of paramount national citizenship. Like the wounded arm Jack later carries in a sling, the scratches amount to a lasting sign of the war that the
captain needs to have tended.

In Marsdale's story, however, Jack Harrington discovers no trustworthy nurse in his fetching hostess, despite her good looks ("the prettiest
girl I ever saw in all my life" [714]). After all, he could have taken her
fancy only if he had left his Yankee overcoat on and only if he had bowed
to the imposition of Northern troops in the regularly trafficked corridors of Miss Calline's heterotopian manor. Instead, the Confederate officer returns "home" from the "theatre of war" to marry his cousin.
Against all odds ("I was running like the mischief from about forty
million Yankees" [713]), he makes his way back to a household of Southern women who are busy knitting his future to their past and thus his
lightfooted energy to their family credentials. In the process, the sphere
of Marsdale's war, where even pretty girls are skirmishing, infiltrates her
household arena, which for the Harrington refugees is makeshift, ra-
tioned, and given to skirmishing for the narrative floor. Demanding his
right to talk ("Miss Mollie Harrington, I should like to know which of us
is to tell this story!" [715]), Cousin Jack fights for dibs on what is his,
much as James Parton fought for authors and William Hand Browne
fought for "the South." For Marsdale, the exiled Confederate household
is caught up in the public promise of Reconstruction, and the fight that
Cousin Jack brings home itself becomes theatre, the surprisingly heterogeneous space of Civil War stories in literary magazines that took the

war to the homefront and took "home" to Browne's short-lived southern theatre of postwar opportunity.

Examining the relocation of conflict to rural Louisiana as well as the narrative demand to come "home from the theatre of war" to perpetual border territory in the *Southern Magazine* makes it easier to understand those tropes by which the Civil War would later become known: the emergence of divided kinsmen as fictional embodiments of the "house divided" in Civil War novels of the 1880s and 1890s; the broad appeal of industrializing the South and of a wholly Southern romance of Reconstruction in *Gone with the Wind* decades later; and the continued contest between kinship affiliations and national allegiance that the outbreak of war sharpened and that regional literature has complicated ever since. During and after the Civil War, the audacious magazine industry, sprawling beyond Boston and New York and Philadelphia, was singularly positioned to articulate how the Civil War would finally be remembered and how a prickly national citizenship would thereafter be defined.

NOTES

1. Varying perspectives on the war's first clash may be found in Frank Towers, "'A Vociferous Army of Howling Wolves': Baltimore's Civil War Riot of April 19, 1861," *Maryland Historian* 23 (Fall–Winter 1992): 1–27; Edmund Wilson, *Patriotic Gore: Studies in the Literature of the American Civil War* (New York: Farrar, Straus, and Giroux, 1962), 395–401; Matthew Page Andrews, "Passage of the Sixth Massachusetts Regiment through Baltimore, April 19, 1861," *Maryland Historical Magazine* 14 (1919): 60–76; and George William Brown, *Baltimore and the Nineteenth of April, 1861: A Study of the War* (Baltimore: N. Murray, 1887), which also examines the legal and political consequences of Baltimore's insubordination.

2. This discussion of Baltimore's early commercial development is drawn from Sherry H. Olson, *Baltimore: The Building of an American City* (Baltimore: Johns Hopkins Univ. Press, 1980), 41–101; Jane N. Garrett, "Philadelphia and Baltimore, 1790–1840: A Study in Intra-Regional Unity," *Maryland Historical Magazine* 55 (1960): 1–13; Writers' Program of the Work Projects Administration in the State of Maryland, *Maryland: A Guide to the Old Line State* (New York: Oxford Univ. Press, 1940), 196–212; and J. Thomas Scharf, *History of Baltimore City and County* (Philadelphia: Louis H. Everts, 1881), 281–310. For a more ample discussion of Baltimore's domestic trade corridors, see James Weston Livingood, *The Philadelphia-Baltimore Trade Rivalry, 1780–1860* (Harrisburg: Pennsylvania Historical and Museum Commission, 1947); and for specific information on the city's growing international trade, see Marshall W. Fishwick, "*The Portico* and Literary Nationalism after the War of 1812," *William and Mary Quarterly* 8 (1951): 239.

3. In addition to Marshall Fishwick's remarks on the *Portico*, see Sam G. Riley, *Magazines of the American South* (Westport, Conn.: Greenwood, 1986), 173–76; Kent Ljungquist, "*The Portico*," in *American Literary Magazines: The Eighteenth and Nineteenth Centuries*, ed. Edward E. Chielens (Westport, Conn.: Greenwood, 1986), 323–28; John C. McCloskey, "A Note on *The Portico*," *American Literature* 8 (1936–37): 300–304; and Frank Luther Mott, *A History of American Magazines* (New York: Appleton, 1930), 1:293–96. For substantive attention to Baltimore's cultural growth, see Rollo G. Silver, "The Baltimore Book Trade, 1800–1825," *Bulletin of the New York Public Library* 57 (1953): 114–25; William R. Taylor, *Cavalier and Yankee: The Old South and American National Character* (New York: Harper and Row, 1957), 177–201; William D. Hoyt, "The Monday Club," *Maryland Historical Magazine* 49 (1954): 301–13; and Ottilie Sutro, "The Wednesday Club: A Brief Sketch from Authentic Sources," *Maryland Historical Magazine* 38 (1943): 60–68. For a useful corrective to J. Thomas Scharf's engaging but occasionally inaccurate description of the Delphian Club and its activities, see John Earle Uhler, "The Delphian Club: A Contribution to the Literary History of Baltimore in the Early Nineteenth Century," *Maryland Historical Magazine* 20 (1925): 305–46.

4. On the eve of the journal's momentous change in title, retiring editor and publisher Lawrence Turnbull noted in "A Parting Word" that his intent had been "to develop the nascent literature of the South," a goal that the new host of editors fully shared. See *New Eclectic Magazine* 7 (Dec. 1870): 766–68. For the broader statement of Baltimore's postwar stake in journal production, see Ray Morris Atchison, "Southern Literary Magazines, 1865–1877" (Ph.D. diss., Duke University, 1956), 28. An overview of Baltimore's commercial success on the heels of the Civil War, here just begun, may be found in Olson, *Baltimore*, 149–97; and Carl Bode, *Maryland: A Bicentennial History* (New York: Norton, 1978), 149–73.

5. For information on the emergence of international copyright legislation in the United States, see R. R. Bowker, *Copyright: Its Law and Its Literature* (1886; rpt. Littleton, Colo.: Fred B. Rothman, 1986), 1–42; James J. Barnes, *Authors, Publishers, and Politicians: The Quest for an Anglo-American Copyright Agreement, 1815–1854* (Columbus: Ohio State Univ. Press, 1974); Barbara A. Ringer, *The Demonology of Copyright* (New York: R. R. Bowker, 1974); Perry Miller, *The Raven and the Whale: The War of Words and Wits in the Era of Poe and Melville* (New York: Harcourt, Brace, 1956), 88–103; Andrew J. Eaton, "The American Movement for International Copyright, 1837–60," *Library Quarterly* 15 (1945): 95–122; and *Meeting of Authors and Publishers, at the Rooms of the New York Historical Society, April 9, 1868, and Organization of the International Copyright Association* (New York: International Copyright Association, 1868). For indications of the shifting royalty arrangements struck at various American publishing houses during the nineteenth century, see Sidney P. Moss, "Charles Dickens and Frederick Chapman's Agreement with Ticknor and Fields," *Papers of the Bibliographical Society of America* 75 (1981): 33–38; Heyward Ehrlich, "The Putnams on Copyright: The Father,

the Son, and a Ghost," *Papers of the Bibliographical Society of America* 63 (1969): 15–22; and James J. Barnes, "Edward Lytton Bulwer and the Publishing Firm of Harper and Brothers," *American Literature* 38 (1966): 35–48. For postwar congressional debates, see John Y. Cole, "Ainsworth Spofford and the Copyright Law of 1870," *Journal of Library History, Philosophy, and Comparative Librarianship* 6 (1971): 34–40; Thorvald Solberg, "International Copyright in Congress, 1837–1886," *Library Journal* 11 (1886): 250–80; and the *Congressional Globe*, 36th Cong., 2d sess., 1861, 30, pt. 1; *Congressional Globe*, 42nd Cong., 2d sess., 1871–72, 45, pts. 1 and 3; and *Congressional Record*, 51st Cong., 2d sess., 1891, 22, pt. 3.

6. Browne to Hayne, 30 July 1870, cited in Jay B. Hubbell, *The South in American Literature, 1607–1900* (Durham, N.C.: Duke Univ. Press, 1954), 718. Otherwise, the most valuable sources on Browne are Leonard Butts, "*The Southern Review* (Bledsoe's)," in *American Literary Magazines*, 409–13; Richard J. Cox's sketch in the *Biographical Dictionary of American Educators*, ed. John F. Ohles (Westport, Conn.: Greenwood, 1978), 1:187; John Martin Vincent's sketch in the *Dictionary of American Biography*, ed. Allen Johnson and Dumas Malone (New York: Scribner's, 1929), 2:170–71; and James W. Bright, "In Memoriam, William Hand Browne, 1828–1912," *Johns Hopkins Univ. Circular* 252 (Feb. 1913): 3–28.

7. Michel Foucault, "Of Other Spaces," *Diacritics* 16 (Spring 1986): 23.

11

NOT JUST FILLER AND NOT JUST SENTIMENTAL
Women's Poetry in American Victorian Periodicals, 1860–1900

PAULA BENNETT

•

ONE of the truisms of American literary criticism is that nineteenth-century magazine verse, especially that by women, served as filler for editors burdened with random amounts of space at the ends of articles and stories. On this basis, critics have dismissed the ubiquitous presence of women's poetry in national and regional periodicals, particularly in the second half of the century, as lacking substantive significance. When the quality of these poems is discussed at all, it is usually to support early modernist contentions that American poetry was in a parlous state as the century drew to a close. With a few exceptions (most notably, Lizette Woodworth Reese and Louise Imogen Guiney), women magazine poets—along with the bulk of their male peers—are treated as an eminently forgettable horde whose contributions to the enrichment of American literature were negligible at best.[1] Even Cheryl Walker, in her groundbreaking study of nineteenth-century American women's poetry, *The Nightingale's Burden: Women Poets and American Culture before 1900* (Bloomington: Indiana Univ. Press, 1982), has relatively little to say about the magazine poets as a group or, even more tellingly, about the role periodicals played in circulating women's poetry generally throughout the century.

In this essay, I will argue that nineteenth-century periodicals' receptivity to women's poetry, especially in the second half of the century, was pivotal to the evolution of women's poetry in the United States, whether this poetry was filler or not. Indeed, this receptivity was essential if writers such as Amy Lowell and H.D. were to play the leading role they did in the development of early modernist verse. As points of entry into the process of circulation, late-nineteenth-century periodicals provided space for and helped train a well-defined cohort of professional women poets. As Joanne Dobson has argued, without the efforts made by these nineteenth-century precursors and by women poets generally in the century, early-twentieth-century women writers would not have had the knowledge, let alone the venues, to sell their wares.[2] What is equally important but never acknowledged, however, is that they would not have had the necessary precedents on which to build their own careers as risk-taking, stylistically experimental writers.

Even if every woman-authored poem appearing in national and regional periodicals between 1860 and 1900—literally thousands of poems—were "filler" (in itself, a dubious assumption),[3] it would not obviate the significance of the following facts:

1. Every periodical that included poems in these years carried poems by women, sometimes in numbers exceeding those by men, especially as the century progressed.

2. Even the most prestigious American periodicals tended to carry five or six poems per issue.

3. As a result, hundreds of women's poems were published each month in the United States during this time.

4. Almost all American periodicals discontinued the convention of anonymous authorship by 1860, so that not only was the author's sex readily identifiable, but so was her status as a professional writer.

5. Contrary to common critical opinion, the periodicals did publish "innovative" writing. Indeed, where women's poetry is concerned, they track with remarkable fidelity stylistic and thematic changes as they occurred from one end of the century to the other.

6. And finally, the periodicals carrying these innovative poems reached nationwide into the bourgeois homes from which most early modernist women poets came, thus helping to foster the next generation of explicitly revolutionary writers, whether or not the latter acknowledged their debt.

In *The Labor of Words*, Christopher Wilson observes that publishing history has generally relied "upon the accounts (and the yardsticks) of the newer progressive elites" for its version of "Gilded Age magazines." As a result, he writes, "the magazine revolution of these years is described rather one-dimensionally as the overthrow of a stale and narrow-minded tradition in favor of Progressive politics and literary 'realism.'"[4] Wilson's remarks were directed toward publishing history's treatment of the emergence of early-twentieth-century naturalistic fiction (Jack London, Upton Sinclair, et al.). But his words apply equally well to the way in which the emergence of early modernist women's poetry is conventionally depicted. Here, too, we are told that a "stale and narrow-minded tradition"—usually identified with domestic sentimentalism and, somewhat later in the century, with genteel style—was overthrown by a progressive elite that, writing for small avant-garde magazines, brought to their poetry, as Suzanne Clarke put it, "the revolution of the word."[5]

The enormous stylistic achievement of early modernist women poets cannot be gainsaid, and I have no wish to do so. Nevertheless, the thrust of this argument depends on comparisons worked in reverse, and it distorts accordingly. No matter how stultifying the domestic ideology of early-nineteenth-century sentimentalists may seem to us or how limited their poetic range, these women were bold, new voices in their own day. They, no less than their politically active sisters, helped transform the social and moral values constituting their sphere into a discourse of power that justified women's active participation outside as well as inside the home.[6] And late-nineteenth-century women poets were the direct heirs and perpetuators of this discursive commitment to claiming new ground for women.

Far from being uniformly genteel or relying, as their immediate precursors had done, on domestic sentimentalism's unified and by then stale set of social and rhetorical values, much late-nineteenth-century poetry by women is what I would call heavily negotiated. That is, it is by turns ironic, oblique, angry, sexual, parodic, cynical, politically astute, questioning, "realistic," and, as in the work of Sarah Piatt, who was all the above, despairing. As such, it is very much a reflection of the late-nineteenth-century "new woman" who was then in the process of cultural formation. As a number of these poets expressly recognized, this was a woman who by 1900 could pride herself on being, as one disgruntled male reviewer put it, a member of the "unsentimental sex" (*Chapbook*, Sept. 1897, 323).

The erasure of this poetry from cultural memory has, therefore, been one of the most thoroughly disruptive events in the history of women's writing in the United States. Not only has it entailed the loss of poems worthy of study in themselves, but it has also obscured the close and necessary connection between the cultural work done by late-nineteenth-century feminism and the production of early modernist women writers. In breaking the bond between women's political and artistic enfranchisement, the erasure of late-nineteenth-century women's poetry has made the flowering of women's poetry at the beginning of the twentieth century seem a far more autonomous and self-contained event than it actually was.[7]

History, as Cary Nelson observes in *Repression and Recovery*, "is never simply given but is always politically, rhetorically, and institutionally constituted."[8] In literary history as elsewhere, we read the version of those who won. In describing the emergence of strong women's poetry at the beginning of the twentieth century, literary historians have colluded with the early modernist women whose triumph they record—a triumph that rendered not just old-fashioned but unread the work of hundreds of earlier women poets. In the process, these historians have helped early modernist women "kill the mother."[9] That is, they have effectively silenced earlier generations of women writers, from whose poetry early modernist women wanted to distinguish their own verse.

If this silence is to be ended—the silence not of women but of the history of women's words—and if we are to understand how a large number of highly professional and competitive American women poets were able to assume a leading role among the next generation of writers, female and male, then we must first recover the knowledge of what, in Nelson's succinct formulation, "we no longer know we have forgotten,"[10] appreciating late-nineteenth-century women's poetry not just for its precursor status but also for the substantive stylistic and developmental achievement it represents in its own right.

The story of late-nineteenth-century women's periodical poetry begins, of course, a good fifty years earlier in the host of national and regional women's magazines (Carl Degler estimates about a hundred)[11] that sprang up between 1784 and 1860, magazines such as the *Ladies' Literary Cabinet* (1819), *Ladies' Magazine* (1828), *Godey's Lady's Book* (1830), *Ladies' Companion* (1834), *Ladies' Garland* (1837), and so on. Made viable by the enormous increase in bourgeois women's literacy through the first half of the century[12] and by the felt need on the part of America's new citizen class to educate itself—largely through the instrumentality of educated mothers—these magazines flourished well into the 1860s and '70s. Not only were they read by thousands of women, but, more important for my purposes, they were written, edited, and—albeit far more rarely—published by women as well, thus making a significant number of bourgeois women professional or money-making writers for the first time.[13]

If by 1860 women had engaged in every aspect of the writing game, no facet was better suited to their gifts than the writing of poetry, according to the gender theory of the day. Given that women had been designated by domestic ideology the empresses of the heart, not the head, the lyric expression of religious, domestic, and even political (i.e., nationalistic) affections seemed, inarguably, part of their domain.[14] And once women poets had staked out this turf—or had it staked out for them—they produced poems in great numbers. Made familiar to editors and publishers through their regular appearance in women's magazines (and in local newspapers), these poets were soon picked up by mainstream publications as well: *Knickerbocker* (created in 1833), *Graham's Magazine* (1840), *Harper's Monthly Magazine* (1850), among others. In a new country, hungry for a literature as well as an identity of its own, books followed and reputations were built: Lydia Huntley Sigourney, Hannah Gould, Anna Maria Wells, Maria Gowen Brooks, Lucretia Davidson, Frances Osgood, the Cary sisters, to name a few.

It is not just the numbers, however, but also the professionalism of these early nineteenth-century women poets that impresses. As Joanne Dobson has pointed out, far from emulating the cultural stereotype of women poets as retired domestic singers (nightingales), who wrote out of personal pain, both as individuals and writers, women such as Sigourney, Brooks, and Osgood were highly sophisticated public figures with wide national and even international followings.[15] Both constrained and empowered by the domestic ideology that inspired their verse and legitimated them as writers, they became spokespersons during their lifetimes for the values, complaints, and potentials of their sphere. If they were sentimental, their sentimentalism was morally and epistemologically based. They spoke the intuitions and precepts of the heart—not simply heartfelt and excessive maunderings, as our own definition of the sentimental would suggest.[16] And they were heeded accordingly, even by such esteemed men as Ralph Waldo Emerson. At a time when religious enthusiasm was at its height and intuition and feeling were deemed legitimate forms of knowing, these poets were able to carve out a considerable niche for themselves in the society they served.

By 1860, however, the United States was suffering from a series of profound cultural upheavals that rendered the intuitive truths and moral insights, as well as the national appeal, of domestic sentimentalism problematic. The events at Seneca Falls in 1848 had brought to the surface deep ideological differences among women that undermined domestic sentimentalism's epistemological claim to truth as well as to the self-evidentiary nature of its ethical prescriptions. Even more profoundly, the country itself was caught in the throes of a sectionalism that would soon break out in civil war, putting, for those who thought about it (Herman Melville and Emily Dickinson, for example), all truth in doubt. The time was ripe for change. While many women poets, like their male peers, still clung to older forms and older ways of knowing, for others poetry became a flexible medium through which to explore, question, and redefine their world and the fissures now characterizing it.

Freed by the epistemological uncertainty that the collapse of domestic sentimentalism brought about, these women poets began to move toward what I would call protomodernism. That is, they moved toward a poetry of obliqueness and doubt that undermined the idealism on which traditional nineteenth-century American poetics, whether practiced by men or women, was based. Dispensing with the patriotic, the romantic, and the visionary—the dominant strains in nineteenth-century American verse whether written by women or men—these women writers produced poems that were instead ironic.[17] Subtly or in some cases blatantly, their poems challenged the social, political, religious, and rhetorical values that had been fundamental to antebellum poetry and to bourgeois ways of antebellum life.

To take what may at first seem like a very unprepossessing example, I will begin with a poem published in the November 1861 *Atlantic Monthly,* "The Wild Endive" by Annie Fields, wife of James T. Fields, the *Atlantic's* editor. To us, Fields's poem may not seem particularly interesting or novel, perhaps at best a bland echo of the deeply moving first section from William Carlos Williams's "Spring and All" that lacks the latter's marvelous verbal specificity:

> Only the dusty common road,
> The glaring weary heat;
> Only a man with a soldier's load,
> And the sound of tired feet.
>
> Only the lonely creaking hum
> Of the Cicada's song:
> Only a fence where tall weeds come
> With spiked fingers strong.
>
> Only a drop of the heaven's blue
> Left in a way-side cup;
> Only a joy for the plodding few
> And eyes that look not up.
>
> Only a weed to the passer-by,
> Growing among the rest,—
> Yet something clear as the light of the sky
> It lodges in my breast.

The fact that this poem, among others that Fields wrote, does seem to anticipate Williams ceases to be so bland, however, when one reads it in context (something that her recent biographer, Judith A. Roman, who follows earlier critics in dismissing Field's poetry out of hand, apparently failed to do.)[18] Seven months before "Wild Endive" appeared in the

Atlantic, in April, the war that people thought would only last three months had begun when Confederate forces under General P. G. T. Beauregard fired on Fort Sumter. By November, things were clearly not going well for the Union side, to which the *Atlantic* from its inception as a proabolition journal was fiercely devoted. Nevertheless, or perhaps as a result, the *Atlantic*'s pages were filled with fervently patriotic poetry of the kind that later would justly earn Edmund Wilson's sobriquet "patriotic gore,"[19] such as the following, from Oliver Wendell Holmes's "The Flower of Liberty," published in the same issue as "Wild Endive":

> In savage Nature's far abode
> Its tender seed our fathers sowed;
> The storm-winds rocked its swelling bud,
> Its opening leaves were streaked with blood,
> Till, lo! earth's tyrants shook to see
> The full-blown Flower of Liberty!
>   Then hail the banner of the free,
>   The starry Flower of Liberty!
>
> Behold its streaming rays unite
> One mingling flood of braided light,—
> The red that fires the Southern rose,
> With spotless white from Northern snows,
> And, spangled o'er its azure, see
> The sister Stars of Liberty!
>   Then hail the banner of the free,
>   The starry Flower of Liberty!
>
> The blades of heroes fence it round;
> Where'er it springs is holy ground;
> From tower and dome its glories spread;
> It waves where lonely sentries tread;
> It makes the land as ocean free,
> And plants an empire on the sea!
>   Then hail the banner of the free,
>   The starry Flower of Liberty!
>
>   (*Atlantic Monthly,* Nov. 1861, 550)

Despite the reality of national division and the horrifying reasons behind it, no doubt, no questioning, and, perhaps most strikingly, no disunity, are allowed to enter Holmes's poem. Neither the blood-streaked Indian wars, to which the speaker archly alludes when referring to "savage Nature's far abode," nor the blood-streaked backs of slaves are permitted to mar this vision of America as a "holy ground" or cast their blight upon the "tender seed our fathers sowed." If, as George Santayana claimed, genteel poetry was characterized by an absence of passion (a highly debatable point in itself), then Holmes's poem is not genteel, for it overflows with passion.[20] But it is passion inspired by and in service to a nationalist ideal. Romantic and visionary, a poem such as "The Flower of Liberty" makes no room for distance and irony as it goes about its ideological work. On the contrary, it all too closely embraces the shibboleths of its own era. In doing so, it is no different from the vast bulk of poetry written in response to the war, whether by men or women, from the perspective of the North or the South, whether in 1861 or long after the war itself was over.

But what then does one make of Fields's little poem? How does it fit in?

When read against "The Flower of Liberty" and its ilk, the first thing that astonishes in "Wild Endive" is the economy of its author's techniques as she strives to achieve rhetorical power (the repeated "onlys" onomatopoetically mimicking the burden the soldiers carry even as, by repetition, they mimic the cadence of plodding feet). Next, for a poem written in the early 1860s, "Wild Endive" exhibits striking specificity. If it is not Williams or Dickinson, nonetheless, when measured by the canons of late Victorian poetry that tended to elevate the generic, Fields has depicted an individual scene, a particular place. The road, the soldiers, the weeds, and the speaker's response to them are all carefully drawn.

Finally, however, not economy or specificity but thematic and tonal restraint, with all the ambiguity they bring to her poem, sets Fields's work a world apart from that of Holmes. Like Holmes, Fields does not directly address the war. But where Holmes does not do so because he wants to assert a higher, presumably unifying, transcendent ideal (the nation's birth in liberty), thus supporting his own side (the Union cause), with Fields this silence is the product of a studied and deliberate indifference, indeed, a resistance, to taking sides at all. She does not tell us who these soldiers are, or whether there is a war going on, or even which side God is on—if indeed, the references to the sky's light and heaven's drop of blue are allusions to God—not because she expects us to know these things already and agree with her position on them but because, in terms of this poem's strategies, none of these things should or do matter.

For Fields's poem, unlike Holmes's poem, is not a justification for the war, implicit or otherwise. Indeed, in some sense, though soldiers are central to the means by which it achieves meaning, it is not about war at all. Rather like the opening of the first section of Williams's "Spring and All," where the contagious hospital is mentioned only (seemingly) to be dropped, "Wild Endive" deliberately backgrounds death (the war) to discuss something else, "spiked fingers" and "stark dignity," "the way-side cup" with its "drop of . . . heaven's blue" and "the stiff curl of wildcarrot leaf,"[21] and human beings who in their weariness and despair either will or will not take hold of the significance of the life in the natural world around them, as Fields puts it, the "joy" available only to the "eyes that look not up."

In voiding the political, the transcendent, the romantic, and the visionary, the main staples of nineteenth-century poetry, whatever the ostensible subject, and discovering life and hope—or heaven's "drop of . . . blue"—in one of nature's most despised forms, roadside weeds, Fields, like Williams, was, I would suggest, voicing the weltanschauung of another era, an era in which irony would be the only acceptable garb for "truth." For both writers, poetry, like hope and life, is located not in romantic dreams or patriotic visions but in the meanest apprehensions of the here and now. Both can offer only the bare simplicities of nature by way of consolation to a blasted (whether war-torn or disease-ridden) world.

As an ironic, antiheroic war poem, "Wild Endive" suggests that by 1861, there were other women poets in the United States beside Dickinson who were prepared to step back from the idealizing as well as the sentimentalizing strategies characterizing so much nineteenth-century poetry. Another example, from the opposite end of this period, is Ella Wheeler Wilcox's "Her Prayer," published in *Frank Leslie's Popular Monthly* in May 1894. Although radically different from Field's poem in diction, tone, and subject, "Her Prayer" exhibits a similar inclination to the ironic and resistance to the ideal. Indeed, in this modern updating of the Petrarchan (love) sonnet, Wilcox takes pains to deny the possibility of transcendence to both her lovers. Instead, in what skirts perilously close to a parody of the form she employs, Wilcox uses the Petrarchan sonnet's conventional break between octet and sestet to mark her own deep split with the romantic love tradition from which, formally speaking, she draws and to which the octet itself is lavishly, if quite deceptively, devoted.

> She let down all the wonder of her hair;
> Its dusky clouds fell round her, and her form
> Shone like a Grecian statue through a storm.

One gleaming shoulder, beautiful as bare,
Leaned to the lips that used to sigh "How fair!"
   And the white beauty of one perfect arm,
   As ivory polished and as velvet warm,
Twined round his massive neck.

                     O Heart's despair!
In his cold eyes there lay no least desire,
   And not a thrill shot through him, though his head
   Lay pillowed on her breast. In days scarce fled
One touch of hers could set his blood on fire.
   "Hast thou no hell? Make one, O God!" she said.
   "Twere heaven, to earth with love and passion dead."

                                (530)

However uneven Wilcox was as a poet—and the excesses of her worst work were ridiculed even in her own day[22]—in this sonnet, she has made superb use of her form. Re-visioning the Petrarchan format, she has deployed its rich historical associations to depict (by way of unstated contrast and implicit parody), love's fate in the modern world. Like Petrarch, the male figure in this poem appears not to be married to his mistress, but unlike the archetypal medieval lover, whose name, by the sixteenth century, had become a watchword for enduring passion, the modern lover is not faithful. Nor does his desire refine him and make him a better man. On the contrary, having sexually consummated his passion for the lady, he has grown cold, losing all interest in her. Like male fidelity, male romantic love, it seems, remains what it always was, directly dependent on female unavailability. No road to higher knowledge, in this poem, at any rate, it is a matter of the flesh. Nothing more.

Yet what of the lady? As the woman in "Her Prayer" belatedly discovers, Laura yielding ceases to be Laura. Like the "dusky" (i.e., ambiguous) fall of her hair, whose unloosening hides as much as it reveals, her modern freedom is a self-contradicting boon at best, winning her little beyond the privilege of her despair. If the male lover has failed, then so, perhaps, has she, and so, perhaps, has modern love, which, in encouraging women to claim their sexual passion, seemed to promise so much and ends up giving so little—indeed, which ends up converting "heaven" (i.e., the bliss accessible through consummated passion) into something worse than hell. Is the lady, however great her pain and however sympathetically portrayed, not also responsible for this debacle? Is the blame entirely his?

Wilcox (or her speaker) does not say, and, as in "Wild Endive," this ironic resistance to taking sides, to resolving issues, is essential to the poem's strategy and point. The lovers are presented as they are in the midst of what appears to be a double folly. The poem offers no solution to the dilemma it poses, neither moralizing on the woman's folly nor condemning the man for his infidelity. Despite the lushness of her rhetoric, which harks back to a long line of male sonneteers, and despite what appears to be her own passionate identification with the woman in the poem, Wilcox's speaker is, to use modern parlance, simply telling it like it is and letting readers make of it what they will.

Mary B. Cummings does the same in much more up-to-date terms and with a far more cynical and blatantly parodic attitude in "Possession," published in December 1875 in the *Atlantic Monthly:*

I.

Summer and blossoms are lavish, my dearest;
    See this red rose!
Look how its buds press upon you; the nearest
Tries for your mouth with the gayest, sincerest
    Wish to unclose!
You were always a little neglectful, my brother,
    But why are you cold?
Take my word for it, Francis, there is n't another
To equal this roselet, for any flower-lover
    To have or to hold.

II.

Yes, but I've had it so long, and it bores me;
    What is its name?
Lifting its head in that way, it implores me
To care for it, look at it; see! it adores me
    Always the same!

(665)

It is, of course, not just the use of a brazenly conversational tone that startles in this poem but the explicitly antisentimental message, the almost Wildean perspective. The naive young "roselet" who thinks that love is all hearts, flowers, dependence, and adoration is doomed from the start. The reductive and essentialist cultural assumptions shaping her (bourgeois) female behavior have encouraged her to present herself as sweet, demur, adoring, and good. In the process, she has suppressed all traces of independent character, ironically degendering herself in her lover's eyes. To him, she is an it, without rights or personality of her own whom since he "possesses" he also feels free to dismiss.

Constructed as a dialogue between two speakers (a brother, Francis, and his unnamed sister), "Possession" is a singularly bitter poem and a ruthless debunking of some of the central tenets of "true womanhood" as well as the premises of many a romantic love story. Placed beside Wilcox's later sonnet, it suggests that the women of feminism's first wave, like those of its second, discovered early that the liberation of their sexuality could cut two ways: giving them freedom (a sense of rights), on the one hand, and opening them up to exploitation on the other. But, like "Wild Endive" and "Her Prayer," the effectiveness of Cummings's poem depends on the author's restraint and on her refusal to resolve the dilemma that her poem poses. Bitter, ironic, and oblique, the message of "Possession" is there but it is up to the reader to get it. The two speakers in this poem could be discussing roses, after all.

So could the speaker in Sarah Piatt's "There was a Rose," a poem that, appearing in the February 1872 *Atlantic Monthly*, recalls the horror of the Civil War only to sacrifice it, in an act of extraordinary poetic courage, to the enormity of personal desire, the insatiability of personal pain.

> "There was a Rose," she said,
> "Like other roses, perhaps, to you.
> Nine years ago it was faint and red,
>   Away in the cold dark dew,
>   On the dwarf bush where it grew.
>
> "Never any rose before
> Was like that rose, very well I know;
> Never another rose any more
>   Will blow as that rose did blow
>   When the wet wind shook it so.
>
> "'What do I want?'—ah, what?
> Why, I want that rose, that wee one rose,
> Only that rose. And that rose is not
>   Anywhere just now? God knows
>   Where all the old sweetness goes.
>
> "I want that rose so much:
> I would take the world back there to the night
> Where I saw it blush in the grass, to touch
>   It once in that fair fall light,
>   And only once, if I might.
>
> "But a million marching men
> From the North and the South would arise?
> And the dead—would have to die again?

And the women's widowed cries
Would trouble anew the skies?

"No matter. I would not care?
Were it not better that this should be?
The sorrow of many the many bear,—
Mine is too heavy for me.
And I want that rose, you see!"

(139)

While the rose in this poem could be contextualized in terms of the speaker's presumed biography—some event or loss that occurred nine years before (possibly around 1860 or 1861)—the poet herself refuses to do so. The only hints we are given are that the rose is "wee" and that the speaker values it far beyond its intrinsic worth. Indeed, the obscene excess of the speaker's desire is what is at stake in this poem. Otherwise, no hints or cues are provided to explain why she feels what she feels or says what she says.

Precisely because Piatt's speaker withholds this information, however, the rose in this poem becomes a good deal more than a rose. Without context to pin down what it presumably represents, the flower serves as an indeterminate symbol for loss itself, loss so great it divorces the speaker from her previous framework of values. To have this "rose" back—whatever it is—she would sacrifice the world and everyone in it. Her desire is as ruthless as her need.

Taken thus, Piatt's "rose" appears to signify less something in itself than a state of mind: a stability of value and sense of moral order that the war seems to have destroyed. That is, as in so much modernist poetry, the rose appears to be a private symbol for an imaginative construction of the world whose passing the poet mourns, as the oven bird was for Robert Frost and Helas was for H.D. At the gate between these two worlds, the imagined past and the diminished or blasted present, stands the angel of history with her flaming sword, barring the way.

In this poem, as in so much modernist poetry, irony and nostalgia derive from the fact that however much the speaker wishes, she knows she cannot go back.[23] Piatt's speaker is therefore left with an insatiable desire and unappeasable grief so great that, together they wipe out all other considerations. By the poem's end, everything is reduced to this one point of intense, compacted longing—not because the speaker is excessively attached to something that is worthless (a common definition of sentimentality)—but because in the loss of this "rose," all other losses are comprehended. All the speaker has left is her own desire. Nothing else matters. Indeed, within the field of vision established by this poem, nothing else exists. Time, loss, and desire have stripped her of everything. Even her vocabulary is stripped, as she brings the poem to a close in a series of Steinian monosyllables that stand for nothing outside themselves.

Like Fields's and Wilcox's irony and Cummings's cynicism, the flat tone, self-mockery, and world-weariness of Piatt's concluding stanza suggest that, at least for some literary women, fin de siècle disillusionment had taken hold well before the end of the century itself. For these precursor poets, as for many who would follow them, the traditional consolations and idealizing formulations of an earlier period, whether of love, politics, or religion, no longer worked. Nor did the master narratives and grand designs, formal and otherwise, of more heroic eras. Like those who would come later, they turned instead to irony, parody, and nostalgia.

Heirs of a war that demonstrated how little domestic ideology could do to stem the violence of (male) behavior—violence that women's "spirituality" was theoretically supposed to contain—yet aware that their own "liberation" might prove problematic also, these bourgeois women were far too bruised and too knowing to put their faith in the suasive power of sentiment. There was too much that was uncertain and changing in their lives for them to write as if the old ways or the old forms or even the old feelings and old words still worked. This is true even of such a seemingly sentimental poem as Sarah Orne Jewett's "Missing," published in the March 1882 *Harper's*. Here the silence of the flowers, transferred from the silent pallbearers who lay them on the coffin, replicates the speaker's silence on the subject of religious consolation, a silence that, as it were, ends up speaking for itself and speaking, by implication, for the death of the sentimental tradition from which the poem derives and to which its diction, form, and tone all seem to point:

> You walked beside me, quick and free;
>   With lingering touch you grasped my hand;
> Your eyes looked laughingly in mine;
>   And now—I can not understand.
>
> I long for you, I mourn for you,
>   Through all the dark and lonely hours,
> Heavy the weight the pallmen lift,
>   And cover silently with flowers.

(499)

Given that through the first half of the century (as through much of Christian history), poets, sentimental and otherwise, used flowers as symbols of resurrection, the silence of Jewett's flowers is a heavy weight indeed for this speaker to bear. But it is a weight eloquent in its heaviness and in the absences to which it points: the absence of assurance, the absence of God, and all the other epistemological and ontological absences that modernism has since filled with a torrent of brilliantly crafted words. However sentimental in some respects this poem might seem, a way of thinking, knowing, and speaking is coming to an end in it. Much beside the beloved one herself is missing from the world that "Missing" depicts, much that can never be restored.

With the exception of Sarah Piatt—whose work is far too extensive and complicated to discuss adequately here—none of the poets I have cited in this essay has the scope and volume to qualify as a major poetic voice.[24] This does not mean, however, that the publication of their poetry was without significance or that their writing did not involve acts of courage as well as of innovation. On the contrary, largely unrecognized though their contribution has been, these little-known magazine poets took risks many better-known and more established poets refused to take. Nor is it any wonder, given their achievement, that they were followed by poets such as Amy Lowell and H.D., however much the latter, for their own reasons, failed to acknowledge them. By breaking with early-nineteenth-century sentimentalism, epistemologically, morally, and in terms of their poetic strategies, these poets helped make the achievements of the later writers possible. Their passion, their independence, their disillusionment, their irony, and their distrust of both language and feeling were indispensable foundational elements for early modernist women's poetry.

No matter how different the poets are from those who preceded them or, equally important, from each other (for as noted earlier, late-nineteenth-century women's poetry was not homogeneous but heavily negotiated), the line from Sigourney to Osgood, to Fields, to Piatt, to Cummings, to Wilcox, to H.D. and Lowell is clear: each of these women helped prepare the public ear and thus make room in the public arena for the themes and strategies of the women poets who followed her. In this sense, we can say that the work of these nineteenth-century poets was never truly lost. Disseminated by the periodicals in their own lifetimes, it is alive today in the multitude of women poets now writing, and will remain alive as part of the contribution American letters has made to women poets yet to come.

NOTES

1. Since Edmund Clarence Stedman first called the late nineteenth century a "twilight interval" in American poetry, in *An American Anthology: 1787–1900* (Boston: Houghton Mifflin, 1900), xxviii, critics have followed this general line regarding work in this period. See, for example, David Perkins, *A History of Modern Poetry from the 1890s to the High Modernist Mode* (Cambridge: Belknap Press of Harvard Univ. Press, 1976), 88; Frank Luther Mott, *A History of American Magazines, 1885–1905* (Cambridge: Belknap Press of Harvard Univ. Press, 1957), 120–21.

2. Joanne Dobson, *Dickinson and the Strategies of Reticence: The Woman Writer in Nineteenth-Century America* (Bloomington: Indiana Univ. Press, 1989), 26–40.

3. The length of some women's poems alone would preclude their being used simply as filler. See, for example, Harriet Prescott Spofford, "Pomegranate-Flowers," *Atlantic Monthly* 7 (1861): 573–79 and Sara Piatt, "A Voyage to the Fortunate Isles," *Harper's* 47 (1873): 452–53.

4. Christopher Wilson, *The Labor of Words: Literary Professionalism in the Progressive Era* (Athens: Univ. of Georgia Press, 1985), 41.

5. Suzanne Clarke, *Sentimental Modernism: Women Writers and the Revolution of the Word* (Bloomington: Indiana Univ. Press, 1991), 3, 6. Clarke herself took the phrase from a 1929 essay of that name by Eugene Jolas.

6. The paradoxically political thrust of domestic sentimentalism has been studied extensively by Carl Degler and Glenna Matthews. See Carl Degler, *At Odds: Women and the Family in America from the Revolution to the Present* (Oxford: Oxford Univ. Press, 1980), 144–77, 279–327; and Glenna Matthews, *Just a Housewife: The Rise and Fall of Domesticity in America* (Oxford: Oxford Univ. Press, 1987), 35–91.

7. This critical perspective is now being actively challenged by a number of different critics on a variety of grounds. See, for example, Paula Bennett, "Late Nineteenth-Century American Women's Nature Poetry and the Evolution of the Imagist Poem," *Legacy* 9 (1992): 1–15; Clarke, *Sentimental Modernism*, 19–41; and Cheryl Walker, *Masks Outrageous and Austere: Culture, Psyche, and Persona in Modern Women Poets* (Bloomington: Indiana Univ. Press, 1991), 1–15.

8. Cary Nelson, *Repression and Recovery: Modern American Poetry and the Politics of Cultural Memory, 1910–1945* (Madison: Univ. of Wisconsin Press, 1989), 5.

9. Walker has attributed early modernist women's hostility to their precursors' poetry to a Bloomian anxiety of influence. See *Masks*, 19–20. The analogy seems just. Late Victorian women poets were an enormously powerful group, and early modernist women needed to separate themselves clearly from them. Unfortunately, the way in which they did so (by effectively denying their existence) helped the cause of neither group of women.

10. Nelson, *Repression and Recovery*, 3.

11. Degler, *At Odds*, 377.

12. According to Degler, by 1850, when the census first recognized figures

on literacy, 87 percent of all white women could read and write. By 1860, 94 percent of white men and 91 percent of white women could do both; by 1880, literate white women had overtaken their male counterparts, at least in the North (*At Odds*, 308).

13. See ibid., 377–79; Susan Coultrap-McQuin, *Doing Literary Business: American Women Writers in the Nineteenth Century* (Chapel Hill: Univ. of North Carolina Press, 1990), 2–48; and Cynthia White, *Women's Magazines, 1693–1968* (London: Michael Joseph, 1971), 23–57.

14. See Rufus Wilmot Griswold, *The Female Poets of America* (Philadelphia: Perry and McMillan, 1854), 7–8; and Frederic Rowton, *Cyclopaedia of Female Poets, with Additions by an American Editor* (Philadelphia: J.B. Lippincott, [1875]), xi–xviii.

15. Dobson, *Dickinson and the Strategies of Reticence*, 26–40.

16. See, for example, [Paul Fussell], "Sentimentality," in *The New Princeton Encyclopedia of Poetry and Poetics*, ed. Alex Preminger and T. V. F. Brogan (Princeton: Princeton Univ. Press, 1993), 1145. The seriousness with which nineteenth-century readers took "best-selling" texts such as Elizabeth Oakes-Smith's "The Sinless Child," in which a prepubescent girl exhibits intuitively moral wisdom to rival that of sages, should speak for itself. Women, as Barton Levy St. Armand points out in his article on nineteenth-century spiritualism, were deemed the appropriate vehicles for higher spiritual knowledge. But this knowledge could take either a social turn, as in "the Sinless Child," or a distinctly political turn, as in the "Declaration of Sentiments." Such intuitive knowledge was not limited to matters of love or religion. See St. Armand, "Veiled Ladies: Dickinson, Bettine, and Transcendental Mediumship," in *Studies in the American Renaissance*, ed. Joel Myerson (Charlottesville: Univ. Press of Virginia, 1987), 1–51. For the political thrust of sentimental poets, see Nina Baym's chapter on Sigourney in *Feminism and American Literary History: Essays* (New Brunswick, N.J.: Rutgers Univ. Press, 1992), 151–66; and Aaron Kramer, *The Prophetic Tradition in American Poetry, 1835–1900* (Rutherford, N.J.: Fairleigh Dickinson Univ. Press, 1968).

17. While the definition of modernism is very much in debate, that irony (as opposed to romantic idealism and / or Victorian sentimentalism) was central to its deflationary strategies seems fairly settled and helps to account for many modernists' obsession with the ambiguous and the oblique. What is missing from late-nineteenth-century women's poetry is the linguistic panache of modernist poetry. Free verse brought with it a distilled emphasis on the use of figurative language that changed the face of poetry irrevocably between 1910 and 1920 and rendered most of what was written in the previous century strikingly old-fashioned to the ear, fairly or not.

18. In her biography of Fields, Judith Roman refers to "Wild Endive" as "Blue Succory," the name Fields gave the poem in *The Singing Shepherd and Other Poems* (1895). Fields probably changed the title less for reasons of botanical accuracy (since the poem is not about the weed, she does not seem to have seen accurate

naming as crucial in this instance) than to underscore the contrast between nurturance and violence, life and death. The fact that Roman uses the later name and calls the poem a nature poem both suggest that she did not read the poem in its original context. Had she, her judgment of it might have been less slighting, or at least one would hope so. See Roman, *Annie Adams Fields: The Spirit of Charles Street* (Bloomington: Indiana Univ. Press, 1990), 130.

19. Edmund Wilson, *Patriotic Gore: Studies in the Literature of the American Civi'l War* (New York: Oxford Univ. Press, 1962), 466–79.

20. George Santayana, *The Genteel Tradition: Nine Essays by George Santayana* (Cambridge: Harvard Univ. Press, 1967), 73. One of the ironies of literary history is that critics have since come to attach this label, which Santayana reserved for antebellum poetry, to his own work—perhaps with greater justice and applicability than he showed when applying it to his antebellum precursors.

21. William Carlos Williams, *The Collected Earlier Poems* (New York: New Directions, 1951), 241, 242.

22. Wilcox holds a peculiar and unenviable place in the history of women's poetry. According to Douglas Sladen, her *Poems of Passion* (1883) sold 65,000 copies, presumably by virtue of its "amatory" strain, but she herself has been remembered in literary history as the epitome of the inept late-nineteenth-century sentimental poetess (a sort of Emmeline Grangerford of the erotic). See Sladen, *Younger American Poets: 1830–1890* (New York: Cassell, 1891), xlviii. Wilcox's best poetry is a good deal better than her reputation indicates, but she should not be taken as representative. There were many women poets who were far more effective as writers and whose names her reputation has, unfortunately, eclipsed.

23. See David Porter, *Dickinson: The Modern Idiom* (Cambridge: Harvard Univ. Press, 1981), 9–24. Porter sees this sense of living in the "aftermath" as central to modernism, and I would concur. Unlike Porter, however, I do not see its presence in nineteenth-century American poetry as peculiar to Dickinson. Rather, it appears to be a function of postbellum nostalgia that many writers exhibited, Dickinson and Piatt among them. I am also indebted to Porter for the image of the angel, although I use the figure somewhat differently.

24. I have discussed Piatt's achievement at much greater length in "'The Descent of the Angel': Interrogating Domestic Ideology in American Women's Poetry, 1858–1890," *American Literary History*, forthcoming, and in "John James and Sarah Morgan Bryan Piatt," *The Garland Encyclopedia of American Nineteenth-Century Poetry*, ed. Eric Haralson (New York: Garland, forthcoming).

12

AMBROSE BIERCE AND THE TRANSFORMATION OF THE GOTHIC TALE IN THE NINETEENTH-CENTURY AMERICAN PERIODICAL

GARY HOPPENSTAND

•

THE period in American literature during the career of Ambrose Bierce (1842–1914?) is a significant one in terms of the evolution of the late-nineteenth-century macabre Gothic tale. Prior to Bierce, the Gothic spectral "chain rattler" had become a clichéd staple of the popular press in both Europe and America. Recognizing the severe artistic limitations of the Victorian ghost story, Bierce attempted to transform the genre, in the process paralleling the developing literary modes of realism and naturalism and anticipating the macabre fiction of H. P. Lovecraft in the early twentieth century. In essence, Bierce helped to create the changing American Gothic tale by introducing into the narrative frame of the traditional Victorian ghost story a modern-day scientific empiricism that displayed an American preoccupation with a developing scientific and technological cultural vernacular. The language of Bierce's transformed American Gothic tale became sparser and less ornate, controlled, in part, by the evolving journalistic vernacular of a print medium pressured by such things as publication deadlines, considerations of space, and the changing tastes of an expanded readership. This essay will examine Bierce's relationship with the San Francisco periodicals, specifically addressing the powerful influence that Bierce exerted upon these publications and upon the writers who brought the Gothic tale into the twentieth century. In addition, this essay will discuss several important themes and conventions evident in his two short Gothic tales—"The Damned Thing" (1893) and "Moxon's Master" (1903)—that illustrate Bierce's significant impact on the transformation of the macabre Gothic tale in the nineteenth-century American periodical, a transformation that was nurtured by Bierce's West Coast literary community.

When Bierce arrived in San Francisco and began considering a career as a writer in 1867, he discovered a city that prospered from the then abundant riches of the American frontier. From the period before the Civil War, immense wealth generated from gold and silver mining—as well as the successful exploitation of these and other natural resources and the transportation of these resources to the East by ship and by railroad—helped to make San Francisco the financial mecca of the Far West. In San Francisco, workers were paid the best wages in America, and the city's per capita income was unmatched. A portion of this great wealth was reinvested back into San Francisco in the form of social and cultural improvements. Theater took root and prospered. Numerous libraries, schools, and churches were quickly built. In 1849, an elementary education was made free to the general population by decree of the California state constitution,[1] and an educated, financially prosperous public, in turn, provided a dedicated readership able and willing to be entertained by journals and magazines.

Paralleling San Francisco's dramatic rise to commercial and cultural prominence on the West Coast during the mid-nineteenth century was the equally dramatic proliferation of the city's literary journals. These journals—including the *Californian,* the *Golden Era,* the *Hesperian,* the *Overland Monthly,* and the *News Letter,* among others—essentially imitated the types of stories, sketches, and poems that appeared in the top periodicals published in Boston, Philadelphia, and New York City. Narrative prose and poetry that featured romantic melodrama, social manners, political humor, and the macabre were very popular with readers on both coasts. Literary cliques that discovered a certain measure of notoriety in the East, such as the Bohemian movement that thrived in New York City prior to the Civil War, eventually moved west to discover better markets for their work and found themselves in California, contributing to San Francisco magazines.

Yet there existed an important difference between what was being published in West Coast journals and what was being published in the East. Media historian John Tebbel claims that San Francisco's periodicals, as part of the larger "national market" for the emerging magazine industry, were unusually open to new ideas.[2] Not surprisingly, the topic that generated the most interest among the city's readers was the frontier. Indeed, many of the city's residents had traveled from the East through the frontier and had experienced the numerous hardships of that rough landscape. Thus, several of San Francisco's most prominent young authors, including Mark Twain and Bret Harte, discovered that their writings featuring frontier settings or characters found a sympathetic audience and tended to sell very well. Twain even utilized the narrative folklore traditions of the American frontier, such as the tall tale, in his work, while Harte endeavored to create a sense of frontier realism in his fiction. Conversely, in New York City, stories about the frontier were relegated to the pages of the dime novel, the entertainment mass medium of the lower social classes between 1860 and 1900. Adventures featuring the fictionalized exploits of Jesse James and Buffalo Bill that appeared week after week in dime novels tended to make the American frontier into a pejorative term for the middle class. In the East, both the frontier adventure and the dime novel became equated with the worst sort of hackneyed, potboiling writing, and stories of social manners—as written, for example, by Henry James and Edith Wharton—continued to receive the most positive type of critical attention, while in the West the frontier narrative became an important type of story frequently employed by San Francisco's developing middle-class literary community.

Like Twain and Harte, Bierce also employed the frontier as the setting for a number of his popular tales. By the 1880s, he had become the "West Coast dean of literature."[3] Gertrude Atherton, Charles William Doyle, John Herbert Evelyn Partington, Edwin Markham, George Herman Scheffauer, and George Sterling were included among his numerous literary protégés.[4] He was, however, a notoriously uneven mentor. At times, he provided his student of the moment with kindness and support, while at other times he could be quite cruel and abusive. Bierce's great ego, which was a strength for him as the controversial newspaper columnist, in other literary matters often interfered with better judgment. Nonetheless, his impact upon American literature went far beyond his effect on his immediate circle of admirers (none of whom ever seemed to achieve Bierce's stature). Along with Edgar Allan Poe, Bierce was the foremost American author of the macabre Gothic short story during the nineteenth century. Tales such as "The Damned Thing" influenced the direction of the American Gothic narrative well into the twentieth century. Bierce was an important early author of American science fiction as well. "Moxon's Master," for example, was one of the first robot stories to have appeared in America,[5] and it served to establish the motifs employed by contemporary writers of the genre. Along with such authors as Robert Duncan Milne, Bierce was the most famous of a thriving literary community of imaginative writers who helped to make the city of San Francisco the center of science fiction and fantasy literature in America. Science fiction historian Sam Moskowitz states, "San Francisco in the decades before and after the turn of the century cultivated a remarkable group of superb literary stylists, dealing heavily in the 'forbidden' lore and the dark side of man's conscience. Among the better known were Ambrose Bierce, Frank Norris, Gertrude Atherton, Gelett Burgess, and W. C. Morrow."[6] In fact, a number of eminent San Francisco periodicals—such as the *Argonaut*, the *Overland Monthly*, the *San Franciscan*, and the *Examiner*—published a surprising amount of fantasy and science fiction stories.

Today, Bierce's critics give his short fiction a mixed reception. Cathy N. Davidson finds in Bierce's macabre fiction a well-defined artistic purpose, stating that "Bierce's fictional innovations are more than literary pyrotechnics. They are, instead, the key to his unique view of life and art."[7] Holding the opposing view is Stuart C. Woodruff, who argues in *The Short Stories of Ambrose Bierce* that there is little artistic value in Bierce's non-Civil War Gothic short stories: "While a few of [the macabre Gothic tales] are well done, none of them equal the best of Bierce's war tales, and several are almost unreadable. In all of them, in fact, there is a discernible reduction in imaginative power and control."[8] Woodruff's position seems to represent the prevailing opinion among Bierce scholars: the Civil War stories are more highly regarded than are Bierce's non-Civil War Gothic tales. Certainly, the best of his Gothic stories compares favorably to the best of his Civil War stories, so perhaps it is the Gothic genre itself that lends itself to such a harsh scholarly evaluation. After all, the Gothic narrative in both Europe and America has traditionally been subversive, attacking as it does institutional authority (like religion) and social taboos (such as incest and murder). Perhaps the lurid nature of the Gothic narrative makes it suspect. Overtly macabre stories of death and the supernatural that lack any socially redeeming value other than mere entertainment appear, at first glance, to possess little artistic sophistication. Bierce's Gothic tales, however, do present themselves for elaborate thematic analysis, and a blanket condemnation of their worth is regrettable and wrongheaded.

A number of Bierce's critics (both during the author's lifetime and now) have perhaps attempted a too-close psychological examination, attempting to equate the author's macabre writings with his personal life. An overly simplistic interpretation of Bierce's work—an interpretation that postulates easy relationships between such things as Bierce's estranged relationship with his family and the theme of family violence that sometimes appears in his writings—denies the social and historical context of Bierce's journalism and fiction. In the financially competitive San Francisco newspaper editorial market between the Civil War period and the turn of the century (a market that Bierce dominated), to remain on top Bierce had to give his readers the type of sensational writing that would continue to sell newspapers. Richard Saunders claims that "by 1870 [Bierce's] reputation as a vicious yet uniquely talented cynic had spread across the country. Indeed, his near-sadistic personal attacks and brutal handling of many sensitive topics made him a great many enemies."[9] Bierce knew that morbid tales depicting family violence was one among many types of exploitative journalism that attracted and held his readers' interest.

Bierce's fictional output, when compared to his journalistic writings, is indeed meager, and yet, when he infrequently turned his hand to writing fiction, he selected the Gothic tale as the type of story with which he preferred to work. Historically, the macabre Gothic tale underwent a significant transformation in both England and America as it evolved in the seventeenth and eighteenth centuries and entered the nineteenth. From its early origins in Horace Walpole's *The Castle of Otranto* (1764), to Ann Radcliffe's massive Gothic novels such as *The Mysteries of Udolpho* (1794), Matthew Gregory Lewis's *The Monk* (1796), Mary Shelley's *Frankenstein* (1818), and Charles Brockden Brown's transplanted American variants of the Gothic tale—*Wieland* (1798) and *Edgar Huntly* (1799)—the macabre Gothic narrative tended to be quite lengthy (with a single novel often published in several volumes) and frequently was written in a florid style that complemented its ponderous bulk. However, with the advent of less expensive and more productive printing technologies in the nineteenth century—such as the steamroller press—Gothic tales began to appear in a variety of publications instead of being restricted, in the main, to the novel as book. A growing number of authors, sensing the relatively lucrative markets of the newspaper, the journal, the magazine, and the serial, directed an increasing percentage of their efforts to these new markets.

The two major American authors of the macabre Gothic tale in the nineteenth century—Poe and Bierce—were both profoundly affected by the growing commercial influence of periodicals. Both men earned their livings by writing for magazines and newspapers, and because the editorial requirements of these media encouraged the writing of short fiction, these authors specialized in publishing short stories rather than novels. In a letter written either in December 1892 or January 1893, Bierce explained the commercial appeal of the popular magazine: "Do you know?—you will, I think, be glad to know—that I have many more offers for stories at good prices, than I have the health to accept. (For I am less nearly well than I have told you.) Even the *Examiner* has 'waked up' (I woke it up) to the situation, and now pays me $20 a thousand words; and my latest offer from New York is $50."[10] Due in large part to the growing prominence of the popular magazine and newspaper in America during the nineteenth century, the macabre Gothic tale—one of many types of fiction and nonfiction that were published in the periodicals of the time—was restructured by its authors to better accommodate the space limitations of the periodical format. Even though the Gothic remained as popular as ever, nineteenth-century authors had to shorten the length of their fiction as well as streamline the way in which they told their narratives. The short story, rather than the novel, became the dominant narrative form of the Gothic tale. In addition, the language of the Gothic tale became sparser and less ornate.

But the length and stylistic nuance were not the only things to change in the nineteenth-century American Gothic tale. The supernatural subjects of these stories changed as well. In fact, from Poe to Bierce several pronounced changes are evident. For example, the macabre Gothic tale became less European and more American. Poe tended to look back to the Old World for his settings and characters, while Bierce frequently employed the American frontier as the setting of his stories, and his characters were definitely taken from his present rather than the distant past. In such stories as "The Damned Thing" and "Moxon's Master," Bierce also made frequent use of science or technology as the foundations for his narratives. Granted, Poe infrequently tinkered with the science fiction tale, as evidenced in his story "The Unparalleled Adventure of One Hans Pfaall," but his efforts were defined more by fantasy rather than by science or technology.

In addition, whereas Poe tended to incorporate strong elements of allegory in his fiction, which thus frequently made the settings of his narratives bizarre, indistinct, and surreal, Bierce was more comfortable working with realistic elements in his short fiction. The manner in which Bierce frequently narrated his macabre tales implied a type of journalistic technique. The Bierce narrator tended to explain fantastic events in the simplified, straightforward language of the newspaper reporter. The European style of Gothic writing that relied upon an elaborate prose (a technique employed by Poe himself in many of his own Gothic tales) was conspicuously absent in Bierce's fiction. Bierce's ghost stories often thus read as they might appear as a feature on the newspaper page, objectively described. In fact, the newspaper provided the central literary metaphor for Bierce's fiction. The lurid, real-life depictions of life in wild San Francisco no doubt provided the newspaperman Bierce with ample material for his Gothic fiction. A sample from one of his editorials, entitled "San Francisco's Advantages for Suicide" and published in

1877, illustrates the wryly gruesome flavor of his journalistic work: "A well known San Franciscan has blown out his brains in the streets of St. Louis. And yet no city in the world presents greater advantages to the suicide than San Francisco. We have an efficient and accommodating coroner, and a comfortable, though rather badly lighted, dead-house. Our undertakers have engaging manners, and their hearses easy springs. There is a charming view from every cemetery. In addition to these advantages, San Francisco is itself a very good motive."[11]

Bierce's non–Civil War macabre Gothic tales may be easily divided into four general categories. A number of Bierce's Gothic stories may be described as haunted house or ghost tales. Bierce, however, employed the traditional ghost story to suit his own purposes. Sometimes, as in "The Secret of Macarger's Gulch" and "The Stranger," he Americanized the traditional Victorian ghost story by placing it in a frontier setting, thus enabling himself to comment about the harsh realities of living (and dying) in a wilderness environment. Sometimes, as in "The Isle of Pines" and "An Arrest," Bierce utilized the ghost story as a critical dialogue about the evils of human avarice and the dire supernatural consequences of greed. Sometimes, as in "A Fruitless Assignment" and "The Spook House," Bierce used the ghost story simply as a device to challenge smug satisfaction with an empirical understanding of reality. Bierce tells his reader in these ghost stories that surface appearance is meaningless, that the world contains untold frightening mysteries, and that fate may be a capricious victimizer of the morally innocent as well as the guilty.

Another category of Bierce's macabre tales may be termed stories of family violence. Perhaps the most famous of these stories is "The Death of Halpin Frayser," in which a young man is destroyed by an Oedipal complex brought to a terrifyingly supernatural realization. What on the surface may be interpreted as a misogynist's tale of infanticide is, in reality, an effective condemnation of overt parental permissiveness and of adolescent ingratitude. "A Vine on a House," a story about a wife's brutal murder and the supernatural revelation of that murder by the roots of a vine, is in the tradition of Poe's Gothic tales of retribution such as "The Black Cat" and "The Tell-Tale Heart." "The Middle Toe of the Right Foot"—one of Bierce's most effective macabre stories—depicts a knife duel in a haunted house (which is, in reality, a grim joke), an event that subsequently provides the opportunity for a murdered wife to enact her just retribution against her abusive husband, a supernatural retribution that, as metaphor, defines at the most fundamental level the moral obligations and responsibilities of marriage.

In Bierce's stories that portray some type of ironic twist of fate—the third major category of his macabre short fiction—satire is employed frequently to debunk social institutions or base human iniquities like greed or lust. Bierce's "A Baby Tramp," for example, recounts the story of a boy orphan who wanders back to the site of his mother's grave to die; the tale is an effective though somewhat melodramatic condemnation of society's apparent inability to care for its more vulnerable members. Other ironic twist-of-fate stories include Bierce's notorious "The Boarded Window," which is reminiscent of Poe's "The Fall of the House of Usher"; "The Suitable Surroundings," which provides Bierce's reader with an argument for the correct way to read ghost stories; and "The Man and the Snake," which reveals his fascination with the effects of profound psychological terror on the human psyche.

The fourth category of Bierce's tales, those that feature a scientific methodology as the central thematic structure of the story, are among his most innovative narratives as well as among his most influential. Though Bierce did not invent the Gothic tale of science fiction in America, he did master and perfect this type of story and eventually became an important influence upon later authors of Gothic fiction and science fiction. For example, Bierce borrowed and expanded upon Fitz-James O'Brien's utilization in "What Was It?"[12] of a scientific or quasi-scientific interpretation of the supernatural by developing in "The Damned Thing" a horror tale also featuring an invisible creature that possesses an actual, physical presence. In his essay entitled "Some Disadvantages of Genius," Bierce defends his predilection for the macabre tale by writing, "Tales of the tragic and the supernatural are the earliest utterances in every literature. When the savage begins to talk he begins to tell wonder tales of death and mystery—of terror and the occult. Tapping, as they do, two of the three great mother-lodes of human interest, these tales are a constant phenomenon—the most permanent, because the most fascinating, element in letters."[13] Bierce also cites in this essay as evidence of the macabre Gothic tale's pedigree such authors as Horace Walpole, Monk Lewis, Honoré de Balzac, E. T. A. Hoffmann—and Fitz-James O'Brien. As did O'Brien in "What Was It?" Bierce intended in "The Damned Thing" to provide the traditional trappings of the ghost story and then to befuddle his readers' expectations by providing a scientific rationale for a supernatural creature.

The narrative of "The Damned Thing" (first published in the 1893 Christmas issue of *Town Topics*) begins with a coroner's inquest into the mysterious death of Hugh Morgan. A group of seven men are seated in shadow around Morgan's corpse; they are members of the inquest, farmers and woodsmen from the vicinity, which is described by Bierce as being a "wilderness." The coroner is examining Morgan's diary when a young man named William Harker enters the room. Harker is a reporter and an author of short stories. He was also a friend of Morgan, and while visiting Morgan witnessed the man's death. Harker explains that while he and Morgan were hunting, they heard the sound of an animal thrashing about. Morgan appeared grim and cocked his weapon. When they arrived at the source of the noise, no creature was visible, but an area of a field of wild oats was crushed down, as if some large creature were walking through the field. When Harker inquired about this strange event, Morgan replied that it was the "Damned Thing," fired his weapon, and ran away. Harker was knocked to the ground by something invisible, and his friend Morgan was attacked and killed not more than thirty yards away. While Morgan was wrestling with something much larger and stronger than himself, Harker noted that Morgan's body at times became invisible, as if something unseen had come between the two men. Morgan died, and the mysterious movement in the wild oats departed the area, progressing toward the edge of the woods. When Harker finishes his story for the inquest, the coroner examines the mutilated throat of Morgan's corpse. Before the coroner's jury arrives at its verdict, the foreman asks Harker what asylum he has escaped from, and the coroner himself repeats the question. Offended by the insult, Harker petitions to leave the inquest. Yet before he leaves, he asks the coroner if he could see Morgan's diary. The coroner refuses. A verdict of death from an attack by a mountain lion is falsely determined.

After this verdict is reached and the narrative action is concluded, Bierce provides his reader with a closer look at Morgan's diary. The author tells us that the coroner did not include the diary as evidence because he perhaps did not want to "confuse the jury." Bierce states that the diary contains "certain interesting entries" that have a "scientific value." These entries are incomplete, some having been torn or ripped out of the book, but they nonetheless provide an account of Morgan's earlier contacts with an invisible monster that he calls the "Damned Thing." Even though these entries—dated sporadically from 2 September through 7 October—reveal Morgan's growing terror about the invisible creature, they also provide a type of scientific inquiry into and debate about the physical nature of the Damned Thing. For example, in an undated entry (because its date has been torn out), Morgan describes his dog attacking the invisible creature; employing a form of scientific observation, Morgan speculates about whether dogs can "see" with their noses. In the 2 September entry, Morgan notes that while looking into the evening sky, stars disappear and reappear, as if something has moved in front of them, blotting them out. Diary entries covering the next several weeks are missing, but the next entry, dated 27 September, indicates Morgan's growing sense of fear. He discovers fresh footprints made by the creature. He cannot sleep, and he thinks that he is going mad. In the 3 October entry, Morgan vows not to leave, and in the 5 October entry, Morgan states that he has invited his friend Harker, who has a level head. In Morgan's last entry—dated 7 October—he offers a scientific hypothesis for the bizarre evidence that he has collected about the creature over the past several months. Morgan argues in his diary that just as there are sounds that the human ear cannot hear (as evidenced in the natural world by how animals—like blackbirds and whales—can communicate with each other via sounds beyond the range of human hearing), there must, by deduction, also exist colors that the human eye cannot see. Morgan thus proclaims that he is not going insane, that, in his words, "the human eye is an imperfect instrument; its range is but a few octaves of the real 'chromatic scale.' I am not mad; there are colors that we cannot see. . . . And, God help me! the Damned Thing is of such a color!"

Bierce has thus offered his reader a scientific hypothesis for a supernatural being, and he has fortified this hypothesis with physical evidence. He has achieved a frightening effect in his story by counterpoising a bizarre scientific anomaly with a commonplace American wilderness setting and stock American frontier characters. In "The Damned Thing," Bierce has veered away from the formulaic ghost story prerequisites of the crumbling Gothic castle and the ancient family curse (as originally prescribed by Horace Walpole). "The Damned Thing" is a decidedly American story featuring American protagonists (such as the county coroner and the newspaper journalist), and its narrative effectiveness hinges upon an overriding American fascination with scientific methodology.

One formulaic prerequisite in the traditional Victorian ghost story was a framing device—typically a discovered document that recounts the story, or the living narrator of the tale itself—that was intended to provide a sense of verisimilitude for what was to be an otherwise fantastic discussion of vengeful spirits and haunted houses. Henry James, in his mock Victorian ghost story "The Turn of the Screw," effectively parodies this framing device technique, thus paying a type of homage to the tradition by imitating it. Despite the relative brevity of "The Damned Thing," Bierce establishes two elaborate framing devices in the narrative. The first involves the coroner's inquest into Morgan's mysterious death, where newspaper reporter Harker is invited to provide his unusual eye-witness account of Morgan's final moments. The second framing device involves Morgan's incomplete diary, which, having been found among the personal effects of the deceased, is reviewed (and eventually dismissed as evidence) by the coroner. Both framing devices intrude on the story's plot, dominating it by several times interfering with the narrative flow. Even after the action of the story concludes with the inquest's verdict, the story itself does not end until the reader is allowed to read Morgan's diary. Bierce not only wants the sense of verisimilitude that the traditional Victorian ghost story framing device provides to surround his story, but he also wants reality continually to intrude into the story, dominating from within as well as from without. Bierce sweeps away the cobweb-infested occult mummery of the Victorian ghost story in favor of scientific inquiry into the unknown. Bierce perhaps deduced that a horror story featuring a monster with an empirical physical reality (yet that remains inexplicable despite its obvious existence) would be more frightening to his readers than the overused conventions of the ghost tale. In "The Damned Thing," Bierce thus anticipates the science fiction-inspired horror story as practiced by H. P. Lovecraft in tales like "The Colour Out of Space" and "The Shadow Out of Time" published in American pulp magazines during the 1920s and 1930s.

Bierce's tale "Moxon's Master" (first collected in the 1903 edition of *Can Such Things Be?*) further explores his investigation into the narrative relationship between science and horror. The story begins during a conversation between the anonymous narrator and a scientist figure named Moxon. The narrator and Moxon are debating the theoretical point of whether a machine can think. The narrator assumes the role of the skeptic, the same role that Bierce intends for his reader. Moxon challenges his companion's incredulity when he asks the question, "What is a machine?," then answers it by stating that man is a machine—and man thinks. Uncomfortable with this seemingly bizarre line of reasoning, the narrator challenges Moxon's point by defining a machine as something that has been constructed and controlled by man. Undaunted, Moxon proclaims, "I do believe that a machine thinks about the work that it is doing."

Upon hearing this statement, the narrator assumes that Moxon's mind is "affected" from spending too much time working in his "machine-shop." The narrator then raises the point that a machine does not have a brain and therefore can't think, a scientifically legitimate objection that Moxon counters by presenting examples from the natural world. Specifically, Moxon uses observations of certain plants—such as the climbing vine and roots of the eucalyptus—to prove that these plants exhibit a type of "consciousness" and that, by inference, machines also possess consciousness. When the narrator again objects, stating that plants are different than machines, Moxon raises another scientific example to further his argument. Moxon suggests that the symmetrical and mathematical properties evident in crystallization indicate an "intelligent cooperation among the constituent elements of the crystals."

The narrator's and Moxon's animated debate is suddenly interrupted by a noise ("a singular thumping sound, as of some one pounding upon a table with an open hand") that comes from the "machine shop," a place that Moxon keeps secret, allowing no one else to see it. Moxon leaves the narrator, only to return after what sounds like a scuffle in the adjoining room with four parallel wounds on his left cheek (as if he were scratched by the nails on a hand). Moxon apologizes for having to leave so abruptly, adding that he had a "machine in there that lost its temper and cut up rough." Ignoring the narrator's jesting reply, Moxon goes on to provide an additional scientific rationale, which is the philosophical crux of Bierce's science fiction Gothic tale: "Doubtless you do not hold with those (I need not name them to a man of your reading) who have taught that all matter is sentient, that every atom is a living, feeling, conscious being. *I* do. There is no such thing as dead, inert matter; it is all alive; all instinct with force, actual and potential; all sensitive to the same forces in its environment and susceptible to the contagion of higher and subtler ones residing in such superior organisms as it may be brought into relation with, as those of man when his is fashioning it into an instrument of his will. It absorbs something of his intelligence and purpose—more of them in proportion to the complexity of the resulting machine and that of its work." Moxon resumes the philosophical debate about what constitutes life, with Moxon drawing the analogy that if a man is alive when he is active, then so too is a machine.

The narrator (thinking that Moxon is perhaps hiding a woman in the machine shop) inquires of Moxon who is in the next room. Moxon replies that nobody is there except for a machine that was left "in action with nothing to act upon." Disgruntled, the narrator abruptly leaves Moxon's house, but he quickly returns after viewing the light from the window to Moxon's machine shop, a window that presented to the narrator a "mysterious and fateful meaning." The narrator returns to Moxon's house a transformed convert. He now believes in Moxon's theories and wants to "seek further light from him whom . . . [the narrator] now recognized as . . . master and guide." Soaked by the rain, the narrator enters Moxon's house and returns to the room where he and Moxon conducted their discussion. Moxon is nowhere to be seen, so the narrator opens the door to the forbidden machine shop and witnesses a terrible event that quickly purges the narrator of all "philosophical speculation."

Moxon is sitting at a small table in the machine shop, facing the narrator. At the other end of the table is another "person," his back to the narrator. The two are playing a game of chess. The narrator describes Moxon's chess companion as being short in height, stout, "with proportions suggesting those of a gorilla," wearing a "crimson fez" on his squat head, and sitting on some type of box. The game is being played rapidly. Something about the precise, "mechanical" movements of Moxon's companion as the chess pieces are moved across the board disturbs the narrator. The narrator soon deduces that this strange individual is a machine, an "automaton chessplayer" that the narrator remembers Moxon as having built. The automaton chessplayer appears, to the narrator's unbelieving eyes, to be upset at losing the game, and when the "startled" Moxon pronounces checkmate, the machine begins to convulse in what appears to be anger.

After leaping to its feet, the machine grasps Moxon about the throat. The narrator attempts to intervene but is impeded by a "blinding white light that burned into [the narrator's] brain and heart and memory a vivid picture of the combatants on the floor." Before the narrator faints, he observes on the face of the automaton "an expression of tranquil and profound thought, as in the solution of a problem in chess!" Three days later, when the narrator regains consciousness in a hospital, he recognizes Moxon's "confidential workman," a man named Haley. Haley tells the narrator that he had been removed from Moxon's house, which had caught on fire, and that the origin of the fire (as well as the narrator's presence there) is still a mystery. Haley states that Moxon was buried the previous day. When the narrator inquires about the circumstances of his own rescue, Haley claims to be the saviour. And when the narrator then asks the workman if he saved the "automaton chess-player that murdered its inventor," Haley's response is guarded. The workman asks the narrator "Do you know that?," and the narrator replies that he witnessed the killing. Bierce abruptly concludes the tale in an equivocal manner that is typical of a number of his other stories by having the narrator question the reality of what he observed those "many years ago": "If asked to-day" about the circumstances of Moxon's death, "I should answer less confidently."

Once again, as Bierce had done with "The Damned Thing," in "Moxon's Master" he employs previously utilized Gothic formulaic traditions as part of his story's narrative frame, only later to radically modify the

Gothic formula to suit his own artistic ends. For example, Bierce biographer Carey McWilliams identifies several literary sources for this Gothic science fiction tale: "Bierce's 'Moxon's Master' is suggestive . . . of Poe and his automatic chess player, which in turn relates back to the frequent appearance of the Frankenstein monster in German and English fiction."[14] Mary Shelley provided an arguably greater influence upon "Moxon's Master" than did Poe; indeed, the story deliberately echoes Shelley's classic Gothic horror novel *Frankenstein* (1818). Both Shelley's novel and Bierce's short story recount the exploits of scientists who seek forbidden knowledge. After employing this knowledge to bring life, in God-like fashion, to otherwise inanimate matter, they suffer the moral consequences for their colossal vanity; they are themselves thus destroyed because of their dangerous ambition and false pride. The parallels between the two stories are obvious. In essence, Bierce has written his own interpretation of the Frankenstein's monster archetype, but while the similarities are interesting to note, the differences in Bierce's rendition are even more intriguing and ultimately are more revealing about his artistic methods and the late-nineteenth-century American audience for which he wrote.

First, Bierce chose to employ the short story to tell his version of the Frankenstein tale. Bierce disliked the novel, defining it in his *Devil's Dictionary* as "A short story padded."[15] In addition, Shelley's novel is written in the epistolary form and in an elaborate style that was consistent with the fiction written during the early part of the nineteenth century. By contrast, the language of Bierce's short story is terse, compact, and direct. He forsakes any sort of detailed character description that is a strength in Shelley's novel. Unlike Shelley, whose narrative pace in *Frankenstein* is more leisurely, Bierce places the reader directly in the middle of a conversation between the two central characters when he begins his story, essentially leaving the question of interpreting previous narrative events up to his reader. And whereas Shelley provides the appropriate length necessary to tell her morality tale and to present a clear picture of the dire ethical consequences of Frankenstein's forbidden acts, Bierce rushes the reader headlong toward the abrupt conclusion in his short story, delivering an ambiguous conclusion at the story's end that indeed fails to present any type of expected message and, in fact, denies a moral reading.

Because Bierce was trained as a journalist and because he desired to meet the needs of a newspaper readership, he approached the writing of his macabre Gothic tales with a considerably different mind-set than did Shelley, who published *Frankenstein,* her most famous novel, nearly a century before Bierce's own literary work began appearing in American West Coast periodicals. Bierce understood the importance of keeping his language and the length of his narrative plots within the acceptable parameters of the expectations of a periodical readership. He preferred the short story because it was the literary form most similar to the newspaper sketch that he wrote with great success for his "Prattle" columns. Bierce's terse writing was the compact language of late-nineteenth-century American newspapers, and his audience was part of that newly educated growing American middle class whose literary appetites were increasingly satisfied by the short story published in the magazine or journal. Shelley intended her fiction to be read by quite a different type of audience, one that tended to be highly educated, upper class, and wealthy enough to afford the luxury of books.[16]

Ultimately, "Moxon's Master" reflects an American pragmatic attitude about science, while Shelley's *Frankenstein* is firmly entrenched within the worldview of British romanticism. Shelley clearly defines Frankenstein's "scientific" experiments as evil. Her monster thus functions as an emblem of the evils of scientific progress. Her novel advocates mystery over science, God over the scientist. Bierce's tale, on the other hand, though essentially duplicating Shelley's pessimistic conclusions about the unchecked pursuit of scientific research, departs radically from Shelley's dismissal of science in general. Both of the major characters in Bierce's narrative—the narrator and Moxon—recognize in their heated debate the metaphoric significance of the natural world and the importance of pursuing knowledge of nature. While Frankenstein is portrayed as being misguided (and essentially wrongheaded), Bierce's Moxon is precisely correct with his definition of what constitutes life. While Frankenstein's monster is demonic because it represents a perversion of nature, Moxon's living machine is the product of Moxon's theories taken to their logical conclusion. Frankenstein's monster is evil because it subverts religious mystery. Moxon's machine becomes evil because it lives and acts beyond human control.

Moxon himself is the embodiment of the stereotypical American inventor figure. Like Thomas Edison, Henry Ford, or the Wright brothers, Moxon maintains a workshop sanctum where he does his scientific tinkering. His tinkering results in devices that may one day soon profoundly affect his culture and his society. Moxon's seemingly bizarre theories about machines possessing life and being able to think are the product of the lone inventor's scientific observations about basic environmental laws. His philosophy shapes the pragmatic side of his work, which presents a typically American notion of the scientist. Moxon's scientific methods, when begun to be understood by the story's narrator, reveal a sublime truth that redefines the narrator's (and, Bierce hopes, his readers') understanding of reality. Bierce views science in "Moxon's Master" as possessing a reality independent of religion or politics, also a very American idea. Moxon's own destruction results because he fails to fully understand the logical conclusion of his efforts—that this new machine life will want to exert its own will upon its environment. Bierce's message in the tale is not so much allegorical as it is problematic.

This distinction between the European and American perceptions of science reflects a crucial difference between Shelley's audience and that of Bierce. Shelley's readers (i.e., her European and upper class audience) no doubt desired in their lives a type of social status quo. Political revolutions of the type seen in America and France the previous century certainly engendered in the privileged classes a powerful antipathy to radical change. As an emerging body of knowledge, the growing field of science was perceived with a certain measure of mistrust. After all, science was but another type of revolution that sought either directly or indirectly to alter the dominant role of autocratic religion and politics in English society. Bierce's readers (i.e., his middle-class, pragmatic audience) probably perceived science and technology as beneficial to their lives. Indeed, technology had become a significant element of American culture during the hundred years since *Frankenstein*'s publication. Improved technology had helped to create the very middle class that had come to define American society as it entered the twentieth century. As an American journalist, Bierce understood the fundamental relationship between science and communication, and science thus became a significant thematic motif in his fiction, both as an affirmation of a New World paradigm and as an effective attack on the Old World and its literary traditions. West Coast periodicals embraced Bierce's unique approach to the writing of imaginative fiction, just as San Francisco's newspapers had embraced the scathing political and social commentary in his editorials. The East Coast journals and magazines, on the other hand, remained controlled by past literary traditions. Science fiction would not find a wide audience in the East until the advent of the pulp magazine in the early twentieth century.

Bierce's fascination with quasi-scientific methodology in a number of his Gothic stories like "The Damned Thing" and "Moxon's Master" reflects his desire to incorporate elements of scientific reality in his horror fiction, subsequently producing in the process a type of Gothic tale that breaks away from the conventions of the traditional (British) Victorian ghost story. E. F. Bleiler argues in his introduction to the anthology *Ghost and Horror Stories of Ambrose Bierce* that Bierce dared to write macabre fiction that was atypical for its time.[17] Bierce's British contemporaries like Algernon Blackwood and M. R. James persisted in following the past traditions of the ghost story and failed to pursue Bierce's initiative. Unlike Poe, who wrote his fiction for the magazines of his period with the intent of making money and was thus somewhat constrained by the limitations of popular taste, Bierce's secure employment as a celebrated newspaper columnist allowed him to be selective about the type of fiction he wrote. He attempted to tie the Gothic tale to reality by suggesting in a number of his macabre stories that there are many levels or dimensions of reality and experience that humanity might apprehend or confront under unusual circumstances. Perhaps a possible explanation as to why later American authors like Lovecraft and his circle of imitators in the popular American magazines were more influenced by Bierce's work than by the fiction of British ghost story writers during the late nineteenth and early twentieth centuries might be related to the idea that Bierce's type of macabre Gothic tale—because it relies on scientific documentation of physical reality—parallels the developing literary modes of realism and naturalism in American literature. Both realism and naturalism were outgrowths of "nineteenth-century scientific thought, following in general the biological determinism of Darwin's theory, or the economic determinism of Marx."[18] Bierce's sketches and short fiction—as they appeared in the same West Coast literary venues that helped to nurture such authors as Bret Harte and Jack London—reflected these narrative modes of realism and naturalism that had begun to become established as new schools of American literature. The British masters of supernatural fiction were perhaps too far removed from these new types of American fiction to be influenced by a dependence on science and nature as significant narrative elements.

In fact, John A. Kouwenhoven argues in *The Arts in Modern American Civilization* that a fascination with science and technology is a characteristic American cultural trait. He suggests that American art in its many forms was determined in large part by a New World reliance on a "democratic-technological vernacular."[19] According to Kouwenhoven, such things as American architecture, music, and literature have all been affected by the functional worldview of an American people who have depended on technology for their survival in an often harsh and dangerous frontier environment. Within this context, it makes sense, then, that the New World ghost story—initiated by Bierce and perfected by Lovecraft—should concern itself with scientific and technological motivations. Indeed, the deciding cultural symbol for the transformed nineteenth-century American Gothic tale was the mass-produced magazine and newspaper, media created by technology that celebrated technological subjects. Within the context of a vernacularized nineteenth century, the shape of Bierce's robot in "Moxon's Master" reveals itself to resemble the shape of the American short-story author compelled to produce work that was dominated by a commercially pervasive American print media that would come to profoundly influence both the function and form of American art and science. The image of Bierce's invisible monster in "The Damned Thing" resembles the nineteenth-century realist breaking tradition with traditional ghost story formulas, in the process anticipating the twentieth-century Lovecraftian nightmares of American social estrangement from rampant technology that have become in our modern world both fascinating and frightening because of their pervasiveness.

NOTES

1. Franklin Walker, *San Francisco's Literary Frontier* (Seattle: Univ. of Washington Press, 1969), 13.

2. John Tebbel, *The Media in America* (New York: Crowell, 1974), 242–43.

3. Richard Saunders, *Ambrose Bierce: The Making of a Misanthrope* (San Francisco: Chronicle Books, 1985), 42.

4. M. E. Grenander, *Ambrose Bierce* (New York: Twayne, 1971), 62–63.

5. Though the robot motif is a popular thematic device in contemporary American science fiction, the word *robot* originated from a Czech word and was first used in the 1921 play *R.U.R.* by Karel Capek.

6. Sam Moskowitz, *Science Fiction in Old San Francisco: History of the Movement from 1854 to 1890* (West Kingston, R.I.: Donald M. Grant, 1980), 25.

7. Cathy N. Davidson, *The Experimental Fictions of Ambrose Bierce: Structuring the Ineffable* (Lincoln: Univ. of Nebraska Press, 1984), 2.

8. Stuart C. Woodruff, *The Short Stories of Ambrose Bierce: A Study in Polarity* (Pittsburgh: Univ. of Pittsburgh Press, 1964), 116.

9. Saunders, *Ambrose Bierce*, 16.

10. Bertha Clark Pope, ed., *The Letters of Ambrose Bierce* (New York: Gordian Press, 1967), 20.

11. Ernst Jerome Hopkins, ed. *The Ambrose Bierce Satanic Reader: Selections from the Invective Journalism of the Great Satirist* (Garden City, N.Y.: Doubleday, 1968), 116.

12. Fitz-James O'Brien was an Irish immigrant who rose to a measure of distinction as one of the leaders of the pre–Civil War Bohemian literary movement in New York City. Though largely forgotten today, during his time O'Brien was a popular poet, playwright, and short story writer. O'Brien's tale entitled "What

Was It?" (first published in the March 1859 issue of *Harper's*) was one of his most popular (and subsequently one of his most reprinted) tales.

13. Ambrose Bierce, "Some Disadvantages of Genius," in *The Collected Works of Ambrose Bierce* (New York: Neale, 1911), 10:296.

14. Carey McWilliams, *Ambrose Bierce: A Biography* (New York: Albert and Charles Boni, 1929), 230.

15. Ambrose Bierce, *The Devil's Dictionary* (New York: Dell, 1991), 122.

16. Before the advent of less expensive printing technology (such as the steam-driven roller press), books were virtually inaccessible (because of their prohibitive cost and their general lack of availability) for the lower classes in Europe during the early years of the nineteenth century, the period in which Mary Shelley published *Frankenstein*. The middle and lower socioeconomic classes in both Europe and America began to have greater access to fiction when that fiction was published in the less expensive formats of the newspaper and the magazine. Thus, as the turn of the twentieth century approached, magazines began to dominate the U.S. entertainment publishing industry, while short stories and serialized novels began to dominate readers' attention (subsequently becoming more profitable for the newly evolving class of professional authors). In essence, then, the short story's popularity matched the demographic rise of a middle-class readership that had the basic education and could afford an inexpensive publication.

17. E. F. Bleiler, introduction to *Ghost and Horror Stories of Ambrose Bierce* (New York: Dover, 1964), xix.

18. James D. Hart, *The Concise Oxford Companion to American Literature* (New York: Oxford Univ. Press, 1986), 282.

19. John A. Kouwenhoven, *The Arts in Modern American Civilization* (New York: Norton, 1967), 13.

13

THE NORTH-SOUTH RECONCILIATION THEME AND THE "SHADOW OF THE NEGRO" IN *CENTURY ILLUSTRATED MAGAZINE*

JANET GABLER-HOVER

•

> *"We all white folks al'ays set heap o' sto' by one nurr."*
> —Thomas Nelson Page, "Meh Lady"

IN 1885 *Century Illustrated Magazine* published installments or excerpts from three American masterworks: Henry James's *The Bostonians,* William Dean Howells's *The Rise of Silas Lapham,* and Mark Twain's *Adventures of Huckleberry Finn.* I have wondered persistently how readers of the time might come upon these serials. How might they have read these installments in the context of other essays and literature appearing in the *Century*? The question is irrelevant with *The Bostonians,* which remained unknown to the majority of *Century*'s audience. In a famous 1886 anecdote, senior editor L. Frank Tooker overheard an editor on the *Century* ask another if *The Bostonians* would finish serialization in February. "'Yes,' [he] replied, not looking up from his own work. 'James says it does, and so does Tooker, and they ought to know: they are the only ones who have ever read it.'"[1]

Strangely enough, the plot of the once unread *Bostonians* speaks eloquently today about the context of the *Century* in the 1880s. One reason James may have been disappointed that *The Bostonians* failed, for example, was that he had changed his New England–bound hero from a Westerner into a Mississippian specifically to accommodate and take advantage of an enfant terrible in the pages of the *Century*—the popular Civil War series running concurrently.[2] James's seemingly casual use of the Civil War series provides a key for readers today to the text and subtext of the *Century* magazine and its fiction in the 1880s. For one thing, James used the Civil War theme to try to make *The Bostonians* more popular, and profitability was an incentive to *Century* writers to use the series or its accompanying theme of North-South reconciliation.[3]

James's Civil War novel, insofar as it was one, also followed the other predictable pattern of the North-South reconciliation theme in the *Century;* oddly—or perhaps not so oddly—treatment of the war between the North and South was marked by no mention of the African-American presence for whom the war was at least in part ostensibly fought. From its inception, the Civil War series in the *Century* was conceived with the ethical motive of reconciling the white North and South; profitability was presented as a minor happy consequence. Unfortunately, the *Century* ethics of reconciliation was an exclusionary ethics. If the presence of African Americans was not so dominant in the 1880s *Century*,[4] then it might not be so apparent how much this presence was resisted by the Northern editors who continued to deny in *Century* editorials that racial injustice in the South was still a problem. Indeed, there are eloquent arguments made in prose and fiction during this time in the *Century* for the fair treatment of African Americans, but ironically, these arguments are usually made by Southern writers invited into the *Century* for their profitability and endorsed by the enthusiasm of antisectional fervor. Although there are a plurality of voices in the *Century* that would suggest an openness to engagement and controversy on the issue of Euro-American treatment of African Americans during the 1880s, the influential pervasiveness of the reconciliation theme indicates a strong psychological pull toward ethnic homogeneity and a resistance and denial of racial difference. Hence, a notable characteristic of the contextual ambience of the *Century* in the 1880s was a pathological attitude toward the African-American race and its place in America. This pathology extended to the pages of *Century's* fiction, even to *The Bostonians, Silas,* and the selection of excerpts from *Huckleberry Finn.*

I

To understand the environment of the 1880s *Century*, one must first turn to the *Century's* Civil War series. By the mid 1880s, the *Century* had become the forum for the first real North-South discussion of the Civil War. The Civil War series, which took up a good third of each monthly issue of approximately 160 pages, ran in the *Century* from November 1884 through November 1887.[5] As explained by associate editor Robert Underwood Johnson, it "included contributions from nearly all the surviving officers of high command on both sides of the struggle—Grant, Sherman, McClellan, Pope, Rosecrans, Franklin and many others on the

Union side, with Beauregard, Joseph E. Johnston, Longstreet, Hill, Wheeler, Law, and other leaders of the Confederates" on the other.[6]

The Civil War series, launched as an experiment, was an astounding financial success. Tooker commented on the initial reserve of wily business manager Roswell Smith about the project: "Now, though Mr. Roswell Smith was a man of far-sighted mental vision and bold almost to the point of riskiness . . . he doubted that the proposed War Series would be of material advantage to the magazine, which he thought had attained its potential growth." Yet, remarkably, in the series's second year, *Century*'s circulation rose from 127,000 to 225,000. Tooker remembers that "there were times when the normally quiet editorial rooms were like the headquarters of an army on the eve of a great battle, with generals and privates, Confederates and Federals, coming and going."[7]

Proceeds from the series and subsequent published volumes ultimately earned more than $1 million for the *Century* company. But with the Civil War series the *Century* took on not only a financial boon but an accompanying sense of mission. The full consequence of the series for the *Century* can only be understood by remembering that culture in late-nineteenth-century America, especially lucrative culture, could not be justified by profit margins alone. *Century* editors (perhaps more than their audience) had to be convinced that moral purpose was the driving force behind their art. One scholar notes the paradoxical conflation between art, morality, and economics in late-nineteenth-century America. America saw "the emergence of a rhetoric that deployed the 'cultural' and the 'aesthetic' as advertising slogans, as part of a naive but nevertheless effective strategy for advertising commodities that would at once glorify and efface the act of consumption itself by grounding even the most mundane acquisitive choices in the nonmaterial realm of transcendent value designated by the aesthetic."[8] The idea of North-South reconciliation "saved" the Civil War series with its transcendent mission of reconciling the regions and hence creating a post–Civil War unity. Actually, reconciliation was so embedded in the series as its motivating force that it is not altogether clear that the moral urge did not precede profit motive as the series's inspiration.

The editors certainly realized early on that, with timely albeit perhaps unwitting brilliance, they had tapped into a great need in the still regionally divided country for a moral catharsis. Exposed was the still-raw wound of North-South division and perhaps the North's need to absolve itself of the responsibility of decimating the South. The series, confirms one editor, "did more to bring together North and South than anything that had happened since they were torn apart in 1861."[9] Editors later reminisced about the ethical goal of their Series, to "soften controversy"[10] between the North and the South. General editor Richard Watson Gilder used this ethical argument in his solicitation of contributors: "Please," he begged one officer, "don't say 'no' to our war series request! This is the time for the 'unveiling of all hearts.' If the North can see the heart of the South, and the South of the North's, they will love each other as never before! This is truth and no sentimentalism."[11]

But even with North-South reconciliation as the series's guiding force, it seems almost inevitable that, once a Pandora's box of profit motive was opened, the ethical reasons for urging North-South reconciliation were complicated considerably. A more sophisticated member of *Century*'s audience certainly might feel cynical about the basis for the series. One society friend of editor in chief Richard Watson Gilder—Mariana Griswold van Renssalaer, to be specific—commented slyly to her friend in personal correspondence about the gold mine that the series had provided: "What would you all have done if the contemporaries of the last war had used up all the material at the time instead of letting [it] lie in camphor for you?"[12]

As revealed above, ethical motives aside, the Civil War series and its implicit goal of reconciling North and South was of tremendous financial importance to the *Century*. Gilder explained in a letter in 1886 that "what makes a magazine 'go' in a business and moneyed point of view" is the combination of materials in its pages: "We put a poem or an artistic story in next to a war article and that number of the magazine has a huge circulation, but it is the war article that gives it the circulation and is the power to pay authors, rather than the individual story."[13] Gilder and the rest of the staff had come to depend on the series. It had gained the power of an addiction; withdrawn, Gilder may well have feared for the *Century*'s prosperity. Tooker commented ruefully on his own provisional stability after the end of the series: "To learn every detail of the routine work of the office appeared highly advisable, for the flood-tide of activity and prosperity that the War Series had caused was certain to be followed by the ebb, when poorly piloted craft might be stranded."[14]

The *Century*'s mixture of economic and moral reasons for the Civil War series can be seen in the editorial attitude about how to package it. The Civil War series was the invention and subsequent responsibility of associate editor Johnson. Johnson came on board after Gilder succeeded founding editor Josiah Gilbert Holland as the editor in 1881. Holland had been the morally conservative co-owner, with business manager Smith, of the original *Scribner's Monthly Magazine*, which changed its name to the *Century* after the periodical owners split with Scribner's so that they could have their own publishing company.[15] A Gilder biographer notes that although "Gilder had been a liberal influence on Holland [as his assistant editor], . . . Johnson was probably the most prudish editor on the staff of *The Century*."[16] And Johnson apparently orchestrated the reconciliatory tone of the series. Johnson wrote to Gilder during the series's halcyon days, "Dear RWG: We have come across a most excellent Ms. account of life with the Army of the [?] by the author of our Andersonville article—full of color and humor and with fine descriptions of the fighting at Fredericksburg, Antietam, Gettysburg and in the Peninsula. It is *exactly the sort of thing we want the generals to write*" (italics his).[17] It is disconcerting to find Johnson not only approving but mandating that battle accounts of Gettysburg and Antietam be filled with color and with humor. Undoubtedly Johnson is striving for a reconciliatory effect, however; it would be impolitic to linger too long on the negative. Given the moral agenda of reconciliation, Johnson's formula of mixing battle accounts with humor seems targeted toward transforming the potentially bitter memories of *Century*'s sectional audiences into nostalgic reminiscences.

The *Century* war series proofs on file at the New York Public Library are not complete; one cannot determine how much prepublication editing took place at the *Century:* the extant article editing, which seems to be in Gilder's handwriting, relates to wordiness and historical accuracy. Probably much of the encouragement for a reconciliatory tone in the articles happened verbally, in pre-writing correspondence or in the office of the *Century.* Johnson explained that many "acrimonious" controversies sprang up between generals and soldiers during the course of the series, "particularly on the Confederate side." Yet because the controversies were apparently subdued by the *Century* staff, "the general reader never knew the violence of them." Johnson recalled the instance when Generals J. E. Johnston and P. G. T. Beauregard argued over the victory at Bull Run: "In the heat and flame of such discussions Buel [the assistant editor] and I would recall to each other, humorously, from the public announcement of the series, the statement that one of its aims would be to 'soften controversy.' As between the warring parties, this was true, since the contemplation of sacrifice, resourcefulness and bravery in foes (upon which we took every occasion to lay stress) became an element of intersectional reconciliation. This was promoted, if not insured by our rigid enforcement of our main principle, the exclusion of political questions."[18] This sort of reconciliatory rhetoric even appears in the *Century* article "The Battle of Shiloh" by Ulysses S. Grant. Although Grant cannot help himself from confrontationally calling the Union troops "National" and the Southern troops the "so-called Confederate," he later temporizes: "The troops on both sides were American, and united they need not fear any foe. It is possible that the Southern man started in with a little more dash than his Northern brother; but he was correspondingly less enduring" (Feb. 1885, 593, 609).

II

THE Century's open-door policy toward southerners in the Civil War series extended to southern fiction writers. Nowhere is the Gilded Age's fascination with America's diverse regions—which included the outermost regions of the far-flung world—more evident than in the Century, which navigated a fine line between being the arbiter of fine taste and expressing the currents of popular judgment. Of all these diverse places, the Century most aggressively pursued the South. About the time of the Civil War series, the Century welcomed impoverished southern writers into its pages, and for the new regional writers of the South, such as Joel Chandler Harris, George Washington Cable, and Thomas Nelson Page, the Century's endorsement meant refuge in northern magazines from the dry southern markets.

The Century's tradition of opening the door to and reconciling with the "Great South" actually began with a special series bearing that name by Edward King in the 1870s under the editorship of Holland. Robert Scholnick has noted that "the 'Great South' series was widely acknowledged to be a most successful publication, demystifying the region and establishing the grounds for the reconciliation of the former antagonists."[19] The phrase "Great South," amended by Sidney Lanier in Scribner's in 1880 as the "New South,"[20] implied among other things a South reformed in its attitude toward slavery. The "New South" would have to possess changed attitudes toward African Americans if the North were to open itself up to southern writers: the Century inherited the legacy of moral views of pre–Civil War abolitionist rural New England.[21]

The "New South" concept included a South reformed from racism. The Century extended this impression in the later 1880s. With Gilder and Johnson as editors, the Century became increasingly conscious of the profitability as well as ethical dimensions of imagining the New South as reformed. The editors tended to minimize, in editorials and in their consideration of the work of southern writers, sectional disagreement on racial questions. In June 1880, despite the optimism of the New South series, Holland wrote candidly about racial problems in the United States: "The shadow of the negro," Holland wrote in his editorial of the same title, "lies upon the North as upon the South. . . . It cannot be disputed that the great obstacle that stands to-day in the way of the negro is the white man, North and South" (*Scribner's,* June 1880, 304).[22] By January 1885, however, Gilder wrote much more temperately and consolingly about America's racial problems: "There are, indeed, many indications . . . that the old lines of color, and of geography also, are soon (though none too soon) to fade from sight in American politics" (*Century,* Jan. 1885, 462). This optimism obviously flew squarely in the face of the facts, even as they were being addressed by southern writers in the *Century.*

Century's optimism about the South and racism allowed northern readers to turn their gaze, without compunction, to a consideration of the South. There are a variety of possible reasons why northern readers wanted to do so. At a time when America was fascinated with its diverse regions, interest in the South is not surprising. Perhaps more fundamentally, however, the North felt a prurient and exculpatory fascination with the land that they had conquered and an unconscious guilt for privileging a "foreign" element—African Americans—over their own white brethren in the South. Perhaps on an even more sinister level of unconsciousness, northerners were themselves resisting the "shadow of the Negro."

Century's acceptance of the fiction of Thomas Nelson Page is one example of how it gave wide berth to its own stated commitment to anti-slavery sentiment. Although Page had published dialect poetry in *Scribner's* in 1877, his two most famous stories appeared in the *Century,* "Marse Chan" in April 1884 and "Meh Lady" in June 1886, both during the run of the Civil War series. Tooker disclosed in his memoirs that Johnson suggested to Page the North-South reconciliation theme of "Meh Lady"—"the happily ending love-story of a Virginia girl and a Northern soldier."[23] Meh Lady, her brother, Marse Phil, and the Mistis suffer the travails of a Southern plantation-owning family during the Civil War. Phil is killed fighting bravely in battle, his sister and mother travel against odds to the battle site to give him final alms, and Meh Lady is finally reduced to teaching "niggers" in the nearby school and faces the anxiety of losing the plantation, while her declining mother languishes away in increasing dependency upon her daughter. Salvation comes from the Yankee Captain Wilton, who just happens to be half-Virginian, distantly related to Meh Lady's family, and in love with Meh Lady. Wilton had extended all the courtesies of the South during the war, protecting Meh Lady's plantation from Yankee marauders. Meh Lady, predictably, falls in love with him after she nurses him back from ailing health. However, only on Mistis's death bed does Mistis release Meh Lady to marry a Yankee. Wilton returns one final time to the plantation not to be rebuffed, and the day is saved.

Northern readers, of course, noticed that Page had made his hero not quite a Yankee, but "Northern readers, however, had shown no partizan feeling, and had accepted the compromise in their eagerness to believe that the breach between the two erstwhile hostile regions was closed."[24] And "Meh Lady" certainly obliged. The tone of appeasement in General Grant's lauding of the bravery of both sides in the Civil War is also present here: "Meh Lady she ax one de doctors ef many o' de cav'lry wuz into de fight, an' he say she'd think so ef she'd been dyah; dat de cav'lry had meck some splendid charges bofe sides."[25]

Present also but unacknowledged by delighted northern readers, was the profound irony that Page's telling the story of the fall of southern aristocracy through the voice of an ex-slave makes for a better story. Thanks to Shelley Fisher Fishkin's consciousness-raising about the presence of the African-American voice in *Huckleberry Finn*, we can see how much of the lyricism of the southern voice comes from its African-American influence, a point that nineteenth-century American authors such as Page, Harris, Cable, and Twain seemed to intuit. Although "Meh Lady" is framed in brief by a presumably white nonvernacular southern speaker sometime after the Civil War, the storyteller in this tale about fallen southern aristocracy is the ex-slave Uncle Billy, who in old age still identifies himself as one of the "boys—Meh Lady's" (78).

Billy exhibits traits of African-American dialect that Fishkin notes make African-American storytelling so interesting, including a proliferation of "slang and figurative expressions," for example, that make for a speaker's "lucidity and directness," and his lyricism, his "breath of life caught from his surroundings," as one linguist put it.[26] Here is one example of figurative language from the African-American persona in "Meh Lady": "'Well, suh, dat night de plantation wuz fyah 'live wid soldiers—our mens; dee wuz movin' all night long, *je' like ants,* an' all over todes de gre't road *de camp-fires* look *like stars;* an' nex' morning' dee wuz movin' 'fo' daylight, gwine 'long' down de road, an' bout dinner-time hit begin, an' from dat time tell in de night, right down yander way, *de whole uth wuz rockin'.* You'd a-thought *de wull wuz splittin open* an' sometimes ey you'd listen right good you could *heah 'em yellin', like folks in de harves'-fiel' holleri' after a ole hyah'*" (italics added) (96).

Page's narrators also mark tense nonredundantly, a trait of African-American dialect, according to Fishkin. Nonredundant narration applies tense shifts erratically as long as a stabilizing time cue denoting the real time is established.[27] African-American dialect also includes the use of serial verbs, or "the tendency to describe every detail of an action or event from start to finish with its own special verb, a trait that has been traced to a number of African languages."[28] The following example from "Meh Lady" illustrates both nonredundant and serial narration: "De Cap'n he *wuz* [past tense cue] in he room and he head me, and he *come* [shift to present tense, nonredundant] out wid he cap on, *bucklin'* on Marse Phil' s'o'de whar he done *teck* down off de wall, and he *order* me to come 'long, and *tell* Meh Lady not to come out; and down de steps he *stride* out and *'cross* de yard out th'oo de gate in de road to whar de mens wuz wid meh horses at de fence. . . . Well, suh, de Cap'n' eye *flash;* he ain' *say* a wud; he jes *rip* out Marse Phil' s'o'de an' *clap* it up 'ginst dar man' side, and *cuss* him once" (serial and nonredundant verbs in italics) (104).

I do not intend here to authenticate Page's use of African-American dialect or to prove that the narrators in Page's "Marse Chan" and "Meh Lady" are African American. Obviously, unlike Huck, these narrators are established as such in Page's tales. Page's appropriation of the African-American voice to tell the Southern story is certainly offensive: not only does Billy in "Meh Lady" empty out his identity by empathizing with his enslavers—condemning the black slave Ananias as a "weevly black nigger" because he tells the Yankees where the plantation horses are and joins the Yankee forces (109), devoting his life to the romantic happiness of Meh Lady—but he also abandons himself by identifying himself as white ("like we all white folks"[133] and "We all white folks al'ays set heap o' sto' by one nurr" [105]).

Perhaps as egregious because more insidious is Page's relaying of his propaganda through the African-American voice—"the new and picturesque dialect."[29] Such use of dialect was invariably patronizing in an age that equated grammaticality with social and moral stature.[30] Yet, paradoxically, a great part of the charming simplicity that northerners enjoyed in "Meh Lady" and "Marse Chan" is created by the "indescribably suggestive" ("Meh Lady," 7) lyrical point of view of the world as focalized through Billy in "Meh Lady" and Sam in "Marse Chan." It might seem paradoxical, then, to say that African-Americans are absent in these stories, but the African-American voice is more than absent. "Marse Chan" is a story told by former slave Sam about his young Master Channing, to whom Sam is still devoted. Although Sam is the focalizer of the story, the value-centered character in the story is the young white plantation master. Although in Sam's dialect, which is exploited for its storytelling properties, the tale is in effect read through to hear the story of Master

Channing. In essence, African-Americans are absent in this fiction, which is relayed right through them as if they were invisible.

"Marse Chan" stereotypes the African-American slave as naive, simple, kind, and devoted to his master, with whom he is engaged in a benevolent patriarchal relationship. As such, the story represents the Old South rationale against which the North fought so vocally. "Meh Lady" and "Marse Chan" are unreconstructed southern stories that pretend that slaves are back in their place and that the Civil War has not even been fought: "Marse Chan's" outer frame narrator literally dreams himself back into the story of the Old South, where "time was of no consequence to them,"[31] and Billy in "Meh Lady" says his story "cyars me back sometimes, I mos' furgit de ain' nuver been no war nor nuttin'" (79). One would assume that post–Civil War northern readers would strongly resist such a message.

Yet famous post–Civil War readers loved the story. The abolitionist Henry Ward Beecher was moved to tears when "Marse Chan" was read to him. Thomas Wentworth Higginson also cried over the story, perhaps because " 'Marse Chan' was a story of a vanished way of life so remote in time and space that [it] had a romantic charm. Or perhaps [this story] recalled to readers in huge Northern cities memories of a simpler life they had known or heard their parents or grandparents speak of."[32] How we shudder today to read the fond description by one "antislavery" *Century* editor of a story like "Marse Chan": such stories present "the hospitable, patriarchal life; the new and picturesque dialect; the half-humourous clashes between master and man; the heroic devotion shown to 'ol' Miss' and the children by faithful old servitors even at the moment of the dissolution of the bond that held them together—all these things the Northerner read with delight, and with a half-conscious softening of his former hostility. And the Southerner, awakened to hope, and thrilled by the successes of his latest conquest, felt a new glow of fraternity. Justification seemed no longer necessary."[33]

The northern reader's oversimplification of the racist nuances in "Marse Chan" can be juxtaposed with the way it was understood by some of Page's unreconstructed contemporary southern readers, who imputed to "Marse Chan" the value of a historical document that justified, as one southern woman put it, "the slave plantation and made the lost cause seem in many ways the right one."[34] That African Americans would have rejected the implications in this story about the benevolent Marse is suggested by the only known essay by an African-American that appeared in the 1880s *Century:* "My Master," says Frederick Douglass scornfully, in "My Escape from Slavery," with quotation marks around the word "master" (Nov. 1881, 128).

Both in yearning for an agrarian past that was simpler and in relegating southern patriarchal treatment of African Americans to "distance," northern readers and *Century* critics unconsciously expressed a desire to transcend the fragmented self. Beecher's reconciliatory yearning for the Old South days represents an Anglo-American myth of sameness and a desire for a simplifying plenitude that would deny that the nation was fractured by internal division. In the positing of unity, something is, of necessity, repressed. What was repressed in this "cathartic recapitulation of a plenitude of being?"[35] The shadow of the Negro.

Perhaps the phrase the "shadow of the Negro," used by Holland in his 1880 *Century* editorial, came originally from George Washington Cable's *The Grandissimes,* which was accepted by the *Century* in 1879 and was serialized beginning that November. Cable was discovered by King during his Great South series. Given the startlingly radical nature of the novel's pronouncements about racism, one wonders whether the novel would have been accepted for serialization during the run of the Civil War series. Lawrence Berkove notes that Cable exposed in *The Grandissimes* "the travesty of equality that blighted the lives" of free men of color, both before and after the Civil War. Cable's novel, Berkove suggests, influenced antiracist works serialized in the *Century* by Mark Twain and Joel Chandler Harris.[36]

The Grandissimes is a story about honor, love, and caste prejudice in old New Orleans to which I cannot do justice here. There are, indeed, the requisite white southern belles and southern heroes. But the novel also features Bras-Coupe, an African slave of royal lineage in love with the beautiful mulatto Palmyra, who is in turn in love with the white Honore Grandissime and who plots to use Bras-Coupe's love to incite insurrection. Through Bras-Coupe and his tragedy readers see "a type of all Slavery, turning into flesh and blood the truth that all Slavery is maiming."[37]

Yet it is the black Honore—half-brother to the white—who is referred to as the "shadow" in a lengthy and monumental passage between the white Honore and the apothecary-narrator Frowenfeld. It is a reference made so prominently in *The Grandissimes* that it would have been difficult for Holland to miss it. The white Honore sees his half-brother and remarks to Frowenfeld that "civilization [is] sitting in a horrible darkness, my-de'seh!" Frowenfeld immediately responds, "The shadow of the Ethiopian," and the white Honore responds that he "had said the very word":

"Ah! my-de'-seh, when I try sometimes to stand outside and look at it, I am *ama-aze* at the length, the blackness of that shadow! . . . It is the *Nemesis* w'ich, instead of coming afteh, glides along by the side of this morhal, political, commercial, social mistake! . . . It brheeds a thousan' cusses that nevva leave home but jus' flutter-h up an' rhoost, my-de'seh, on ow *heads;* an' we nevva know it!" (155–56). The phrase is subsequently internalized into the narrative frame to describe "the other Honore . . . like [the white Honore's] shadow" (185).

This connection between African Americans and the image of the shadow powerfully suggests the way in which blacks in Anglo-American culture and literature sometimes become not just the "type" of slavery but emblematic of Anglo-Americans' own archetypal guilt. One sees a kind of biblical sense of this, for example, in the writings of William Faulkner. In addition to Holland's and Cable's use of "shadow" during the nineteenth century, William Dean Howells also labeled slavery the "dark shadow of our shameful past" in an 1886 *Harper's Monthly*.[38] He reiterated the phrase possibly because of his intimate acquaintance with the *Century*'s use of it when Howells worked with the magazine in the early '80s. Perhaps nothing is intrinsically wrong with this archetype. Indeed, conceiving of African Americans as shadows constitutes an acknowledgment of historical guilt for the ill treatment of slaves. Nevertheless, this phrase and the thinking it implies suggests the objectification of black people as something less than complex human beings; as shadows, their quintessence is reduced to an allegorical function for someone else.

One possible repercussion of this way of thinking is that African Americans become enslaved to whites' impressions of themselves, in particular to the unpleasant, guilt-ridden parts that they might likely seek to repress. Cable's speaker fixates on the blackness of that shadow as if it were some sort of horror with a life external to that of the speaker. Hence, the evil within becomes expelled and becomes the shadow without. In an odd twist of fate, the shadow, African Americans, becomes responsible for the guilt, which is expunged by a fantasy of white homogeneity.

If such conceptualization of the shadow with its accompanying repression and denial brings to mind for the reader the psychoanalysis of Carl Jung, this is not surprising. Jung himself remarked in 1912, "I have frequently observed in the analysis of Americans that the inferior side of the personality, the 'shadow,' is represented by a Negro or an Indian, whereas in the dream of a European it would be represented by a somewhat shady individual of his own kind."[39] The African-American writer

Frances Watkins Harper invoked this psychoanalytical iconography of shadow in *Iola Leroy or Shadows Uplifted* (1892). Harper uses "shadow" with overwhelming rapidity in the novel in a confusing—confuting—number of ways. Harper's ingenuity deserves an essay of its own. Suffice it to say here that Harper firmly reattaches shadow to the person who "owns" it, regardless of ethnicity, and that the shadow is something clearly outside African-American ethnicity in a historical, global sense.

III

CABLE'S *Grandissimes* aside, more often than not the *Century* editorial strategy during the run of the Civil War series was to relegate racial intolerance to the antebellum South and to deny that in the New South racial injustices still existed. At no time was this affirmation of a white homogenous way of thinking more fervent than in 1885, as is evident in a sudden surge of *Century* editorials and open letters about African Americans during this time. These essays, in line with the reconciliation theme, reiterated the mutual gallantry of the North and South in Civil War battle; they suggested that this recognition could now be made because there was a New South of racial tolerance.

The *Century* printed a letter from a "Southern Democrat" in January 1885 that even praised the South for its past of slavery: "There is not a thinking man at the North who will not admit that American slavery seems to have been a provision of Providence for the advancement of a large part of the negro race. This is a phase of the slavery question worthy the attention of reflecting minds. The negroes came to this country barbarians. They were savages; but they were not savages when freedom found them out" (471). Gilder in "Let Us Have Peace" wrote in the succeeding month that there was an "improved condition and spirit [in] the South, and [a] new era of common interests and mutual sympathy and respect" (Feb. 1885, 638). Later in the year Gilder again wrote appeasingly about the "need for patience and tolerance in judging the movements of Southern opinion upon this question [of racism]. It is clear that the cause of the negro may safely be left to such champions as those who have now risen up on Southern soil to defend his rights" (Oct. 1885, 967).

The 1885 date of these editorials was probably strategic. They mediated between Cable's agitationist writings, which Gilder perhaps printed in deference to his longtime contributor, and the vehement Southern response to Cable's work. The tinder for the political fire was the 1883 U.S. Supreme Court decision that rendered unconstitutional the Civil Rights Act of 1875, which had given African-American citizens unconditional access to public accommodations. Suddenly, the North in its legal collusion seemed no more enlightened than the South. As W. E. B. Du Bois observed about the late 1880s, "The rich and dominating North . . . was not only weary of the race problem, but was investing largely in Southern enterprises, and welcomed any method of peaceful cooperation."[40]

It took a Southerner, Cable, in his two *Century* essays, "The Freedman's Case in Equity" (Apr. 1885, 409–18) and "The Silent South" (Aug. 1885, 674–91), to enjoin both North and South to take notice that the "separate but equal" policy imposed in the South was just a more subtle and insidious version of African-American enslavement based on the same southern belief that the black race was inherently inferior. Thinkers in the South were furious at Cable. As Jay Hubbell notes, "Even Southern liberals like Henry W. Grady found altogether unacceptable the views of the Negro question which Cable was freely expressing— [Southern] conservatives regarded him as a traitor to the South."[41] The *Century*, which invited *Atlanta Constitution* editor Grady to write a rebuttal on behalf of southern sentiment, continued nevertheless to support Cable. Yet the support ended after these three articles. Gilder rejected Cable's suggestion that Charles Chesnutt's voice be added to the discussion: "Mr. Chesnutt's paper—'The Negro's Answer to the Negro Question,' is a timely political paper. So timely and *so* political—in fact so partisan—that we cannot handle it. It should appear at once somewhere." Herbert Smith observes of this response, "Editors do not *enjoy* printing unprofitable and controversial articles in the pages of their magazines, and Gilder was no exception."[42]

The *Century* persisted with its claim that race prejudice was a bygone issue for both the North and the South. In its desire to deflect focus from divisive controversy, the *Century* consistently refused to acknowledge racism. And the northern readers, who Cable insisted shared in the more insidious racism of post-Reconstruction America, "even tinctured by that race feeling whose grosser excesses it would so gladly see suppressed" (*Century*, Jan. 1884, 409), turned away from the "shadow of the Negro" as much as their Southern counterparts. Ironically, it was two Southerners, Harris in his fictional "Free Joe and the Rest of the World" (*Century*, Nov. 1884, 117–23) and Cable in his essays, who exposed the old South slave-master ideology for the exploitative system that it was and who uncovered still lurking in the collective unconscious of the entire nation the implicit racist assumptions.

Nevertheless, even Cable and Harris were not immune from the effects of northern apologistic rhetoric. Regardless of how one presently judges the level of racism, intentional or otherwise, in Harris's "Uncle Remus" tales, a review in the *Century* understood the tales from a racist, apologistic perspective: the stories presented "a type familiar to us all—the old plantation negro. . . . The gentle old darky—shrewd, yet simple-minded, devoted to the people who once owned him as a slave. . . . Even the occasional mild little apologies for the patriarchal system which the author scatters through his work will offend no one. They lend it a pleasant old-time, 'befo'-the-wah' flavor; so to speak, they give the picture 'distance' " (Apr. 1881, 961).

It is also true that *The Grandissimes* was an early '80s serial and that Cable's *Dr. Sevier* finished serialization in the *Century* only one month before the beginning of the Civil War series. Is it coincidental that a central theme of *Dr. Sevier* is North-South reconciliation? In *Dr. Sevier,* southerner John Richling is disinherited before the war because of "simple sectional prejudice": he marries a northerner.[43] The last third of the novel takes up the reunion of John and his wife, Mary, behind enemy lines and concentrates also on the bravery of the Southern troops. The one nod to the Northern faction that its "cause [was] just" (377) provoked angry Southern response, which suggests how volatile sectional difference still was during this time of supposed appeasement.[44] Just as noteworthy is the fact that this novel by the creator of Bras-Coupe makes African Americans barely a minor footnote in this work, Cable's novel of the Civil War.

IV

THE question of the absence of African Americans can be put, finally, to the great works by Twain, Howells, and James that can now be read within the context of the North-South reconciliation theme in the mid-1880s *Century*. Where did these works stand on the "shadow of the Negro?" The *Huckleberry Finn* excerpts chosen by Gilder[45] included the Sheperdson-Grangerford feud, the episodes with the duke and the king, and Huck and Jim's conversation about the wisdom of King Solomon. Although there is certainly an intertextual challenge in Twain's debunking chapter on the Grangerfords (1885) to Page's glorification of southern chivalry in his '84 "Marse Chan," Gilder's selection of this excerpt takes no chances with racial questions. When the slave Jim is involved in the excerpts that Gilder apparently selected, his presence serves as minstrel farce or plot enabler. And, significantly, the section in the duke-king episode that in Fishkin's reading "signifies" Jim's humanity beyond the minstrel tropes—Jim's discussion of his deaf daughter and his own human pain—is edited out for the *Century*.[46] Absent is the one clear instance in these scenes where Jim's humanity is shown and Huck forced to acknowledge it.

In Howell's *The Rise of Silas Lapham,* although one could argue that the presence of the Civil War theme in the novel is so minimal that such questions as have been considered in this essay need not be addressed, one might recall that the subplot of the novel is fueled by the hero's debt to a Civil War soldier who sacrificed his own life for the hero. This kind of Civil War heroism and nobility was central to the ideology of the Civil War series, so it is a significant omission that there is no mention of the moral issue that compelled the Civil War.

Finally, in James's *The Bostonians,* southerner Basil Ransom speaks in tribute to the fallen Union heroes who are honored in Harvard's Memorial Hall. Though the North-South reconciliation theme is predictably problematized by James, and thus in one sense *The Bostonians* implicitly undermines the *Century* ideology, there remains a notable absence of African Americans in this novel and a predictable valorization, vis-à-vis the reconciliation theme, of the Anglo-Americans who fought on both sides of the Civil War. One could conclude that these works, as serialized in the *Century,* are as Anglocentric as were the northern readers fixated on Anglo-American presence and ignoring the "shadow of the Negro."

Nevertheless, as Toni Morrison has so eloquently informed us,[47] even through omission the African-American presence is manifested in American literature, as it was in the 1880s *Century.* When Henry James wrote of his white southern hero that "his discourse was pervaded by something sultry and vast, something almost African in its rich, basking tone, something that suggested the teeming expanse of the cotton field,"[48] James goes one step further than the southern writers of his time by actually appropriating African-American dialectical identity to enhance the character of his Anglo-American hero. No more strongly, one could argue, could the need of an Anglo-American writer for identity cancel out and simultaneously exploit the African-American presence.

NOTES

1. L. Frank Tooker, *Joys and Tribulations of an Editor* (New York: Century, 1924), 227.

2. See Herbert F. Smith and Michael Peinovich, "*The Bostonians:* Creation and Revision," *Bulletin of the New York Public Library* 73 (1969): 300.

3. For a complete discussion of the popular subgenre of Civil War novels, see Robert A. Lively, *Fiction Fights the Civil War* (Chapel Hill: Univ. of North Carolina Press, 1957).

4. Articles on African-American ethnicity included Henry King, "A Year of the Exodus in Kansas," *Scribner's* 20 (1880): 211–18; "In the M. E. African," *Scribner's* 20 (1880): 423–29; Eugene V. Smalley, "In and Out of the New Orleans Exposition," *Century* 30 (1885): 185–99; George Washington Cable, "The Dance in Place Congo," *Century* 31 (1886): 517–53.

5. Tooker, *Joys and Tribulations*, 321.

6. Robert Underwood Johnson, *Remembered Yesterdays* (Boston: Little, Brown, 1923), 190.

7. Tooker, *Joys and Tribulations*, 190, 46.

8. Jonathan Freedman, *Professions of Taste: Henry James, British Aestheticism, and Commodity Culture* (Stanford, Calif.: Stanford Univ. Press, 1990), 108–9.

9. William Webster Ellsworth, *A Golden Age of Authors* (Boston: Houghton Mifflin, 1919), 233.

10. Johnson, *Remembered Yesterdays*, 194.

11. Rosamund Gilder, *Letters of Richard Watson Gilder* (Boston: Houghton Mifflin, 1916), 130–31.

12. Van Renssalaer to Gilder, 8 June 18??, Richard Watson Gilder Letter-Press Book 1 (16 Nov. 1880–13 Jan. 1886), Gilder Collection, New York Public Library.

13. Quoted in Carol Klimick Cyganowski, *Magazine Editors and Professional Authors in Nineteenth-Century America* (New York: Garland, 1988), 190.

14. Tooker, *Joys and Tribulations*, 112.

15. For an account of the origins of *Scribner's / Century*, see, for example, Cyganowski, *Magazine Editors*, 179–227; or "The Century Magazine 1870–1924," *Pan-American Magazine* 37 (1924): 341–45.

16. Herbert F. Smith, *Richard Watson Gilder* (New York: Twayne, 1970), 154.

17. Johnson to Gilder, 7 July 1884, Gilder Papers, New York Public Library.

18. Johnson, *Remembered Yesterdays*, p. 194.

19. Robert Scholnick, "*Scribner's Monthly* and the 'Pictorial Representation of Life and Truth' in Post-Civil War America," *American Periodicals* 1 (1991): 61.

20. "The New South," *Scribner's* 20 (1880): 840–51.

21. Scholnick, "*Scribner's Monthly*," 50.

22. One should note, however, that although Holland could speak in such an enlightened manner about the condition of African Americans, *Scribner's* published more than a dozen poems in black dialect by Irwin Russell between 1875 and 1880 that "assumed an unbridgeable gulf between blacks and whites," as Elsa Nettels observes in "The Problem of Negro Dialect in Literature," in *Language, Race, and Social Class in Howells's America* (Lexington: Univ. Press of Kentucky, 1988), 73.

23. Tooker, *Joys and Tribulations*, 203.

24. Ibid.

25. Thomas Nelson Page, "Meh Lady," in *In Ole Virginia or Marse Chan and Other Stories* (New York: Scribner's, 1968), 98. Further references to this work are to this edition and will be cited in the text.

26. Shelley Fisher Fishkin, *Was Huck Black? Mark Twain and African-American Voices* (New York: Oxford Univ. Press, 1993), 43, 44.

27. Ibid., 44–45.

28. Ibid., 47.

29. Tooker, *Joys and Tribulations,* 42.

30. See Nettels, *Language, Race, and Social Class,* 7–40.

31. Thomas Nelson Page, "Marse Chan," in *In Ole Virginia or Marse Chan and Other Stories* (New York: Scribner's, 1968), 1.

32. Jay Hubbell, *The South in American Literature, 1607–1900* (Durham, N.C.: Duke Univ. Press, 1954), 801–2.

33. Tooker, *Joys and Tribulations,* 42.

34. Hubbell, *South in American Literature,* 802.

35. Psychoanalytic phrasing quoted from Donna Przybylowicz, *Desire and Repression: The Dialectic of Self and Other in the Late Works of Henry James* (University: Univ. of Alabama Press, 1986), 23.

36. Lawrence Berkove, "The Free Man of Color in *The Grandissimes* and Works by Harris and Mark Twain," *Southern Quarterly* 18: (1980): 60–61.

37. George Washington Cable, *The Grandissimes, A Story of Creole Life* (New York: Sagamore, 1957), 171. Further references to this work are to this edition and will be cited in the text.

38. "Dostoevski Discovered," in *W. D. Howells as Critic,* ed. Edwin R. Cady (Boston: Routledge and Kegan Paul, 1973), 95.

39. Carl Jung, "The Origin of the Hero," in *Symbols of Transformation,* trans. R. F. C. Hull (Princeton: Princeton Univ. Press, 1976), 183.

40. W. E. B. DuBois, "Of Mr. Booker T. Washington and Others," in *The Souls of Black Folk* (New York: Vintage, 1990), 42.

41. Hubbell, *South in American Literature,* 815.

42. Smith, *Richard Watson Gilder,* 71.

43. George Washington Cable, *Dr. Sevier* (New York: Garrett, 1970), 449. Further references to this work are to this edition and are cited in the text.

44. See, for example, "Old Questions and New," *Century* 29 (1885): 471–72.

45. See Cyganowski, *Magazine Editors,* which suggests that Gilder chose the selections.

46. See "Royalty on the Mississippi," *Century* (Feb. 1885): 544–67. The episode begins several pages into chapter 19 with the arrival of the duke and king. On p. 553, one notes that the entire end of chapter 23 is deleted. The *Century* text stops after what would be the second paragraph of p. 202 in the *Adventures of Huckleberry Finn,* ed. Walter Blair and Victor Fischer (Berkeley: Univ. of California Press, 1986), and picks up with chapter 24, p. 203.

47. Toni Morrison, *Playing in the Dark: Whiteness and the Literary Imagination* (Cambridge: Harvard Univ. Press, 1992).

48. Henry James, *The Bostonians* (New York: Random House, 1956), 5.

14

CHARLES CHESNUTT, THE *ATLANTIC MONTHLY*, AND THE INTERSECTION OF AFRICAN-AMERICAN FICTION AND ELITE CULTURE

KENNETH M. PRICE

•

IN March 1899 Charles Chesnutt wrote to one of his editors at Houghton, Mifflin Company, pinpointing the kind of work he was writing against: "I have been reading the March *Atlantic.* . . . The dialect story ["Chief"] is one of the sort of Southern stories that make me feel it my duty to write a different sort, and yet I did not lay it down without a tear of genuine emotion."[1] These remarks clarify the importance of context for understanding Chesnutt's own racial representations, class biases, dialect usage, and partial participation in the very cultural norms he strove to oppose.

James B. Hodgkin's "Chief" is a dialect tale treating a slave (known as "Chief Justice John Marshall") who is in the North, working for his master's brother, when the Civil War begins. During the war he earns a remarkable amount of money as a hotel porter and instead of enjoying his wealth is convinced that it belongs to his master. Stretching credulity further, the story depicts slavery not as a destroyer of families but as the unifier of Chief's family. His mother had belonged to a neighboring plantation and would have been sold from Virginia to Georgia if his master, Mr. Marshall, had not purchased her (lacking sufficient cash, he pays by providing a "deed of trust" on his plantation). This act comes back to haunt the Marshalls; the plantation has to be auctioned when Mr. Marshall dies in battle and this debt cannot be repaid. With the conclusion of the war, Chief returns in time to buy the old plantation and immediately sign it over to Mrs. Marshall and "de young marster."

This story could have offended Chesnutt, with good reason, on any number of grounds. Perhaps most preposterous, from his viewpoint, was one exchange with the northern narrator in which Chief laments the losses entailed in freedom: " 'Then the war brought you your freedom,' I suggested. 'Well, suh, fur's dat,' he replied, 'Chief ain' wantin' no better freedom en I gits right at home. I's had ter scuffle thu some tough places sence de wah, but 't wuz easy times fer er lazy nigger at home. De warn' no boss hurryin' you up all day; nor, suh, dat de warn'. De han's on de plantation teck de time, yaas, plenty time, time fer eatin; en sleepin', en holidays 'nuff fer anybody. De marster wuz easy man wi' easy ways, en he did n' hurry nobody, en de did n't hurry dese'ves 'sep'n in de harves', en de 'bleeged ter hurry den ter git de crap in" (*Atlantic Monthly,* Mar. 1899, 376). In this fantasy, only the masters ever hurried. Chief's yearning for the soft days of slavery violated Chesnutt's own knowledge of the cruelties of bondage. Plantation mythology denied the reality of slave suffering and family rupture by stressing the dedication of black "servants" to their white masters both before and after the Civil War.[2] Many writers from both North and South created self-sacrificing planters and genial, appreciative, and docile slaves.[3]

We still must account, however, for Chesnutt's mysterious tear. His response marks him as a stranger to our common assumptions and emphasizes the need to historicize our analysis of the *Atlantic* and Chesnutt's work within it. Only then can we appreciate how he produced an alternative not out of thin air but with the tools and assumptions, thick with impediments, provided by a white-dominated culture.

The racial attitudes expressed in "Chief," commonplace in the *Atlantic* of the 1880s and 1890s, had not always been characteristic of the magazine. In fact, the magazine began in the late 1850s as the brainchild of Francis Underwood, a passionate follower of the Free Soil Party. The original *Atlantic* promoted literary culture with a special emphasis on New England, and—just as significantly—it advanced the antislavery cause. From its birth, the magazine vigorously opposed accommodating the "slave powers," and throughout the war it supported Lincoln, lamenting only that he was not adequately aggressive in conducting the war and swift in his declaration of emancipation. Charles Sumner and others later detailed the radical Republican program for reconstruction in the *Atlantic,* which consistently viewed the Republicans in the 1860s and 1870s as "the party of righteousness."[4]

Much had changed, however, by the 1880s.[5] The *Atlantic* had always represented a relatively small cultural elite, but whereas an earlier elite formation was energized by what it saw as the powers and responsibilities of privilege, the post-Reconstruction *Atlantic* writers displayed the fears of an embattled few.[6] Their political commentary in the 1880s displays a sense of estrangement and loss of power in a political process they felt had been debased by an uninformed majority and by corrupt politicians in both parties.[7] Moreover, commentary on racial matters had clearly changed. E. V. Smalley's January 1884 essay on "The Political Field" asserted that "the public mind is no longer interested in the affairs of the negro race. A generation of controversy and four years of terrible war gave the negro in America freedom and the ballot. Now the common sentiment is that enough has been done for him, and that he should make his own way upward in the social scale. There is no demand for a constitutional amendment which will put the machinery of federal courts at work to secure him good seats at the theatres, good beds in hotels and sleeping-cars, and the right to be shaved in the fashionable barber-shops. People are content . . . to leave such matters to state legislation" (130). The apathy of this column represented a general mood: political coverage was on the decline in the *Atlantic*, and the magazine abandoned its once-powerful backing of the Republican Party. The idea that civil equality might bring social equality for blacks provoked hostility both in the *Atlantic* and in the northern press at large.[8]

Chesnutt's stories appeared when many in the South (with the acquiescence and sometimes overt support of northerners) strove to counter any tendency toward equality by reinstituting the basic functions, if not the form, of slavery. Although direct commentary on governmental matters was on the wane in the *Atlantic*, the political valence of other material was clear. It was not a neutral matter, for example, when in June 1888, right in the middle of Chesnutt's run of stories, the magazine published a lengthy review of *Memorials of a Southern Planter*, Susan Dabney Smedes's biographical record of her father, Thomas Gregory Dabney. This review stressed the "liberal" and "patriarchal" relation that "Mr. Dabney bore to his [500] negro slaves" and concluded that the "humane relations of master and slave formed the most impregnable defense of the system" (839). The book under review, published in Baltimore, was an extended apology for the Old South and received respectful attention from a magazine situated in what was once a stronghold of abolitionist sentiment.

To be sure, the *Atlantic* in the 1880s conveyed mixed signals on racial issues. There were reviews of books about William Lloyd Garrison and John Brown that, in muted form, echoed sentiments to be found in the *Atlantic* of old. But other items, such as "Race Prejudices" by N. S. Shaler (October 1886), expressed the reactionary attitudes that newly dominated the magazine. Appearing only a year before Chesnutt's first dialect story in the *Atlantic*, this article contended that "speaking a different dialect" limited sympathy and could well evoke the "instinctive repugnance [of races] to each other" (513, 516). Shaler further remarked that "the one condition in which very diverse races may be brought into close social relations without much danger of hatred, destructive to the social order, is where an inferior race is enslaved by a superior. . . . The sense of possession which the mastering race has in the slave awakens a new avenue for sympathy. We all prize the things which we absolutely possess; the more human they are, the stronger their hold on the affections" (516). He concluded, blithely, that slavery in the United States was "effective in the prevention of race hatreds" (516).

Despite printing essays like "The Political Field" and "Race Prejudices" and reviewing books like *Memorials of a Southern Planter*, Thomas Bailey Aldrich in one crucial way advanced African-American interests during his editorship of the *Atlantic* (1881–90). Near the end of his tenure, Aldrich published three of Chesnutt's stories, "The Goophered Grapevine" (1887), "Po' Sandy" (1888) and "Dave's Neckliss" (1889). The net effect of this editor-author relationship, as William Andrews observes, was "to use the white-controlled mass media in the service of serious social fiction on behalf of the black community." No African-American writer of fiction could compare with Chesnutt's success in gaining the support and promotion of the white publishing establishment.[9]

Of course, it is ironic that Aldrich seems to have had no idea that he was publishing an African-American author. Chesnutt kept silent on this issue until 1891, when he proposed a book to the prestigious house of Houghton, Mifflin, the parent company of the *Atlantic Monthly*. With slight historical inaccuracy, Chesnutt described his projected volume as "the first contribution by an American of acknowledged African descent to purely imaginative literature."[10] Chesnutt's success in working with Aldrich on equal terms was a crucial step in the process that led a first-rank publishing house to the unprecedented decision to offer African-American fiction to a large market.[11]

Why did the *Atlantic* initially agree to publish Chesnutt? And why did he choose to publish in the *Atlantic?* By considering both questions, we can better appreciate the importance and the ironies of the intersection of African-American fiction and elite culture.

Although Aldrich inherited from his predecessors James Russell Lowell and William Dean Howells a magazine with a distinguished history, and although he possessed considerable renown as a writer,[12] he faced difficulties at the *Atlantic*. Aldrich received the editorship in part because of his respectful, even reverential attitude toward the Brahmin immortals,[13] but the Brahmins, unfortunately, were writing less and less, and what they were producing was often lost to higher-paying journals.[14]

By the late 1880s Henry Houghton, the owner of the *Atlantic,* was ready to find new talent that he could pay at the relatively low rate of between six and ten dollars a page. (The *Century,* in contrast, paid about twenty dollars per page of nonfiction and, for some contributors, several times that for fiction.)[15] Whatever his shortcomings, Aldrich successfully maintained his independence as an editor. He rejected contributions by such notables as Charles Eliot Norton, Thomas Wentworth Higginson, and Harvard president Charles Eliot. He also possessed sufficient vision to support established writers who lacked wide market appeal (for example, Henry James) and to locate at least one previously unknown and truly gifted writer within his "sludge pile" of unsolicited manuscripts.[16] As far as literary approach is concerned, Aldrich was predisposed to discover work like Chesnutt's because of his own aesthetic values: a love of polished style, an aversion to the harsher forms of realism and naturalism, and a fondness for surprise endings.

The politics of Aldrich's support of Chesnutt remain intriguing, however. Not only had the *Atlantic* become more conservative (both in tone and substance), but Aldrich's personal views on race and ethnicity were hardly advanced. Of course, the *Atlantic* was not solely an expression of Aldrich's tastes and ideas because his outlook was qualified by his assistant, Susan Francis; his associate, Horace Scudder; the owner, Henry Houghton; and other factors, including the tradition of the magazine, its backlog of acceptances, and his own sense of editorial professionalism.[17] Still, for a decade, Aldrich fundamentally shaped a magazine possessing extraordinary literary prestige.[18] Hence, his own views, implicit in his selections and emphases and explicit elsewhere, deserve study.

As a young man, Aldrich had been shunned by a ward of Wendell Phillips because of his tepid interest in abolitionism. He was also given to ethnic slurs masquerading as witticisms, in one instance placing more value on his dog, Trip, than on the Irish population of Boston.[19] Dapper and wealthy, he thought of himself as staying largely aloof from politics. Accordingly, the *Atlantic* under Aldrich's direction was marked by an ostensible withdrawal of concern from social issues. The poetry featured in the magazine, for example, was the nature poetry of Edith Thomas or the traditional lyrics of Edward Roland Sill rather than more daring or politically challenging poetry.[20] Only matters of race and ethnicity broke the facade of Aldrich's detachment. His one political affiliation was a lifetime membership in the anti-immigration league. After his days editing the *Atlantic,* he published his notorious "The Unguarded Gates" (*Atlantic Monthly,* July 1892, 57), a poetic plea for restriction of immigration, a "cry to keep out the alien, sinister races."

For Chesnutt, whose knowledge of Aldrich's personal politics would have been limited, publication in the *Atlantic* served (as it did for other writers) as a mark of singularly high literary achievement. This success, one of many in Chesnutt's pursuit of self-improvement, also affirmed his sense of class consciousness. Chesnutt had considerable self-possession stemming from his perception of himself as a gifted individual and as part of a noteworthy group. Both of his parents were free blacks who traced their lineage to the "old issue free Negroes" of North Carolina.[21] Both parents had white ancestors as well. Chesnutt himself was of very light complexion, in fact light enough to "pass" had he wanted to. He commented as a young man, "I am neither fish[,] flesh, nor fowl—neither 'nigger', poor white, nor 'buckrah.' Too 'stuck-up' for the colored folks, and, of course, not recognized by the whites."[22] He was educated at Howard School in Fayetteville, North Carolina, a free public grade school for blacks established in 1867 and one of the best schools of any kind in the state.[23] While still a teenager, he began teaching rural blacks; his journal entries are marked by some condescension and a characteristic sense of distance.[24] Chesnutt was a town-bred sophisticate (self-taught in Latin, French, and German) facing rural ways, a confrontation that evoked his sense of racial and class superiority. At age twenty-two, after a "meteoric rise into the ranks of black educators in the state" he became principal of the normal school, one of the two teacher-training schools in the state.[25] Eventually, of course, he became not only an author but a stenographer, a lawyer, and one of the wealthier African Americans living in Cleveland.[26]

In the early 1880s Chesnutt felt cramped at Fayetteville despite notable successes within the educational world. On 26 March 1881 his journal records his "mixture of motives" in pursuing a career as an author. "I want fame; I want money; I want to raise my children in a different rank of life from that I sprang from. In my present vocation, I would never accumulate a competency. . . . But literature pays—the successful."[27] Along with an economic interest in authorship, Chesnutt saw writing as a tool for reform. Yet he recognized, as early as 1880, the difficulty of effecting positive change in a time of reaction: "The subtle almost indefinable feeling of repulsion toward the negro . . . cannot be stormed and taken by assault." Prejudices, he continued, "must be mined, and we will find ourselves in their midst before they think it. . . . It is the province of literature to open the way . . . unconsciously step by step to the desired state of feeling."[28] Adhering to this view, Chesnutt later published in the *Atlantic* by approaching sensitive racial matters indirectly. He sought space in an elite magazine because of its visibility and authority with the audience he most wanted to reach, the white reader: "The object of my writings would be not so much the elevation of the colored people as the elevation of the whites,—for I consider the unjust spirit of caste which is so insidious as to pervade a whole nation, and so powerful as to subject a whole race and all connected with it to scorn and social ostracism—I consider this a barrier to the moral progress of the American people; and I would be one of the first to head a determined, organized crusade against it."[29] Chesnutt clearly faced the recurrent dilemma of the African-American artist—how to reach a white audience without compromising his message.[30]

The strategy Chesnutt adopted was to borrow the outlines of his literary form from Joel Chandler Harris. Harris himself is often dismissed because his Uncle Remus tales invite social condescension on the part of white readers. Yet we should also note the double nature of Harris's creation: as Robert Hemenway remarks, "Uncle Remus is literature, artifice, a Victorian relic whose plantation manners embarrass the modern reader. Brer Rabbit is folklore, a communally created universal outlaw whose revolutionary antics satisfy deep human needs."[31] Chesnutt himself seems to have had a divided response to Harris, on the one hand, admiring him and reading Uncle Remus tales to his children and on the other signifying on his work in "Mars Jeems's Nightmare" and faulting elsewhere his creation of a "devoted negro who prefers kicks to halfpence."[32]

Some critics argue—incorrectly, I think—that Chesnutt is tainted because he employed a form utilized in plantation fiction. Such arguments illustrate the shortcomings of assuming a one-to-one relation between politics and literary form. Plantation stories and stereotypical figures were limiting in most hands, but Chesnutt was remarkably adept at turning Harris's technique to his own purposes. Harris's Uncle Remus tales encouraged white readers to belittle or dismiss unfamiliar cultural experiences and complacently maintain the superiority of their own ways. Chesnutt invokes this formula to subvert it. Harris presents black dialect as the language of an ignorant slave incapable of equality with his master; in contrast, Chesnutt presents dialect as the language of a crafty individual who steers his employer to a desired way of seeing. Repeatedly in Chesnutt's stories, John, who commands the language commonly associated with intellect and advancement, is duped by Julius, whose language masks his cunning. Dialect keeps John from taking Julius seriously, to the white man's detriment.

My understanding of Chesnutt's attitude toward his characters is implicit in the above comments regarding his revision of Harris. Before going further, I want to emphasize the problematic nature of interpreting Chesnutt's tales. How do we understand his subjectivity, his position relative to the double narrative line? In reading Chesnutt, questions proliferate: does he identify with the black man, Julius? With the white man, John? With neither? Does he oscillate between the two? And how are readers to respond? Because the form gives John the first and last word, many people have taken the white man to be an authoritative commentator on Julius's yarns. It seems safe to conjecture that Aldrich read Chesnutt this way. In the past century, the assumption that Chesnutt's view matches John's has been, if not dominant in the criticism, certainly a recurrent idea. Writing in 1976, Hemenway noted that with only one exception, "folklorists who have considered *The Conjure Woman* have been totally misled by adopting the white perspective of John towards Julius's conjure tales."[33] Literary critics as a group have been more cautious, though some critics even into the late 1980s continue to collapse Chesnutt into John.[34]

It is not surprising that people have had doubts about Chesnutt's attitude toward Julius. Arguably, Chesnutt is closer to John than to Julius in more than just physical ways. Like John, he is middle class and has experienced both North Carolina and Ohio. Like John, Chesnutt in his letters and essays favors learned diction and an urbane elegance of construction. Like John, as we have seen, he is occasionally given to condescending attitudes toward the "true Negro." Yet even if we grant Chesnutt's sense of superiority and acknowledge his absorption of some racist tenets of his culture, it does not follow that a sense of superiority kept him from admiring Julius or, more generally, limited his efforts to advance black interests and rights.

What I take to be the dominant line of criticism on Chesnutt—including Andrews, Houston Baker, David Britt, Richard Brodhead, Melvin Dixon, Robert M. Farnsworth, SallyAnn H. Ferguson, Hemenway, Joyce Hope Scott, Robert B. Stepto, and Eric Sundquist—offers a compelling and persuasive understanding of his tales.[35] Nonetheless, it seems dubious for Hemenway to conclude that the other camp—those who identify Chesnutt and John—are "completely misled." I agree with Hemenway about the ultimate purpose of the conjure tales, but he underestimates the complexities of Chesnutt's form. That is, because Chesnutt had to penetrate a type of unofficial censorship, he built a duality into his early tales that virtually asked that he be "misunderstood" by some readers. Duality was a price Chesnutt paid—probably had to pay—to place his work in a leading monthly in the 1880s.[36] At the outset of his career, he wrote to allow certain readers to see his irony and others not. Chesnutt's method, as Britt observes, is a "study in duplicity that masks or reveals its meaning according to the predisposition of the reader."[37]

The widely divergent meanings are the key to the success of Chesnutt's tales in bringing sophisticated African-American fiction to the attention of elite culture. Until he established himself (and to some extent afterwards), a framed tale making use of characters resembling minstrel types—with all the ambiguities attendant on these formal choices—was the main avenue available.[38] Thus, it is misleading for Michael Flusche to conclude, "By writing fiction akin to the plantation genre, Chesnutt chose to do battle on unfavorable terrain. . . . There was no way he could be heard so long as he remained on his opponents' territory. His own imagination was shackled by the character types common in the plantation literature."[39] To the contrary, there was no way he could be heard unless he entered the opponent's field. It is not as if he could choose different cultural circumstances. Chesnutt wanted to be heard by white readers at America's racial nadir: they needed the uplift. Or as Albion Tourgée remarked at about this same time, "I am inclined to think that the only education required is that of the *white* race." On that side of the racial divide one could find the "hate, the oppression, the injustice."[40]

To the extent that Chesnutt saw writing as a crusade for social change and to the extent that he wrote with his own circumstances in mind, he was concerned less with the advantages of his class position than with the disadvantages of his racial position. Chesnutt's own process of identification was probably a fluctuating one, leaving him able to sympathize with—and be amused by—both Julius and John. Chesnutt operates between John and Julius, and, intriguingly, as his stories developed over time, he made both characters more like himself. First, John, though initially obtuse, develops in moral understanding over the course of several stories, as Robert Stepto has observed. Julius changes from being simply a "colored man" in the *Atlantic*'s first version of "The Goophered Grapevine" to being a mixed-race character when the tale was revised. In the version in *The Conjure Woman* (1899), Julius is "not entirely black" and possesses a "strain of other than negro blood. There was a shrewdness in his eyes, too, which was not altogether African, and which, as we afterwards learned from experience was indicative of a corresponding shrewdness in his character."[41] The mixed-race status of Julius is one of many clues suggesting that Chesnutt, though his sympathies shuttle back and forth, identifies more powerfully with Julius than with John.

The initial *Atlantic* story, "The Goophered Grapevine," provides additional reasons to think Chesnutt inclines toward Julius. Julius tells the tale of the bewitched grapevine to discourage John from taking away his livelihood, the income he makes gathering grapes at the abandoned plantation. Julius also seeks to dispel the white man's assumed racial superiority. Julius's comment about the scuppernong grape—"Ef dey's an'thing a nigger lub, nex' ter 'possum, en chick'n, en watermillyums, it's scuppernon's"—can be regarded as minstrel dialect, the words of a stock comic darky.[42] But we need to think beyond that. Julius, like slaves before him, employs wit, indirection, and subterfuge in "putting' on ol' massa." Julius invokes stereotypical notions to lull John into feeling assured about his existing beliefs. Hearing Julius's tale, John mistakenly believes that the ex-slave thinks nostalgically about the past: "He became more and more absorbed in the narrative, his eyes assumed a dreamy expression, and he seemed to lose sight of his auditors, and to be living over again in monologue his life on the old plantation" (*Atlantic Monthly*, Aug. 1887, 255). For John, thoughts of life on the plantation might be dreamy, but nothing in any of the conjure tales indicates that it was a dreamy experience for Julius. Julius is not drifting off languidly but calculating his chances in the present. As Richard Baldwin notes, "The tale . . . consistently presents white men bested by blacks or acting in ways whose folly is clearly perceived by the blacks. . . . Julius thus has the pleasure of effectively calling the white man a fool to his face, yet he fails to make any impression because the narrator is too blinded by racism to be able to perceive what Julius is up to."[43] What John fails to understand emphasizes the point and helps Julius to preserve his livelihood, because John—had he recognized the insults—would not likely have hired Julius. Something analogous must have occurred when Aldrich first read the manuscript sent in by an unknown Charles Chesnutt with a Cleveland return address. Here, apparently, was another white writer "playing in the dark," exploring black dialect in quaint and humorous ways. Here was another writer whose story, at a glance, seemed to fit with work such as Frances E. Wadleigh's "Mistah Famah," (Sept. 1888, 377–82) S. M. P.'s "Voodooism in Tennessee" (Sept. 1889, 376–80) and, slightly later, Hodgkin's "Chief."

For Chesnutt, there was a clear problem with his form: a subversive current that avoided Aldrich's detection might also elude too many of the white readers he hoped to change. If a nationally recognized judge of intellectual matters like Aldrich missed Chesnutt's point, was the form effective? Chesnutt had serious doubts, as he wrote to Tourgée on 26 September 1889, "I think I have about used up the old Negro who serves as mouthpiece, and I shall drop him in future stories, as well as much of the dialect."[44] Chesnutt's declining interest in Julius tales resulted, one assumes, because he regarded these tales as too dubious in their effects, too prone to play into stereotyped thinking, too restricted in terms of racial types, too limited in their depiction of the diversity of black social standing and educational attainment. He wanted to deal more directly with people like himself on the color line. It was only at the bidding of Houghton, Mifflin that he returned to vernacular fiction to compile *The Conjure Woman.*

Chesnutt's form, whatever misgivings he had about it, was an attempt to wrest back from white writers a black cultural form: the story told in black dialect. Chesnutt's attempt was made at a time when malevolent caricaturing was widespread and when the United States was suffering through the most virulent racism in its history, affecting representations of blacks in profound ways. One should be surprised not that he proceeded cautiously but that he succeeded so well in exploding myths.

On the surface, Chesnutt felt obliged to leave the caste system of the South unchallenged.[45] He hoped and expected that various readers would understand his tales in differing ways, as is revealed by the contrasting responses of John and Annie to Julius's conjure tales. Julius's tales are framed by the preliminary remarks of a well-educated, white narrator. This frame established distance and, one gathers, a type of safe haven in which (white) nineteenth-century readers could feel comfortable considering the doings of the social and racial other. Yet for those sensitive to the injustices of a patriarchal and paternalistic culture—and most readers of regionalist fiction were women—Chesnutt interwove additional meaning centering on the prevailing brutality of racial relations.

The interplay between the inside and outside narrative can be seen by considering "Po' Sandy" (*Atlantic Monthly*, May 1888, 605–11). The central story, told by Uncle Julius, gives an account of Sandy, a young slave deeply in love with his wife Tenie, a conjure woman. Mars Marrabo regularly sends Sandy to work on distant plantations, and when Sandy gets tired of this shuffling about, Tenie turns him into a tree to keep him near home. Sandy, an apparent runaway, is tracked to the tree, where the dogs become confused. In time the danger passes, and Tenie is able to return Sandy to his human form at night. But Tenie is sent away to nurse Marrabo's daughter-in-law, and during her absence Sandy is cut down. Tenie returns just in time to watch her husband milled into lumber to build a new kitchen on the plantation. The experience drives Tenie insane. The kitchen remains haunted by Sandy's ghost, so it is eventually torn down and the lumber used to build a schoolhouse. John plans, yet again, to tear down the school for lumber to build Annie a new kitchen. After Julius completes his tale, John and his wife, Annie, have the following conversation:

> "What a system it was," [Annie] exclaimed, when Julius had finished, "under which such things were possible!"
>
> "What things?" I asked, in amazement. "Are you seriously considering the possibility of a man's being turned into a tree?"
>
> "Oh, no," she replied quickly, "not that"; and then she murmured absently, and with a dim look in her fine eyes, "Poor Tenie!" (610)

John's unimaginative response is characteristic of his failure to see beyond the surface of the tales. Annie's sympathetic "Poor Tenie" points readers who are ready for the cue to a deeper meaning involving the inhuman agonies and violations entailed in slavery.

Chesnutt's tale is not realistic in an ordinary sense. It is, however, graphic, painful, and compelling. Through the allegory of the mutilated tree, Chesnutt gets at the truth of the physical and emotional brutality of slavery. Aldrich, not a fan of realism himself, once complained that too many realists endorsed the tedious, the mundane, the disagreeable, and the homely. Chesnutt's reliance on metamorphosis certainly kept him from the mundane. Although the white narrator John—and probably Aldrich, too—saw in "Po' Sandy" only a charming flight of fancy, "an absurdly fantastic yarn," Chesnutt's tale was also structured to enable sensitive readers to detect profound commentary on race relations.

"Dave's Neckliss" was the most radical of the three early stories Chesnutt published in the *Atlantic* (Oct. 1889, 500–509). Interestingly, Aldrich published it, but the seemingly more supportive Walter Hines Page kept it out of the *Conjure Woman* volume. Page, one of Aldrich's successors at the *Atlantic* and a key decision-maker at Houghton, Mifflin, may have excluded the story on legitimate grounds of focus: the story does not deal with conjuring. Yet one wonders if a story that was acceptable to Aldrich when he assumed it was the work of a white man became too threatening once a later editor knew the author to be black. In this story Chesnutt depicts a more impressive and commanding black character than elsewhere in the tales. Dave is fully literate and the tale carries a harsh (implicit) indictment of the enduring harm done to blacks by slavery. The tale involves a lower-class white overseer jealous of Dave's talents who strives successfully to mangle his personality. Dave is forced, on suspicion of stealing, to wear a ham around his neck. The degradation leads Dave to lose all sense of his identity and to commit suicide.

Ellery Sedgwick's recent study of the *Atlantic Monthly* characterizes Aldrich's editorship as retrospective, reactionary, and opposed to both aesthetic and social change. Such a conclusion certainly seems generally valid because, unlike Howells, who grew in sympathetic understanding of the social and economic outsider, Aldrich "grew progressively more bigoted and misanthropic towards those outside the pale of his own social circle." Thus the irony of his (unintended) support of African-American writing. Aldrich has sometimes been blamed as an editor for failing to secure any "major new writers for the magazine or the house."[46] Chesnutt stands as the exception to this statement.

What are we to make, finally, of Chesnutt's tear over Hodgkin's "Chief"? Racist, manipulative, implausible, "Chief" bristles with flaws that are only too apparent. Yet the story also displays in miniature the same fascination-repulsion at things black that generally characterized the *Atlantic*.[47] The story, the magazine, and (as Eric Lott has recently shown) the culture at large were shot through with this type of contradiction. "Chief" denigrates black people and caters to destructive white illusions even as it longs for a racial utopia of love uniting black and white.[48] Chesnutt probably read through "Chief" to the potential resident in the subject and its resolution, finding (more in himself than in the text) a vision of relations purged of one-sided sacrifices and marked by true mutuality, and thereby deserving a "tear of genuine emotion."

NOTES

1. Quoted in Helen Chesnutt, *Charles Waddell Chesnutt: Pioneer of the Color Line* (Chapel Hill: Univ. of North Carolina Press, 1952), 107.

2. The criticism on the plantation myth is extensive. Two works that I have found useful are Eric Sundquist, *To Wake the Nations: Race in the Making of American Literature* (Cambridge: Harvard Univ. Press, 1993), esp. 332, and Melvin Dixon, "The Teller as Folk Trickster in Chesnutt's *The Conjure Woman*," *CLA Journal* 18 (1974): 186–97.

3. Northern writers, including Sarah Orne Jewett, also participated in this myth making. See Jewett's "The Mistress of Sydenham Plantation," *Atlantic Monthly* 62 (1888): 145–50.

4. Ellery Sedgwick, *"The Atlantic Monthly,"* in *American Literary Magazines: The Eighteenth and Nineteenth Centuries*, ed. Edward E. Chielens (New York: Greenwood, 1986), 505–7.

5. This paragraph has benefited from Ellery Sedgwick, *The Atlantic Monthly 1857–1909: Yankee Humanism at High Tide and Ebb* (Amherst: Univ. of Massachusetts Press, 1994), 102–4, 161–64. I am grateful to him for showing me portions of this work in manuscript.

For further information on Aldrich's editing of the *Atlantic*, see Charles E. Samuels, *Thomas Bailey Aldrich* (New York: Twayne, 1965); Donald Tuttle, "Thomas Bailey Aldrich's Editorship of the *Atlantic Monthly*: A Chapter in the Belles-Lettres Tradition," Ph.D. diss., Case Western Reserve Univ., 1939; Charles

R. Mangam, "A Critical Biography of Thomas Bailey Aldrich," Ph.D. diss., Cornell Univ., 1950.

6. By the time of Aldrich's editorship, the Brahmins regarded themselves as anything but complacent controllers of power in a safe, comfortable world. Protestant Yankees in Boston were in retreat politically and economically, yielding to rising immigrant pressures. The Brahmins could still hold out in their clubs and cotillions, in certain banks and businesses, and to some extent at Harvard. But in the 1880s and 1890s Boston was becoming less and less theirs: one-third of the population was foreign born, and Irish Americans were capturing nearly complete control of city government. When Aldrich, a New Hampshire native of "sound colonial stock" (as an early biographer assures us) moved into town, he began calling himself Boston-plated. In doing so, he of course identified himself only with a select portion of a city fractured along class and ethnic lines. He was not identifying with the districts that would soon elect Patrick "Honey Fitz" Fitzgerald, the grandfather of John F. Kennedy, as the first Irish-American mayor of a major U.S. city.

7. See Herbert Tuttle, "The Despotism of Party," *Atlantic Monthly* 54 (1884): 374–84.

8. As C. Vann Woodward notes, "It was quite common in the 'eighties and 'nineties to find in the *Nation, Harper's Weekly,* the *North American Review,* or the *Atlantic Monthly* Northern liberals and former abolitionists mouthing the shibboleths of white supremacy regarding the Negro's innate inferiority, shiftlessness, and hopeless unfitness for full participation in the white man's civilization" (*The Strange Career of Jim Crow,* 3d ed. [New York: Oxford Univ. Press, 1974], 70).

9. William L. Andrews, *The Literary Career of Charles W. Chesnutt* (Baton Rouge: Louisiana State Univ. Press, 1980), 273–74.

10. Chesnutt, *Charles Waddell Chesnutt,* 68.

11. Chesnutt's progress toward book publication dragged on slowly. His initial proposal was based on the "Rena Walden" story, now known as *The House Behind the Cedars.* After redirecting Chesnutt (with their own idea of appropriate racial discourse in mind) Houghton, Mifflin agreed to publish a group of conjure tales based on two of the three stories originally printed by Aldrich in the *Atlantic.* The publication history of *The Conjure Woman* (1899) has been insightfully treated in Richard Brodhead's introduction to *The Conjure Woman and Other Conjure Tales* (Durham: Duke Univ. Press, 1993), 1–21. However, Brodhead focuses on Chesnutt's relationship with Walter Hines Page, leaving unexplored the earlier, groundbreaking relationship with Aldrich.

12. At the age of twenty-nine, in 1865, Aldrich's poetry was enshrined by Ticknor and Fields in their distinguished Blue and Gold series. He thereby was elevated into the company of James Russell Lowell, Henry Wadsworth Longfellow, William Cullen Bryant, and John Greenleaf Whittier. Through the end of the century Aldrich's status remained high. In 1884, when the *Harvard Crimson* polled its readers about who should make up an American academy, Aldrich

ranked second in the voting, placing well ahead of Howells, Mark Twain, Henry James, and Walt Whitman. See Kenneth M. Price, "Thomas Bailey Aldrich," in *American Literary Critics and Scholars, 1880–1900*, ed. John W. Rathbun and Monica M. Grecu (Detroit: Gale Research, 1988), 3–8.

13. Carol Klimick Cyganowski, *Magazine Editors and Professional Authors in Nineteenth-Century America* (New York: Garland, 1988), 121, and Price, "Thomas Bailey Aldrich."

14. In the 1880s the *Atlantic* printed many critical essays on Nathaniel Hawthorne, Longfellow, Oliver Wendell Holmes, and Ralph Waldo Emerson to make up for a shortage of original contributions by these figures.

15. Sedgwick, *Atlantic Monthly*, 177–79.

16. See ibid. for a more complete discussion of some of these matters. By the mid-1880s, James's ability to sell his wares to the magazine market had declined considerably, though Aldrich and the *Atlantic* stood by him loyally. In fact, James appeared in 65 of the 110 issues Aldrich edited.

17. Susan Francis noted that Aldrich was "very fair-minded towards articles treating of subjects which did not appeal to his personal tastes, if the writers thereof were clear-headed and had a reasonable amount of literary skill" (quoted in Ferris Greenslet, *The Life of Thomas Bailey Aldrich* [Boston: Houghton Mifflin, 1908], 144). Aldrich solicited work from E. L. Godkin (editor of the *Nation*) and Carl Schurz, even though both held views quite different from his own. In May 1886, following the Haymarket bombing, he invited Terence Powderly to state labor's position at a time when the leader of the Knights of the Labor was denounced by the *Century* as a charlatan (Sedgwick, *Atlantic Monthly*).

18. Despite the *Atlantic*'s relatively small audience—circulation in the 1880s never exceeded 20,000 and hit a low of just over 10,000 in 1886, when the *Century* reached 200,000—the magazine retained an unfaltering grip on cultural prestige. Oliver Wendell Holmes remarked that from a "literary point of view [the *Atlantic*] is recognized as the first of the monthlies." Helen Hunt Jackson explained her attraction to the magazine somewhat differently: for her, gaining the highbrow "*Atlantic* audience was part of the pay." E. R. Sill also considered the *Atlantic* audience the "'illuminati' from whom ideas would 'work down' into popular thought and practice." The *Critic* and *Nation* "continued to find [the *Atlantic*], on balance, more intellectually challenging, more aesthetically sophisticated, and of higher literary quality than the other monthlies" (Sedgwick, *Atlantic Monthly*, 181).

One of Chesnutt's own comments from the 1890s may shed light on his attitude toward the magazine in the previous decade: he told Walter Hines Page that, if he had to choose, he would prefer to publish stories separately in the *Atlantic* than as part of a book of his own stories (Chesnutt, *Charles Waddell Chesnutt*, 84).

19. He remarked after the death of his beloved dog, Trip, "The dear little fellow. He had better manners and more intelligence than half the persons you meet 'on the platform of a West-End car.' *He* wasn't constantly getting drunk

and falling out of the windows of tenement houses, like Mrs. O'Flararty; *he* wasn't forever stabbing somebody in North Street. Why should he be dead, and these other creatures exhausting the ozone?" (Greenslet, *Life of Thomas Bailey Aldrich*, 169).

20. Aldrich had little use for experimental work like that of Whitman and Emily Dickinson or for the radical work of Sarah Piatt. He did publish at least one Piatt poem, but it was not one of her more radical ones.

21. David Dodge's essay on "The Free Negroes of North Carolina"—a piece that may have caught Chesnutt's eye in the year before he first published in the *Atlantic*—provides this explanation of the terms *old issue* and *new issue:* "At the close of the war the appellations 'Old Issue' and 'New Issue,' to distinguish the free from the freed negroes, were invented by the latter. The blacks are quick at appropriating new words, and sometimes very original in applying them; and this instance came about as follows: Early in 1864, when Confederate money had greatly depreciated in value, it was rumored that the government was about to make a new issue of notes, whose purchasing value would be fixed by law, and that they would bring back the good old time prices. While those competent to judge must have known better, popular expectation was on tiptoe. Wonders were fondly hoped for from this magic 'New Issue.' It came. Almost the only effect was at once to still farther depreciate the 'Old Issue' while prices went steadily upward. The war ended while these terms were still fresh in the popular mind, and the only result of this great financial scheme was to add two words—'Ol' Isshy' and 'New Isshy'—to the negro's scant vocabulary. The terms were expressive and appropriate and no one now thinks of using any other" (*Atlantic Monthly*, Jan. 1886, 28).

22. Richard Brodhead, ed. *The Journals of Charles W. Chesnutt* (Durham: Duke Univ. Press, 1993), 157–58.

23. Ibid., 7. Brodhead further observes, "Two facts suggest the extreme prestige that attached to this well-managed, well-financed school in the 1870s. First, when the movement to introduce grade schools to white education caught on in North Carolina in the late 1870s, it was led by Alexander Graham, a white teacher from Fayetteville who was trying to match the quality of black schooling in his town. . . . Second, when the state of North Carolina decided to create state-supported normal schools for the training of white and black teachers in 1877, . . . it chose Fayetteville's Howard School to become the state's normal school" (8).

24. On 16 March 1880 Chesnutt wrote in his journal, "There is something romantic, to the Northern mind, about the southern negro, as commonplace and vulgar as he seems to us who come in contact with him every day" (Ibid., 125).

25. Ibid., 17.

26. Harry Forrest Lupold observes that, in Cleveland, Chesnutt's "life style was . . . that of the black elite; . . . the family enjoyed an expensive touring car, dancing lessons for their daughters, were served by white immigrant servants,

and sent their children to the integrated Central High School. Two daughters attended Smith College, a son Harvard." It is also true that Chesnutt complained that he did not "know more than one place downtown where [he] could take for luncheon a dark-colored man." See Lupold, "Charles W. Chesnutt: A Black Writer Caught in Two Worlds," *Ohiona Quarterly* 29 (1986): 6.

27. Brodhead, ed., *Journals,* 154.

28. Ibid., 140.

29. Ibid., pp. 139–40.

30. For a discussion of Chesnutt and the problem of reaching a white audience, see Richard E. Baldwin, "The Art of *The Conjure Woman,*" *American Literature* 43 (1971): 385–98.

31. Robert Hemenway, Introduction to Joel Chandler Harris, *Uncle Remus: His Songs and Sayings* (New York: Viking Penguin, 1982), 9.

32. See Sundquist, *To Wake the Nations,* 327, 357.

33. Robert Hemenway, "The Functions of Folklore in Charles Chesnutt's *The Conjure Woman,*" *Journal of the Folklore Institute* 13 (1976): 300. For examples of critics who regard John as expressing Chesnutt's own attitudes, see Donald Winkleman, "Three American Authors as Semi-Folk Artists," *Journal of American Folklore* 78 (1965): 132; Ruth Miller, *Blackamerican Literature, 1760–Present* (Beverly Hills: Glencoe, 1971), 160–61; and David Littlejohn, *Black on White* (New York: Grossman, 1966), 27.

34. Recent examples include Donald B. Gibson, *The Politics of Literary Expression: A Study of Major Black Writers* (New York: Greenwood, 1981), 125–54; and R. V. Burnette, "Charles W. Chesnutt's *The Conjure Woman* Revisited," *CLA Journal* 30 (1987): 438–53.

35. See Andrews, *Literary Career,* 50–65; Houston Baker, *Modernism and the Harlem Renaissance* (Chicago: Univ. of Chicago Press, 1987), 43–47; David Britt, "Chesnutt's Conjure Tales: What You See Is What You Get," *CLA Journal* 15 (1972): 269–83; Richard Brodhead, *Cultures of Letters: Scenes of Reading and Writing in Nineteenth-Century America* (Chicago: Univ. of Chicago Press, 1993), 177–210; Dixon, "Teller as Folk Trickster," 186–97; Robert M. Farnsworth, introduction to Charles Chesnutt, *The Conjure Woman* (1899; Ann Arbor: Univ. of Michigan Press, 1969), v–xix; SallyAnn H. Ferguson, "Chesnutt's 'The Conjurer's Revenge': The Economics of Direct Confrontation," *Obsidian* 7 (1981): 37–42; Hemenway, "Functions of Folklore," 283–309; Joyce Hope Scott, "Who 'Goophered' Whom: The Afro-American Fabulist and His Tale in Charles Chesnutt's *The Conjure Woman,*" *Bestia: Yearbook of the Beast Fable Society* 2 (1990): 49–62; Robert Stepto, "'The Simple but Intensely Human Inner Life of Slavery': Storytelling, Fiction, and the Revision of History in Charles W. Chesnutt's 'Uncle Julius Stories,'" in *History and Tradition in Afro-American Culture,* ed. Gunter H. Lenz (Frankfurt: Campus Verlag, 1984), 29–55; and Sundquist, *To Wake the Nations,* 271–454.

Other works, less central to this study but important for understanding *The Conjure Woman* include Robert Bone, *Down Home: A History of Afro-American Short*

Fiction from Its Beginnings to the End of the Harlem Renaissance (New York: Putnam's, 1975), 74–105; Lorne Fienberg, "Charles W. Chesnutt and Uncle Julius: Black Storytellers at the Crossroads," *Studies in American Fiction* 15 (1987): 161–73; Sylvia Lyons Render, introduction to *The Short Fiction of Charles W. Chesnutt* (Washington, D. C.: Howard Univ. Press, 1981), 3–56; and Werner Sollors, "The Goopher in Charles Chesnutt's Conjure Tales," *Letterature d'America: Rivista Trimestrale* 6 (1985): 107–29.

36. However great the difficulties for Chesnutt at the *Atlantic,* they were worse at the *Century.* In a famous letter of 5 June 1890 to George Washington Cable, Chesnutt complained that "Mr. Gilder finds that I either lack humor or that my characters have a 'brutality, a lack of mellowness, lack of spontaneous imaginative life, lack of outlook that makes them uninteresting'" (quoted in Robert M. Farnsworth, introduction to Charles Chesnutt, *The Marrow of Tradition* [1901; Ann Arbor: Univ. of Michigan Press, 1969]). Chesnutt concluded that Gilder did not want anything approaching realism in the treatment of black characters. See also Janet Gabler-Hover's discussion in this volume of Gilder's unwillingness to print Chesnutt's essay "The Negro's Answer to the Negro Question."

37. Britt, "Chesnutt's Conjure Tales," 269.

38. On the ambiguities of minstrel performance, see Eric Lott, *Love and Theft: Blackface Minstrelsy and the American Working Class* (New York: Oxford Univ. Press, 1993).

39. Michael Flusche, "On the Color Line: Charles Waddell Chesnutt," *North Carolina Historical Review* 53 (1976): 23.

40. Quoted in Ronald C. White, Jr., *Liberty and Justice for All: Racial Reform and the Social Gospel (1877–1925)* (New York: Harper and Row, 1990), 3.

41. Chesnutt, *The Conjure Woman,* 9–10.

42. The problems and controversies involved with the use of black dialect are discussed in many works. Some of the more useful are: Elsa Nettels, *Language, Race, and Social Class in Howells's America* (Lexington: Univ. Press of Kentucky, 1988), 72–86; Henry Louis Gates, Jr., *The Signifying Monkey: A Theory of African-American Literary Criticism* (New York: Oxford Univ. Press, 1988), 127–216; and Shelley Fisher Fishkin, *Was Huck Black? Mark Twain and African-American Voices* (New York: Oxford Univ. Press, 1993), esp. 3–127.

43. Baldwin, "Art of *The Conjure Woman,*" 388.

44. Quoted in Andrews, *Literary Career,* 21.

45. Britt, "Chesnutt's Conjure Tales," 471.

46. Sedgwick, *Atlantic Monthly,* 168.

47. The fascination is displayed in many of the works I have mentioned and also in the account of "The Black Madonna of Loreto," *Atlantic Monthly* (Sept. 1889): 410–15.

48. See Hemenway, introduction to *Uncle Remus,* 19, for the importance of a racial utopia in a different, though relevant, context.

CONTRIBUTORS

INDEX

•

CONTRIBUTORS

•

PAULA BENNETT is an associate professor of English at Southern Illinois University, Carbondale. She is the author of *Emily Dickinson: Woman Poet* (Iowa City: Univ. of Iowa Press, 1990) and *My Life, a Loaded Gun: Female Creativity and Feminist Poetics* (Boston: Beacon Press, 1986). She is co-editor of *Solitary Pleasures: The Historical, Literary, and Artistic Discourses of Autoeroticism,* forthcoming from Routledge, as well as the editor of *Nineteenth-Century American Women's Poetry: A Critical Anthology Providing Texts and Contexts* and a volume of the selected poetry of Sarah Morgan Bryan Piatt.

KATHLEEN DIFFLEY is an associate professor of English at the University of Iowa. Her most recent publication is *Where My Heart Is Turning Ever: Civil War Stories and Constitutional Reform, 1861–1876* (Athens: Univ. of Georgia Press, 1992), a study of the short stories published during the Civil War and Reconstruction in sixteen magazines of the South, West, and Northeast.

JANET GABLER-HOVER is an associate professor of English at Georgia State University. She has published *Truth in American Fiction: The Legacy of Rhetorical Idealism* (Athens: Univ. of Georgia Press, 1990) and numerous articles on American literature in such journals as *Texas Studies in Literature and Language, Journal of Narrative Technique, Henry James Review,* and *Philological Quarterly.*

EZRA GREENSPAN is an associate professor of English at the University of South Carolina. He is the author of *The Schlemiel Comes to America: A Reading of Jewish-American Fiction* (Metuchen, N.J.: Scarecrow Press, 1983) and *Walt Whitman and the American Reader* (New York: Cambridge Univ. Press, 1990). He is editor of *Cambridge Companion to Walt Whitman.*

GARY HOPPENSTAND is an associate professor in the Department of American Thought and Language at Michigan State University. In addition to publishing numerous articles on American literature and popular culture, he is the author of *Clive Barker's Short Stories: Imagination as*

Metaphor in the Books of Blood *and Other Works* (Jefferson, N.C.: McFarland, 1994). His *Popular Fiction* is forthcoming from Harper Collins. He is currently vice president of the Popular Culture Association.

CAROLYN L. KARCHER, a professor of English at Temple University, is the author of *The First Woman in the Republic: A Cultural Biography of Lydia Maria Child* (Durham: Duke Univ. Press, 1994). She is the editor of *Hobomok and Other Writings on Indians* (New Brunswick, N.J.: Rutgers Univ. Press, 1986) and the author of *Shadow over the Promised Land: Slavery, Race, and Violence in Melville's America* (Baton Rouge: Louisiana State Univ. Press, 1980).

PATRICIA OKKER is an assistant professor of English at the University of Missouri, Columbia. She has published essays on Henry David Thoreau, Sarah Hale and Lydia Sigourney, and Zitkala-Sa and is the author of *Our Sister Editors: Sarah J. Hale and the Tradition of Nineteenth-Century Women Editors* (Athens: Univ. of Georgia Press, 1995).

SHEILA POST-LAURIA is an assistant professor of English at the University of Massachusetts, Boston. She has written several articles on Herman Melville for the *Journal of American Culture, Nineteenth-Century Literature, College Literature,* and *American Periodicals.* Her book, *Correspondent Colorings: Herman Melville and Nineteenth-Century Culture,* is forthcoming (Amherst: Univ. of Massachusetts Press).

KENNETH M. PRICE is a professor of English at the College of William and Mary. He served as editor of the *South Central Review* from 1988 to 1992. He is the editor of books on Walt Whitman and George Santayana and the author of *Whitman and Tradition: The Poet in His Century* (New Haven: Yale Univ. Press, 1990).

DAVID S. REYNOLDS is a professor of English at Baruch College and at the Graduate Center of the City University of New York. He is the author of *Faith in Fiction: The Emergence of Religious Literature in America* (Cambridge: Harvard Univ. Press, 1981), *George Lippard* (Boston: Twayne, 1982), *Beneath the American Renaissance* (New York: Knopf, 1988), and *Walt Whitman's America: A Cultural Biography* (New York: Knopf, 1995).

LARRY J. REYNOLDS is the Thomas Franklin Mayo Professor in Liberal Arts at Texas A&M University. He is the author of *James Kirke Paulding* (Boston: Twayne, 1984) and *European Revolutions and the American Liter-*

ary Renaissance (New Haven: Yale Univ. Press, 1988). He is also the co-editor of *"These Sad but Glorious Days": Dispatches from Europe, 1846–1850* (New Haven: Yale Univ. Press, 1991) and *New Historical Literary Study* (Princeton: Princeton Univ. Press, 1993).

ROBERT J. SCHOLNICK is a professor of English at the College of William and Mary, where he also serves as dean of graduate studies of the Faculty of Arts and Sciences. The founding president of the Research Society for American Periodicals, he is the author of numerous studies of nineteenth-century American periodicals and writers. He wrote *Edmund Clarence Stedman* (Boston: Twayne, 1977) and recently edited *American Literature and Science* (Lexington: Univ. Press of Kentucky, 1992).

SUSAN BELASCO SMITH is an associate professor of English at the University of Tulsa, where she also directs the University Writing Program. She is the author of several essays on women in nineteenth-century American literature as well as the introduction to Margaret Fuller's *Summer on the Lakes, in 1843* (Urbana: Univ. of Illinois Press, 1991). She is the co-editor of *"These Sad but Glorious Days": Dispatches from Europe, 1846–1850* (New Haven: Yale Univ. Press, 1991).

JOYCE W. WARREN is an associate professor of English at Queens College. She is the author of *Fanny Fern: An Independent Woman* (1992) and *The American Narcissus: Individualism and Women in Nineteenth-Century American Fiction* (1984) and the editor of *Ruth Hall and Other Writings* (1986) and *The (Other) American Traditions: Nineteenth-Century Women Writers* (1993), all published by Rutgers University Press.

INDEX

•

Duganne, Augustine, 82
Dwight, Timothy, 20, 31–32n

"Each Has His Grief" (Walt Whitman), 39
The Early Black Press in America, 1827–1860
(Frankie Hutton), 8
Eastman, Mary, 161
Edgar Huntly (Charles Brockden Brown),
224
Edgeworth, Maria, 113n
Edinburgh Review, 186
Education, 262, 272n
"The Eighteenth Presidency!" (Walt Whit-
man), 48
Eliot, Charles, 261
Eliot, George, 72
Ellison, Julie, 28
Emerson, Lidian, 23
Emerson, Ralph Waldo, 14, 35, 52, 184,
206, 271n; "The Fugitive Slave Law,"
3–4; Fuller and, 19, 20–21, 23–26,
29–30, 31–32n, 33n; *Round Table* on,
177
Emory, William H., 193
"The End of All" (Walt Whitman), 39
An Epic of the Starry Heaven (Thomas Lake
Harris), 47
Erkkila, Betsy, 48
"An Escape from Johnson's Island," 190
Essays, Second Series (Ralph Waldo Emer-
son), 29–30
Estes, Dana, 6–7
Etchings of a Whale Cruise (J. Ross Browne),
123
Europe, 75–76, 80–82, 129
*European Revolutions and the American Liter-
ary Renaissance* (Larry J. Reynolds), 75
Evangeline, 144
Evening Gazette, 168
Evenings at Home (Anna Letitia Barbauld),
113n
Evenings in New England (Lydia Maria
Child), 92–93
Everett, Edward, 5, 59, 60–61
Ewbank, Henry, 190

Faler, Paul, 102
"The Fall of the House of Usher" (Edgar
Allan Poe), 227

"A Family Scene" (Caroline Howard Gil-
man), 90, 91
"Fanny Ford" (Fanny Fern), 55–56
Farnsworth, Robert M., 264
Farrington, Samuel, 53, 54
Farrington, Sara, *see* Fern, Fanny
Father Abbot (William Gilmore Simms), 150
Faulkner, William, 250
Feminism, 17–18
Ferguson, James, 112n
Ferguson, SallyAnn H., 264
Fern, Fanny, 6, 11–12, 51–68
Fern Leaves (Fanny Fern), 55
Field, Kate, 176
Fields, Annie, 207–10, 215, 216, 218–19n
Fisher, G. P., 176
Fishkin, Shelley Fisher, 246, 253
Fitzgerald, Patrick "Honey Fitz," 270n
"The Flower of Liberty" (Oliver Wendell
Holmes), 208–10
Flusche, Michael, 265
Forman, B. R., 190
Foster, Charles H., 41
Foucault, Michel, 51, 67, 190–91
Fowler, Lorenzo, 47
Fowler, Orson, 47
Fowler and Wells, 47
Francis, Convers, 32n, 93
Francis, Susan, 261, 271n
Frankenstein (Mary Shelley), 224, 233–34,
235, 238n
Frank Leslie's Popular Monthly, 210
Franklin, Benjamin, 95–96, 120, 124–25,
129
Franklin, William B., 240
Franklin Evans or the Inebriate (Walt Whit-
man), 47
"The Freedman's Case in Equity" (George
Washington Cable), 252
The Freedmen's Book (Lydia Maria Child),
112n
"Free Joe and the Rest of the World" (Joel
Chandler Harris), 252
"The Free Negroes of North Carolina" (Da-
vid Dodge), 272n
"Friendship" (Henry David Thoreau), 22
Frost, Robert, 214
The Frugal Housewife (Lydia Maria Child),
95–96, 113n